ARCHITECTURE AND
THE CRISIS OF
MODERN SCIENCE

Alberto Pérez-Gómez

The MIT Press

Cambridge, Massachusetts

London, England

Fifth printing, 1990

© 1983 by
The Massachusetts Institute of Technology

Originally published under the title *La
génesis y superación del funcionalismo en
arquitectura*, copyright © 1980 by Editorial
Limusa, S. A. Translated and revised by the
author.

T

This book was set in Palatino
by The MIT Press Computergraphics
Department
and printed and bound by Halliday
Lithograph
in the United States of America.

Library of Congress Cataloging in
Publication Data

Pérez Gómez, Alberto, 1949–
    Architecture and the crisis of modern
science.

    Revised translation of: La génesis y
superación del funcionalismo en
arquitectura.
    Bibliography: p.
    Includes index.
    1. Architecture, Modern—17th–18th
centuries—Europe. 2. Functionalism
(Architecture)—Europe. 3. Architecture—
Philosophy. I. Title.
NA956.P413 1983 720'.1 82–18010
ISBN 0–262–16091–9

ACKNOWLEDGMENTS

The theme of this book was originally presented as a doctoral dissertation to the University of Essex, England. My greatest debt is to my teachers, Joseph Rykwert and Dalibor Vesely. Professor Rykwert patiently brought to bear his great erudition upon often unfocused hypotheses, while Dr. Vesely's incisive and profound criticism was crucial in the formulation and evolution of the major themes. I obviously owe much to the great modern scholars who have studied this period, often more than what I could acknowledge in polemics or bibliographical references.

The subject matter of this book has been discussed with Daniel Libeskind, Kenneth Frampton, and Werner Oechslin. I have profited from the comments and advice of Anthony Vidler and Alan Colquhoun. In presenting the material in lectures and courses, I was inspired by the enthusiasm of John Hejduk and the sensitive response of architecture students at the Cooper Union School in New York and the Cranbrook Academy of Art in Michigan. Oriol Bohigas, Vittorio Gregotti, Antoine Grumbach, John Perry, and Robert Griffin have offered supportive remarks and suggestions. I am particularly grateful to my colleague Bruce Webb, who kindly read the manuscript and provided valuable recommendations. I feel fortunate in having met, spoken, and taught with these creative designers and artists, whose work and whose vision of contemporary and future architecture have aided me in defining relevant questions and hypotheses.

During almost eight years of preparation, I have received many insights from my students in England, Canada, Mexico, and the United States. Among the many deserving special acknowledgment are Lauren Letherbarrow, Bahram Shirdel, Steve Parcell, Marina Stankovič, and Douglas Disbrow.

The staffs of various libraries have been helpful, especially those of the University of Essex, the Warburg Institute, Bibliothèque Nationale, and the British Library, where I did most of my reading.

Invaluable help in the initial editing of the manuscript came from Arthur Kristal, who gave me as much trouble as I deserved.

The last stages in the production of the manuscript were made possible through the decided support provided by the College of Architecture of the University of Houston. I was often encouraged by my faculty colleagues, whose excitement at facing the challenge and the paradoxes of "the last great American city" is a strong stimulant.

Finally, my appreciation to my wife, who helped with typing and revisions, and to my daughter, who justly wondered why I sat at my desk thinking about geometry and architecture instead of building her a castle out of wooden blocks.

ARCHITECTURE AND
THE CRISIS OF
MODERN SCIENCE

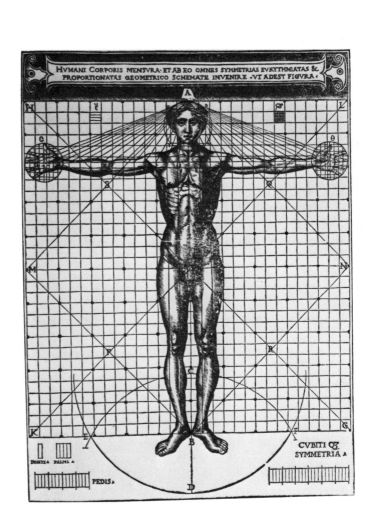

INTRODUCTION: ARCHITECTURE AND THE CRISIS OF MODERN SCIENCE

The creation of order in a mutable and finite world is the ultimate purpose of man's thought and actions. There was probably never human perception outside a framework of categories; the ideal and the real, the general and the specific, are "given" in perception, constituting the intentional realm that is the realm of existence. Perception is our primary form of knowing and does not exist apart from the a priori of the body's structure and its engagement in the world. This "owned body," as Merleau-Ponty would say, is the locus of all formulations about the world; it not only occupies space and time but consists of spatiality and temporality. The body has a dimension. Through motion it polarizes external reality and becomes our instrument of meaning; its experience is therefore "geo-metrical." The extension of this "geometry of experience," in Husserl's phrase, beyond the body's (and the mind's) spatiality constitutes the thrust of architectural design, the creation of an order resonant with the body's own.

The historical awareness and utilization of geometrical form among architects has by no means resulted in a consistent or universal approach to architecture itself. In fact, the malaise from which architecture suffers today can be traced to the collusion between architecture and its use of geometry and number as it developed in the early modern period. An analysis of the architectural intentions of the seventeenth and eighteenth centuries in relation to the changing world view ushered in by Galilean science and Newton's natural philosophy is necessary before we can understand the dilemmas still confronted by architects. Such an analysis becomes particularly significant in light of the prevalent obsession with mathematical certainty in its various forms: design methodologies, typologies, linguistic rules of formalism, any sort of explicit or disguised functionalism. Contemporary architects, who encounter a proliferation of these forms whenever they make design decisions, find it difficult to reconcile mathematics' demands for invariance (the *mathemata*) with their conception of architecture as an art rather than a science.

The assumption that architecture can derive its meaning from functionalism, formal games of combinations, the coherence or rationality of style understood as ornamental language, or the use of type as a generative structure in design marks the evolution of Western architecture during the past two centuries. This assumption, whose implication is no less than the algebraization or "functionalization" of architectural theory as a whole, the reduction of architecture to a rational theory, began to gain ascendancy toward the middle of the seventeenth century, culminating in the theories of Jacques-Nicolas-Louis Durand and his critics. Durand's functionalized theory is already a theory of architecture in the contemporary sense: replete with the modern architect's obsessions, thoroughly specialized, and composed of laws of an exclusively prescriptive character that purposely avoid all reference to philosophy or cosmology. Theory thus reduced to a self-referential system whose elements must be combined through mathematical logic must pretend that its values, and therefore its meaning, are derived from the system itself. This formulation, however, constitutes its most radical limitation since any reference to the perceived world is considered subjective, lacking in real value.[1]

This functionalization of architectural theory implies its transformation into a set of operational rules, into a tool of an exclusively technological character. Its main concern becomes how to build in an efficient and economical manner, while avoiding questions related to why one builds and whether such activity is justified in the existential context.[2] The inception of functionalism coincided, not surprisingly, with the rise of positivism in the physical and human sciences. This set of circumstances, according to Edmund Husserl, marks the beginning of the crisis of European science.[3]

When a physician talks about a crisis in the condition of a patient, he is describing a moment when it is unclear whether the patient will survive or succumb. In a true sense, this is now the condition of Western culture. In the last century and a half, man has done his utmost to define the human condition and ironically has lost the capacity to come to terms with it; he is unable to reconcile the eternal and immutable dimension of ideas with the finite and mutable dimension of of everyday life.[4] Moreover, contemporary man, while recognizing this dilemma, seems incapable of deriving from this tension the ultimate meaning of his existence.[5]

The elucidation of this crisis marks the writing of the most profound thinkers of our century, but perhaps only Husserl has been able to reveal its unique character.[6] According to Husserl, the beginning of the crisis coincides with the end of classical geometry, still a geometry of the *Lebenswelt*, the world as lived, and the appearance of non-Euclidean geometries, which occurred around 1800. This development in mathematics augured the possibility that the external world of man could be effectively controlled and dominated by a functionalized theory subsumed by technology.[7] One result of the crisis has been an unprecedented inversion of priorities: Truth—demonstrable through the laws of science—constitutes the fundamental basis upon which human decisions are made over and above "reality," which is always ambiguous and accessible only through the realm of "poetics."[8] Today, theory in any discipline is generally identified with methodology; it has become a specialized set of prescriptive rules concerned with technological values, that is, with process rather than ultimate objectives, a process that seeks maximum efficiency with minimum effort. Once life itself began to be regarded as process, whether biological or teleological, theory was able to disregard ethical considerations in favor of applicability. Modern theory, leaning on the early nineteenth-century model of the physico-mathematical sciences with their utopian ideals, has designated the most crucial human problems illegitimate, beyond the transformation and control of the material world.[9]

According to Husserl, there are two dimensions from which every system derives its meaning: (1) the *formal*, or syntactic, dimension, which corresponds to the structure of the system itself, that is, to the relations among its elements; and (2) the *transcendental*, or semantic, dimension, that is, the reference of each element to the reality of the *Lebenswelt*, including its historic constitution.[10] Although not without difficulty, Western thought managed to reconcile these two dimensions of logic until about 1800. The radical ambiguities of existence were always explained by acknowledging a residual but most important *mythos*.[11] It has only been during the last two centuries that the transcendental dimension of meaning has been questioned. Culminating perhaps in the recent structuralist approach to the human sciences, Western thought seems to be floundering in the excessive formalism of systems, unable to accept the reality of specific phenomena. The already classic failure of C. Norberg-Schulz's *Intentions in Ar-*

chitecture and other applications of linguistics to architectural theory over the past ten years reveal a passion for structural rules and their limitations. In terms of architecture, structuralism has consciously rejected the importance of the transcendental dimension, thereby denying the importance of the historical horizon of meaning.

The problem that determines most explicitly our crisis, therefore, is that the conceptual framework of the sciences is not compatible with reality.[12] The atomic theory of the universe may be true, but it hardly explains real issues of human behavior. The fundamental axiom of the sciences since 1800, as well as of the humanities, has been "invariance," which rejects, or at least is unable to cope with, the richness and ambiguity of symbolic thought.[13] This attitude is endemic to the modern crisis and is reinforced by those scientists and intellectuals who still believe in a utopian future, who maintain that regardless of present limitations, a time will come when their specific disciplines will arrive at a full understanding of phenomena and thereby become at last truly meaningful for mankind.

The consequences of all this for architectural theory are enormous. The poetical content of reality, the a priori of the world, which is the ultimate frame of reference for any truly meaningful architecture, is hidden beneath a thick layer of formal explanations. Because positivistic thought has made it a point to exclude mystery and poetry, contemporary man lives with the illusion of the infinite power of reason. He has forgotten his fragility and his capacity for wonder, generally assuming that all the phenomena of his world, from water or fire to perception or human behavior, have been "explained." For many architects, myth and poetry are generally considered synonymous with dreams and lunacy, while reality is deemed equivalent to prosaic scientific theories. In other words, mathematical logic has been substituted for metaphor as a model of thought. Art can be beautiful, of course, but only seldom is it understood as a profound form of knowledge, as a genuine, intersubjective interpretation of reality. And architecture, particularly, must never partake of the alleged escapism of the other fine arts; it has to be, before anything else, a paradigm of efficient and economical construction.

This inversion of priorities that originated in the scientific and philosophical speculations of the seventeenth century has never, at a popular level, been corrected. Although Cartesian dualism is no longer a viable philosophical model, faith in mathematics and logic as the only legitimate way of thinking is still commonplace. Decisions concerning planning or the establishment of new towns, for example, continue to be made on the basis of statistics. The immediate perception of the reality of quality of place is disregarded as a subjective interpretation of traditional urbanism. The evident shortcomings of such a view could not be more dramatic; our cities are becoming a vast world village where the external reality of man is at odds with man himself and whose reason for being is to express a mute universal process embodying the values of technology rather than to establish a meaningful framework for man's finite existence. The well-known failures of modern planning continue to be a source of embarrassment. And still the modern professional waits for a set of objective and universal standards, either formal, ideological, or functional, that will determine his design and contribute to truly meaningful buildings.

Many years have passed since architects began their search for a universal theory grounded in absolute rational certainty. Gottfried Semper, for one, drawing on some of the insights first expressed by Durand, postulated functionalism as a fundamental premise of architectural intentionality. In those of his writings that appeared toward the middle of the nineteenth century, Semper clearly attempted to make the process of design analogous to the resolution of an algebraic equation. The "variables" represented the manifold aspects of reality that architecture had to take into account; the solution was simply a "function" of these variables.[14] This reductionist strategy has since become the fundamental framework of architectural theory and practice, whether one examines the forms of structural determinism or the more subtle attempts to utilize psychological, sociological, or even aesthetic variables. More recently, various sophisticated methodologies and even computers have been applied to design, always failing, however, to come to terms with the essential question of meaning in architecture.[15]

The main problem of architectural intentionality is the genesis of form. Prior to the nineteenth century, the architect's concern for *mathemata* was never merely formal. Even the traditional Vitruvian categories: *firmitas*, *commoditas*, and *venustas*, were not perceived as independent entities, as values in their own right. Architectural intentionality was transcendental, necessarily symbolic.[16] Its mode of operation was therefore metaphor, not mathematical equations. Not only did form not follow function, but form could fulfill its role as a primary means of reconciliation, one that referred ultimately to the essential ambiguity of the human condition.

A simplistic view of human experience, derived from the projection of scientific models onto human reality, exemplified by certain aspects of behaviorism and positivistic psychology, has hampered our understanding of the essential continuity between thought and action, between mind and body.[17] Because architectural theory is assumed to imply absolute rationality, it has been considered capable of standing on its own, free of all relations to fundamental philosophical questions.[18] Subject to the values of technology, its interest is not in meaning, but in a conceptual or material efficiency dominating design and construction. This naturally has created a peculiar tension between theory and practice. Theory may work smoothly on a formal level, but it is unable to come to terms with reality. Correlatively, practice has been transformed into a process of production without existential meaning, clearly defined aims, or reference to human values. Or else practice has ignored its connections to theory in order to recover its poetic dimension. This last situation is evident in some of the best examples of contemporary architecture. Obviously, certain buildings by Le Corbusier have very little to do with stated theoretical intentions.

The illusion remains, however, that practice can be reduced to a system of rational prescriptive rules. This is particularly evident in architectural education and obstructs our perception of how the relation between theory and practice operated until the end of the eighteenth century. This uniquely modern relation should not be taken for granted; it epitomizes the crisis of contemporary architecture. Consequently, we must examine its historical origin, studying the process of the transformation of theory into a set of technical rules (*ars fabricandi*) and the implicit intentions in other works related to architecture. An analysis of the changing meaning of geometry and number for architectural intentionality during the seventeenth and eighteenth centuries will illustrate the development of the mathematization of theory.

The Mythical Horizon

Geometry and number, prototypes of the ideal, since time immemorial have been symbols of the highest order, their immutability contrasting with the fluid and changing reality of the sublunar world. The concept of *mathesis* appeared in preclassical Greek culture around the seventh century B.C. It referred to what could be taught and learned: the invariable, the familiar, the accessible; its exemplar was number. *Mathesis* was also the first step toward *theoria*, the apprehension of reality at a distance; as such, it was the first symbol of reality, becoming the basic element in a coherent conceptual system that enabled man to disengage himself from the involvement of his embodied being in ritual, allowing him to come to terms with the external world and his own existence within an independent universe of discourse.

Originally, the knowledge of *mathesis* was confined to the magician. Only he dared to manipulate numerical entities, affecting the world on a level separated from physical reality. Traditional numbers were always material entities, never purely formal. To engage them was equivalent to tampering with the order of the real world, a powerful form of magic.

Positing the invariable in the universe of perception corresponded to ancient astronomical thinking. It was in the supralunar sphere that absolute truths of Euclidean geometry were to be found. Astronomers discerned in the heavens logicomathematical systems, and throughout most of human history such invariable laws were perceived as transcendental symbols. Astronomy was never free of ontological presuppositions; it was traditionally astrobiology, with implications of a magical or religious nature.[19] Reality was perceived as an organic totality directed by the regularity of the heavens, and knowledge was synonymous with the elucidation of the transcendental order of the cosmos.

Before the seventeenth century, the primacy of perception as the ultimate evidence of knowledge was never questioned. *Mathesis* explicitly maintained its symbolic connotations, and the hierarchical structure of the cosmos established by Aristotle remained valid. It was a world of predominantly mythical character, qualitatively different from our present universe of precision.

The discovery of *theoria* in Greece permitted the beginnings of architectural theory, a *logos* of architecture. Such theory, however, always contained the necessary complement of *mythos*, maintaining it explicitly until the end of the Renaissance and implicitly during the seventeenth and eighteenth centuries. Alberti postulated a distance between theory and practice, between design and real building. Vignola and others, during the second half of the sixteenth century, emphasized the prescriptive character of the rules of the classical orders rather than their meaning. Nonetheless, the Renaissance was a profoundly traditional world. Liberated from theological determinism, the architect became conscious of his power to transform the physical world. He was often a *magus*, but his intention was reconciliatory; art was a privileged form of metaphysics—metaphysics made into matter. Architecture was not concerned exclusively with the cathedral or temple, but the physical configuration of the new human world had to conform to the *mathesis* that linked microcosm and macrocosm.

During the Renaissance, theory was not merely a series of technical precepts but was underlined by metaphysical preoccupations often implicit in the mathematical rules themselves. The mythical, ancient world embodied in the writings of Vitruvius and the visible ruins was never lost sight of. In this Aristotelian world, there could be no split between architectural theory and practice. The former maintained its role as the elucidation and justification of the latter, while practice retained its primordial meaning as *poesis* (not merely *praxis*), as a form of reconciliation between man and the world, which were perceived as the two poles of a sacred, living totality.

Geometry descended from the heavens and lost its sacred character as a result of the epistemological revolution brought about by Galileo's speculations during the first decades of the seventeenth century.[20] The "spatiality" that referred to the immediate network of intentions relating man's embodied being with the *Lebenswelt*, and that allowed for the apprehension of his place in a hierarchical order, could now be replaced by geometrical space.[21] At this historical juncture, geometry and number were able to become instruments for the technical control of practical operations and, eventually, for an effective technological domination of the world. Through the new science of mechanics, man began to subject matter to his will.

| **The Rational Horizon** | The present work argues that modern architecture, and the crisis it faces, has its roots in a historical process touched off by the Galilean revolution, a process whose development is marked by two great transformations, the first of which occurred toward the end of the seventeenth century, and the second, toward the end of the eighteenth. |

The present work argues that modern architecture, and the crisis it faces, has its roots in a historical process touched off by the Galilean revolution, a process whose development is marked by two great transformations, the first of which occurred toward the end of the seventeenth century, and the second, toward the end of the eighteenth.

In the first transformation, the assumption, which had been inherited from medieval and Renaissance cosmology, that number and geometry were a *scientia univeralis*, the link between the human and the divine, was finally brought into question by philosophy and science. At the same time, technique and the crafts were freed from their traditional magical associations. In architecture, this laid the basis for a new approach. Architects began to consider their discipline a technical challenge, whose problems could be solved with the aid of two conceptual tools, number and geometry.

But in the eighteenth century, the transcendental dimension of human thought and action was sustained through the myth of Divine Nature. This myth lay at the root of Newtonian natural philosophy. The eighteenth century rejected as fiction the closed geometrical systems of seventeenth-century philosophers, but accepted Newton's empirical methods as universally valid. The influence of Newton paved the way for the systematization and mathematization of knowledge, a knowledge that held that immutable, mathematical laws could be derived from the observation of natural phenomena, and that would eventually take on the form of nineteenth-century positivism. Implicit in eighteenth-century Newtonianism, though to the modern mind it may seem thoroughly empiricist, was a Platonic cosmology, usually complemented by some form of deism, in which geometry and number had transcendental value and power in and of themselves. Architectural theory absorbed the fundamental intentions of Newtonian science, and in doing so, it sidetracked earlier developments.

Around 1800 a second great transformation took place. Faith and reason were truly divorced. Scientific thought came to be seen as the only serious and legitimate interpretation of reality, denying any need for metaphysics. Euclidean geometry was functionalized. Infinitesimal calculus was purged of its residual symbolic content. Geometry and mathematics were now purely formal disciplines, devoid of meaning, value, or power except as instruments, as tools of technological intentionality.[22]

It is around this time that the great obsessions of contemporary architecture were first clearly expressed. Practice was supposed to follow theory since theory now assumed that one day, through the fruits of mathematical reason, it would thoroughly control design and building. Eventually, the split between thinking and doing became a critical problem. The belief in the symbolic richness of the external world, in a Divine Nature that ultimately revealed its meaning through observation, was replaced by the notion, by now familiar, of the material world as a mere collection of inanimate objects. In such a framework, architecture could no longer be an art of imitation. Once it adopted the ideals of a positivistic science, architecture was forced to reject its traditional role as one of the fine arts. Deprived of a legitimate poetic content, architecture was reduced to either a prosaic technological process or mere decoration.

It was now that style, that is, the articulation and coherence of architectural "language," became a theoretical problem. The obsession to find immutable laws also invaded the field of aesthetics. But once architecture was reduced to the status of material structure, even the best architects concerned with the problem of meaning could not avoid insurmountable contradictions. History of architecture itself came to be regarded during the nineteenth century as the evolution of rational structure, and style, or *mélange*, was judged on purely rational terms. The problem "In which style should we build?" was not a problem of traditional architecture; an invisible *mathemata* had guaranteed the value of its work, and a symbolic intention had generated both structure and ornament. Only after 1800 do we find a distinction between "necessary" structure, that is, prosaic construction, and "contingent" ornament; the *École des Beaux Arts* did not merely continue a traditional "academic" practice in France. The transformation after Durand was profound, and the illusion of stylistic continuity between the eighteenth and nineteenth centuries has created much confusion in our understanding of modern architecture.

Even today, architects who recognize an affinity between their profession and art usually play formal games, but fail to understand the transcendental dimension of meaning in architecture. The lively discussions over the possibility of applying typological or morphological strategies in design also betray the same illusion. Before 1800 the architect was never concerned with type or integrity of a formal language as a source of meaning. Form was the embodiment of a style of life, immediately expressive of culture and perhaps more analogous to a system of gestures than to articulated language. Today architects often work under the absurd assumption that meaning and symbol are merely products of the mind, that they can be manufactured a priori and that they possess somehow the certainty of number.

Historical Method Finally, some remarks about historical method. I shall address myself to architectural intentions, not merely to theoretical issues or to buildings and projects understood as objects of art or products of materialistic determinism. Nothing can be gained from historical perspective basing itself on simplistic formal or stylistic comparisons. Equally irrelevant is the assumption that the theory of architecture is a specialized discipline whose components exist in hermetic isolation. The intentional realm is the real operating dimension of human existence. In spite of its ambiguities, it has to be addressed through historical research.[23] The illusion that history could refer scientifically either to buildings or ideas as independent data is itself part of the contemporary crisis to which I have alluded.

Specifically, attention will be paid to the implications of number used as either a technical tool or a symbol in proportional systems, or both. Geometry will be examined in its applications to statics, mensuration, and stereotomy and in its use as a vehicle of meaning in Baroque architecture and late eighteenth-century French projects. I shall make a close study of French sources; I shall also examine, though only marginally, English and Italian sources. Although it is well known that French culture was normative for Europe during this period, the discussion is concerned with the most important ideas in the history of Western architecture at that time and their reference to a world view that was essentially European. The connections between the architectural uses of geometry and number and their scientific and philosophical contexts are crucial. It is hoped that a thorough understanding of these relations will touch on the basic intentionality that determined the theory and practice of architecture in this period, thereby casting light on the genesis of modern architecture as a whole.

Intentions have to be understood in reference to their epistemological contexts.[24] Architectural history should not therefore be filtered through a pattern of evaluation whose judgments of success and failure corresponds only to a latter-day ideology. A Gothic cathedral, for example, *is* the City of God on earth, regardless of contemporary religious convictions, structural preoccupations, concerns with efficiency and stylistic coherence, or opinions about useless formal elaboration. The point is to disclose the transcendental intentions that generated form. The continuing conception of architectural history as a collection of material monuments, classified in terms of formal style, has further obstructed a clarification of contemporary problems.

Making a case for historical interpretation would be preposterous without drawing on the writings of such philosophers as Dilthey and Gadamer.[25] Also, there is no question here of a neutral scientific or objective fact-finding operation apart from interpretation. Categories derive from history, but they are ours; they cannot help but qualify interpretation. This circle is not a limitation in the negative sense; it does not condemn history to subjectivity, but is, in fact, part and parcel of human knowledge. Even the exact sciences are ultimately based on interpretation insofar as perception itself must affect the object being studied. The problem is to close the circle, to come to terms with the categories of interpretation. With this in mind, I have allowed the texts that I examine to speak for themselves wherever possible. Being aware of the dangers involved in identifying order in history, I have nevertheless done so convinced that this is a fundamental dimension of historical research.

I

NUMBER AND ARCHITECTURAL
PROPORTION IN THE
SEVENTEENTH AND
EIGHTEENTH CENTURIES

1

CLAUDE PERRAULT AND THE INSTRUMENTALIZATION OF PROPORTION

Il n'est point de secret dans la Nature entiere
Ny dans les Arts qu'Il n'ayt connu
Et modeste Il n'vsa de toute la lumiere
Que pour voir non pour estre vû

Not until recently has the significance of Claude Perrault's work in relation to the origins of modern architecture been properly appreciated.[1] My concern will be to examine his contribution to the process of mathematization of architectural theory, the meaning of his progressive position in the famous Dispute of the Ancients and the Moderns (*Querelle des Anciens et Modernes*), and the almost total rejection or misinterpretation of his work by eighteenth-century architects.

It is important to emphasize that during the seventeenth and eighteenth centuries, architectural theory was not founded on independent premises but existed within an epistemological framework in which not even the distinction between the sciences and the humanities was clear-cut. Architectural theory had enjoyed an autonomous universe of discourse since the Renaissance, but its ultimate frame of reference remained outside itself. In this sense, Claude Perrault's universal interests were in the best tradition. He was not only the author of an important architectural treatise, editor and commentator of a new translation of Vitruvius's *Ten Books*, and the reputed architect of the eastern facade of the Louvre, but possessed a brilliant and far-ranging intellect. Originally trained as a physician, he devoted a great part of his life to scientific research, and his understanding of seventeenth-century science and philosophy was thorough. He wrote on many scientific topics and participated in the activities of the Royal Academy of Science. His achievements should not be considered independently; a coherent intention lay behind his scientific and architectural interests.

Perrault's writings date from the last third of the seventeenth century. This was a period in the history of Western culture in which most implications of the Galilean scientific revolution were generally accepted. Thought was no longer perceived as a closed process, leading by necessity to universal truths prescribed by divine revelation. Modern science, as opposed to its ancient and medieval counterpart, had ceased to be a hermetic discipline whose transcendental conclusions existed beforehand.[2] In his *Novum Organum*, Francis Bacon denied the authority of ancient writers. Qualifying traditional philosophical systems as "comedies," evocative of imaginary worlds, Bacon proposed a new type of knowledge that derived from the observation of natural phenomena and was independent of transcendental issues. This implied the possibility of a philosophy in constant development, moving toward the utopian perfection of absolute rationality.[3] The history of science was regarded by Bacon as progress, an accumulation of valuable experience gleaned from the past, to be used by a community of intellectuals looking toward the future. Knowledge could thus become a collective task of humanity, capable of being shared and transmitted, constantly increasing and growing. The result would be a single scientific tradition, a product of necessity, the only true knowledge, in contrast to the long-standing conflict among philosophical systems.[4]

The "new science" of Galileo was more than just another cosmological hypothesis; it implied a radical subversion of the traditional astrobiological world view. The new science pretended to substitute for the reality of the live world, infinitely diverse, always in motion and defined essentially by qualities, a perfectly intelligible world, determined exclusively by its geometrical and quantitative properties. An idealized, geometrical nature replaced the mutable and mysterious *physis* that man had always perceived. In Galilean thought, visible reality loses importance in order to come to terms with a world of abstractions, relations, and equations. In this world, truth becomes transparent, but only to the degree to which it avoids the irregularities of lived experience. Galileo meant to describe in mathematical language the relations among the diverse elements of natural phenomena.

Following upon the work of Galileo, scientific phenomena came to be regarded not simply as what can be perceived, but primarily as what can be conceived with mathematical clarity. Things became numbers, not understood as their Platonic or Pythagorean transcendental essences, but as objective and intelligible forms. The book of nature was written in mathematical terms, and man began to think that he could manipulate and dominate effectively this objective, external reality. Galilean science thus constitutes the first step in the process of geometrization of lived space; it was the beginning of the dissolution of the traditional cosmos.

But the seventeenth century was not positivistic. It was a time of divided epistemology. The Platonic systems of philosophers were deeply rooted in an Aristotelian world. Only a few exceptional scientists such as Galileo or Gassendi were able to realize the limitations of hypotheses. In contrast to the old occult disciplines, the new science would learn what knowledge was within its province and what knowledge was unattainable. But this awareness was never universal during the seventeenth century. Most scientists and philosophers were simultaneously traditional and progressive.[5] True, they all had greater confidence in the

Claude Perrault and the Instrumentalization of Proportion

Claude Perrault, engraved by G. Edelink (1690). The
inscription praises his modesty, stating that no secret
in nature or the arts has remained beneath his reach.

Number and Architectural Proportion

The hierarchical and animistic Aristotelian cosmos. An image of the world provided by Cesare di Lorenzo Cesariano in his edition of Vitruvius's *Ten Books* (1521).

evidence presented by mathematical reason than in the authority of ancient writers, which bespoke a belief in scientific progress,[6] but most philosophers still believed that mathematical thought constituted a privileged channel of communication between human minds and the divine mind.

Cartesian philosophy and the new science of Galileo postulated the initial split between the perceptual and conceptual spheres of knowledge. Afterward, Western science and philosophy concentrated its attention on truth rather than on reality. The value of a system depended on its clarity and the evidence for its ideas and relations. During the seventeenth century, however, the necessary correspondence between the ideas of the subject and the reality of the object was guaranteed by a benevolent God who had created the universe on the basis of geometrical laws. Scientists and philosophers built vast conceptual systems based upon a mechanistic logic of causes and effects that explained the phenomena of nature. But these systems were always closed and concerned ultimately with final causes.

The notion of progressive knowledge (open to the future), empirical and not hypothetical, became much more explicit in the intellectual climate of the last third of the century. The creation of the academies and the Dispute of the Ancients and the Moderns are two very important events that embody this transformation. In both, Claude Perrault played a major role.

Perrault was a founding member of the French Royal Academy of Science (1666) and the author of its original research programs in anatomy and botany.[7] The academy, as well as its English counterpart, the Royal Society of London, regarded itself as a contributing factor in Bacon's utopia: each member working in his specific area of knowledge for the benefit of mankind. The importance of these new institutions cannot be overemphasized. In sharp contrast to the Christian universities that rejected Cartesianism during the seventeenth and eighteenth centuries, the academies, patronized by the civil authoritites, provided an ideal framework for the development of the new science.

The Dispute of the Ancients and the Moderns divided French intellectuals on the issue of ancient authority. Claude and his famous brother, the writer Charles Perrault, defended the moderns. The meaning of their position is obviously complex. Some authors have emphasized the literary origin of the *querelle* and the dimension of personality conflict it contained.[8] The moderns were mostly French, and the Perrault brothers were very close to the court. Their passionate defense of modern science, however, had further implications.

Charles Perrault described the conflict in the four volumes of his *Parallèle des Anciens et Modernes*.[9] After acknowledging in the preface that there were excellent ancient authors, he quickly proclaims the superiority of the moderns. Charles was well aware that the old order of natural philosophy had discouraged experimentation in the belief that it was sufficient to take the truth from literary sources, learning from Aristotle and his interpreters. Perrault considered this attitude to be inadequate, favoring instead the moderns who searched for the immediate knowledge of nature's works.

The position of the Perrault brothers in relation to Descartes is illuminating. Charles had credited this *homme extraordinaire* with the refutation of Aristotelian philosophy, while Claude used Cartesian models for his work in physics. But Charles also criticized those who believed in the Cartesian system literally, assuming that it disclosed the final causes of nature.[10] Charles was referring to the system of the world postulated by Descartes in his *Principles of Philosophy*.[11] As an introduction to this text, Descartes wrote a dissertation on the principles of human knowledge emphasizing the existence of certain notions, "so clear in themselves . . . that they cannot be learned . . . being necessarily innate." We might question the truth of the sensible world, but can be assured that God would never intentionally fool humanity. Since knowledge is God given, all that we perceive clearly and distinctly, "with mathematical evidence," must be true. The text, rejected as pure imagination by the eighteenth-century *philosophes*, is a collection of amazing and often beautiful mechanical dreams that attempt to explain all possible phenomena: from the constitution of the universe to the essence of fire, magnetism, and human perception. Descartes believed that his mechanistic system, one that explained in a clear and distinct manner the phenomena of nature through causal relations, must be true and had priority over any perceptual evidence.

The difference between the intellectual positions of Descartes and the Perrault brothers had a theological dimension. Although Descartes proposed that "we should prefer divine authority over our reasoning,"[12] his work was condemned by the Church. This condemnation, like Galileo's famous trial, referred not only to a specific philosophy or astronomical system but to the total subversion of the traditional order. While Descartes still tried to rec-

Claude Perrault and the Instrumentalization of Proportion

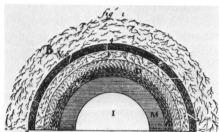

Frontispiece of Claude Perrault's *Histoire des Animaux* (1671). This engraving by Sebastien Le Clerc shows the king visiting the Academy of Science. The observatory, for which Perrault supplied the design, is being built in the background.

Plate from Descartes's *Principes de la Philosophie*, illustrating the different density of matter and its effects in the author's vortex theory.

oncile philosophy and theology in an almost medieval fashion, the Perrault brothers were clearly more modern in their attempt to separate faith and reason, thereby avoiding insoluble conflicts.

This difference in their methods reflects their positions in relation to the ultimate validity of a priori conceptual systems. While Descartes had criticized the open and unsystematic character of Galileo's work,[13] the Perrault brothers clearly recognized the limitations of closed hypothetical systems. In the epistemology of the modern world, the sphere of transcendental causes becomes increasingly more alien. The domain of God is outside reason. Thought concentrates its interest on how things come about and stops asking why. An investigation of laws, of necessary and mathematically determined relations, was more appealing than seeking final causes. Claude Perrault defined phenomenon as "that which appears in Nature and whose cause is not as evident as the thing."[14]

Such a distinction is symptomatic of a true protopositivism and was evident in French intellectual circles between the last decades of the seventeenth century and the 1730s, when the natural philosophy of Newton became generally accepted in Europe. Claude and Charles Perrault were able to distinguish truth from illusion, dissociating scientific knowledge from mythical thought. After discussing astronomy, telescopes, and microscopes in the *Parallèle*, Charles dismissed astrology and alchemy as purely fantastic and whimsical disciplines, lacking any real principles. "Man," he wrote, "has no proportion and no relation with the heavenly bodies . . . infinitely distant from us."[15] Perrault made a distinction here between the new science and traditional hermetic knowledge, disciplines that were usually confused in the earlier part of the century. It may be remembered that between 1570 and 1630, approximately 50,000 women were burnt at the stake, accused of witchcraft. Aside from sociological conditions, this atrocity was a consequence of the confusion between magic and science, linked to the Renaissance discovery of man's power to transform his internal and external reality. It was only in 1672 that the minister Colbert passed a decree stipulating the illegality of such accusations.[16]

Charles already finds it incredible that some modern authors do not accept the irrefutable evidence of blood circulation or the astronomical systems of Copernicus and Galileo. After discussing the values of modern and ancient arts and sciences, including war, architecture, music, and philosophy, he concludes that with

Claude Perrault and the Instrumentalization of Proportion

the exception of poetry and eloquence, the moderns were always superior.[17] The Dispute was therefore much more than a literary quarrel or an apologia for French seventeenth-century authors. It was an affirmation of faith in progress and militant reason, a faith that rejected the type of knowledge that Descartes still upheld, founded on belief in the transcendental power of thought and immediate access to divine truth.

In his *Essais de Physique* (1680), Claude Perrault distinguished between theoretical and experimental physics, emphasizing the secondary value of conceptual systems or hypotheses postulated a priori.[18] Referring to the explicative systems that he himself puts forward, he admits that their value does not derive from their superiority to other similar ones; their worth is, in his opinion, more a result of their novelty. In this manner, Perrault admits total freedom to the construction of hypothetical systems and even justifies the "extravagant imaginative discourses of some celebrated philosophers." He believed that ultimately "truth is but the totality of *phenomena* that can lead us to the knowledge of that which Nature wanted to hide. . . . It is an enigma to which we can give multiple explanations, without ever expecting to find one that is exclusively true."[19]

Perrault considered exactness in the inductive process to be much more important than deductive constructions. His notion of system was no longer linked with that of a cosmological scheme; he repudiated the claim that it had transcendental power as a *clavis universalis*, a key to universal reality.[20] System now designated merely a principle of constitution, a structural law.[21] Emphasizing his distinction between perceptually evident truths and illusory causes, he pointed out that although many readers might disagree with his philosophical explorations, his *Essais* still contained a great number of positive and constant discoveries that would stand on their own.[22] Perrault believed that it was better to accept many hypotheses to explain the different aspects of nature than to try to postulate a single, exclusive explanation.[23] This relativistic dimension of systems is always evident in his work. True causes, he believes, are always occult, and probability can be the only result of reasoning.

Nevertheless, Perrault emphasized in different contexts the impossibility of "philosophizing without putting forward propositions of a general character."[24] He seemed to be aware of the dilemma of modern science: "Philosophical physics reveals an ambition of synthesis and deduction at a moment in which acquired knowledge is still insufficient," while "historical physics" collects precise information through an inductive method, being excessively humble and prudent.[25] It is significant that in spite of his recognition of the limitations of systems as artificial and non-transcendental, Perrault always presented his discoveries precisely in this fashion—an attitude that could be qualified as simultaneously positivistic and traditional.

It is well known that Perrault designed very few buildings; even his authorship of the Louvre Colonnade has been questioned. Undeniable, however, is his profound influence upon successive generations of architects.[26] Beyond his formal contributions, which were fundamental models for French Neoclassical architecture, is a basic architectural intentionality that can only be understood in relation to his epistemological presuppositions. Perrault's theoretical writings on architecture, the preface and notes to his edition of Vitruvius, and his treatise, *Ordonnance des Cinque Espèces de Colonnes* constitute a fundamental point of departure for modern architecture.[27] Perrault questioned the most sacred premises of traditional theory, especially the idea that it was something given beforehand. In a note on his edition to Vitruvius, where he justifies his use of double columns in the facade of the Louvre, he refuted François Blondel's criticism: "His main objection . . . is founded on a prejudice and on the false supposition that it is not possible to abandon the habits of ancient architects."[28] Perrault admitted that opening the way for beautiful inventions could be dangerous, encouraging excessive freedom and giving rise to extravagant or capricious buildings. But, in his opinion, ridiculous inventions would destroy themselves. If the law that stipulates the necessary imitation of antiquity were true, he wrote, "we would not need to search for new means to acquire the knowledge which we are lacking and that every day enriches agriculture, navigation, medicine, and all the other arts."[29]

In the epistemological revolution of the seventeenth century, it was knowledge as a whole that became an unfulfilled task. The arguments that Perrault considered convincing in scientific thought were to his eyes equally valid when applied to architecture. In his preface to the *Ordonnance*, he concludes that "one of the first principles of architecture, equal to the other arts, is that it has not yet arrived to its final perfection."[30] In spite of his unquestionable pride and his belief in the perfection of his own theory, Perrault expressed a desire that his conclusions on the rules of the classical orders could be made some day even more precise

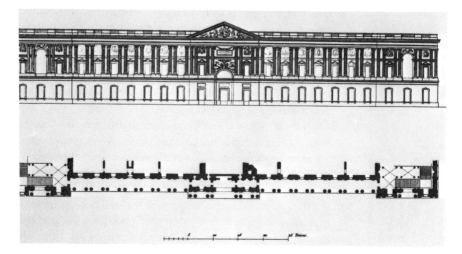

Perrault's design for the eastern facade of the Louvre
with its controversial paired columns, from Quatremère de Quincy's *Histoire de la Vie et des Ouvrages
des Plus Célèbres Architectes* (1830).

Number and Architectural Proportion

and easier to remember. The relevance of this position, obviously in accord with his defense of the moderns in the Dispute, cannot be overemphasized. Notions about the perfectibility of the arts had been expressed before, particularly during the second half of the sixteenth century, but these were mostly echoes of ancient doctrines. Perrault turned his face toward the future, conceiving his theory of architecture as a stage in a continuous line of development in a process of ever increasing rationalization; possessing the accumulated experience of the past, modern architecture was necessarily superior.

This truly modern ideal of a progressive architecture was one of the most profound reasons behind the foundation of the Royal Academy of Architecture in 1671. The direct role that Perrault played in it has never been clear,[31] but the academy was the first institution devoted to the rational discussion of the fundamental problems of architecture and the structured education of future architects. Traditional apprenticeship or the training in the mechanical arts provided by the medieval masonic guilds was obviously inadequate.[32] The architecture of the modern world put an unprecedented emphasis on rational theory; the superiority of modern architecture became a fundamental premise, and this belief, often implicitly, is still prevalent today. The way in which the menacing and contradictory implications of this belief were reconciled with traditional values during the eigthteenth century will be discussed in the following chapters.

After declaring his faith in a progressive architecture, Perrault established in the *Ordonnance* a system of proportions for the classical orders that he considered to be perfect and conclusive. His dimensional system is truly novel. Rejecting all other systems generally accepted in his own time and criticizing their complicated subdivision of modules, he postulated a method that consisted in dividing the major parts of the building in relation to whole numbers. A considerable section of the *Ordonnance* is taken up by Perrault's calculations of the most appropriate dimensions for each of the parts of the classical orders. His method consists in finding an average between two extreme dimensions, taken from buildings, designs, or treatises by the best ancient and modern architects.[33] The arithmetic mean, a most appropriate conceptual expression of the *juste milieu*, was for Perrault a rational guarantee of perfection. In view of the fact that he considered architecture not determined "by proportions that might be true in themselves . . . we must examine the possibility of establishing *probable* dimensions, set firmly on the basis of positive reasons, but without distancing ourselves excessively from the proportions that we have received and are normally used."[34]

An examination of Perrault's text immediately betrays a great number of errors and discrepancies in the determination of the average proportions. His mathematical calculations are ultimately immaterial since his conclusions are barely affected by them. The system of dimensions postulated by Perrault is, in effect, an a priori invention, conditioned only by the most general appearance of the traditional classical orders. The theory of the *juste milieu* and the invocation of famous architects are only a means to render his proposition legitimate. But Perrault was fully conscious of the subversive implication of his system, which amounted to an arbitrary and conceptual construction that was, in essence, disrespectful of the rules of the great masters.

What was then the real motive behind Perrault's complex and time-consuming task? In the *Ordonnance*, he characterized the opinions of his contemporaries about the five classical orders as "confused." He complained that there were no certain rules of proportion, remarking on the great discrepancies that existed among the well-known systems of Vitruvius and the Renaissance authors. Although they all depended on the same transcendental justification, Perrault was quick to point out that the dimensional relations among the parts of the classical orders always differed and never corresponded to the measurements of real buildings.

Although several authors of the seventeenth century, particularly Roland Freart, had already noticed this problem, it is significant that such discrepancies were never considered a fundamental problem before Perrault. In the *Parallel of the Ancient Architecture with the Modern* (1650), Freart wanted to demonstrate how the classical orders had been used in diverse manners by different authors.[35] But his criticism was directed precisely against those authors who "pretended to modify the classical orders through fantastic interpretations." Perrault, on the contrary, criticized "all those treatises that compared proportional systems from the past, without proposing a new conclusive one."[36] He believed that the treatises that recommended only one system were better. The problem had always been that no single architect "has had sufficient authority to establish laws that would be invariably followed."[37]

The observed divergencies became unacceptable to the critical rationalism of Perrault. In the preface of the *Ordonnance*, he ex-

Number and Architectural Proportion

pressed a wish to create a system of architectural proportions so simple and universal that it would solve the problem once and for all. It was to be a system that any architect, regardless of his talent, could easily learn, memorize, and apply, controlling through reason the irregularities of practice.[38] Unquestionably, the proportional rules established by Perrault fulfill his basic intentions. His *petit module*, a third of the diameter of a column instead of the traditional semidiameter, is the regulating dimension of the most important elements of each order. It allows for a sequential relation of pedestals, shafts, capitals, and entablatures. All the dimensions are presented as whole natural numbers, constituting a system of prescriptive instructions, easy to memorize and apply.

In order to achieve his objectives, however, Perrault had to *reject* the traditional symbolic implications of architectural proportion. In the same preface, he criticized the "spirit of submission and blind respect for antiquity" that was still prevalent in the arts and sciences. He then contended that, apart from the truths of religion, which should not be discussed, the remainder of human knowledge could be subjected to "methodical doubt."[39] Architectural proportion lost in Perrault's system its quality of absolute truth. Numbers no longer had their traditional magic power, their connotations as an essential form of divine revelation. Perrault was thus able to reduce the problem to the immanent discourse of reason, and at the same time question proportion's immemorial role as the ultimate justification of *praxis*.

Perrault also rejected the traditionally recognized relation between architectural proportion and musical harmony. In the *Ordonnance*, he asserted that "positive" beauty did not depend directly on proportion, but was generated by visible aspects. He cited three fundamental categories: (1) the richness of building materials, (2) the exactness and propriety of execution, and (3) a general symmetry or disposition. Numerical proportions, on the other hand, could not be accepted as a guarantee of beauty. According to Perrault, these changed constantly, "like fashion," and were dependent only on custom.[40] For the first inventors of proportion, imagination was the only rule, and when "this *fantasie* changed, new proportions were introduced that were also pleasing."[41]

In the *Parallèle*, Charles also pointed out that proportions had been modified through history. He assertively rejected the existence of any kind of relation between human proportions and the dimensions of columns, attributing this modern belief to a

Claude Perrault and the Instrumentalization of Proportion

false interpretation of Vitruvius's *Ten Books*.[42] Vitruvius had mentioned the perfection of human proportions, dictated by Nature, as a model for architecture. In Charles's opinion, however, this never implied that buildings were to derive their proportions from the human body. In a short essay on ancient music, Claude meanwhile denied the mythical perfection of this art, traditionally a symbol of preestablished harmony in an Aristotelian cosmos.[43] In Claude Perrault's theory, architectural proportion lost for the first time, in an explicit way, its character as a transcendental link between microcosm and macrocosm.

Vitruvius had recommended the use of optical adjustments to correct the distortion of dimensions that occurred when buildings were viewed from certain positions. This argument had been taken up by most architects before Perrault to justify the discrepancies between the proportions stipulated in theory and the dimensions of real buildings. The resolution of such differences between the ideal and the real worlds had never been a problem for architects. They were seen as proof of the architect's ability to face the specific character of each building task. But Claude systematically refuted this interpretation. After showing in the *Ordonnance* how, in most cases, these discrepancies between theory and practice were not intentional, he questioned the validity of optical corrections. In light of his epistemological position, Perrault was confident in man's ability to perceive directly the undistorted mathematical and geometrical relations in a world that is already "given" in perspective.

Traditional optical correction (*perspectiva naturalis*) referred to a world where visual aspects of perception were not assumed to have absolute supremacy.[44] The optical dimension had to be matched to the primordial (preconceptual) embodied perception of the world, with its predominantly motor and tactile dimensions. In Perrault's theory, the ideal had absolute priority over physical reality. Theory thus became a set of technical intructions whose fundamental objective was to be easily and directly applicable.

Claude Perrault was obsessed with the transformation of theory into an *ars fabricandi*. His proportional system clearly reveals this intention. Due to his peculiar position in a metaphysical vacuum, he could be more radically modern than many of his successors. Nevertheless, it is important to remember that his protopositivistic attitude was never free from contradictions and has to be carefully qualified. Living in the time of Louis XIV, he had faith in the structure and ornament derived from classical antiquity. He never

Typical illustration of the need for optical correction
in design, from the first French edition of Vitruvius's
Ten Books by Martin and Goujon (1547).

Claude Perrault and the Instrumentalization of Proportion

questioned the validity of the classical orders themselves and appeared to accept their essential role in architectural practice. He even tried to justify his new system of proportion by declaring that it only modified minimally a few details "not important for the overall beauty of buildings."[45] Perrault's architectural intentions thus appear inconsistent on many levels. In the most profound sense, however, these are already the contradictions of modern architecture, appearing most explicitly in Perrault's still traditional world.

Perrault frequently resorted to the myth of ancient authority as a justification of his own theory. He even affirmed that his system of proportion, being the most rational, was a type originally recommended by Vitruvius.[46] This antique proportion, based on whole numbers and easy to remember, had been abandoned by modern architects only because it did not coincide with the artifacts and ruins of antiquity. Significantly, Perrault blamed the carelessness of craftsmanship for this lack of correspondence, imagining again a one-to-one relation between a rational theory and architectural practice.

Perrault had defined architectural beauty in terms of its visible aspects. For him the visible, or the phenomenon, is clearly distinguished from the invisible, or the speculative cause, with the former always having priority over the latter. Perrault's theory of architecture is the first in which the distance between a visible form and an invisible content becomes problematical. Such a disparity could only exist after the inception of Cartesianism. Many of the contradictions apparent in Perrault's work derive precisely from his different attitudes toward the perceptual and conceptual dimensions. In terms of visibility, Perrault accepted the conventional forms of traditional architecture while rejecting the magical implications of numerical systems as the invisible cause of beauty.

Although Perrault could point to the relativity of architectural proportions, he never questioned the traditional symbolic connotations of the classical orders. But it is important to note that architectural meaning was never perceived in terms of a style's formal coherence. Perrault used the term "Gothic order" to describe a church in Bordeaux and admitted that French taste was somewhat Gothic, differing from that of the ancients: "We like airiness, lightness and the quality of free-standing structures."[47] His "sixth order" of coupled columns was meant to reflect this taste, an obvious precedent of Neoclassical intentions. A good number of Perrault's contemporaries, both his immediate predecessors and his successors in France and England, were prepared to admit and appreciate the value of alternative systems of ornamentation, for example, Gothic and Chinese. The most important condition was always the presence of an invisible *mathesis*, which assured the role of architecture as a true art of imitation. Thus the relevance of Perrault's position on this issue. The question about the origins of modern architecture cannot be simply a matter of evaluating the extent to which the classical orders were used or rejected.

Charles Perrault was even more extreme in his *Parallèle*, in which he recognized the historical relativism of the forms and ornamentation of classical architecture. He believed that architectural ornament had the same character as rhetorical figure in language,[48] which is why all architecture must use it. The merit of an architect, however, was not in his ability to use columns, pilasters, and cornices, but in "the placement of these elements with good judgment in order to compose beautiful buildings."[49] The actual form of such ornament "could be totally different . . . without being less pleasant, if our eyes were equally accustomed to it."[50] Charles seemed ready to declare that beauty derived only from a formal or syntactic relation among the elements of a given ornamental system. Although he never did so, the way had been opened for others to question the traditional symbolic role of architecture as a whole.

Clearly, the Perrault brothers believed in the perfection of their own time.[51] In the preface to his edition of Vitruvius's *Ten Books*, Claude identified the Golden Age of Louis XIV with the mythical excellence of the Roman Empire. Architecture had to be conceived in terms of Roman prototypes.[52] Perrault particularly admired the richness and splendor of Imperial Rome. He believed that grand modern architecture had to recover those qualities of ancient building. This ideal, as well as his conviction that theory was absolutely essential, compelled him to translate and comment upon the treatise of Vitruvius. At the time, there was no adequate French edition of the Latin text, and Perrault believed that ignorance of the "original precepts" of architecture was a great obstacle to the revival of this art.[53]

Perrault was aware that the rules of Vitruvius constituted only one possibility among many. He justified his preference for the Roman by emphasizing the necessity of theoretical precepts: "Beauty has no other foundation than the imagination.... It is [therefore] necessary to establish rules that would form and correct the idea [that each one of us has of perfection]."[54] Perrault was convinced that rules are so necessary that if nature did not provide them for certain disciplines, then it was the responsibility of human institutions to supply them, "and for that there should be agreement on a certain authority as having the character of positive reasons."[55] But Perrault also adopted a critical attitude and pointed out that the authority of Vitruvius did not derive from a blind veneration of antiquity or from his association with a historical period identified with perfection. Nevertheless, in spite of his tone of scientific objectivity, Perrault certainly would not have embraced the gigantic task of translating and commenting upon the text of Vitruvius if he had not been convinced that it constituted "the original source of architectural rules"[56] and that "the precepts of this excellent author . . . are absolutely necessary to guide all those who want to attain perfection in the art of architecture."[57]

Perrault sincerely believed in the importance of Vitruvius's theory as the *fons et origo* of the great symbolic wealth that he admired in the architecture of the Roman Empire. Concerning the issue of proportion, however, Perrault declared in the *Ordonnance* that no author of the past had sufficient authority. The rules of proportion derive from custom, but are fundamental. It is here that the most revealing contradiction in Perrault's intentionality appears.

According to Perrault, a thorough knowledge of the rules of proportion is essential because they form the "taste that any true architect must have."[58] In Perrault's definition, "positive beauty" is visible; but precisely for this reason, it can be discerned by anyone with a minimum of common sense. It is simple enough to distinguish between rich and poor architecture, between a building executed with excellent craftsmanship and one badly constructed.[59] To succeed in his design, the architect must know the more subtle rules governing "arbitrary beauty." Although proportion might be arbitrary, established through custom and use, although it might not lead necessarily to positive beauty, it is still essential for the practicing architect. The accord or consensus derived from custom is still considered a positive frame of reference. The ambiguity, never fully understood by most eighteenth-century architects and theoreticians, is made explicit in a footnote to Perrault's edition of Vitruvius[60] in which he claims that customs are powerful enough to warrant the belief in some architectural proportions as being "naturally approved and loved." Identified with musical harmony, these proportions are assumed to possess true beauty.[61]

Perrault's designs for a triumphal arch and the Louvre, appearing in the background of the frontispiece of his edition of Vitruvius's *Ten Books*.

Claude Perrault and the Instrumentalization of Proportion

In Perrault's theory, proportions were identified through *association* with positive beauty. He is the first architect to question the traditional belief that meaning appears immediately through perception. Instead, he provides an associative, conceptual explanation of architectural value. His understanding of perception is already akin to that of modern psychology's: *partes extra partes*, which affirms the separation of optical, tactile, and auditive sensations, synthesized only in the mind.

Perrault invoked the authority of Vitruvius in an effort to escape the irreconcilable contradictions of his theory. The writings of the Roman architect were believed to embody the visible aspects of classical architecture. But proportion, the essential invisible cause, became as relative as any other conceptual explanatory system in Perrault's thought. This splitting of the architectural "phenomenon" would be taken for granted only in the practice of nineteenth- and twentieth-century architecture.

Perrault never denied the importance of *mathesis* in architecture. But conscious of the scientific revolution and its implications, he gave number a totally different role, using it as an operational device, as a positive instrument for simplifying the process of design or avoiding the irregularities of practice. His theory of proportion demanded absolute and direct control over the dimensions of the orders. The fundamental intention betrayed by such use of number is totally modern. His theory pretended to be a set of perfect, rational rules whose express objective was to be easily and immediately applicable. Perrault never went further. He did not attempt to mathematize human behavior or the structural stability of buildings, but he did lead the way toward a progressive architecture. Progress since then has become synonymous with the further reduction of architecture to mathematical reason.

It is well known that the technological dream of effective domination of matter through number and geometry became a reality only after the Industrial Revolution. But as soon as number had lost its symbolic connotations in philosophy toward the end of the seventeenth century, Perrault used it in his proportional system with the same intention. At the time, traditional systems of proportion were only "applied" through the personal experience of the architect and were postulated, essentially, as an elucidation of the reconciliatory nature of architecture and its meaning. In sharp contrast, Perrault's system pretended to be as perfect and universal as reason itself. Analogous to his physical systems, his set of a priori rules of proportion was devoid of all transcendental overtones. Its objective was to guide architectural design "in the least bad possible way," rejecting its traditional role as a source of absolute certainty.

<table>
<tr><td>François Blondel's Reaction</td><td>

Most architects of the seventeenth and eighteenth centuries were interested more in the physical dimension of architecture than in ideal solutions. Consequently, they rejected or misunderstood Perrault's writings. His substitution of the practical realm for a conceptual, a priori system could not be easily admitted. Some architects simply ignored the more profound implications of his theory and considered the *Ordonnance* just another treatise on the orders.[62] Still others doubted the conviction behind his arguments. It was not difficult to find discrepancies between his theory and his few but famous buildings. It is important to remember that architectural *praxis* generally kept its traditional *modus operandi* during the seventeenth and eighteenth centuries.

</td></tr>
</table>

Nevertheless, Perrault's writings created a significant theoretical discussion in which architects were to take sides for more than a hundred years. His theory was criticized initially by François Blondel, the engineer and architect responsible for the construction of several fortifications and who was the author of a course on mathematics, a treatise on bombs, a book on the mechanism of clocks, and a history of the Roman calendar. Like Perrault, he wrote an influential treatise on architecture and was a member of the Royal Academy of Science. He was not only a founding member of the Academy of Architecture but also the first official professor at that institution.

In spite of these similarities, however, Blondel's architectural intentions were still deeply rooted in the Baroque world of the seventeenth century. His understanding of science, philosophy, and mathematics is basically different from Perrault's, based as it is on a fundamental synthesis of the perceptual and conceptual dimensions of knowledge.

Blondel's epistemological context is indeed akin to Galileo's. But it must be remembered that even the Italian scientist was incapable of discerning clearly between "true causes" and "illusions" of an observed "effect." Although he could posit isolated discoveries without concern for final causes, rejecting the hierarchical and animistic cosmos of Aristotle, Galileo still believed that the human mind and the world were linked through geometrical structure, the result of preestablished harmony. It is now believed that a great number of Galileo's discoveries were the result of "experiments" that took place only in his imagination.[63] In the *Dialogue of the Two Sciences*, Galileo pointed out that the circle was perfect not only from an aesthetic or mathematical point of view but also where it concerned physical science.[64] His synthetic understanding of value as embodied in geometry was shared by seventeenth-century artists and architects.[65] Galileo identified geometry with nature. He believed the idea of a sphere or a circle was perfectly realized in each specific sphere or circle. The world was perceived as a constant materialization of geometry. During the seventeenth century, the mathematical sciences became a means of achieving the most abstract, and therefore the most valuable, imitation of nature.

Traditional Aristotelian philosophers distinguished the qualitative places of the central, permanently fixed world of man from the geometrical space of the stars and planets, which was conceived as a truly ideal entity. The hierarchy of places of the sublunar world could be identified with geometrical space only after man became a subject, a rational mind separated from the objective reality of the world. Only then could man pretend that real phenomena should be understood in the framework of an ideal space. This implied substituting an independent entity governed by the properties of geometrical space for the original and undifferentiated field of intentions where reality was constituted. In the modern universe, bodies become aggregates of material points, behaving mathematically in an infinite and homogeneous extension.

Seventeenth-century philosophers, scientists, and artists accepted that the book of nature was written in a mathematical alphabet. Because the figures of Euclidean geometry related to the perception of the real world, they were ultimately a product of intuition,[66] and thus geometry could become a *scientia universalis*, a symbolic science *par excellence*. Innate, God-given ideas were believed to derive from geometrical prototypes, as was the divine alphabet that had been impressed on the things of the visible world by the Creator. Seventeenth-century geometry provided a link with the higher realities that gave ultimate meaning to human existence. As a vehicle for the constitution of symbols, geometry became normative in the arts, music, and literature. Moreover, it became accepted as the only true mode of perception, a condition that one day would provide the context for the desecration and technological exploitation of the world.

Baroque architectural intentions, apart from the specificity of their cultural embodiment, such as the diverse buildings of Christopher Wren, Guarino Guarini, and François Blondel, were founded in this epistemological context. They shared to a greater or lesser degree this necessarily ambivalent interest in geometry and mathematics.

In the *Cours d'Architecture*, the first textbook for the students at the Royal Academy of Architecture, François Blondel criticized Perrault's theoretical assumptions from many revealing angles. Blondel reaffirmed the belief, commonly held since the Renaissance, of the great importance of theory.[67] Realizing, however, that the writings of Vitruvius only reflected the doctrines of the Greek architects that had preceded him and did not coincide "with the most beautiful remains from antiquity," Blondel also provided the rules given by other excellent architects, such as Vignola, Palladio, and Scamozzi.[68] His intention was to examine and compare these rules, showing where they concurred or differed, in order to establish those precepts that could be more universally accepted. This was, in his opinion, the only way to fashion the contemporary architect's taste. Clearly, Blondel's attitude contrasts with Perrault's desire to establish an exclusive, simple, and rational system of architectural proportion. Blondel did not believe that the difference of opinion among the great architects of the past constituted a real problem. He understood their writings to be essentially true insofar as they referred to the theoretical dimension of their unquestionably valuable work. The problem was always one of personal interpretation. The architect had to choose the most appropriate rules and apply them in each case through his personal experience.

Blondel discussed at length the problem of optical corrections, which he considered of great importance. He openly criticized Perrault on this issue. Using as evidence some famous buildings, he emphasized the need to adjust the dimensions of buildings so that their proportions might appear correctly in perspective.[69] Writing in italics, he asserted that the successful determination of the real dimensions of a building, once the increments and reductions of the original proportions had been considered, was precisely the aspect that revealed the architect's strength of intellect (*esprit*): "The result depends more on the vivacity and genius of the architect than on any rule that might be established."[70]

Claude Perrault had rejected optical adjustments, indicating that the human mind immediately corrected these distortions; his attitude was motivated by an obsession to reduce the distance between his rational theory and traditional practice. Blondel, on the other hand, still understood theory primarily as a transcendental justification of practice, recognizing a profound and noncontradictory continuity between both aspects. He emphasized the importance of personal expression and decision in architecture, an emphasis that Perrault's *ars fabricandi* would have gladly eliminated in favor of reason. The discrepancies between the diverse systems of proportion and the real dimensions of executed buildings, which became intolerable for Perrault, were perfectly justified in Blondel's theory.

In view of all this, it is significant to note Blondel's interest in mathematics. His passion for geometry was much greater than Perrault's. In a small book entitled *Résolution des Quatre Principaux Problèmes de l'Architecture*, Blondel pointed out that architecture was, in fact, a part of mathematics.[71] This was not an uncommon attitude among architects and philosophers of the seventeenth century, and Blondel, for one, maintained that all that was "good and magnificent" in architecture came from mathematics. The "principal" and most difficult problems were indeed propositions concerning statics and geometry.[72] He was convinced that much would be gained if architects studied mathematics and mathematicians studied architecture. The course of architecture that Blondel taught at the academy included, aside from the rules of the classical orders, geometry, arithmetic, mechanics, hydraulics, gnomonics (solar clocks), fortifications, perspective, and stereotomy (stonecutting).[73] In his short treatise on fortifications, geometrical tracings are used to determine the configuration, angles, and location of every element according to the regular polygon selected as a plan for the building.[74]

Although Blondel recognized the virtue of mathematics as a technical instrument, a careful examination of his work reveals his inability to distinguish between the symbolic and merely technical uses of geometry and number. In his book on the principal problems of architecture, he discusses on equal terms certain "errors" he has found in the mechanics of Galileo and the attributes of harmonic proportion. Similarly, in his *Cours*, following upon the traditional rules of proportions for the classical orders is a method for finding the dimensions of a pier or other vertical structural element in relation to the geometry of the supported arch or vault.[75] After several impressive plates that show elaborate geometrical methods for the determination of elliptical and parabolic arches, Blondel reproduced the proportions Vitruvius recommended for the design of doors and compared them to corresponding Renaissance rules.

In the *Cours*, Blondel expressed his opinion about the Dispute of the Ancients and the Moderns. He believed that both sides

Geometry as a transcendental revelation, discovered
by the philosopher Aristippus after a happy landing.
An allegory on the meaning of mathematics from J.
Ozanam's *Récréations Mathématiques* (1696).

Claude Perrault and the Instrumentalization of Proportion

had good arguments. Antiquity, being the source of modern excellence, deserved to be esteemed, even venerated. But this veneration should never be slavish. Adopting a very moderate position, he concluded that "all beautiful things should be appreciated, regardless of when or where they had been produced, or who had been their author."[76] Consequently, Blondel upheld both the perfection of his own century and that of the Roman Empire.[77] And he could also admit, like Perrault, the possibility of progress in architecture.[78] But Blondel never accepted that progress was inevitably linked with an acceptance of relative values.

The fundamental problem was not, in his opinion, the greater or lesser merits of ancient and modern authors, but the absolute or relative nature of architectural value. Blondel accepted the existence of diverse tastes and appreciations of beauty, but he rejected the notion that beauty might ultimately be the result of custom. He firmly believed "with most authors" in the existence of a natural beauty, capable of producing everlasting pleasures, a natural beauty derived from mathematical or geometrical proportions. This was true not only for architects but also for poetry, eloquence, music, and even dance. The arrangement and proportion of the elements among themselves and in relation to the whole resulted in "harmonic unity," allowing the diverse parts of the work to be perceived simultaneously and without difficulty. Harmony was, therefore, the source of true pleasure.[79]

Blondel devoted a whole chapter of the *Cours* to discussing and proving the importance of proportion in architecture.[80] He collected opinions of the most prestigious Renaissance authors, espousing many of their traditional beliefs. He affirmed the existence of a profound analogy between human proportions and the dimensions of the classical orders. The proportions of buildings, therefore, could not be arbitrarily altered. Commenting on Alberti's theory, Blondel emphasized that harmony had a deep-seated relation to the human soul (*âme*) and reason. Architecture had always tried to follow the rules of nature, and "nature is invariable in all its aspects." Consequently, "the numbers that make sound agreeable to the ear are the same that make objects pleasant to the eyes."[81]

After devoting a large section of the *Cours* to proving graphically the existence of geometrical proportions in the most prestigious buildings of antiquity and the Renaissance, Blondel finally confronted Perrault's theory. Summarizing Perrault's ideas on beauty, Blondel categorically rejected Perrault's fundamental assumption that "it matters little to architects whether the beauty of a building derives from nature or custom."[82] This point, Blondel stated, is

Number and Architectural Proportion

of the greatest importance and should be clarified. He then espouses the contrary opinion, sharing the ideas "of most, if not all the authors that have written about architecture."[83]

Both Blondel and Perrault believed in the unquestionable value of classical architecture. Blondel could also admit the ephemeral and mutable character of some architectural elements, such as the capitals of columns, which, in his opinion, did not derive from nature. The pleasure these elements provided was, indeed, dependent upon custom. But Blondel always believed that number and geometry, the regulating principles of nature and the embodied human being, linked both poles of the Creation and were therefore a cause of positive beauty: "External ornaments do not constitute beauty. Beauty cannot exist when the proportions are missing."[84] Even Gothic buildings, according to him, could be beautiful when they were determined by geometry and proportion. Relying on the traditional belief that our perception of the world is a projection of the human body, Blondel maintained that geometry and proportion, being transcendental entities, guaranteed the highest architectural meaning, apart from the specificity of ornament or style. For example, the bilateral symmetry in any building provided a positive delight precisely because it was an imitation of the disposition of a beautiful face or human body.[85] While Perrault believed that the systems of architectural proportion were not "true" but only "probable," Blondel's theory argued that geometry and mathematics, being invariable, assured the truth and beauty of architecture at all levels; by relating man's immediate perception of the world with absolute values, they became a tool for fulfilling architecture's fundamental symbolic role.

Also, Blondel insisted that number, in spite of its invisibility, was a primordial source of beauty: "Although it is true that there is no convincing demonstration in favor of proportions, it is also evident that there are no conclusive proofs against them."[86] Not content with a simple declaration, Blondel devoted a chapter of his *Cours* to trying to substantiate his belief scientifically. The title of this section is in itself significant: "Proofs That Proportions Are the *Cause* of Architectural Beauty and That This Beauty Is Founded in Nature, Like That Produced by Musical Accords."[87] Using as examples several well-known physical phenomena, Blondel showed how invisible causes of a mathematical nature (such as the relation between a force and the dimensions of a lever or that among angles of incidence as in reflection and refraction in optics) proved and explained effects that occurred in the real world. Applying these observations to architecture, he

Claude Perrault and the Instrumentalization of Proportion

The proportions in the section of Milan Cathedral,
from F. Blondel's *Cours d'Architecture*.

Number and Architectural Proportion

wrote, "Experience has shown that there are proportions in beautiful buildings that we cannot find in disagreeable ones. . . . My emphatic affirmation of proportions as a cause of beauty and elegance in architecture should not be surprising. . . . Architecture, being a part of mathematics, should possess *stable and constant principles*, so that, through study and meditation, it might be possible to derive an infinite number of consequences and useful rules for the construction of buildings."[88]

Blondel, however, could not distinguish between architectural proportion and the mathematical laws of optics or mechanics. Invariable geometrical principles derived in both cases "from induction and experience." He was also unable to distinguish between the proportions of a building resulting from technical concerns and proportions motivated by aesthetic considerations. His confusion contrasts with the protopositivistic lucidity of Perrault, who, in trying to convince the readers of his *Ordonnance* that the proportions of the orders should be fixed and rational, stated that such an achievement should not be so difficult since "architectural proportions are not of the same nature as those required in military architecture or the manufacture of machines."[89] Perrault emphasized the difference between the arbitrary proportions used in architecture and the necessary mathematical strictures in other disciplines. While the dimensions of a detail of the orders could be changed without detriment to the general appearance of a building, lines of defense in fortifications or the dimensions of levers had to be absolutely fixed. Perrault distinguished speculative cause from observed phenomenon. Blondel, reflecting in a more conventional way the Baroque epistemological world view, did not recognize the difference between true physical cause and illusion, between magic and an effective technique.

Blondel realized that Perrault's theory questioned the fundamental metaphysical justification of architecture. His own refutation of an architecture that lacked absolute principles was obsessive. Three times he wrote in italics that the human intellect would be terribly affected if it could not find stable and invariable principles. Without such principles, man could have no satisfactory idea of unity and would be restless and anguished. Blondel was thus compelled to support the traditional theory of proportion, one that provided "stable and invariable principles," which in effect justified architecture's *raison d'être*. He categorically rejected relativism as a dangerous and senseless possibility.

Claude Perrault and the Instrumentalization of Proportion

2

SYSTEMS OF PROPORTION AND NATURAL SCIENCE

The famous dispute between Perrault and Blondel touched upon a fundamental issue, one that concerned the very meaning of architecture itself. The new theory, ultimately founded on the modern mechanistic world view, was haunted by an incipient subjectivism, which caused it to question its own ability to provide absolute and rational justifications of *praxis*. I have already pointed out that during the period between 1680 and 1735, the new epistemology ushered in by Galileo was felt with particular intensity. During the first decades of the eighteenth century, architects were generally very interested in technical problems and in their mathematical solutions.[1] This protopositivistic interest generally went hand in hand with criticism of traditional theory.

In 1702 Michel de Fremin published an astonishing little book entitled *Mémoires Critiques d'Architecture*, in which he defined architecture as "the art of building according to the object, the subject, and the place."[2] Taking to their logical conclusion some of the ideas expressed by Claude and Charles Perrault, Fremin questioned, for the first time in the history of Western architecture, the traditional primacy of the classical orders. He pointed out that a knowledge of the orders and their proportions constituted only a minimal part of what architecture truly was.

Fremin's book deals essentially with problems of construction but also emphasizes that the architect is not a mason; his role is to coordinate rationally all the operations of building.[3] Fremin believed that the architect had to control mentally the totality of the process of design and construction, making sure that all he imagined possessed absolute unity and coherence. He thought that good architecture had to be rational and used Gothic examples to illustrate what he had in mind. Fremin preferred Notre-Dame or the Sainte-Chapelle over the recent Baroque architecture, which he disliked and criticized, including the work of Blondel.

Fremin was also suspicious of seductive architectural drawings that were merely nicely rendered but lacked "architectural consistency."[4] This implied an understanding of drawing as a reductive technical tool, an understanding that would only become widespread in the nineteenth century.[5] While drawing had always expressed an architectural intention, the distance between its specific universe of discourse and that of "real building" had never been a problem.

Fremin's understanding of theory, his perception "of that which constitutes true architecture," his attitude toward drawing, and his derogatory comments about "insignificant" architects who speak only about the classical orders, betray a truly protopositivistic attitude. He was totally oblivious to the metaphysical dimension of theory.

Perrault's influence appeared most explicitly in Abbé Cordemoy's *Nouveau Traité* (1706),[6] in which the defects and bad taste in most buildings are attributed to a lack of knowledge of the principles of architecture.[7] Believing that traditional treatises were useless because it was impossible to take from them the dimensions and proportions of the orders, Cordemoy praised Perrault's *Ordonnance*: "This book is the only one from which craftsmen can profit. [Perrault] provided a certain and comfortable rule for the dimensions and proportions of each order. He has even inspired the idea of beauty."[8]

Cordemoy invariably avoided any discussion of the critical questions concerning the relation between proportions and beauty. In this respect, he found Perrault "too verbose, confused, and rather obscure."[9] He never examined in his treatise the implications of proportion, except for a definition of the term that he included in the *Dictionary* added to the second edition.[10] After transcribing some opinions of Vitruvius, Cordemoy affirmed the importance of establishing a module that would allow the spectator to judge the dimensions of a building. This dimensional comparison permitted the beauty, majesty, and impact of the building to work upon the intellect. However, Cordemoy ignored the transcendental implications of proportion. He never seemed interested in establishing the actual numerical value of the module. Proportion and beauty seemed to have become problems of intellectual judgment, of relative scale rather than absolute value.

The lack of importance that Cordemoy attributed to the issue of proportion is in itself significant. He reproduced in the *Nouveau Traité* Perrault's simplified system based on the *petit module*, repeated the story about it being the most primitive, and blamed defective craftsmanship throughout history for its abandonment. Cordemoy also believed that mathematical precision was indispensable in theory. But the meaning of proportion was not even worth discussing. He seemed to be interested in the virtues of Perrault's system only as an *ars fabricandi* for craftsmen.

Perrault's immediate impact can also be discerned in the work of Sebastien Le Clerc, whose diverse interests ranged from the formulation of a cosmological system in which he tried to reconcile the Bible with Descartes's physics, to the invention of a curious theory of perception, in which only the right eye was capable of

Systems of Proportion and Natural Science

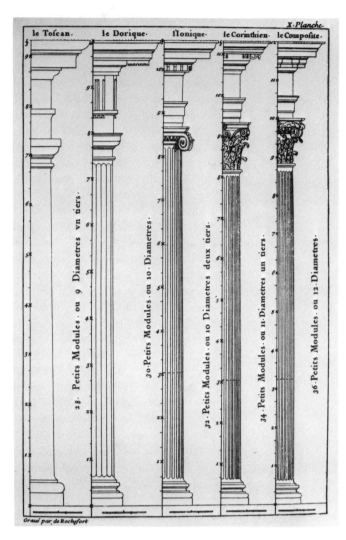

Perrault's system of proportion, reproduced by Cordemoy in his `Iouveau Traité.

Number and Architectural Proportion

clear vision.[11] In his *Traité d'Architecture* (1714), Le Clerc repeated Blondel's plea for all architects to learn mathematics and its related disciplines, including mechanics, leveling, hydraulics, perspective, and stonecutting.[12]

After comparing the proportions for the classical orders recommended by Vignola and Palladio, Le Clerc concluded that their rules were arbitrary, a product of their own taste and genius.[13] He also observed that it was possible to change the proportions of smaller elements such as triglyphs and metopes without offending even those most knowledgeable in architecture. Le Clerc insisted on the "absolute necessity of geometry" in architecture and described this science as the foundation of the principles that guide architectural practice.[14] Like Perrault, Le Clerc distinguished between a necessary "rational" geometry and the contingent proportions of the classical orders.[15]

Building upon these conclusions, Le Clerc decided to postulate his own system. Significantly, however, this is where the similarities with Perrault end. Le Clerc established his proportions through discussion and observation. Although there were often different proportions recommended for the same order, "it is unquestionable that among them some are more pleasing and receive universal approval."[16] He believed that his own personal taste could discern the better rules. Thus, instead of postulating an a priori mathematical system, Le Clerc thought that his rules had to be constituted a posteriori. His more humble attitude evinced no interest in controlling practice through a rational theory, and on the surface his discussion of proportions seemed merely traditional. In fact, however, his thought started to reveal a different set of epistemological presuppositions. In his theory, taste was already capable of stemming the menace of relativism while maintaining the possibility of reason—an early sign of the Neoclassical world.

Amédée-François Frezier, author of a famous treatise on stonecutting, was a long-lived architect and military engineer.[17] Interested in science and construction, he was aware that geometry and mathematics were the basic disciplines providing the means for the implementation of technical operations. For Frezier, architecture was mainly a problem of rational building, and in several literary disputes with the most famous Neoclassical theoreticians, he argued that arches and piers were more suitable for stone construction than the column and lintel systems preferred by the architects and patrons of the Enlightenment.[18] It is particularly interesting, therefore, to observe the way in which he interpreted Perrault's ideas in his *Dissertation sur les Ordres d'Architecture* (1738).

Frezier recognized along with Perrault that there were no fixed rules in architecture. Ornament changed constantly, and therefore "it has no real beauty."[19] He admitted that "fashion reigns over the classical orders" and that it often determined our idea of beauty. But unlike Perrault, he never accepted custom as a positive force: "Fashion is not always a certain rule for judging what is beautiful or deformed."[20] Custom no longer determined a choice of proportions, which were then identified with "positive beauty" through association. Instead, it became a negative factor that prevented the appreciation of true natural beauty.

Frezier believed that the classical orders should be strictly subjected to rational laws, which could guide architecture toward "purely natural beauty."[21] And he believed it was possible to establish such rational principles, independent of the diversity of personal tastes and opinions: "Everyone would accept that the imitation of a natural thing is a cause of pleasure . . . and being perfect, a copied object derived from a beautiful nature is a cause of even greater pleasure than the original. . . . If it exists, the universal rule of the orders should be founded on the imitation of Natural architecture."[22] The point was, in Frezier's opinion, to establish the principles of this "great art . . . which has often even been called a science" and to obtain them from the most simple things. This, in turn, would lead architecture back to its origins. Natural architecture was simple, like Nature itself in eighteenth-century science.

After an evocation of primitive architecture taken from Vitruvius, Frezier discussed the appropriate number of architectural orders.[23] Inspired by the methods of natural philosophy, he declared his intention to reduce the number of principles to the least possible. Acknowledging only three ways to build: heavily, lightly, or in an intermediate manner, he concluded that there should also be only three orders: Doric, Ionic, and Corinthian. The Tuscan and Composite, normally accepted since the Renaissance, were rejected.

Frezier believed that man had a natural idea of the proportions between the dimensions of a column and the weight it carried. It was obvious that columns more squat than Doric or taller than Corinthian could be built. But the former lacked "grace," while the latter, although perhaps physically stable, would appear as dangerous and thus be unacceptable to the human intellect. Building should possess not only real stability but also "visible solidity."[24]

With this in mind, Frezier applied his natural common sense and experience to the determination of the maximum and minimum acceptable proportions and attributed them to the Doric and Corinthian orders. The proportions of the Ionic order were obviously the *juste milieu* between the two extremes and resulted from an arithmetical average of their dimensions. Frezier pointed out that in applying this system, it becomes possible to determine the proportions of the essential parts of each order: the column and the entablature. The greater weight should always be carried by the wider columns. But the adjustment of dimensions, he added, should be left to the good taste of the architect.[25]

Discussing the issue of proportion, Frezier recognized the great differences among traditional systems. Architects had chosen diverse modules, dividing their dimensions in extraordinarily complicated ways. However, Frezier questioned the "scientific" thoroughness of his predecessors, suggesting that perhaps their irrationality was intentional, "as if they had tried to complicate this frivolous issue and give an air of mystery to this art, which is almost totally arbitrary in that concerning the small subdivisions."[26] Frezier thus rejected the inveterate symbolic connotations of architectural proportion, maintaining that the dimensions recommended by architects and writers of the past were based only on their particular tastes. Numerical relations, then, did not constitute a mysterious guarantee of architectural beauty.

Like Perrault, Frezier believed that the "causes" of beauty should be visible and not merely speculative. But Perrault had postulated an a priori, mathematically perfect system of proportions, emphasizing its formal rather than its transcendental dimension. This, of course, was the only possible scientific solution to the problem in the epistemological context of the late seventeenth century. During the Enlightenment, however, the meaning of life itself would become visible in the operations of Nature, as revealed by the new empirical science. Frezier could therefore assert that the principles of architecture should be founded on the laws of nature and stem invariably from observation and not from a merely conceptual operation.

Thus Frezier established the essential proportions of his three orders, defining the relations among the heights of columns, their diameters, and the dimensions of their entablatures.[27] His proportions were simple, but they were never intended to become

Systems of Proportion and Natural Science

a mere tool of design. They were not arbitrary but natural and were therefore believed to be the most perfect, constituting a true source of pleasure. Even with regard to minor details, Frezier ended up admitting the existence of proportions, "which it is not possible to alter considerably."[28] The dimensions of doors and windows, for example, cannot be changed because their beauty "derives from a natural sentiment through which we relate everything to the dimensions of our body and to our needs, even before reason has determined their convenience."[29] To prove his point, Frezier stated that if humans had the proportions of sheep or birds, they would prefer square or circular openings. But because humans are approximately "three times as tall as . . . wide," these are the proportions that are considered beautiful. This phenomenological return to reality, with its emphasis on preconceptual perception as a fundamental source of meaning, would become normative in the natural philosophy of the Enlightenment.

Frezier provided an excellent summary of his own position when he declared himself "only partially (*de moitié*) in accord with Perrault on the insufficiency of proportions as a source of real beauty."[30] His theory of architecture, founded on the epistemological framework defined by eighteenth-century empirical science, sought to recover an explicit, traditional interest in absolute value (identified with mathematics) while accepting without contradiction the increasing power of reason.

A similar attitude was adopted by Père André in his influential and popular *Essai sur le Beau* (1741). André believed there were two types of rules in architecture: (1) rules that were necessarily equivocal and uncertain, resulting from the observations of diverse masters in different times; and (2) rules that were visible and conducive to positive beauty. André thought that the proportions of the classical orders were in the first group, but he also stressed the geometrical character of the second type of rules, which were "invariable like the science of architecture itself."[31] Essential geometrical principles, such as the perpendicularity of columns, parallelism of floors, symmetry, and perceptual unity, were always to be observed. In fact, André considered all regularity, order, and proportion to be attributes of essential beauty.

As the century grew older, Perrault's precocious distinction between technical necessity and contingent aesthetic considerations seemed to vanish from architectural theory. The dimensions of number and geometry as technical instruments or symbols began to be perceived as complementary in considering architectural value. Around 1750 preference for François Blondel's position in the famous dispute was practically universal, whereas Perrault's ideas often evoked criticism. The most explicit refutation of Perrault's theories appeared in Charles-Etienne Briseux's *Traité du Beau Essentiel* (1752), which sought to show the falsity of Perrault's ideas through the opinions of prestigious writers and evidence derived from "physical explanations and experience."

Briseux accepted that progress in art and science was prompted by a healthy expression of diverse opinions, but he believed extreme subjectivism was dangerous. An obstinate adherence to a certain position, "frequently motivated by the false honor of defending a singular system," often makes men lose sight of their own internal convictions.[32] Briseux speculated that Perrault's defense of a system of proportions "that had absolutely no relation to the beauty of buildings" might have been prompted by such human weakness. In Briseux's opinion, Perrault, perhaps offended by Blondel, had become insensitive to his own knowledge, the opinions of other authors, and the unquestionable evidence of experience. What caused him the most concern was the vast influence he thought the *Ordonnance* had exerted on other architects. Significantly, Briseux was aware that Perrault's system of proportion never became popular with eighteenth-century practicing architects. The issue was not simply one of immediate application. Briseux understood that the potential freedom from traditional principles, implicit in Perrault's theory, had made itself felt during the first half of the century. The ornamental exaggerations of Rococo, popular after 1715, were a clear manifestation of this influence.[33] Distinct from Baroque architecture (though certain formal similarities remain), Rococo eschewed theory. Only pattern books were used as sources of images. Taking their cue from Perrault, some architects felt themselves liberated from the authority of antiquity and resorted to a superficial, purely visible understanding of nature as a source of forms. By midcentury the nonmetaphysical nature of *rocaille* had been replaced by the Nature of Newtonianism, of which more will be said later. At this point, Rococo was universally condemned as decadent by the theoreticians of Neoclassical architecture.

The impact of Perrault's incipient *ars fabricandi* was also felt in the Royal Academy of Architecture, where discussions during the first half of the century dealt mainly with technical questions. This obviously reflected the general interest of architects and caused Briseux to complain that the true "principles of architecture" were no longer taught by professors who followed the banner of Perrault.[34] Briseux considered the *Ordonnance* to be exceptionally obscure and full of contradictions. His refutation seems traditional at first glance. He asserted the analogy between the causes and effects of beauty in architecture and music and carefully justified his belief. In music, the harmonic relations, although not generally understood by the public, were nevertheless the source of pleasure. Equally, in architecture, the observer did not measure "geometrically" the building with his eyes before receiving the "sensation" of beauty. But "a sort of natural trigonometry" seemed to play a large role in the judgment of "the spectator who possesses a natural taste."[35] "The sensation of beauty" always depended on the observance of proportions, whose knowledge was the responsibility of the architect.

Briseux firmly stated that reason underlined all those products of "art and Nature" that were beautiful. This is an indication of Briseux's fundamental belief in a transcendental Nature and in the absolute character of its laws. His *Traité* attempted to prove the visibility of harmonic proportions in architecture and to show their origin in the mathematical laws that governed nature itself. Such proportions might then be said to be "analogous" to the human intellect, which perceives them with pleasure, and thus be posited as the unquestionable cause of essential beauty.

Briseux's text begins with a poetic glorification of Nature, "our fecund mother that leaves nothing to chance."[36] Nature is described as a projection of the human body, the ultimate model of just proportions, providing the true idea of harmony and symmetry. Harmonic proportion, moreover, had its origin in nature. The famous experiments of Pythagoras, who had subdivided a string into fractions producing harmonic consonances, clearly proved this point. Briseux then related how the ancients "inferred" from this observation a common principle of beauty, one that derived from the law of harmonic proportion, which was itself part of nature and did not depend on the visual or auditive character of our sensations. The human intellect, the judge of all "sensations," thus received from each of the senses uniformly pleasant or disagreeable "impressions".

But it was clear to Briseux that "the Creator established a natural sympathy between certain sounds and our emotions" that was not as explicit with regard to the inanimate objects of the visible world. The traditional justification of antiquity no longer seemed sufficient. Briseux was then forced to reformulate the question of this relation in a more rigorous and scientific manner. His conclusions reveal the most fundamental sources of his thought: "The rainbow provides an excellent example; its colors are clearly distinguishable, but everything is reduced to unity. According to the experiments of the renowned Newton, this marvelous effect originated from the correspondence between the proportions of the spaces occupied by the seven colors and that which regulates the intervals between the seven musical tones: a natural 'tableau' that the Creator offers to our eyes, in order to initiate us in the system of the arts."[37]

By invoking the name of Newton, Briseux hoped to give legitimacy to his "intuitions." It was evident that Nature always operated with the same wisdom and in a uniform manner. Therefore no one could question that both auditive and visual pleasure consisted "in the perception of harmonic relations analogous to our human constitution" and that this principle was true not only for music but for all the arts since "one same *cause* cannot have two different *effects*."[38]

Briseux also stressed his rejection of Perrault's distinction between the specific characteristics of visual and auditive sensations from the point of view of the subject: "The mind is touched in a uniform fashion by all commensurable objects."[39] This is significant because both Briseux and Perrault clearly shared the notion of perception *partes extra partes*, understood as an intellectual association of sensations transmitted by independent, specific senses. But Briseux, believing in the existence of a mathematical structure that linked the external world with the human intellect, could "recover" the primordial sense of preconceptual, embodied, and undifferentiated perception: "The mind judges all types of impressions in a similar and uniform way, this being an indispensable necessity, a sort of law that has been imposed by Nature."[40]

Briseux may not have fully appreciated the importance that proportions and arbitrary beauty had in Perrault's system.[41] However, his main criticism was perfectly valid in his own epistemological context. Perrault's proportions were not derived from the observation of nature, and so his system was despised by most architects precisely because it was totally intellectual and a priori. This explained, in Briseux's opinion, why Perrault's relatively small variations had "visibly altered the beauty" of the classical orders.

Briseux accepted the existence of a diversity of tastes, but he always reconciled any divergences with his belief in an absolute beauty that depended on "geometrical principles" and was derived

Systems of Proportion and Natural Science

from Nature. He thought that the rules of proportion, founded on "calculation" and "experience," constituted invariable principles that allowed the architect to "operate justly" and were indispensable for perfecting his innate talent: "In vain have the followers of Perrault pretended that there are no rules but those of taste."[42] On the other hand, Briseux emphasized that it was not sufficient to follow certain theoretical proportions literally in order to design a meaningful building. The architect's taste, perfected through experience, was ultimately responsible for the appropriate choice of dimensions. Taste was not synonymous here with pure, arbitrary subjectivity. It was perceived by Briseux as capable of correcting any conceptual system, including Perrault's. Resulting from experience and the observation of Nature, it had a transcendental and intersubjective character, and was thus incapable of distorting the true natural systems of proportion.

In sharp contrast with the intentions of Perrault's *ars fabricandi*, Briseux never pretended to reduce practice to theory. This is evident in the second volume of his *Traité*, where he illustrated his harmonic proportion applied to the classical orders without the use of numerical dimensions. Briseux merely drew graphic scales along buildings and elements of the orders demonstrating the existence of dimensional relations. He did not provide specific measurements or a module that might allow the translation of any illustration into a building. It is clear that his theory deliberately kept a distance from practice. Unquestionably, Briseux understood the values of the latter, which accounts for the apparent contradiction in his statements about taste. True taste was a warrant of architectural meaning at the level of practice, and Briseux's theory was an indispensable complement and guide, not a substitute. The role of theory as a justification of practice prevails here over its utility as a technical instrument.

Other architects and theoreticians during the second half of the eighteenth century adopted similar attitudes. Germain Boffrand, for example, believed that although acceptable buildings might be constructed without using the orders, proportions were absolutely indispensable.[43]

Boffrand, a member of the Royal Academy of Architecture and the successor of Jacques Gabriel in the leading post of the *Corps des Ponts et Chaussées*, published in 1745 his *Livre d'Architecture* along with an interesting technical study on how to cast in one piece a bronze equestrian statue of the king. Interested in a wide variety of technical and artistic subjects, including machinery, the centering of bridges, lock construction, methods of mensuration, and Gothic and Arab architecture, Boffrand, like François Blondel, attributed the beauty of some Gothic buildings to their just proportions. For him, the most important function of the architect was to choose appropriate rules of proportions. He thought that nature formed the germ of the arts, but that reflection and experience nurtured it and allowed it to develop. "Perfection derives from an excellent imitation of the *belle Nature*", which was also the origin of the principles of Greek and Roman architecture. Ancient models could, therefore, become once again a legitimate source of meaning.

Boffrand's small treatise examines certain relations between the classical orders and the different styles and genres described by Horace in his *Art Poetique*. His analogy was still clearly metaphoric. Architecture was a poetic activity in the sense of Aristotle's *poesis*, an action with transcendental objectives, determined by an implicit thrust to reconcile man with a cosmic order. Boffrand's primitive semiological study, however, stemmed from a belief that, once divorced from metaphysical concerns, would become the very source of modern structuralism. The fundamental point of departure for his work was the identity between the principles of the arts and those of the sciences, both of which are founded on mathematics and geometry. Geometry, he thought, could be applied to any science, so that "a study of one subject can bring new knowledge to another."[44]

The abbé and *homme des lettres* Marc-Antoine Laugier, the most influential theoretician of French Neoclassicism, also believed that architecture should have as sound principles as does science.[45] In the preface of *Essai sur l'Architecture* (1753), Laugier rejected the notion of a theory reduced to an *ars fabricandi*. He stated that in all those arts that are not purely mechanical like architecture, it is not sufficient to know how to proceed; the author should learn to think. An artist should be able to explain to himself why he does what he does: "For this reason, he needs fixed principles to determine his judgments and justify his choices."[46]

Laugier maintained that architecture had never been founded on true, rational principles. Vitruvius and all his modern followers, with the exception of Cordemoy, had only recounted the practices of their own times, but had never penetrated the mysteries of architecture. To Laugier, practice often misleads artists from their true objectives: "Every art or science has a definitive objective. There is only one way of doing things right."[47]

In order to establish "evident" principles that could be the basis of invariable precepts for practice, Laugier adopted an empirical method. He used "experiments" and observations to ascertain that the most beautiful buildings and objects produced the same positive or negative impressions on himself and others. After repeating these experiments a number of times, he became convinced that there were essential beauties in architecture, independent of custom and convention.[48]

Laugier was an eminent historian, so confident in his rational judgment that he could criticize the traditional political status quo.[49] He openly admitted his faith in the progress and evolution of architecture. But the abbé also believed that his *Essai* contained infallible and truly fixed rules, and that his efforts to discover "the causes of the effects" produced by certain famous and beautiful buildings were totally successful. Laugier's *logos* was certainly rigorous and inquisitive, thoroughly shaping his theory, but never betraying a superficial interest in formal or technical control. His fundamental concern was to disclose the possibilities of meaning in an activity that appeared increasingly in crisis because of its lack of principles but that was, according to him, crucial for the coherence of culture. Following from his premise that there was meaning in the world (*Nature*), Laugier aspired to understand the act of creation, and thus looked back to the origins of architecture. The final answer to his metaphysical question was necessarily a myth.

In the first chapter of his *Essai*, he described the essential elements of architecture that can be derived from the primitive hut: the architecture of man in an idyllic, unprejudiced, and natural state. The columns, architraves, and pediments that constituted the hut were put forward as the *only* essential elements of architecture. During the earlier part of the century, architects and engineers had been more aware of the differences between the values of *firmitas* (physical stability, durability) and those of *venustas* (beauty). Before Perrault, this fragmentation of value had never played a role in architecture.[50] Striving to save meaning, Laugier emphatically identified the fundamental parts of the classical orders (ornament in Renaissance theory) with the very structure of the building. In spite of his differences of opinion with Frezier regarding what constituted the most rational form of construction, this attempt to reconcile the traditional values responded to the same concerns that the military engineer had first revealed in his *Dissertation*.

Frontispiece of Laugier's *Essai sur l'Architecture,*
showing the primitive hut as a source of architectural principles.

Systems of Proportion and Natural Science

The great impact of Laugier's *Essai* has been widely studied.[51] His "essential elements" became the favorite forms of Neoclassical architecture, and his ideal church was obviously the germ of Soufflot's project for Sainte-Geneviève, later to become the French Pantheon. But Laugier also published some twenty years later a second book, *Observations sur l'Architecture*. In this less popular text, he upholds the fundamental importance of proportions; this is so essential to architecture that, in his opinion, a well-proportioned building will always produce a positive effect, independent of the richness of its materials or ornamentation.

In the *Essai*, Laugier criticized Briseux for having invested so much effort only to prove a self-evident truth. No one with a minimum of knowledge about architecture would deny the necessity of proportions.[52] Furthermore, Laugier thought that Perrault had understood the absurdity of his own argument and defended it only out of stubborness, while Briseux, in his opinion, would have fared better if he had tried to discover and postulate rational rules of proportion.

This is precisely the task Laugier undertakes in his *Observations*. His objective is to establish the "science of proportions" on more solid grounds. A precise rational operation always has to be involved in the choice of dimensions; rules of proportion must be applied to not only the classical orders but many aspects and parts of a building. Laugier was critical of previous authors who had merely copied Vitruvius in their systems of proportion without pondering their importance. He himself wished to provide an adequate justification of proportions, "raising slightly the thick curtain that hides this science."[53]

His text is a rational tour de force that tries to establish a theory of proportion based exclusively on "visual" evidence. Three criteria of judgment are put forward: The first essential requirement for a correct proportion is the "commensurability" of the two compared dimensions, the exactness of their correspondence. The second requirement is "sensibility" and refers to the ease with which the relationship can be perceived, 3 : 5, for example, being better than 23 : 68. The third category is the "proximity" of the proportional relation to the perfect ratio (1 : 1); 10 : 30 is worse than 10 : 20. There is no further rational justification with regard to the choice of proportions. Numbers have to be simple and natural. Most important, however, was Laugier's belief in the essential character of dimensional relations generating meaning in architecture. Proportion, like the essential formal elements of his *Essai*, is ultimately derived from an ordered and harmonious nature whose *mathemata* could be evidently perceived by man.

After Laugier, the contradictions between taste and reason, which had been posited earlier in the century by Cordemoy, Briseux, and the abbé Dubos, were thoroughly reconciled.[54] They both, of course, were derived from Nature. Defending his position from the criticism of Frezier, who had brought up the issue of arbitrary beauty in a review of the *Essai*, Laugier categorically pointed out that there was an essential beauty in art, often difficult to define by reason, but absolutely evident to our hearts and perceptions.

The notion of simplicity as a source of beauty underlined architectural intentions during the second half of the eighteenth century and appeared in many theoretical works. In his *Traité des Ordres d'Architecture* (1767), one of the last manuals of this type ever published, Nicolas-Marie Potain declared his intention to elucidate the origin of the five orders, which are "derived from one common principle."[55] He adopted the prototype of the primitive hut and postulated it as a model for both the essential formal elements of architecture and his own system of proportions. Also, several scientists and philosophers of that period referred to architectural proportion in terms similar to Laugier's, for example, Christian Wolff, whose contribution will be examined in the following chapter, and Leonard Euler, the exceptional mathematician who determined the equations for the buckling of columns long before this phenomenon could be tested experimentally. In his *Letters to a German Princess*, Euler discussed musical harmony, rejecting its cosmological implications. However, he still thought that natural proportions, expressed in small numbers, were more clear to the intellect, thereby producing a feeling of satisfaction. He maintained this was the reason why architects always followed that norm, using the simplest possible proportions in their works.[56]

Compared to philosophers and *hommes des lettres* such as Wolff or Laugier, engineers and architects of this period obviously were more interested in technical problems. But the differences in interest should not hide the profound similarities of their theoretical assumptions. Jacques-François Blondel, the most important architectural teacher in France around midcentury, still conceived of architecture as something of a universal science. In 1739 he instituted a school of architecture, independent of the Royal Academy of Architecture, which taught that the architect should be knowledgeable in science, philosophy, literature, and the fine

Systems of Proportion and Natural Science

arts.[57] And while accepting the differences between naval, civil, and military architecture, Blondel praised the achievements of Frezier, François Blondel, and Vauban, all simultaneously architects and military engineers.

Jacques-François Blondel's ambition may have seemed unwarranted at a time when the first specialized schools of civil engineering (*ponts et chaussées*) and military engineering (*génie militaire*) had already been established in Paris and Mezières. What is significant, however, is the great number of similarities between the program of studies at Blondel's school and the curriculum of the two technical institutions.[58] Blondel's course actually became a requirement for admission to the *École des Ponts et Chaussées*.[59] It included, aside from the theory of architecture, the history of proportions, drawing, ornament, and sculpture, many technical subjects, such as mathematics, geometry, perspective, topography, mensuration, and the properties of the conic sections necessary for stereotomy. In his *Cours d'Architecture*, a vast work that summarized his pedagogical career, Blondel added other subjects to the list, such as mechanics, hydraulics, trigonometry, principles of fortification, and experimental physics "relative to the art of building."[60]

In the first volume of his *Cours*, Blondel emphasized architecture's usefulness, claiming it as the basis of all works that physically transformed the world of man. Not only temples and public buildings but also bridges, canals, and locks fell within its province. Throughout the eighteenth century, engineers and architects still shared a theoretical framework and a basic intentionality derived from common principles, so that their individual areas of action were not mutually exclusive. Many civil and military engineers such as Gauthey and Saint-Far frequently built churches and hospitals. Gauthey, the author of an important book on the structural analysis of bridges, also wrote about architecture and adopted Laugier's principles.[61] Perronet, a renowned civil engineer and founder of the *École des Ponts et Chaussées*, was also a member of the Royal Academy of Architecture. In a similar position was the mathematician Camus, who wrote his *Cours de Mathématiques* for the students at the academy and then saw his text adopted by the military schools.

Jacques-François Blondel's extensive *Cours* pretended to be the first truly universal encyclopaedic work on architecture. The similarity with the aims of the *philosophes* is, of course, not coincidental. Blondel admitted that except for the problem of distribution, all that could be considered as essential in architecture had been discussed previously. His text is basically a compilation and systematization of the most important and prestigious theories of the past.

In the second volume of his *Cours*, Blondel systematically studied the "distribution" in plan of different types of buildings (*genres d'édifices*), such as Greek cross, Latin cross, and centralized churches, cathedrals, markets, and convents. He was fascinated by room combinations and their relation to land use. An interest in typology led him to write the first consistent exposition on the subject in Western architecture. In contrast to nineteenth-century formulations, his types never referred exclusively to utilitarian or formal categories. His general eclecticism notwithstanding, Blondel never affirmed that the value of a building might result simply from the appropriate distribution or combination of its parts in plan.

Blondel recounted in a traditional way the story about the mythical origin of the classical orders and reproduced the proportional systems of Vignola, Palladio, and Scamozzi. His understanding of fashion was very confused, but in the end, he also considered taste as a positive criterion for the appreciation of beauty. Natural taste, although innate, could be perfected through the comparison of great master works, "becoming a banner to guide artists in all their productions."[62]

Blondel often stated that the problem of proportion was the most interesting part of architecture.[63] In his *Cours*, he tried to prove that architectural proportions were derived from nature, citing the opinions of great masters. Although he could understand the differences between visual and auditive sensations, he still believed in the analogy between architectural proportion and musical harmony. Without mentioning Perrault by name, Blondel criticized "those authors that have considered proportions as useless, or at least arbitrary." Basing their theories on independent systems, these authors rejected fundamental laws and traditional principles, pretending that there were no convincing demonstrations in favor of architectural proportions and that a lack of innovation was synonymous with timidity. After measuring many beautiful buildings, Jacques-François Blondel repeated in almost identical words the original refutation of François Blondel, concluding that the source of true beauty in architecture consisted essentially in proportional relations, "even though it might not be possible to prove [this] with the scrupulous exactness of advanced mathematics."[64]

In his *Architecture Françoise* (1752), Jacques-François Blondel tried to show how the most pleasant proportions could be determined from a comparison of the best existing buildings. In attempting to rationalize the problem, he established three different types of proportion. The first was derived directly from human dimensions, such as the measurements of a step; the second referred to the structural stability of a building, prescribing, for example, the thickness of walls; and the third was concerned with beauty, being applied particularly to the classical orders.[65] J. F. Blondel's types of proportion correspond to each of the traditional Vitruvian categories: *commoditas, firmitas,* and *venustas.* His lucid distinction contrasts sharply with the confusion between the aesthetic and technical attributes of proportion in François Blondel's Baroque theory.

Nevertheless, J. F. Blondel always maintained that architecture had access to the sphere of absolute values. He thought beauty immutable and felt that architects, through their open spirit and sense of observation, were capable of extrapolating it "from the productions of the fine arts and the infinite variety of Nature."[66] He believed that excellent buildings possessed "a mute poetry, a sweet, interesting, firm or vigorous style, in a word, a certain *melody* that could be tender, moving, strong, or terrible."[67] Just as a symphony communicated its character through harmony, evoking diverse states of nature and conveying sweet and vivid passions, so proportion acted as the vehicle for architectural expression. Properly used, it presented the spectator with "terrifying or seductive" buildings, allowing for a clear recognition of their essence, be it "the Temple of Vengeance or that of Love."[68]

In an age when enlightened reason was capable of questioning the absolute validity of the forms of classical architecture, the problem of meaning appeared more clearly at the level of theory. For Blondel however, it was never reduced to the issue of evidence of style or type; it was primarily a problem of reference. Blondel believed that "it was ultimately unimportant whether our buildings resembled those of classical antiquity, the Gothic period, or more modern times," as long as the result was happy and the buildings were endowed with appropriate character.[69] Naturally, the expressive and poetic character of architecture was guaranteed by proportion.

The crucial reconciliation between aesthetic and technical interests to which I have previously alluded is particularly evident in the work of Jacques-Germain Soufflot,[70] whose most significant creation, the church of Ste.-Geneviève, represents the culmination of French Neoclassicism, embodying that taste that admired the lightness of Gothic structures and the purity and grace of Greek architecture. In this building, it is impossible to establish where aesthetic motivations end or at what point design decisions were prompted by an intention to rationalize the structural system. In his constant participation in academic deliberations, Soufflot displayed an interest in geometry, mechanics, geology, physics, and chemistry.[71] His best friends were famous engineers like Perronet and Rondelet. Soufflot also designed a machine to test the quantitative strength of stone. His scientific observations were instrumental in determining the proportions of Ste.-Geneviève, particularly the dimensions of the structurally critical central piers under the dome.[72] He defended the daring dimensions of his structure, claiming that they had been established through observation and experimentation. In 1775 he proposed to the Royal Academy of Architecture the construction of other machines to determine the strength of metals and wood. These machines, he thought, should be made easily accessible to architects and engineers.

All this notwithstanding, Soufflot wrote two formal papers on the problems of taste and proportions. His work on the identity of taste and rules in architecture was initially presented to the academy at Lyons in 1744, and read at least twice in the Royal Academy in Paris during 1775 and 1778.[73] According to Soufflot, there existed a reciprocity between taste and rules in architecture; taste had been the original source of rules, which, in turn, modified taste. Rules have always existed; the Greeks simply discovered them. Taste and rules were found in Nature, but they could also be taken from excellent authors. "A force whose cause I ignore," writes Soufflot, "always leads me to the choice of proportions. I build accordingly; my work pleases and becomes a rule for those that come after me." If greater assurance was required, Soufflot recommended precise measurements of beautiful buildings and a careful consideration of the effects produced by their proportions.

Soufflot believed architecture should be simple and guided by the "beautiful correspondence among the parts of the human body." Like Père André a few years before him, he affirmed the existence of an essential geometry, which could be perceived empirically in nature and that was the origin of true beauty. Architecture was bound to respect these universal rules, such as the observation of horizontal and perpendicular lines and the disposition of weaker over stronger elements.

Systems of Proportion and Natural Science

The church of Sainte-Geneviève in Paris, transformed after the Revolution of 1789 into the French Pantheon.

Number and Architectural Proportion

Soufflot's theory again reflects the fundamental paradox of eighteenth-century epistemology: Architectural rules can be determined empirically through taste only after one has accepted the premise of a universal, immutable architectural value to which natural observation has access. Ignoring the relation between cultural or historical context and architectural expression, particularly explicit after the publication of Johann Bernhard Fischer von Erlach's universal history of architecture (1721), Soufflot rejected formal invention: "What was beautiful two thousand years ago is still beautiful." True beauty, in his opinion, was not "an extravagant composition of ornament." Consequently, he disapproved of rococo, baroque, and medieval complexities. Beauty consisted "in a perfect disposition of the most common parts" whose forms and proportions were perfectly known already. The role of the architect was to combine and establish dimensional relations between these absolutely valid classical elements, which would constitute the specificity of each work, its true source of meaning.

In his *Mémoire sur les Proportions d'Architecture* Soufflot discussed the dispute between Perrault and François Blondel.[74] Like Laugier, he questioned the authenticity of Perrault's conviction; both architects, in spite of their differences, had obviously created beautiful buildings. But Soufflot, while admiring Perrault's facade for the Louvre, unhesitatingly sided with Blondel. He thought natural proportions did exist, differences among specific examples notwithstanding. Discrepancies, after all, were the product of optical correction and adjustments. After measuring many famous churches, including some Gothic structures, Soufflot concluded that their general proportions were approximately the same, a product of nature, not custom, and, as in music, constituted a true cause of pleasure.

Soufflot was well aware of the works of Galileo and was capable of using mathematics as a formal instrument in his speculations about statics and structures. His predilection for quantitative experimental results in problems of strength of materials and his ability to disregard the experience embodied in prestigious buildings of the past and the authority of famous architects seems to betray the attitude of a positivistic engineer. The truth, however, is that Soufflot's positions in relation to both aesthetics and mechanics were derived from a belief in a mathematically ordered nature. Scientific observation and experimentation yielded quantitative results that led to the establishment of absolute laws. In a similar way, a transcendental taste had access to the rules of proportion implicit in the same elemental Nature; architecture, a metaphor of divine creation, should therefore be simple and thoroughly ruled by number. And the truth and beauty of any building were endorsed by the presence of number.

Soufflot's most severe critic was Pierre Patte, also an architect and prolific writer, who was mainly interested in the technical problems of building.[75] In the introduction of his most important work, *Mémoires sur les Objets les Plus Importans de l'Architecture* (1769), Patte emphasized that except for the problem of proportion, on which there was no universal consent, the remainder of architecture still needed to be expounded. In his opinion, the most essential, useful, and necessary part of architecture was construction, which still lacked principles. This aspect, Patte conceded, had been traditionally understood by masons. But it was imperative to study its principles in a more profound way "from a philosophical point of view."

Among the many chapters devoted to clarifying technical problems of architecture and urbanism, there is one that addresses the proportions of the classical orders. Patte does not question the fact that "proportions constitute the essential beauty of architecture," and in an earlier work he had drawn a connection between proportion, character, and morality.[76] He thought that beautiful buildings ruled by proportions would inspire noble and even religious feelings. The problem was to determine what these proportions actually were. Patte was convinced that if this became possible, architecture would achieve perfection.

He rejected outright the ancient metaphoric identification of columns with the human body, relating the former to the "disposition" of trees. Repeating Frezier's argument, he replaced the Vitruvian myth of the genesis of the classical orders with a theory based on the intuitive mechanics of primitive building. According to Patte, the Egyptians had used very heavy columns; it was the Greeks who gave columns a thickness relative to their heights and to the loads they had to bear. Thus, he thought, were established the natural proportions of the orders. But here begin the problems. Like Perrault, Patte worried about the discrepancies between theoretical systems of proportion and the dimensions of real buildings. Even during Vitruvius's lifetime these problems existed, and all subsequent attempts to reconcile the differences had failed. Patte attributed this failure to the lack of absolute rules of proportion, which architects had never been able to establish. Two great difficulties existed: finding principles leading

Number and Architectural Proportion

to self-evident or at least probable truths, capable of satisfying both taste and reason, and the impossibility of subjugating the human intellect to determinations whose principles were not derived from nature.

Patte thought that the architect faced problems similar to those of an artist trying to determine geometrically exact relations between the features of a beautiful face. The mathematical law existed; the problem was to discover it from the observation of nature.

From this point of view, Patte devised a devastating criticism of Perrault's *Ordonnance*. Acknowledging Perrault's intention to "reconcile the differences between theory and practice, " Patte maintained that Perrault had failed. He attributed this failure to his predecessor's belief that neither reason or good sense nor the imitation of nature constituted the foundation of beauty. Patte's interpretation of Perrault's ideas is peculiar and significant. Perrault's understanding of proportion as arbitrary, dependent solely on custom, amounted in Patte's opinion to an absolute negation of the existence of positive beauty in architecture.[77]

Perrault had tried to justify his new rational system by identifying it with a mythical, perfect, ancient system that had been ruined by the carelessness of craftsmen throughout history. Patte never took this claim seriously. He thought Perrault's theory was only an extreme example of what had always happened in architecture, perpetuating the discrepancies between theory and practice. But Patte agreed with Perrault in his assessment of optical corrections. It was absurd to pretend, like Blondel had, that true beauty might be derived from those adjustments. Thus Patte emphasized the modern intention to establish a fixed and immutable system of proportions capable of controlling practice.

Both Patte and Perrault shared a concern to solve the problem of architectural proportion through scientific method. The great differences between them corresponded precisely to their divergent beliefs regarding the origin of knowledge in science and its accessibility. Patte declared that instead of trying to establish new, ideal systems, inevitably condemned to fail, it was preferable to define methods for the determination of optimal proportions through practice. Only then would it be possible to postulate a truly rigorous system, capable of reconciling different opinions in one rational whole. Patte believed that Perrault's system was erroneous and had never been used because "it was false that a proportional mean could produce in any case the most agreeable effects, coinciding with true perfection."[78]

Systems of Proportion and Natural Science

Patte distinguished, as did Perrault, between observed phenomena and speculative causes. Nevertheless, he rejected the possibility of inventing a priori systems, choosing instead the empirical method of natural philosophy. While both authors wished to define the mathematical principles of architecture, Patte was the more patient. He repudiated the Platonism of Perrault and insisted that proportions should be derived from nature. Numerical relations were assumed to be visible. For Patte, then, numbers recovered their transcendental dimension and could be postulated as the fundamental means for the imitation of nature, still architecture's task.

The system that Patte finally put forward after his rigorous scientific disquisition was, perhaps not suprisingly, eclectic, confused, and rather disappointing. He established six orders: "rich," or ornamented, and "simple" versions of the three main classical orders. Evidently, Patte had greater faith in his method than in the result. Empirical science progressed to the degree to which observations were accumulated and systematized. He believed that any system based on his method was assured of becoming truly objective, producing real satisfaction.

The last architect whose work I examine in this chapter is Nicolas Le Camus de Mezières. Between 1780 and 1782 he published three books, two concerning technical problems and the other dealing with harmonic proportion. In the introduction to his *Traité de la Force de Bois*, after mentioning several buildings that had suffered structural failures, Le Camus pointed to the existence of mathematical laws derived from the science of mechanics. These laws, in his opinion, should always be respected. In his book, he commented upon the results of many experiments made by Buffon on the strength of wooden beams. Although he did not provide analytical methods for structural design, his intention was technical: the systematization of experimental results with the purpose of designing wooden structures scientifically.

In apparent contrast to this attitude, Le Camus emphatically defended the value of harmonic proportion in *Le Génie de l'Architecture*. Architecture, in his opinion, should have "character," indicative not only of its type but also of its internal composition. Each room in a building is meant to have particular qualities, so that our desire for other rooms may be stimulated: "This agitation occupies the intellect and keeps it in suspense."[79] According to Le Camus, the objective of architecture is to move our souls and excite our sensations. And this could only be achieved through the use of harmonic proportion.

Le Camus was convinced that "there was only one beauty," which could be found in the purity and harmony of proportions. But he never provided a system of dimensions that could be applicable to practice, only some traditional advice and the suggestion to avoid irrational or excessively small proportions, which might be confusing. In a more radical way than his predecessors, Le Camus rejected the possibility of an *ars fabricandi* concerning the fundamental problem of proportions. The immutable *mathesis* was indispensable in architecture, but it could not be made synonymous with a set of rules. Harmony, wrote Le Camus, is only accessible to the genius: "It is a spark of Divinity whose smallest reflection carries the imprint of a dazzling source."[80]

Le Camus tried to provide general prescriptions for the design of buildings with true character, something he perceived as lacking in the work of his contemporaries. Because natural phenomena could produce sensations such as happiness, sadness, sublimity, and voluptuousness, he exorted architects to capture these effects in their forms. Meaning in architecture had to be attained through a careful study of Nature. Proportion was understood as the essence of beauty because number constituted the most explicit form of a natural harmony pregnant with poetry, the ultimate source of architectural expression. Proportion alone could "cast that spell that overwhelmed our souls."[81]

Le Camus was aware of the critical importance of his theory and defended it, not without anguish, from the menace of relativism. He wrote, "Architecture is truly harmonic. . . . Our principles about the analogy of architectural proportions with our sensations are derived from those of the majority of philosophers. . . ."[82] These principles constituted, in the words of Le Camus, "the metaphysics of architecture," upon which followed its progress. The ultimate meaning of architecture depended on the existence of these absolute, natural principles.

After such an emphatic declaration, it is not surprising to encounter a violent criticism of Perrault's theory. Indeed, Le Camus thought Perrault was mistaken in his belief that "immutable proportions should not exist, that taste alone should decide," that too many strict rules restricted and sterilized the genius of the architect.[83] Le Camus identified Perrault's theory with relativism and contested it by establishing a circular argument that was noncontradictory only in the context of eighteenth-century epistemology: It was imperative to establish "immutable points of departure," laws that might set limits to our imagination, which in itself was licentious and incapable of self-restraint. Le Camus was obviously referring to the fundamental philosophical principles of architecture, not to an invariable, merely prescriptive, theory.

Among the traditional works admired by Le Camus were Ouvrand's treatise on harmonic proportion and the commentary on the Book of the Prophet Ezekiel by the Jesuits Prado and Villalpando, who illustrated how the Corinthian order and classical proportions were derived from the Temple of Solomon in Jerusalem.[84] But he also praised the more recent work of another Jesuit, Père Castel, who had been fascinated by Newton's discovery of the mathematical laws of optics and had composed a treatise to prove the analogy between the harmony of color and music.[85] Castel built an organ, or *clavecin oculaire*, in which a special mechanism produced colors relative to the notes played. The instrument was admired by the composer Telemann and also by Le Camus, who saw in it a proof of his own theories. The colors appeared in harmonic succession, he wrote, charming the sight of a well-educated man with the same magic of the well-combined musical sounds that enchanted his hearing.[86]

<table>
<tr><td>

Number in Natural Philosophy

</td><td>

The major architects and theoreticians of the French Age of Reason ultimately accepted the mythical belief in proportion as the source of beauty and values. Looking back, what can we say about this reactionary attitude that always rejected the protopositivism of Perrault and adopted François Blondel's traditional position? First, this preference cannot be interpreted as a mere revival or survival of Renaissance theories. Modern historians of architecture have felt the need either to ignore or to isolate this attitude, perceived as curious and extraneous to the dominant characteristics of the period, which was marked by an ever increasing rationalism and interest in technology.

</td></tr>
</table>

But Neoclassical architecture is not merely a dogmatic and rationalist precedent of contemporary practice. The theory behind this architecture was still prepared to accept an implicit but fundamental mythical dimension, one that allowed reason to elucidate the basic metaphysical questions of architecture while still avoiding contradictions.[87] The increasing rationalization evident in architectural intentions during the second half of the century was only the most conspicuous sign of architecture's adoption of the methods and principles of natural philosophy. The full meaning and implications of this assimilation have never been seriously considered by historians of art, architecture, and engineering since they assumed that their respective disciplines evolved as autonomous entities. Architects, engineers, and philosophers of the Enlightenment explicitly identified the principles of architecture with those of science, presuming a fundamental analogy in the methods and sources that led all human disciplines to the attainment of truth.

The science of the Enlightenment was the natural philosophy of Newton. After 1735, when his methods and premises were generally accepted in Europe, Newton appeared as a hero of superhuman dimensions, having solved once and for all the enigma of the universe. Many popular versions of his philosophy appeared in different languages, and he became a venerated figure among philosophers, scientists, poets, engineers, architects, and even priests. His scheme of the universe became a model for all disciplines, including aesthetics and architectural theory.

It might be said that during the Enlightenment, the science of Newton took the place of philosophy. Rejecting as fictitious the great deductive metaphysical systems of the seventeenth century, Newton declared that science should not make hypotheses or substitute reality as it presents itself to our senses with false or fantastic representations. Natural philosophy, for Newton, constituted a compendium of laws that attempted to explain the behavior of the physical world in mathematical terms and was deduced from phenomena through induction and experimentation. His principles were presented as a discovery of mathematical relations in the observed phenomena. And it was precisely his great success in establishing a connection between mathematical theory and the experience of everyday life that allowed his natural philosophy to be perceived as the final refutation of traditional metaphysics.[88]

Newton always tried to explain with the smallest number of principles the diversity of phenomena in the real world, reducing them whenever possible to one universal law. His model of the cosmos became the only acceptable system for eighteenth-century epistemology: a systematization of knowledge through the observation of nature, rejecting a priori hypotheses while searching for and finding general principles and often a universal *mathesis*.

Newton seemed quite capable of distinguishing between final causes and the mathematical laws derived from quantitative observation and understood as simple formulations of the empirical world. Alluding to the essence of gravity, he declared his interest in establishing the phenomenon's mathematical law, not in dis-

Systems of Proportion and Natural Science

cussing "the cause of its properties." Consciously eschewing metaphysical or transcendental questions, he often disclosed the autonomous formal character of scientific discourse.[89] Consequently, he rejected all symbolic connotations of mathematics and seemed prepared to use it as an instrument for resolving problems in physics. His discovery of infinitesimal calculus derived from this specific practical consideration, which contrasts markedly with the symbolic and universal implications that Leibniz, its almost simultaneous codiscoverer, saw in it. For Newton, the origin of geometry was not intellectual but practical; geometry was only a part of universal mechanics, whose objective was "to postulate and demonstrate with precision the art of measurement."[90]

Around 1750 many scientists and philosophers could criticize the mathematical exterior, or geometrical form of thought, that purportedly had guaranteed absolute truth in the philosophy of the previous century. D'Alembert, for example, disapproved of the work of Euler, Spinoza, and Wolff precisely because their ideas were structured *more geometrico*. Mathematics apparently could be conceived as a mere formal system of relations, with no inherent meaning.

Having proved experimentally the imaginative intuitions of Galileo, Newtonian physics presented a definitive formulation of modern epistemology, becoming a model for all future knowledge. Newton seemed able to recognize truth from illusion, objective science from subjective speculative philosophy. He made available a relation between theory and practice in which the former aspired to be no more than a mere description of the technical means of the latter and not a discussion about its meaning. This opened the way for positivism, or the possibility of acquiring the truth about things without a concomitant theory concerning their natures. Or, more simply, the Newtonian schema encouraged the belief that it was possible to know a part (meaningfully) without knowing the whole.[91]

Although correct from the point of view of its consequences, this interpretation of Newton's thought is totally inadequate in its own terms. The great British scientist devoted much of his life to alchemy and theology, concerning himself with the Rosicrucian texts and the archetypal Temple of Jerusalem.[92] His theological writings were criticized even during the eighteenth century, but the fundamental metaphysical presuppositions of his natural philosophy were implicitly and thoroughly assimilated into all the scientific endeavors of the Enlightenment.

Number and Architectural Proportion

Particularly after Einstein, it became abundantly clear that Newton's "empirical science" worked precisely because it started from hypothetical and absolute premises. The existence of independent, geometrical, and absolute space and time was, indeed, an a priori postulate, indispensable for the success of his physics. In Newton's most important work, *The Mathematical Principles of Natural Philosophy*, observed phenomena from the world of everyday life were explained as relations of geometrical bodies in an abstract, empty, and truly infinite space. Newton was aware that the concept of absolute space was obviously not the space of human experience, and so there seems to be an unavoidable contradiction emerging from the simultaneous adoption of an empirical method and the hypothesis of absolute time and space. In Newton's philosophy, however, absolute time and space were not merely formal mathematical entities implicit in the experimental method. They were unquestionable premises precisely because he perceived them as transcendental manifestations, as symbols of the omnipresence and eternity of almighty God. "God," wrote Newton, "endures forever and is everywhere present; and by existing always and everywhere, He constitutes duration and space. . . . In Him are all things contained and moved; yet neither affects the other."[93] This "primary existing being," whose "emanative effect" is space-time, was consequently responsible for the order, regularity, and harmony of the structure of things.[94] Newton believed His intervention was required constantly, but most particularly, of course, when man was confronted by irregular phenomena that could not be easily explained within the framework of his universal law.

During the eighteenth century, God was still required in the universe of theoretical discourse, and Newton's natural philosophy simply took the place of the traditional metaphysical systems as a foundation of religion. In fact, Newton believed that science would necessarily lead to a true knowledge of the "first cause." This belief became commonplace among writers, scientists, and artists; it was interpreted literally in Craig's *Mathematical Principles of Christian Theology* and in Derham's *Astrotheology*, and in a more sophisticated and rational fashion by Voltaire and Buffon. The religious principles of natural philosophy were also practically identical to those of Freemasonry, the most popular "religion" of the Enlightenment after 1725,[95] and scholars have pointed to the great interest and often clear affiliation of eighteenth-century architects with this society.[96]

Systems of Proportion and Natural Science

The law of universal gravitation summarized the quantitative essence of the cosmos. One principle explained the motions of the heavenly bodies and those of any object in the sublunar world. The order of Newton's universe depended upon the existence of gravity, yet there existed only a relatively small amount of matter in motion within an infinite and homogeneous space. How then could gravity account scientifically for the essential order? Attraction had been a common enough concept in the astrobiological cosmos of antiquity and the Middle Ages, which explained it as a projection of human affection. Animism and inexplicable forces, however, had been rejected by seventeenth-century scientists, who attempted to explain motion mechanically, that is, as the result of immediate and direct physical actions. Newton was unable to explain the nature of gravitational force, but he appeared willing to accept action at a distance through a vacuum. He conceived of gravity as substance, not merely as a mathematical formulation. Gravity could only occur in the absolute space that is God; its universal mathematical law was postulated as a consummate symbol of divine existence.

Deep within Newton's empiricism was a Platonic cosmology. He believed that after having created the great masses composing the universe, God put them in motion within Himself. The creation of matter from pure space is a notion that appeared in Plato's *Timaeus*. This is also Newton's ultimate source for his understanding of the corpuscular structure of matter and the properties of its particles, a conception he shared with other Neoplatonic philosophers, in particular, Henry More. Newton allotted occult properties to particles in his *Opticks* in order to justify the ultimately successful hypothesis of the structural similarity between electricity and gravity. Inspired by Newtonian empiricism, Condillac wrote that physical science consisted in "explaining facts by means of facts." Paradoxically, nothing could be further from this than Newton's own natural philosophy.

Newton's philosophy was based on the proposition that number and geometry were the essence of external reality, their only true form. But having rejected seventeenth-century metaphysical systems, and recognizing the limitations of formal thinking, he opted for inductive methods and asserted that knowledge should always derive from the observation of reality. This created the belief in the possibility of demonstrating the mathematical and geometrical essence of reality through the observation of nature. The metaphysical preoccupations implicit in Newton's traditional cosmology

Number and Architectural Proportion

retained, often surreptitiously, but always forcefully, their essential role in the realm of theoretical discourse. The order manifested by the mathematical regularity evident in nature became an immediate symbol of divine presence in the world of man. Physical reality, although excluding all supernatural phenomena, was still capable of revealing the ultimate meaning of human existence.

Newtonian physics was evidently successful in the experimental field. This was instrumental in the arts and sciences of the Enlightenment adopting both its methods and its implicit beliefs. During the eighteenth century, most thinkers rejected the traditional link between human and divine reason, generally renouncing all hypotheses and the authority of ancient texts and envisioning truth as the goal of experience. In this sense, enlightened reason was more humble than Baroque philosophy, believing that truth belonged in the world and was part of empirical reality. The task of theory was to disclose the rationality evident in the natural order. This meant that such operations were never merely motivated by a technological interest, but were grounded in metaphysical necessity. In short, the ancient myth of preestablished harmony was now revealed to man through experimentation and technical action.

The use of inductive methods began to be seen in all disciplines as a guarantee of absolute certainty and meaning. Newton had shown that such methods could reveal the mathematical wisdom of Creation. This was a not gratuitous hypothesis, but a fact accessible to immediate perception. Man could now presuppose the integral rationality of reality and assume its validity in any branch of theory. The new empirical method and the systematization of knowledge became an indispensable stage in the process by which theory was transformed into an effective instrument of technological domination in the nineteenth century. The same empiricism, however, gave renewed priority to practice (rather than theory) and permitted the symbolic perception of nature. All those immutable principles that reason "discovered" through the observation of nature were seen as a manifestation of divine will. The reason of the Enlightenment could come to terms with radical problems of meaning only because it had deep roots in the mythical realm.

The method of natural philosophy put a new emphasis on the embodied perception of the physical world. Knowledge about life became inseparable from sentiment, differentiated but consciously integrated in artistic manifestations. The perception of the universe

Systems of Proportion and Natural Science

was truly symbolic, capable of apprehending meaning behind the presence of reality, and thus avoiding the menace of subjectivism. Nature was the place where all human values were to be found, a transcendental reality full of life and movement, where God, man, and things were subject to mathematical harmony. This fundamental belief prevented theory from becoming an instrument of technological domination; man always felt the need to reconcile himself with Nature.

During the eighteenth century, man thought he was capable of discerning the hand of God in His work through the discovery of mathematical and geometrical laws that betrayed His presence. God no longer inhabited a supernatural sphere from which He communicated with the human mind; the Creator of the Enlightenment was a force that endorsed the perpetual miracle of everyday life. Corresponding to this transformation of divinity, geometry and mathematics, which had lost their symbolic power with the end of traditional metaphysics after Leibniz, recovered it from a Divine Nature. Paradoxically, this recovery was precipitated by the growing interest in technical problems that revealed the presence of a symbolic mathematical harmony through quantitative experimentation.

Architecture had traditionally depended upon geometry and number to vouchsafe its role as an immediate form of reconciliation between man and the world, between microcosm and macrocosm. During the second half of the eighteenth century, architectural theory, sharing the basic premises, intentions, and ideals of Newtonian philosophy, adopted an implicit metaphysical dimension. The results appeared as a passionate defense of traditional positions, strengthened by a consciousness of the power of reason to control practical operations. Deriving its fundamental principles from Nature, architectural theory was capable of maintaining its customary role as a metaphysical justification of practice. Thus while respectfully modifying Nature, building *praxis* remained *poesis*, the character of which was determined primarily by its reconciliatory aims.

During the eighteenth century, rationality in architectural theory was capable of disclosing differences of taste and opinion, questioning the absolute value of the classical orders, the authority of ancient and Renaissance texts, and even the specific myths that explained the genesis of forms. In the end, however, architects and theoreticians did not accept subjectivism and relativism. In the last decades of the century, theory became a set of *grands principes*, often impossible to describe, but postulated emphatically as a necessary source of architectural meaning. Apparently subjective notions like taste, once it was established that they originated in Nature and experience, could be invoked as absolutely objective reasons in favor of theoretical arguments.

Perhaps the most explicit work on "Newtonian aesthetics" was Abbé Batteux's *Les Beaux Arts Réduits à un même Principe* (1746). He believed that taste was the foremost principle of the fine arts and that these disciplines were therefore never subject to chance. Batteux stated that "taste is for the arts what intelligence is for the sciences."[97] He thought that the intellect had been created in order to know truth and to love goodness and that we should simply let our hearts choose freely. Each aspect of human consciousness had, in his opinion, a legitimate objective in nature. Even symmetry and proportion were determined by the laws of taste.

Once the transcendental dimension of mathematical reason is established, it becomes evident that there were no contradictions between the technological and the traditional interests of eighteenth-century architecture. In fact, the true meaning of Neoclassical architecture can only be understood after accepting the radical coherence of its technical and aesthetic dimensions. In a similar way, taste reconciled the lightness of Gothic with the purity and grace of classical architecture. It is therefore futile to attempt an elucidation of Neoclassical architecture as a juxtaposition of formal styles, systems, or the specialized interests of architects and engineers.[98]

After 1750 numerical proportions recovered their traditional role in architectural theory. An ever increasing empiricism brought architecture constantly closer to nature. Architects strived to imitate the *belle Nature*, finding it increasingly more simple. This process, which I shall try to clarify from diverse perspectives in the following chapters, already shows the great impact that the Galilean revolution had upon architectural intentions during the seventeenth century and the basically traditional framework of eighteenth-century theory and practice. It should already be clear that modern architecture did not appear around 1750 and that it was not simply generated by the Industrial Revolution. The process of transformation of theory into an instrument of technological domination started with modern science itself. Nevertheless, after adopting the humility of natural philosophy, the architecture of the Age of Reason became motivated primarily by a symbolic intention.

Systems of Proportion and Natural Science

II

GEOMETRY AND
ARCHITECTURAL MEANING IN
THE SEVENTEENTH AND
EIGHTEENTH CENTURIES

3

GEOMETRICAL OPERATIONS AS
A SOURCE OF MEANING

The great role mathematics played in seventeenth-century European architecture has already been hinted at in relation to the theory of François Blondel, Perrault's traditional opponent. The most explicit assimilation of the new geometrical universe by architecture appears in the work of Guarino Guarini, whose fascinating buildings in Turin and the Piedmont unquestionably represent a high point in Baroque architecture. Guarini, a Catholic priest, synthesized the scientific, philosophical, artistic, and religious interests of the day in his architectural theory and practice.

The literary and architectural production of Guarini is prodigious. His writings encompassed the theatre, philosophy, Euclid's *Elements*, astronomy, topography and the mensuration of buildings, as well as an important architectural treatise that appeared posthumously in 1737.[1] Although it is probably fair to say that Guarini was not an original thinker, his understanding of modern philosophy was thorough.

Guarini lived in Paris from 1662 to 1666, where he taught theology and published his philosophical treatise, *Placita Philosophica*. This work explained the crucial relation between the Cartesian *res cogitans* and *res extensa* in the occasionalistic sense: The only real and effective cause is God; finite beings are only the natural and occasional causes for the realization of Divine Will. In two works, *De la Recherche de la Vérité* and *Entretiens sur la Métaphysique* (published after Guarini's *Placita*), the French philosopher Nicolas Malebranche postulated the reconciliation between the human mind and the external world through God; every idea is "in God," and only in Him can the human mind comprehend His work. Malebranche believed that man did not perceive the specificity of things, but rather saw transparent and pristine ideas that were necessarily always in God. Guarini used a similar argument: Our knowledge of things is fulfilled through our apprehension of ideas in God; the ideas thought by man are the same divine ideas, or the archetypes that are contained in the Verb and have been communicated to us only in an imperfect way. For both Guarini and Malebranche, faith was synonymous with mathematical knowledge, and the *mathesis* implicit in all finite beings was equivalent to their immanence in God.[2]

In the *Placita*, Guarini stressed that mathematics constituted the foundation of human reason and that a mathematical knowledge of nature was equal to divine knowledge. But he also believed that spiritual things were ineluctably evident to our senses, so that mathematical rationality never contradicted sensuous experience as a source of knowledge. There was no dilemma because ultimately all knowledge was resolved in God. Thoughts were not real things, however; an authentic science of real essences was reserved for God. Intellectual problems for Guarini thus became a synthesis of reason and sensuous experience; only such a synthesis could effect true transcendental knowledge.

Guarini recognized the limitations of ancient philosophy vis-à-vis modern science. In his opinion, only moderate respect was due to the traditional texts. He openly embraced the geometrization of the universe brought about by the Galilean revolution and adopted the modern belief in the possibilities of mathematical reason and experimental knowledge. It is significant and typically Baroque that having taken this position, Guarini was also able to reject the heliocentric system of Galileo. He perceived no contradictions in this attitude, which also allowed him to accept elements of the traditional Aristotelian cosmology, which were, in fact, more in line with his religious faith. Indeed, the Holy Scriptures were the ultimate frame of reference for Guarini's scientific theories.

Guarini's cosmological system is interesting because it clearly shows the Baroque obsession to synthesize the specificity of perceived phenomena with a geometrical theory. Pre-Copernican astronomy concerned itself with the geometrical nature of planetary orbits; Aristotelian cosmology attributed a geometrical and mathematical regularity to the celestial spheres. The heavens were believed to be immutable, and therefore irregularities were never observed. Guarini rejected Galileo's system as just one more geometrical hypothesis of the traditional kind, unable to explain our actual experience of the universe. His own theory was designed to reconcile the physical, observed nature of the planetary orbits with the immobility of the earth, still perceived as the center of the cosmos. This theory, believed to save all phenomena was, nevertheless, geometrical and based on a geocentric system, with the sun and the planets revolving in sinusoidal orbits around the earth.[3]

Geometry, for Guarini, was not only one science among others; it was the prototypical Universal Science, comprising all dimensions of human thought and action, capable of reaching the truth through intellectual argumentation based on precise relations and combinations.[4] Absolute truth was derived from mathematics, the science that drew its conclusions directly from first principles.[5] Malebranche would add that the universal science of geometry could also open the human intellect, increase its capacity of attention and guide its imagination.[6]

Guarini's geometry had all the implications of an *ars combinatoria*, the traditional science of permutations that was accepted during the Middle Ages and the Renaissance as a true mirror of perceptual reality. These logical systems were believed to possess a magical transcendental dimension, endorsed by God or His agents. Generally, this was still the logic of seventeenth-century metaphysical systems.[7] All that any human could aspire to was a knowledge of relations; thus the geometrization of knowledge was perceived as an urgent task. In Guarini's work, philosophy, astronomy, physics, theology, architecture, engineering, and poetry all converged in geometry.[8] Geometry symbolized the highest values, but it was not opposed to nature. It possessed simultaneously celestial and terrestrial connotations; it was both the science of the stars and topography. Geometrical form guaranteed the truth of theory, while geometrical operations were used as a tool for the transformation of the world, reinforcing the traditional meaning of practice.

Guarini's treatise, entitled simply *Architettura Civile*, represents the first attempt to postulate a theory of architecture subject totally to the laws of geometry and mathematics. There were some precedents to his mathematization of architectural theory, but these were understood as part of the wider context of intellectual disciplines. Guarini himself cited as an important source C. F. Milliet Dechales's *Cursus seu Mundus Mathematicus* (1674), an immense compendium of knowledge *more geometrico* that included architecture. In his *Architettura Civile*, however, Guarini not only asserted that "architecture depends upon mathematics and geometry" but also emphasized that it was a "flattering art" that should never disgust the senses in order to please reason.[9] Thus Guarini defines the essence of architecture to be the synthesis of mathematical reason and sensuous qualities. Architecture depended on rules derived from mathematical reason *and* empirical experience, with no possible contradiction between the two. Moreover, Guarini thought that both the structural safety of buildings and their beauty and proportion, being the most important objectives of architecture, derived from the same rules.

Guarini accepted the possibility of correcting and modifying the architectural rules of antiquity and perceived the discrepancies that existed between Vitruvius's theory and many important buildings of the past. In accordance with the new epistemology,

Guarini preferred mathematical reason and empirical observation to ancient authority. Nonetheless, his deep roots in a traditional cosmology kept him away from any relativism. For Guarini, absolute rules constituted a fundamental point of departure in architecture.

Like François Blondel, Guarini believed that optical corrections were necessary to compensate for the distortions caused by perspective; and believing that a primary aim of architecture was to please and seduce our senses, he further developed the rules for optical correction. Nevertheless, he cautioned that architecture should never go to the extremes of perspective illusionism. A delicate balance had to be maintained since perspective was concerned only with delight and disregarded the structural stability and solidity of buildings. Guarini thought that architecture to be truly pleasant must possess a "real symmetry" that did not attempt to fool our sight.[10] Architecture had to be governed by a rational geometry capable of providing stability to the building, but also a geometry whose combinations and figural transformations could generate symbolic form and space. In this way, the ultimate meaning and beauty of architecture depended on the implementation of geometrical operations.

A major part of *Architettura Civile* was devoted to the description of geometrical combinations and manipulations, applied to all aspects of design and construction. The principles of geometry provided by Guarini were strictly Euclidean.[11] Guarini did not use the incipient projective geometry recently discovered by his contemporary Girard Desargues, of whom more will be said later. The postulate of the nonconvergence of parallel lines was defended by Guarini in the *Architettura*, where he emphasized the importance of intuition in a thoroughly Aristotelian vein. His geometry was never an abstract mathematical discipline, but depended on an intimate relation with the figures (the square, the triangle, the pentagon, and so forth) as perceived initially by our senses. In this respect, Guarini's edition of Euclid's *Elements* is significant. Although this was a treatise on geometrical theory, every single operation, including the most simple arithmetical ones, was presented graphically. Algebra was conspicuously absent. The specific image of each problem was obviously considered essential, making Guarini's geometry not only visible but also tangible, a true science of the real world. Only such a conception of geometry could lead him to assert that "the miraculous creativity of distinguished mathematicians shines intensely through regal architecture."[12]

Geometrical Operations as a Source of Meaning

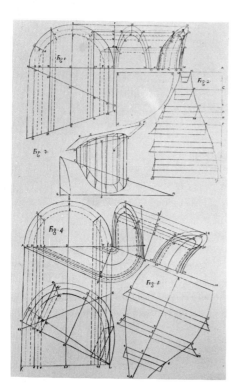

Stereotomic tracings, from Guarini's *Architettura Civile*.

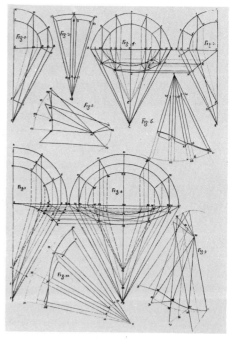

In his *Architettura Civile*, Guarini established a strictly geometrical method for determining the proportions of the classical orders, avoiding numerical relations. He cited as his source the work of a rather unknown figure, Carlo Cesare Osio, who had published his own *Architettura Civile* in 1684.[13] Osio's treatise was devoted entirely to the teaching or application of geometry as an instrument in drawing the five classical orders. After showing how to divide a straight line into a given proportion with the use of the compass, Osio provided detailed instructions for the design of any classical element by means of that simple operation. Although Osio apparently believed in the importance of proportions, it is significant that he never mentioned the great authors of antiquity and disregarded the issue of which were actually the most correct dimensions. Osio declared that his sole aim was to put forward a simple method that would facilitate architectural practice.

The traditional concerns of architectural theory, although ambiguous, were more explicit in Guarini's text. The section on the orders was introduced by showing how to trace some "necessary" curves, such as the spiral and the sinusoid. But then Guarini reproduced Vitruvius's story about the origin of classical forms and their proportions, "derived from the human stature."[14] Compared to previous treatises, the issue of the classical orders was given much less importance by Guarini, who subordinated everything to geometry. And although he believed that beauty depended on proportion, he was skeptical about the possibility of finding what actually caused pleasure in a well-proportioned and symmetrical elevation. He implied that there was an invisible cause, but obviously distrusted number. He defined proportion as a just correspondence between the parts and the whole; but rather than implying a perfect Renaissance fit, his intention was only to avoid excessively large or small pieces. After providing some general rules for the disposition of the orders and pointing out how different authors had divided the module into diverse units, he proposed to divide it into twelve parts for purely practical reasons.

Guarini was aware of the conflicting opinions regarding the orders and their proportions. Although he pretended to respect the authority of certain prestigious authors, quoting them as sources for his own recommended proportions, his own three orders are highly original inventions. Their ornamental detail, which is more exaggerated and conspicuously less abstract and geometrical than that of his sources, attempts to realize the com-

Geometrical Operations as a Source of Meaning

plexities of natural (particularly vegetable) shapes. These plates appear striking, placed as they are between stereotomic projections and manifold geometrical applications. The fundamental coherence of Guarini's theory, impossible to appreciate adequately through the contrast of his rhetorical naturalistic ornamentation and his concern for precise geometrical methods, becomes explicit once the symbolic sense of his geometrization of architecture is fully comprehended.

Technical problems were extensively discussed in *Architettura Civile*. Guarini described methods for leveling and topographic surveying in which buildings were treated as additions of geometrical elements; walls, domes, and columns were actually addressed as geometrical bodies. A similar transformation is evident in a little book that Guarini wrote specifically on the problem of measurement in buildings. His *Modo di Misurare le Fabriche* was conceived as the practical application of the principles he had developed in his *Euclides*. In it he provided methods for measuring and determining the cubic volumes of any part of a building, even of those elements that were hardly regular. However, there is no allusion to any real problems of building; after a brief introduction to mathematics, Guarini merely explained how to measure areas and regular volumes.

After discussing the geometrical nature of vaults, Guarini devoted a whole section of his *Architettura* to stereotomy. The use of geometrical projections to determine the shapes and proportional dimensions of wooden or stone elements of domes, arches, vaults, and stairs had been first introduced into architectural theory by Philibert de l'Orme during the sixteenth century. Guarini emphasized the importance of stereotomic tracings, whose complexity led Rudolph Wittkower to underline the "mechanical" dimension of his architecture. It is clear, however, that Guarini's plans never required any sort of projective geometry to be realized in three dimensions.[15] His stereotomy never implemented the discovery of Girard Desargues, as some scholars have imagined;[16] the significance of this will become clearer from the perspective of later chapters. Guarini's geometry was not a descriptive geometry; every problem generated its own method, as was the case in the traditional treatises of Derand and De l'Orme.[17]

Unlike previous Renaissance treatises, Guarini's subjected all the technical operations of architecture to geometry. This modern attitude, nevertheless, has to be carefully qualified; its meaning can only be understood in relation to the crucial role that geometry

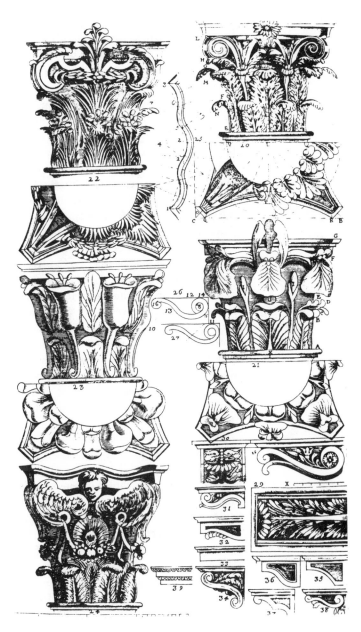

Details of composite capitals, from Guarini's *Architettura Civile*.

Geometrical Operations as a Source of Meaning

played in the totality of his work. Architecture for Guarini combined the objectives of seventeenth-century science and philosophy. His architectural intentions were totally coherent, without conflict or distance between his artistic and scientific interests.

Geometry was used by Guarini as a precise technical tool; it was an instrument, a set of operations, but always implemented to achieve a reconciliation between spiritual values and the world of man. The basic geometrical figures of Euclidean science became the elements of an *ars combinatoria* in which the figures were combined and transformed to design extremely complex and seductive buildings. Created with the most simple elements, a Guarini church becomes a true microcosm, capable of reflecting the order of an Aristotelian world through the qualities of natural perception and the persuasive use of light and textures.

It has been pointed out that Guarini's churches were conceived as monumental models that reproduced the structural system of the universe, registering the influence of the planets, the phases of the moon, and the harmonic motion of the heavenly spheres.[18] His architecture, however, was not merely a reflection of the geometrical structure of the cosmos, but achieved the status of quasi-natural objects, created through the magic of combinations and an emphasis on the sensuous qualities of matter, a process that Guarini considered analogous to that of divine creation. Thus geometry was deemed capable by Guarini of reconciling Platonic symbolism with the Aristotelian world of everyday life and traditional religion.

In Guarini's work, the formal and transcendental dimensions of geometry were perfectly reconciled. The geometrization of the world had been the result of the Galilean revolution; geometrical science became a prototype of true knowledge. But Guarini's Baroque geometry was not merely a formal science; it was an instrument of rhetoric as well as logic. In keeping with traditional, Aristotelian perception, geometrical figures assumed the character of symbolic essences, always derived from sensuous intuitions. The geometrization of *res extensa* was the point of departure of modern science and technology, allowing for an increasing exploitation and desecration of nature. During the seventeenth century, however, the geometrical structure of the cosmos guaranteed the perception of absolute values, establishing an immediate relation between *res cogitans*, *res extensa*, and God.

Baroque architecture emphatically utilized geometrical operations to determine forms and spaces. Geometry replaced the authority of the ancients as the source of ultimate justifications in architecture; it became, in fact, a metaphysic, transforming the world of man into a symbolic universe. Architectural historians have commonly regarded the technical dimension of these geometrical operations as a curious but mistaken precedent for statics and structural mechanics. Thinking in terms of formal styles, they have been unable to recognize the fundamental continuity between intentions that resulted in the sensuous ornamentation and spatial complexity of some buildings and intentions that motivated austere and dominating schemes such as Versailles or the geometrical transformation of cities. Only by accepting the essential symbolic dimension of geometrical operations in architecture within the epistemological framework of the seventeenth century is it possible to discern the coherence of Baroque architectural intentions, containing both rational and sensuous dimensions.

Desargues's Universal Method and Perspective

Any study on the impact of modern science upon the architecture of the seventeenth century would be remiss if it failed to examine the work and ideas of Girard Desargues (1593–1662). Desargues was an architect and engineer, and probably the most brilliant geometrician of the seventeenth century. Many of his works were published around 1650 by his disciple Abraham Bosse, including two treatises in which he proposed a universal method (*manière universelle*) for solving problems of perspective on flat and irregular surfaces and a book on stereotomic projections for stonecutting.[19] His complete works, however, including an important piece on pure geometry, were not published until 1864.

Desargues sought to establish a general geometric science, one that might *effectively* become the basis for such diverse technical operations as perspective, stone- and woodcutting for construction, and the design of solar clocks. These disciplines had always had their own theories, which ultimately referred to the specificity of the techniques themselves. Desargues's interest was exceptional even in the context of the seventeenth century. In order to find universal geometrical principles that would allow him to structure a common theory for the operations of the techniques in question, Desargues disregarded the transcendental dimension of geometry and the symbolic power of geometrical operations. In practical terms, he had to discover the theoretical properties of geometrical perspective (*perspectiva artificialis*). Having identified theory with an *ars fabricandi*, he aspired toward the rational control of practice,

Geometrical Operations as a Source of Meaning

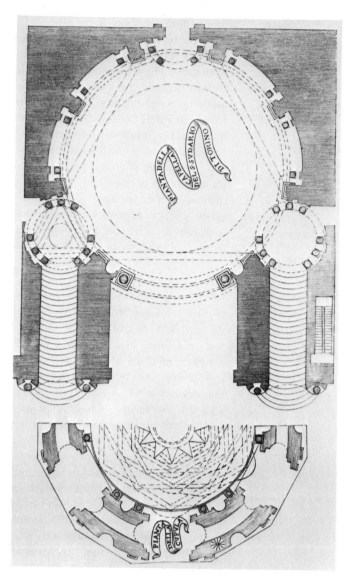

Plan and section of Guarini's design for the Church
of the Holy Shroud (S. Sudario) in Turin, showing
the geometry of the dome, from *Architettura Civile*.

Geometry and Architectural Meaning

Geometrical Operations as a Source of Meaning

not an explanation of its reasons.[20] Consequently, he could ignore the symbolic implications of infinity and was capable of introducing this notion into geometry for the first time in the history of Western thought.

Such an accomplishment is difficult to appreciate from a contemporary vantage point, which regards visual perspective as the only true means of comprehending the external world. In fact, preconceptual perception, evident in the art of children or primitive and non-Western cultures, is not a perspective perception. Parallel lines did not converge in Euclidean space, where tactile considerations, derived from bodily spatiality, are still more important than purely visual information.[21] Euclidean geometry was conceived as a science of immediacy[22] whose principles had their origin in perception. Like Aristotelian categories, its rules were a posteriori. In a real sense, Euclidean theory is almost a practice, with intuition at its roots. Euclid's theorems are exact and true only insofar as the things to which they make reference are accepted as variable and imprecise.

Desargues maintained, however, that all lines converged toward a point at infinity. Thus any system of parallel lines, or any specific geometrical figure, could be conceived as a variation of a single universal system of concurrent lines. Desargues's basic aims would eventually be fulfilled by Gaspard Monge's descriptive geometry toward the end of the eighteenth century. In fact, Desargues's fundamental principle, which stipulated the tracing of perspective projections without the use of arbitrary points of distance, would become the general postulate of projective geometry, a science that would be developed during the second decade of the nineteenth century by Jean-Victor Poncelet. The postulate read, "If placed two by two on three lines converging in one point, the prolongation of their sides will converge in three points of a single line."[23]

In his *Manière Universelle pour Pratiquer la Perspective*, Desargues emphasized that there was no difference between the drawing of a plan and that of a perspective, as long as an appropriate scale of real dimensions projected to infinity was used. A scale of this nature was to be employed for each one of the Cartesian axes in order to construct perspectives that avoided all empirical considerations. The traditional, more or less arbitrary, tracings were, in his opinion, irrelevant complications. Desargues's theory of perspective, in contrast to that of his contemporaries and successors, was precise and autonomous (independent of reality, that is). Thus it could become a general science of geometrical projections, capable of controlling and rationalizing the most important techniques of architecture. The laws of perspective became the first "theory of theory," truly independent of practice. The actual drawing and construction of perspectives, the design of solar clocks and the determination of the shape and dimensions of stone pieces for vaults and arches, all depended upon the same system of oblique projections and thus could be reduced to a methodology. For the first time, regardless of the architect's capacity to visualize the operations, true results were guaranteed by this formal logic, even arriving at "inferred" conclusions that might not be explicit in the "premises" of practice and embodied reality. Desargues *manière universelle* was in fact the first step toward a functionalization of reality that would precipitate the Industrial Revolution and the crisis of European science during the nineteenth century.

The significance of this remarkably early functionalization of three-dimensional reality should be emphasized. Once perspectivism was introduced as a condition of thought by Cartesian dualism, the theory of perspective could become the first autonomous general science. Desargues recognized the *continuity* that existed between the descriptive characteristics of geometrical figures and bodies. He was the first to discover that the conic sections (parabola, hyperbola, and ellipse) were only perspective projections of a circle. In the context of Euclidean geometry, such continuity was never recognized. For each qualitatively different figure, there was a corresponding interpretation and deduction; each geometrical problem was solved according to its specific character.

Functioning independently of reality, Desargues's theory avoided metaphysical concerns. His astounding protopositivism, which was closer to the architectural intentions of the nineteenth century than to those of the Enlightenment, was never accepted by his contemporaries. Artists and craftsmen tended to reject any reduction of theory to the condition of *ars fabricandi*. They continued to use empirical methods for the different techniques of architecture, methods by which practice and rules were closely related.

It is interesting to mention in this respect the problems that Bosse faced in the Royal Academy of Painting and Sculpture when he attempted to teach Desargues's *manière universelle* to

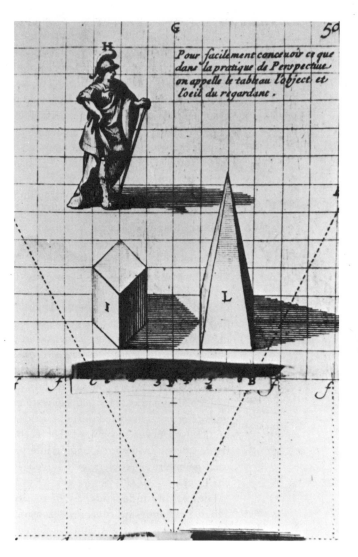

Desargues's simplified perspective method, from
Bosse's *Manière Universelle pour Pratiquer la Perspective* (1648). Desargues's method avoided the use of
vanishing points outside the picture plane.

Geometry and Architectural Meaning

art students. The main point of contention was the universal applicability of Desargues's theory, which was nothing less than an ontological attack against traditional practice. After a lengthy struggle, Bosse was dismissed. It was clear that Desargues's geometry was not the Euclidean science that allowed artists to fulfill their symbolic intentions. Desargues's work was indeed rejected, but it cannot be discounted. It reveals the full and immediate impact of the epistemological revolution, opening the way to an effective technological domination of reality. His intentionality, although explicit only in relation to certain techniques, was already that of modern architecture.

The noticeable return to the phenomena, implicit in the method of physics and natural history during the eighteenth century, reinforced the status of Euclidean spatiality. During the Enlightenment, Desargues's name was forgotten. The Italian geometrician G. Saccheri, editing and commenting Euclid's *Elements* in 1731, had in hand all the necessary technical knowledge to refute the axiom of the nonconvergence of parallel lines.[24] Had he obtained the conclusions that clearly lay in the path of his investigation, Saccheri might have hit upon non-Euclidean geometries a hundred years before their time. It is significant, however, that without any clear logical reason, the Italian geometrician never concluded his speculations. The true cause of this has eluded most historians of science, though it is probably nothing more than a question of true cultural limitations; Euclidean space, still the space of embodied perception, was the horizon of thought and action in the eighteenth century.

After Leibniz, the magical attributes of *ars combinatoria* were discredited and geometry and mathematics lost their symbolic dimension, maintaining only a formal value. This situation advanced the transformation of applied mathematics into a powerful instrument for the technological domination of reality. But this transformation, as I have already explained in the previous chapter, did not actually occur in the eighteenth century. From the point of view of a scientific teleology, the systematization of reality was absolutely imperative as a precondition of the Industrial Revolution and positivism. The process of geometrization that had been initiated by the epistemological revolution ceased during the eighteenth century, restrained by the renewed interest in empirical methods.

Once geometry lost its symbolic attributes in traditional philosophical speculation, perspective stopped being a preferred vehicle for the transformation of the world into a meaningful human order. Instead, it became a simple representation of reality, a sort of empirical verification of the way in which the external world is presented to human vision. The Enlightenment generally abandoned the use of perspectives that had been so crucial for Baroque architecture, urbanism, and gardening. Without its immanent symbolic sense, perspective became synonymous with an objective perception of external reality. This transformation was equivalent to a return to the more traditional empirical methods of perspective construction. Subsequently, the artists and writers interested in the subject during the Enlightenment tried to avoid all conceptual impositions. Their theories never intended to violate or modify perceived reality. Thus the development of a geometrical theory of perspective was arrested during the eighteenth century, and works like·Desargues's, which implied a different attitude to reality, were ignored by practicing artists.

The most influential work showing this transformed notion of perspective was, perhaps paradoxically, Andrea Pozzo's *Rules and Examples of Perspective for Painters and Architects*. This book, published in Latin between 1693 and 1700, was the result of Pozzo's vast practice, itself a significant part of the Jesuit contribution to Baroque art. Avoiding the geometrical theory of perspective, Pozzo's theoretical discourse amounts to a collection of extremely simple rules and detailed examples of perspective constructions, which always begin from the plan and elevation of a building.[25] In 1720 a well-known mathematician, J. Ozanam, defended this revised conception of perspective in his *Perspective Théorique et Pratique*, which maintained that the sole objective of this science was the imitation of nature. Ozanam criticized those authors who had opposed perspective and who accused it of being a useless art, pleasant to the eye, but only through constant deception. True, some charlatans had indeed committed abuses in its name, relating it to magic and superstition, but this, he thought, was nonsense. Perspective was only a vehicle for reproducing "the marvelous world of man" from a given point of view.

Taking their cue from this purification of perspective, architects and artists of the eighteenth century showed no interest in the illusionistic tricks and exaggerations that were so popular during the Baroque period. The world of illusion was distinguished from the world of everyday life. Man's position vis-à-vis the objective physical reality of the world was defined more clearly, and this, in turn, led to the beginning of anthropological speculations.[26]

Geometry and Architectural Meaning

Enlightened reason became a force whose task was to transform reality into a universe of representation. This notwithstanding, a metaphysical channel remained open between the stage and the spectator, between *res extensa* and *res cogitans*. Truth appeared in the observation of phenomena, and intersubjective communication remained possible. This meant that perspectivism, a condition and result of the radical dualism of modern philosophy, could not achieve its ascendency over perception until the end of the eighteenth century.

It is significant that in contrast to the great number of philosopher-mathematicians of the seventeenth century, during the Enlightenment, only d'Alembert, Wolff, and perhaps Euler can be called such. By 1754 Diderot observed a "great revolution" taking place in the sciences and predicted that in a hundred years there would not even be "three geometricians left in Europe. . . . The progress of this science will suddenly stop."[27] Indeed, after mid-century the interest in abstract speculation declined sharply in favor of experimental physics and natural history. Any geometrical system, including Newton's, could be accused of imposing a false structure upon the diversity of nature.[28] Geometry as a formal science was not developed at all during this period and lost its predominant role as a prototype of knowledge.

In this transformed epistemological framework, geometrical operations were seldom used in architectural design, although they were widely applied in other technical disciplines related to architecture, such as surveying, mensuration, stereotomy, and statics. But their use in generating architectural form and meaning was ambivalent and sporadic, usually appearing elsewhere than at Paris or Rome, the cultural and architectural centers of Neoclassicism.

Geometrical Operations in Eighteenth-Century Design

The direct influence of Guarini on Central European architects was considerable during the early eighteenth century. In the Piedmont, Bernardo Vittone followed the example of his master. Vittone was born in Turin in 1705 and was responsible for the publication of Guarini's *Architettura Civile*.[29] Traditionally, his work had been classified with that of other Austrian and German architects as late Baroque. His use of formal elements and his geometrical combinations were clearly borrowed from Guarini, but his buildings seem to betray a less confident and systematic spirit.

Geometrical Operations as a Source of Meaning

Geometry and Architectural Meaning

Perspective constructed from a precise plan and elevation, after A. Pozzo's *Rules and Examples of Perspective* (1709).

However, Vittone's architecture should not be dismissed for these reasons. His important place in the debate between Baroque and Neoclassical architecture has recently been established.[30] Vittone's theory and practice was the result of a conscious, although never rigorous, synthesis of diverse interests. A devout Catholic, he had been impressed by Newton's cosmology, which he knew through Algarotti's interpretation.[31] His library included the most important architectural treatises, several editions of Vitruvius, and other less-known books, such as *Architectura Civil, Recta y Obliqua* by Guarini's enemy, Caramuel de Lobkowitz, and Carlo Fontana's *Tempio Vaticano*. He was passionately interested in rhetoric and science. In his library was a book by A. Bosse on the drawing of the classical orders using a geometrical method (a possible precedent of Osio and Guarini), as well as works on physics, astronomy, mechanics, and optics. He had copies of Galileo's *Dialoghi*, a course on mathematics by Ozanam, and Bélidor's most important work, *La Science des Ingenieurs*.[32]

Vittone, who always added to his signature the title *ingegnere*, was very interested in technical problems of construction and was aware of the recent French contributions on the subject. His theory of architecture was published in two enormous, often redundant, treatises entitled *Istruzioni Elementari* (1760) and *Istruzioni Diverse* (1766), dedicated to God and the Virgin Mary. Both books betray the same interests. In *Istruzioni Diverse*, Vittone dealt with mensuration, hydraulics, property evaluation, bridge construction, "and all types of buildings and ornaments of civil architecture."[33] He included methods of calculating areas and volumes of complex vaults and the precise dimensions of the Italian mile in relation to the spheroidal shape of the earth. In the section on the design and construction of bridges, he mentioned Bélidor's work. Still, Vittone did not refer to quantitative considerations resulting from the strength of materials; his recommendations for the proportions of piers were wholly conventional, taken mostly from the best-known Renaissance treatises. In the chapter on vaults, he pointed out the difficulties involved in determining the "convenient thickness" of the upper sections in order to make them sufficiently resistant.[34] He then tried to apply some principles of statics to the problem, devised a formula, and used it. In the end, however, Vittone repeated L. B. Alberti's advice on the dimensions of vaults. Indeed, if Vittone's work is compared to contemporary French and Italian Neoclassical treatises, including the *Rigoristti*, his lack of interest in mechanics and quantitative experiments is remarkably conspicuous.

Vittone faced great difficulties when trying to provide a method for quantifying and evaluating buildings or property. His categories for determining the monetary value of buildings were mostly qualitative, never merely material or quantitative. His traditional perception of the world created a confusion between qualities and quantities that was already normally avoided in books about mensuration.

One of the more interesting aspects of Vittone's theory is his emphasis on the use of a grid to solve design problems, particularly the distribution of such architectural elements as columns, walls, and openings in plan. He included a great number of plates in which the grid was used for the determination of plans of buildings and gardens, for the composition of elevations, and as the basis for tracing abstract geometrical figures or emblems. Vittone's use of the grid anticipated by more than forty years Durand's "mechanism of composition," a method of design recommended solely for purposes of efficiency. Vittone's grid was obviously no longer the symbolic reticulation of De l'Orme's *Divine Proportion* or that of Cesariano's representation of Vitruvius's man. It was a practical device for providing simple rules for determining the proportions and locations of rooms, doors, and windows. No longer a network of invisible lines to elucidate architectural meaning, the grid became a mere instrument for simplifying the design process.

In view of our previous discussion, however, the technological implications of Vittone's use of the grid should not be overemphasized.[35] For though he seemed genuinely concerned with statics, his comprehension of structural problems was narrow. He may have known Borra's treatise on strength of materials and Poleni's collection of reports on the structural problems of Saint Peter's Basilica in Rome, both published in 1748; but the tracing he provided in *Istruzioni Diverse* for the correct configuration of a dome is a modified version of Carlo Fontana's method, as it appeared in his *Tempio Vaticano* (1694). This was a truly Baroque set of geometrical operations, not derived from mechanical considerations, but endorsed by their immanent symbolic power and the actual existence of exemplary models that embodied this geometry.

Vittone also studied the works of Newton, though he never seemed to understand the importance of empirical, quantitative knowledge. He was concerned mainly with the poetic dimension of Newton's Platonic cosmology. Like Briseux, Vittone identified musical with architectural harmonies and considered Newton's optical theory, which explained mathematically the separation of

Geometrical Operations as a Source of Meaning

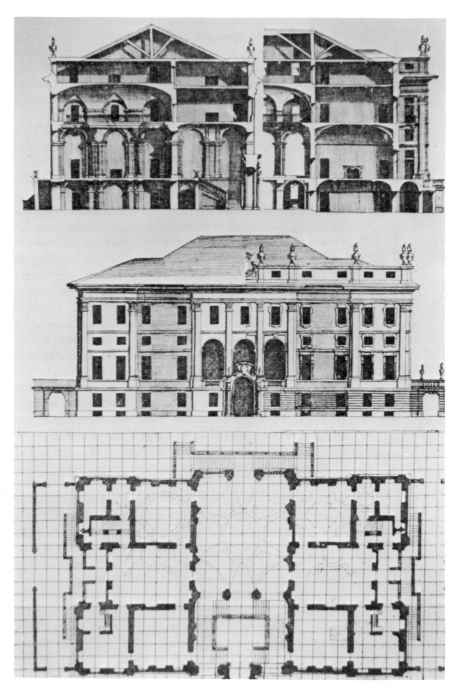

The use of the grid applied to the design of a villa,
from Vittone's *Istruzioni Elementari* (1760).

Geometry and Architectural Meaning

white light into the seven colors of the rainbow, to be the supreme confirmation of traditional theories of proportion. The careful and mysterious use of light in Vittone's churches had its origin in the archaic horizon of Neoplatonic belief. Light was a traditional symbol of divinity, now made explicit through its newly discovered qualities and magical properties. Newton's acute empiricism, however, could never determine the true essence of light. Its mystery, similar to that of the gravitational force, always fascinated Newton, just as it did artists, poets, and architects, for whom it became a source of inspiration.[36]

To the *Istruzioni Diverse*, Vittone added a short piece on the nature of music and harmonic proportion by a close associate.[37] In a short introduction, Vittone evinced skepticism about Plato's and Hermes Trismegistus's idea that music is a "science of order, according to which are disposed all things in nature."[38] He also questioned the marvelous and magical character of a "universal architecture," though he considered an understanding of the universal laws of harmony necessary to establish rules for the design of theatres, communal halls, basilicas, and choirs, where a consideration of acoustics was essential. Thus Vittone endorsed his disciple's piece, which was an attempt to apply "scientific" principles to the problems of harmony and represented, in effect, a corpuscular theory of sound. The author analyzed "extrinsic" and "intrinsic" properties of sound: sonority, propagation, "dilatation" or the "periodic order" of harmonic elements—all of which he defined in terms of "atoms of sound." He compared them to "atoms of light" and imagined them traveling through the ether. He studied their form, elasticity, and dimensions, postulating an analogy between atoms of sound, atoms of fire, and atoms of water. Mathematical harmony constituted the essense of this analogy because, as Galileo had shown, "nature is mathematical in all that concerns physical things and their functions."[39]

These theories were partly derived from seventeenth-century physics, having their roots in a traditional cosmobiology. Not surprisingly, the author also emphasized the symbolic character of certain numbers. The number 2, for example, was "meaningful and mysterious," since it was always present in harmonic consonances; its symbolic character was reinforced by the fact that number 22 determined the "totality of the musical system."[40] This is also the number of letters in the Jewish, Chaldean, and Syrian alphabets; it is the number of ancient canonical texts and the number of patriarchs, judges, and kings. After a similar study of

Geometrical Operations as a Source of Meaning

the character of number 7, the author concluded that "in view of such and so many mystical correspondences," it was unquestionable that harmony was a science in which God had deposited conspicuous signs of His most sublime and admirable secrets.

Vittone's conception of number and his use of geometrical operations were ambivalent; although half-conscious of the implications of modern science, they also derived from traditional considerations. His use of the grid as a tool of design and his interest in Newton and in the works of French engineers seemed to be a move away from the transcendental theories of his Baroque predecessors. But in the end, his profound religious convictions and the formal architectural expression that he had inherited from Guarini prevailed. Assimilated at a certain level with the Platonic cosmology of natural philosophy, his geometrical structures were never as overpowering as Guarini's. In his humble churches, the structure was always subdued by the presence of light.

The use of a grid as an instrument to simplify the design process and to make explicit the proportions of the components of an architectural plan also appeared in a less-known work, the *Instituzioni d'Architettura Civile* (1772) by Nicola Carletti. To Carletti, architecture was a science, and his aim was to guide young architects through "the purest doctrines," toward a "universal practice of their art."[41] Without quibbling, Carletti declared his fervent adherence to Newton's philosophy. His own wish, then, was to implement in architecture the analytical methods that the British scientist had discovered. For Carletti, "the culmination of human knowledge" consisted in a series of observations and experiences from which were obtained general principles through induction.[42]

Carletti claimed that his work was thoroughly modeled on Newton's "system" and gave two reasons for his choice. In the first place, he wanted to provide "simple meditations" founded on few data, instead of a "long series of irritating arguments." His second reason was more interesting. Carletti realized, as did Perrault, that architecture was related to custom. After a brief historical analysis, he expressed a pragmatic view of primitive architecture, showing it to be simple, unrefined, and guided by the sole objective of defending man against the elements. Beauty, solidity, and commodity, the three categories that constituted the main objectives of architecture, were to be founded on the investigations, approval, and institutions of wise men "that had opened the way toward truth, through reasons considered as absolute principles." But while Perrault upheld Vitruvius's treatise

View into the dome of Vittone's Sanctuary of Valli-
noto, near Carignano in the Piedmont (1738–1739).

Geometrical Operations as a Source of Meaning

and provided his own rules in the *Ordonnance*, Carletti took Newton as his source. Geographical and cultural differences notwithstanding, architecture, for Carletti, was an extension of nature and therefore was grounded in absolute principles. The search for truth and its application was the declared motif of his analytical system. Ironically, the form of the text was *more geometrico*, a collection of definitions, observations, experiments, corollaries, schollia, and rules, reminiscent of the previous century.

Carletti surveyed various types of buildings and used a grid to describe his project for a jail, placing the walls on the lines and columns on the intersections. His proportions were stipulated in terms of natural whole numbers. He was genuinely interested in the strength of materials and statics. In the *Istituzioni*, he provided empirical rules concerning the properties of building materials. The second volume of his work was totally devoted to such technical problems as topography, the geometrical determination of the shapes of vaults and arches, mensuration of parts of buildings and quantification of their cubic volumes, and a method for finding the real dimensions of buildings starting from their general proportions.

Yet alongside his modern preoccupations, Carletti also retained traditional notions about proportion. He believed that architectural harmony and proportion had their origin in the human body, which he proved in the Vitruvian fashion. In a section on the determination of proportions of vertical structural elements, he was unable to distinguish between dimensions obtained through the application of statics and those simply prescribed by the traditional rules of proportion. It was only in relation to sacred buildings, however, that he emphasized the crucial importance of harmony and proportion. These buildings, which he saw as being dedicated to the God of the Enlightenment, the "Supreme Maker" or "Divine Unity," should be places conducive to the "perfect adoration and contemplation of INFINITY."[43]

Carletti's understanding of architecture vis-à-vis sacred space has important implications on which I shall elaborate in the following chapter. During the Middle Ages, the symbolic order revealed by architecture concerned fundamentally the cathedral, the City of God, the only immutable and transcendental building. The finite order of the city was not an architectural problem strictly speaking, except perhaps on the occasion of religious celebrations, when the ideal geometrical order was made manifest in the structure and staging of a mystery play.[44] In the Renaissance, human life acquired a new value as lived experience. The architect was concerned with the city as a stage for the drama of humanity, now liberated from religious determinism but nonetheless devout. Through the seventeenth century, the symbolic geometrical order of both secular and religious institutions was indeed the task of the architect, striving to give man a dwelling place for his image, reconciling his finitude with eternity. In order to understand the origins and possibilities of modern architecture, it must be noted that once the human world and its institutions became truly secularized in the eighteenth century, the symbolic intentionality of architecture became strongly associated with theoretical projects of sacred (and funerary) buildings.

Carletti admitted to having been influenced by the work of the German philosopher Christian Wolff, who himself had been the most important disciple of Leibniz. It was Wolff's disregard for the transcendental implications of Leibniz's cosmological synthesis that intimated a philosophy that no longer depended on theology, and would eventually become a critique of reason.

Wolff spent his life attempting to achieve a total systematization of human knowledge. His general metaphysics would become during the nineteenth century the general philosophy of positivism. He tried to organize all available information, transforming it into a "true science." His objective was to create a system in which the principles would be the obvious origin of their own consequences, a system where everything could be "deduced with demonstrative evidence." He wrote that after "having meditated on the foundation of evidence in geometrical demonstrations and on the techniques of research in algebra," he was able to establish "the general rules of demonstration and discovery."[45]

Wolff's philosophy is a good example of how the Newtonian model was applied early on to the human sciences. His numerous writings are all characterized by a mathematical structure, very similar to the metaphysical systems of the seventeenth century, but without their guarantee of absolute transcendence. His formal a priori systems imitated in a sense the perfect intelligibility of Newtonian thought. Wolff's stated intention was to do for metaphysics what Newton had achieved in his physics: to define it through the unification of "reason and experience."[46] In his *Elementa Matheseos Universae* (1713), for example, he tried to implement this synthesis. The text was structured *more geometrico*. Alongside specific sections on civil and military architecture, it included those disciplines that had been or were to become part

Geometrical Operations as a Source of Meaning

of the education of eighteenth-century engineers and architects: mathematical method, arithmetic, geometry, trigonometry, finite and infinite analysis, statics and mechanics, hydraulics, optics, perspective, gnomonics, and pyrotechnics.

This interest to axiomatize knowledge in a world where such operations were still impossible determined the ambiguity of the work of philosophers like Wolff and d'Alembert, an ambiguity that was shared by the infrequent attempts of absolute systematization in eighteenth-century architecture. During the Enlightenment, the dilemma was solved by invoking the transcendental sense of Nature. Both Wolff and Carletti depended upon Newton's discoveries to justify their own geometric and aprioristic intellectual structures—structures that the English scientist himself would have rejected. Induction and encyclopedism normally avoided the contradictions between mathematical systems and empirical reality by discouraging any excessive mathematical formalization of knowledge.

The section on civil architecture in the *Elementa*, like Carletti's *Istituzioni*, was structured *more geometrico*. Wolff's theory was still fundamentally Vitruvian and included the classical orders. Concerning proportion, Wolff made no explicit reference to its symbolic content, but insisted that the optimal dimensional relations were defined by natural numbers "easy to recognize by the human sight." His theory was similar to that which Laugier would put forward in his *Observations*, almost sixty years later. Wolff introduced three categories by which to recognize the perfection of proportions in relation to a mathematical rationalism that, he believed, corresponded to perceptual intelligibility. His fundamental criterion was the clarity with which proportion was presented, becoming better as it approached the square and avoided small fractions.[47]

Wolff reproduced the proportions for the classical orders recommended by Goldmann, one of the least-known traditional authors. However, he also included systematic tables for determining the dimensions of certain ornamental elements, numerical rules for the design of chimneys, and geometrical methods for tracing various details. It is significant that the anonymous translator of the French edition of the *Elementa* (1747) decided to substitute Goldmann's proportions ("in such bad taste") with Perrault's.[48] His decision was explained in a "corollary" to the text that underlined the relative unimportance of following scrupulously the original recommendations of Wolff. The translator thought that

Geometry and Architectural Meaning

proportions could be slightly modified without endangering the beauty of a building, and no doubt recognized certain essential affinities between Wolff and Perrault, particularly their emphasis on mathematical systematization and their understanding of theory as a formal discipline capable of being structured apart from metaphysical speculations. Wolff's own protopositivism, however, was restrained by the implicit metaphysical dimension of Newtonian natural philosophy; his systematization was still a metametaphysics, not an actual positivism.

In eighteenth-century England, there were also some sporadic applications of geometry in architectural design, particularly among the "architect-surveyors". One instance is the work of Robert Morris, who on the surface appears as a very traditional architect, insisting that good taste necessarily derives from an intimate acquaintance with the work of the ancients. His admiration of Palladio, so popular in England during the early eighteenth century, was unconditional. He called him "the chiefest restorer of antiquity."[49]

In 1728 he published *An Essay in Defence of Ancient Architecture*, which was concerned with the criticism of modern "follies" and excessive use of ornament. He added a rather lengthy introduction as a key to his architectural intentions. In an exalted poetic vein, Morris emphasized the symbolic sense of Nature; he referred to it as the "architectural Creation of the World" and as a manifestation of "Divine Power."[50] After praising the Royal Society of London and the Baconian concept of mutual assistance for the advancement of science, he declared his faith in a universal harmony. Morris clearly revealed the poetic dimension of natural philosophy: fantastic visions of microscopic worlds, planets, animals and plants—everything ordered in a cosmic totality where it was possible to perceive "the mysterious act of Divine Wisdom." But apart from this, when he tried to describe the prototypical image of traditional cosmobiology, his words lacked conviction: "We are not a little pleased says a great author . . . when we compare the body of man with bulk of the whole Earth, the Earth with the circle it describes round the sun, the circle to the sphere of the fix'd stars, the sphere of the fix'd stars to the circuit of the whole creation."[51] In the end, his conclusions about architecture were not very ambitious. Like Carletti long after him, he specifically addressed sacred architecture, which he claimed would be more pleasant if it resembled the works of nature.

Geometrical Operations as a Source of Meaning

E S S A Y

In Defence of

Ancient Architecture;

OR, A

P A R A L L E L

OF THE

Ancient Buildings with the Modern :

SHEWING

The Beauty and Harmony of the Former,
and the Irregularity of the Latter.

With Impartial Reflections on the Reasons of the Abuses
introduced by our present Builders.

To which is Annexed,

An Inspectional TABLE, universally Useful.

Illustrated with Sixteen COPPER-PLATES.

By ROBERT MORRIS, *of* Twickenham.

Learn hence for Ancient Rules a just Esteem,
To copy Nature is to copy them.   POPE on Criticism.

L O N D O N :

Printed for D. BROWNE, at the *Black Swan,* without *Temple-Bar ;*
W. BICKERTON, in *Devereaux-Court,.* near *Temple-Bar ;*

Frontispiece and title page of Morris's *Essay.* Notice
the allegory of revelation of ancient rules and Pope's
quotation.

In his *Lectures on Architecture*, Morris wrote more extensively about the use of proportions and geometry. His purpose was to determine what "true proportion and harmony" really were, so that it might be possible to establish practical rules. He believed that, regardless of whether harmony resided "in numbers or Nature, it immediately strikes the Imagination by some attractive or sympathizing property."[52] These were obvious echoes of Newtonian harmony. But Morris also believed that architects should know geometry in order "to delineate regular or irregular plans, etc., to furnish him with reasons for the capacity of supporting weights," and to trace perspectives, sections, and elevations. And they should be acquainted with arithmetic "for estimates, measurements," and "money spended," and be familiar with "Musick . . . to judge their accords and discords and affinity with proportion, in erecting places such as Rooms of Entertainment, Theatres, Churches in which Sound is more immediately concerned."[53]

Morris apparently recognized the formal dimension of mathematics as a technical tool in architecture. His interest in musical harmony, however, did not stem merely from a concern with acoustics. Explaining his system of proportion, Morris pointed out that through music, nature has taught Mankind certain rules of "Arithmetical Harmony." These were the rules of proportion that he adopted for architecture: "The Square in Geometry, the Unison or Circle in Music and the Cube in Building have all an inseparable Proportion; the Parts being equal . . . give the Eye and Ear an agreeable Pleasure, from hence may likewise be deduc'd the Cube and half, the Double Cube; the Diapason and Diapente, being founded on the same Principles in Musick."[54] Immediately thereafter, Morris declared his preference for natural numbers in architectural proportions and established the maximum dimensions of his modular cube. The use of modular cubes unquestionably simplified the conception of architectural volumes. The technical dimension of his concern with proportions was particularly evident in a chapter on chimneys, in which he sought to discover the "arithmetic and harmonic proportions" of chimneys in relation to the dimensions of rooms and to provide simple and universal rules for their design.

Having established an analogy between musical harmony and architectural proportion, Morris decided that to the seven "distinct" notes of the musical scale there corresponded seven proportions in architecture that could be clearly differentiated: Architectural

Geometrical Operations as a Source of Meaning

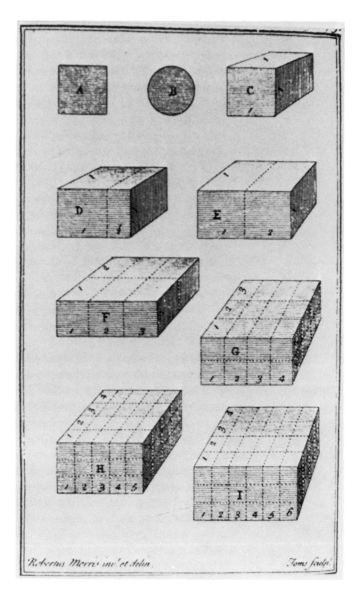

The generation of cubic proportions in architecture,
from Morris's *Lectures on Architecture* (1734).

Geometry and Architectural Meaning

proportion "difuses itself to the Imagination by some sympathizing Secret to the Soul, which is all union, all Harmony."[55] In *An Essay upon Harmony* (1739), Morris emphasized that the harmony of nature consisted in proportions, which originated in the human body. He included a quotation from Shaftsbury: "Nothing surely is more strongly imprinted in Our Minds . . . than the idea or sense of order and Proportion; hence all the force of Numbers, and those powerful arts founded on their Management and Use."[56]

Obviously, Morris was aware of the metaphysical foundation of natural philosophy, and he invoked this outlook to provide the ultimate validity of his architecture. Nevertheless, his use of geometry as a design tool still appeared as a merely technical operation, equivalent to geometrical applications in statics, surveying, and mensuration. It should be remembered that the ambiguity present in the use of mathematics by eighteenth-century architects also appeared in Newtonian science itself. On the one hand, and on a practical level, Newton attested that geometry derives from mechanics; on the other hand, the geometrical order of his Platonic cosmology was a primordial symbol of God's participation in Being, confirming the significance of human action in an infinite universe.

The work of Batty Langley, a defender of the English garden and contemporary of Morris, was developed within a similar framework, but with an additional important dimension. Throughout Langley's work, there is a marked emphasis on the necessity to apply geometrical operations to all sorts of architectural problems. Geometry was not a means for formal innovation, but rather a tool for resolving traditional questions, in the manner proposed by Osio and Bosse. For Langley, geometrical operations were indispensable for the conception and execution of buildings.

In 1726 Langley published his *Practical Geometry Applied to the Useful Arts of Building, Surveying, Gardening and Mensuration*, which provided the definitions, theorems, and axioms of Euclidean geometry as a necessary foundation for all the building crafts. This supposition of a general geometrical theory is quite exceptional during the eighteenth century. Langley applied it to the description of spiral lines in gardening, tracing classical orders, and drawing plans and elevations of labyrinths, groves, cities, parishes, estates, and "wildernesses."

Aware of the different proportions recommended by the great masters for the classical orders, Langley decided, like Perrault, to use approximately average dimensions. But he gave little im-

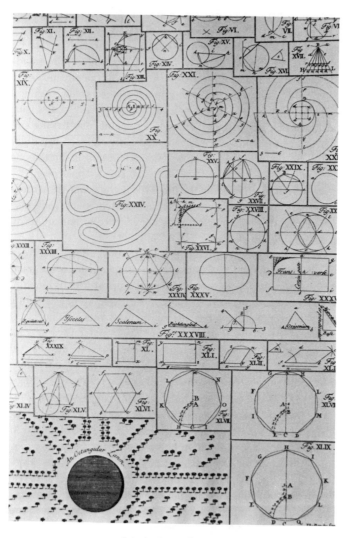

Introduction to the operations of Euclidean
geometry, from Langley's *Practical Geometry* (1726).

Geometry and Architectural Meaning

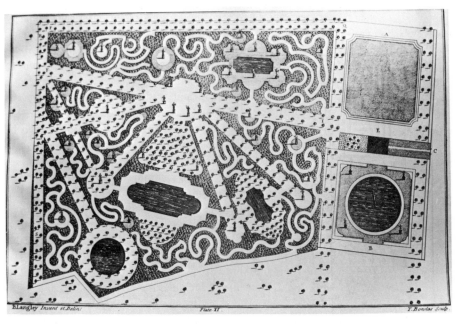

Design for an English garden from Langley's
Practical Geometry.

Geometrical Operations as a Source of Meaning

portance to the specific numerical proportions. Instead, he provided precise geometrical instructions by which to draw the orders and their details, simplifying as much as possible the operation of design. A scale of his own invention was to be used to determine the dimensions of mouldings and flutings in relation to the heights of columns. Significantly, his *Gothic Architecture Improved by Rules and Proportions* advocated the same methods. Geometrical operations were obviously his main concern; they were perceived as fundamental, regardless of stylistic differences. Langley proposed five "gothic orders," which were constructed on the basis of geometrical tracings.

Langley avoided the symbolic implications of geometry. *The Builder's Compleat Assistant* (1738), examined trigonometry, topography, stereometry, and Newton's laws and considerations about statics, mechanics, and hydrostatics. It discussed complex applications of geometry to many problems of construction, such as stairs, vaults, and scaffolding, and included Palladio's system of proportion and one of his own invention. In *A Sure Guide to Builders* of 1729, after a long introduction devoted to geometry, Langley reproduced the proportions of the classical orders by Vitruvius, Palladio, and Scamozzi, adding a geometrical tracing of each one of the respective orders.

In apparent contradiction to his own technical interests and to the views expressed by his Baroque predecessors, Langley *never* questioned the value of ancient authority. His unconditional respect for the texts and buildings of the past, together with his passion for geometrical operations and technical problems of construction, appears as a perfectly coherent aspect of his theory. This can only be explained through Langley's militant affiliation to Freemasonry, whose ideology reinforced the ethical and moral values implicit in natural philosophy. Langley published in 1736 two large volumes entitled *Ancient Masonry Both in the Theory and Practice*, where he provided "Useful Rules of Arithmetic, Geometry and Architecture in the Proportions and Orders of the Most Eminent Masters of All Nations."

The content of this work is, significantly, similar to all his other works on architecture. It included the geometrical tracing of the classical orders and their details, the resolution of diverse construction problems, rules of proportion according to ancient and modern authors, and a whole gamut of applications of geometry to architecture. By identifying the history of architecture with the masonic tradition, however, his collection of geometrical opera-

Geometry applied to the design of openings, from
Langley's *Builder's Treasury of Designs* (1750).

Geometrical Operations as a Source of Meaning

tions takes on a different meaning. Instead of being mere instruments of technology, geometrical operations assume the character of *poesis*, technical procedures with implicit transcendent objectives. Operational Masonry was practical geometry, a science given by God to the People of Israel, which the Masons of the eighteenth century believed they had inherited. A. M. Ramsay, the "philosopher of Freemasonry," put it this way in 1737: "The Supreme taste for Order, Symmetry and projection could not have been inspired but by the Great Geometrician architect of the Universe whose eternal ideas are the models of true Beauty."[57] Ramsay then went on to describe how God, according to the Holy Scriptures, provided Noah with the proportions of his "floating building" and the manner by which the "mysterious science" had been transmitted, by oral tradition, to Abraham and Joseph, who brought it to Egypt. Masonic science then was disseminated throughout Asia, reached Greece, and, after the Crusades, was brought to Great Britain, the modern center of Freemasonry. Ramsay believed that the Temple of Solomon, which reproduced the proportions of the "primordial tabernacle" of Moses, embodied the laws of the "Invisible World," where all is harmony, order, and proportion.

The great interest of architects in the Temple of Solomon as an archetypal building had grown since the end of the sixteenth century, when the syncretism of the Renaissance began to be questioned and a synthesis of the Graeco-Roman and Judeo-Christian traditions had to be justified rationally. The temple was, in Joseph Rykwert's words, "the image of production as path to salvation," the only monument directly inspired by God still visible on earth.[58] The appreciation of the temple's attributes, however, shifted significantly in the seventeenth and eighteenth centuries. In their late-sixteenth-century reconstruction of the temple, the Jesuits Prado and Villalpando attempted to reconcile the Bible with Vitruvius by postulating that building as the origin of the Corinthian order, while its geometrical plan responded to Renaissance cosmobiology.[59] In his *Entwurff einer Historischen Architectur* (1727), J. B. Fischer von Erlach viewed the temple as an archetypal building, the source of the "great Principles" of Roman architecture, which magically reconciled all differences of taste. But Fischer was not interested in *mathemata*. Instead of its proportions, he praised the grandeur and richness of the mythical building. During the eighteenth century, particularly in the masonic tradition, the temple became an embodiment of the perfect geometrical harmony of the universe and of a meaningful *praxis*.

In *The Builder's Compleat Assistant*, Langley provided his own version of the history of Masonry. After defining geometry as "the most excellent Knowledge of the world, as being the Basis or Foundation of all Trade and on which all arts depend," he described its origins in the Old Testament and its utilization by Hermes, "the Father of Wisdom"; Euclid, "the most worthy Geometrician in the World"; and Hiram, "the chief Conducter of the Temple of Solomon."[60] (The source of this identification of geometry with a mythical building craft was probably a famous manuscript dating from the middle of the fourteenth century, the *Constitutions of the Art of Geometry According to Euclid*.[61])

Langley, it should be noted, concentrated his interest on technical problems, ignoring the metaphysical dimension of architectural theory as a liberal art. This attitude, however, betrayed not a positivistic but a traditional position. Langley's techniques were intended to keep the poetic and symbolic values of medieval craftsmanship, and the result was always fundamentally ambiguous. For as soon as geometry was applied to problems of building construction during the Enlightenment, all the secret or transcendent connotations of Masonic science seemed to vanish. Even when compared to previous seventeenth-century works on statics, stereotomy, and architecture, Langley's collections of technical operations seem neutral, lacking in magic and fascination. Following in the steps of natural philosophy, the mythical framework in Langley's theory became implict, reconciling the respect for traditional myths and proportional systems with a fundamental belief in the continued importance of geometrical operations in architectural history.

The ambiguous uses of geometry by Langley and Morris take on an added significance in view of the fact that British architecture had always disapproved of Italian and Central European Baroque. The formal particularities of architecture, fascinating and irreducible, while being the expression of the most profound personal and cultural characteristics of an architect, should not hinder an understanding of the intentions underlying architecture common to eighteenth-century Europe: an architecture that shared in theory the metaphysical principles of natural philosophy and in practice its transcendent objectives.

Geometrical Operations as a Source of Meaning

4

SYMBOLIC GEOMETRY IN
FRENCH ARCHITECTURE IN THE
LATE EIGHTEENTH CENTURY

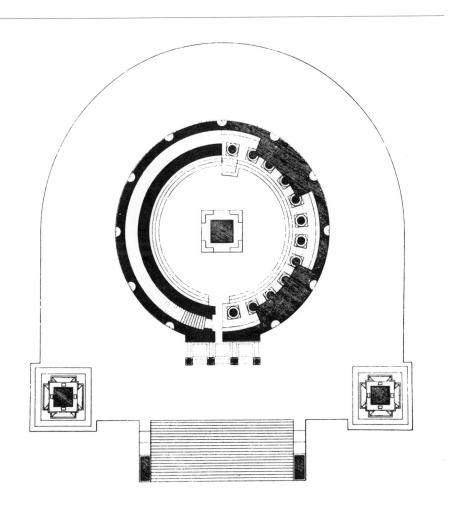

Toward the end of the eighteenth century, which had seen an increasing rationalization of theory, architects frequently questioned the mythical framework underlying traditional forms. The architecture of the French Revolution was characterized essentially by the use of simplified ornamental elements, a frequent disregard of the classical orders, and the employment of volumes in the form of simple geometrical bodies. In 1793 Louis Du Fourny wrote, "Architecture should be regenerated through geometry." Indeed, the primordial role attributed to geometry as a "regenerator" of form, over and above any other consideration, is evident in the now well-publicized "revolutionary" projects.[1]

A thorough understanding of late-eighteenth-century French architecture is crucial in order to clarify the origin of modern architectural intentions. The most influential architects of this period, Etienne-Louis Boullée and Claude-Nicolas Ledoux, produced their work in the years preceding the explosion of technology and industrialism in Europe. It is important to clarify the similarities and differences between their intentions and those of their disciples, particularly Durand.

The great majority of works on the history of late-eighteenth-century French architecture have approached these problems from a merely formal point of view. The label "romantic classicism" has been used to group together indiscriminately French and European architecture spanning the period from the mideighteenth century to the midnineteenth century. Direct relations have been postulated between the pure geometrical solids in Ledoux's projects and the work of Le Corbusier or between Goethe's abstract sculptures in Weimar and the pieces of a chess set produced in the Bauhaus.[2] Such characteristics as austere simplicity, the absence of the classical orders, and the use of Platonic solids and simple geometrical figures in plans and elevations are seen as precedents of twentieth-century architecture. Louis Kahn even wrote a poem in which Boullée and Ledoux have the same importance for architecture as Bach for music or the sun for the universe.[3] This unrestricted identification has often been misleading for the understanding of modern architecture and its origins.

The tendency toward formal simplicity, evident in French art during the second half of the eighteenth century, has been interpreted as the consequence of a reaction against the formal exaggerations of Rococo, resulting from the increasing domination of reason.[4] Taste and rationality, that is, emotional and intellectual considerations, impelled the artist to search for first principles, which often resulted in a conscious primitivism and a tendency toward purism. From this standpoint, the architecture of Boullée and Ledoux can be considered the final embodiment of the Neoclassical reconciliation of taste and reason.

Architects such as Soufflot, De Wailly, and Gondoin emphasized that the simplicity of their prototypes existed in classical antiquity. J. F. Blondel, like most theoreticians, believed that this "noble simplicity" was a fundamental quality of architecture.[5] Marie-Joseph Peyre, in his popular collection of projects (1765), intended to imitate the "magnificent buildings" erected by the Roman Emperors.[6] Nevertheless, his designs were striking not for their grandeur (as were Baroque conceptions), but precisely because they made use of simple elements and geometrical volumes.

Clear formal precedents for these conceptions appeared in Rome about 1740 and probably influenced many young French architects studying there.[7] At the beginning of the century, J. B. Fischer von Erlach was employing historical fragments (Roman columns, obelisks, temple fronts, and so forth) as conceptually independent elements that he combined in his architecture. But the emphasis on elementary geometry evident in late-eighteenth-century French architecture cannot be explained away by these models alone. The search for pure and fundamental forms was unquestionably related to natural philosophy's search for truths of universal validity.[8] In his *Lettres sur l'Architecture des Anciens* (1787), Jean-Louis Viel de Saint-Maux referred to primitive antiquity as "fabulous;" although it had not been recommended by ancient and traditional authors because it lacked beautiful contours, modern architects should look back to it as "the time in which art had its origin."[9] This obsession to establish the principles of art in their natural origins was taken to the limit toward the end of the century, when the Platonic cosmology of Newton had firmly taken hold.

Etienne-Louis Boullée was a rather successful practicing architect.[10] He had a considerable library, comprised of many literary works: books on history, geography, and astronomy; a small collection of architectural treatises; texts by Voltaire, Rousseau, and other *philosophes*; as well as writings on art history and archaeology, including works by Dubos, Winckelmann, and Cleriseau.[11] His own theoretical writings were not published until the twentieth century.[12]

In his *Essai sur l'Art*, Boullée asks, "What is architecture? Is it possible to define it, like Vitruvius, as the art of building?" His

Symbolic Geometry in French Architecture

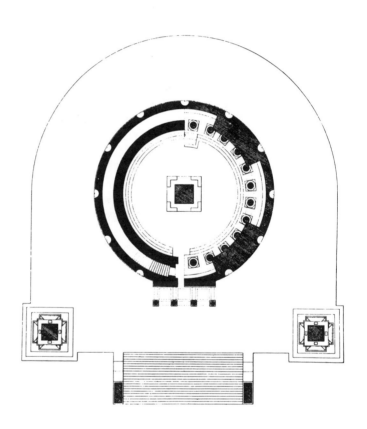

Geometry and Architectural Meaning

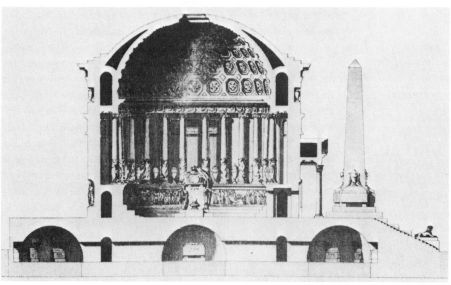

Plan, section, and elevation of a funerary monument, from Peyre's *Oeuvres d'Architecture* (1765).

Symbolic Geometry in French Architecture

answer is categorically negative. Vitruvius, in his opinion, confused the effect with its cause. According to Boullée, it is necessary to conceive in order to execute, and this creation, a "production of the intellect," constitutes architecture. The old Renaissance distinction between design and building became sharp and dogmatic in Boullée's theory. The specificity and value of architecture decidedly pointed to the sphere of design and conception. He thought that architecture was composed of two autonomous parts, "the art itself" and science: "Unfortunately, the majority of authors who have written about architecture have dealt only with the scientific part."[13] Boullée considered as part of "science" all those aspects of architectural theory that had already been made subject to reason, including the canons of the classical orders. Boullée, using scientific inquiry as a guide, then attempted to justify and explain the true act of creation by dealing with the conception of images in the universe of theoretical discourse.

The end of the eighteenth century witnessed the increasing importance of the ideal dimension of architecture. In the *Essai*, Boullée claimed that men gain clear ideas about the figure of bodies only after "possessing" the idea of regularity. The capacity of the artists to reconcile the ideal with reality, however, was also evident during the Enlightenment. Wordsworth identified imagination with "reason in its most exalted mood." And in his article on "genius" for the *Encyclopedia*, Diderot contrasted the elegance and finished quality of something merely "beautiful according to the rules of taste" with a work of genius, which has an "irregular, rugged or savage air." Admiration for genius and its sublime creations did not imply, as it would during the Romantic movement of the nineteenth century, hostility to the rules of art.[14]

For Boullée, mathematical reason, important as it was, had its limitations. Like Le Camus de Mezières before him, he stressed the role of genius in architecture. He pointed out that the beauty of art could not be demonstrated like mathematical truths. To the degree that beauty emanates from nature, it is imperative to possess certain irreducible and innate special faculties, "scarce in nature itself," in order to perceive and happily apply such beauty.

Boullée faced the great dilemma of eighteenth-century architecture: the necessity to reconcile universal reason with a historical and cultural relativism that was becoming increasingly evident. While supporting Perrault's assessment regarding the nonessential character of numerical proportion, Boullée nevertheless proclaimed the existence of absolute beauty. To counteract the relativism implicit, to his thinking, in Perrault's theory, Boullée postulated a theory of his own.

Many pages of the *Essai* are devoted to the discussion between Perrault and Blondel. Boullée accepted the notion of progress in architecture and praised the concrete realizations of modern builders. In fact, he dedicated his work to those artists who believed, as he did, that there was more to architecture than the imitation of antiquity. He also acknowledged the distinction between music and architecture first formulated by Perrault: Whereas harmony provided the basis for the fundamental principles of music, architectural proportion, although an important source of beauty, was not "the first law from which derive the constitutive principles of this art."[15] Boullée then added that while a lack of harmony in music hurts the ear, architecture could not be pleasing to the eye if it was in need of order and symmetry. These were, in his opinion, the fundamental rational principles that should never abandon the architect's genius, for "Nothing is beautiful if all is not wise."[16]

Boullée's position in this respect seems similar to Perrault's, who had also adopted the notion of bilateral symmetry as one of the characteristics of positive beauty. But Boullée could not accept that the fundamental principles of architecture were arbitrary. This was, indeed, his main point of contention with Perrault. Architecture could not be an art based merely on imagination (*un art fantastique et de pure invention*). Having found François Blondel's refutation inconsistent, and realizing that well-educated men had embraced Perrault's ideas, Boullée decided to prove that architecture possessed absolute principles derived from nature, despite the validity of historical or cultural relativism. This appeared as a crucial issue, one not to be taken for granted. For Boullée, metaphysical necessity was a personal existential problem. The meaning of his life and his architecture depended on the presence of such principles. Boullée's theory, for the first time in the history of architecture, was formulated out of fear of "having devoted his life to the study of a chimeric art," a pursuit that might have led him into constant error.[17]

It is still a commonly held belief that after the Renaissance, with the transformation of architecture into a liberal art, building practice became dependent on an eminently prescriptive theory. Such a simplistic assertion has hampered a true understanding of Baroque and Neoclassical architecture. In the aftermath of the Galilean revolution, Perrault and some of his followers could voice this dependence. But, as I have tried to show, architectural practice during the Enlightenment, a true *poesis*, never depended upon a merely prescriptive technical theory. The relation between theory and practice became increasingly critical toward the end of the century, coinciding with the dissolution of the traditional cosmos. Thus when Boullée proclaimed that theory was not an essential instrument for architects, he was openly flaunting tradition. Boullée believed that architects depend on their innate gifts to choose wisely, regardless of their knowledge of principles. He believed that not even "the best reasonings" about the fine arts could be used in artistic education. Reason, according to Boullée, was not conducive to the acquisition of "sensations." Consequently, artists should learn how to exercise their sensibilities, finding a means for developing it through the works of Nature and man. In this way Boullée explained the existence of beautiful buildings in the primitive cultures of Africa and South America before there was any science of architecture.

Theory, for Boullée, was fundamentally a transcendental justification of practice, an explicit metaphysical discourse, or the *first principles* of art, which, he believed, his predecessors had ignored. As philosophers extended reason's domain, its limitations became more dramatic, as did its ultimate dependence upon Nature. Critical of the pretended autonomy of reason in Perrault's theory, Boullée emphasized that architecture's ultimate objective, like that of any other art, was the imitation of nature. Extrapolating certain notions from sensualist philosophy, he believed that all ideas and perceptions came from the "external objects of Nature." In order to affirm, as had Perrault, that "architecture was an art of pure invention," it would be necessary to prove that men could conceive images independently, apart from any relation to these objects. Boullée thought that the external objects produced "diverse impressions" on the subject, according to the "greater or lesser analogy that they had with our organization."[18] The reaction by which man approved beautiful works and rejected others was a direct result of this natural reciprocity.

In a collection of notes, probably not meant for publication, Boullée wrote that the art of producing images in architecture derived from the effect of the *bodies* and that bodies constituted the *poetry* of architecture, allowing the artist to produce buildings full of character.[19] The essential and primordial bodies to which Boullée was referring were regular geometrical solids. Irregular bodies he considered mute and sterile, confusing to the human intellect. Regular bodies, however, possessed symmetry and also variety—the two attributes of order and evidence. Regularity was consequently "the source of beauty in the shape of objects."[20]

Le Camus de Mezières had already expressed concern about meaning in architecture. In Boullée's *Essai*, this preoccupation became paramount. He complained about a lack of expression in the buildings of his contemporaries: works that displayed a lack of concern with "the poetry of architecture." Boullée maintained that architecture, particularly public buildings, "should be, in some way, like poems; the images that they offer to our senses should excite us with sentiments analogous to the use to which these buildings are consecrated."[21] To realize this aim, Boullée studied the "theory of bodies," analyzing their properties, their "power over our senses," and their analogy with our being. Beginning with Nature, the "source of the fine arts," he intended to establish "new ideas" and absolute principles.

Boullée believed, like Le Camus, that the emotional response in architecture depended on the effect of the composition of bodies in their totality; they were not produced by particular details, whose beauty was secondary to the first impression produced by the great volumes. Consequently, the general volumetric composition of architecture was to be determined by the regular bodies. These rational and perfect forms, Boullée contended, were necessarily found in Nature.

All this reveals an intensification of the same intentions generally present in architecture during the second half of the eighteenth century. But Boullée's principles, a true "plastic metaphysics" grounded in the tradition of French Neoclassicism, constituted the first effective possibility of rejecting the value of the classical orders and its proportions *without* loss of meaning.[22] Boullée never tried to explain how the elemental solids derived from nature, believing that the marvelous buildings of primitive cultures that he so much admired spoke for themselves. He respected the ineffable mystery of the origins of a preconceptual geometry, part of the human order since the beginning of time. His geometrical bodies are Euclidean, that is, transcendental. Combining an acute rationalism with artistic sensibility, Boullée revealed the eloquent "figure" of the fundamental principles of Newtonian natural science: the constitutive elements of its Platonic cosmology. Hence the geometrical solids were postulated as symbols of a transcendent order, representing ethical, aesthetic, and religious values, revealing the preestablished harmony between man and the world.

Symbolic Geometry in French Architecture

Boullée's theoretical projects invariably included centralized plans, and their massing was determined by cubes, pyramids, truncated cones, cylinders, and spheres. Their formal expression was characterized by large, smooth surfaces, practically devoid of ornament, and by the infrequent use of columns. "The plan of the universe formed by the Creator," wrote Boullée, "is the image of order and perfection." For Boullée, architecture was God's gift to man to help him make his home on earth. Symmetry, "the image of order and perfection," was the foundation of the "constitutive principles" of architecture. The geometrical solids were therefore explicit symbols of a cosmic order that revealed the presence of the Divine Architect and emulated His creation.

Architecture was not only the mechanical art described by Vitruvius, or even "the art of presenting images through the disposition of bodies," but "considered in all its extension," it also recollected and applied the beauties scattered through Nature. Boullée believed that it was necessary to emphasize that the fundamental role of the architect was to implement (*mettre en oeuvre*) Nature. His work represents the last possibility of an architecture of imitation in the sense of the original Greek *mimesis*, that is, as a metaphor of the a priori order of the world.[23] Boullée's concept of a transcendental Nature also decreed that the perception of natural phenomena was but a vivid projection of such elementary human feelings as admiration, terror, and happiness—these were not merely subjective, "romantic" appreciations. Obviously a profound knowledge of this transcendental Nature was necessary to achieve a model of "architectural poetry." Even the four seasons are examples of "character" (the sadness of winter), which show how a unity of expression results from a combination of diverse perceptual conditions. "[Nature, you are] so true that you are the book of books, the universal science! No, we can do nothing without you! . . . Very few men assist to your lessons and profit from them."[24]

Boullée's Platonic solids were thus derived from "the book of Nature," as was Buffon's system of *histoire naturelle*, which revealed at each step the presence of the Creator. The solids allowed for the constitution of a truly meaningful architecture, where each building had an appropriate character with regard to the institution it represented. This of course represents a metaphoric relation between use or purpose and formal expression, or a more explicit formulation of the traditional *convenance*.[25] Boullée's theoretical projects were intended to "ascertain the measure in which architecture needs to study Nature."[26] In fact, his work embodied the ultimate rational architecture within a traditional cosmos.

Boullée's conceptual scheme is demonstrated, appropriately enough, by the well-known funerary monument for Newton. Boullée had in his house portraits of Newton and Copernicus, and his admiration for the British scientist was passionate and unconditional. In the dedication of his project, he addressed Newton as the "sublime mind! Vast and profound genius! Divine Being! ... If ... you have determined the figure of the earth, I have conceived a project to surround you with your discovery."[27]

Newton's cenotaph was more than a monument to the common objectives of art and science; it was the forceful image of a hierarchical and still undivided cosmos, of a fundamental, intersubjective structure of values.[28] Boullée's own depiction of the cenotaph's internal space is fascinating. He described his anguish when, after going over the "great images of Nature," he could not find means to reproduce them. Finally, he placed Newton in the "abode of immortality," heaven itself, designing something apparently impossible: a monument in which the spectator would be magically transported through the air, beyond the clouds, to be confronted with the immensity of space. The entrance to the vast sphere was through the base of the tomb, the only material object on the inside, thus forcing the spectators to stay away from the endless surface of the wall. This shape, "never used before," favored the creation of marvelous illusions. Appropriately pierced, the vault appeared to be full of scintillating stars and heavenly bodies, and provided a quality of light very similar to that of the clearest night.

Boullée proclaimed that only architecture was capable of reproducing exactly the image of the celestial vault, and that it was precisely this potential to imitate Nature that made it superior to the other arts. Kepler's world machines or astrological *globi* of the seventeenth century have been recently cited as precedents of Boullée's monument.[29] But the cenotaph is not only a symbol of the earth or a cosmological map. It is not merely a representation of Nature, but a true *presentation* of the Newtonian cosmos as it is perceived from the sublunar world.

The sphere is obviously one of the elemental bodies. Analyzing rationally the properties of this geometrical solid, Boullée defined it as the essential polyhedron, incorporating the properties of all the other bodies and reconciling infinite variety with maximum uniformity: "Its contour is the sweetest and most fluid. ... The

Symbolic Geometry in French Architecture

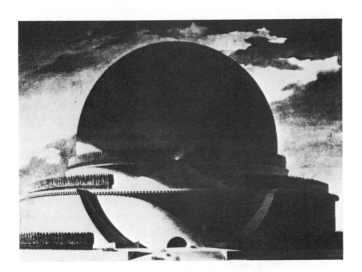

Boullée's design for Newton's cenotaph (Cabinet des
Estampes, Bibliothèque Nationale, Paris; reproduced
by courtesy of the University of St. Thomas,
Houston).

Section of Newton's cenotaph during the day (Bibliothèque Nationale; by courtesy of the University of
St. Thomas, Houston).

sphere is the image of perfection."[30] (Later Vaudoyer, Sobre, Lequeu, Delépine, De Gay, and De Labadie employed it as a symbol
of universal gravitation, immortality, justice, equality, and wisdom.) In a truly Platonic sense, the sphere became the image of
agathon—supreme beauty and goodness. Issuing from Newtonian
cosmology, it symbolized the presence of the infinite *in* nature.

Of course, Boullée's cenotaph was not without theological implications; it was an image of the supreme work of the Creator,
as revealed to mankind through science. Essentially, the monument is an absolutely empty spherical space, the image of an
infinite and immaterial geometrical entity. This is in keeping with
Newton's cosmos, in which the vacuum was a determinant factor.
In opposition to Descartes's Baroque universe, full of a subtle
matter in constant circular motion, Newton predicated an infinite
void.[31] Only a small part of it was full of matter, whose order at
all scales was maintained by the force of attraction. Absolute time
and space, infinity and eternity, were not simple mathematical
figures in an empirical positivistic system. When he referred to
them, Newton frankly abandoned his cherished empiricism: "We
ought to abstract from our senses and consider things themselves . . . . There's besides space and time vulgarly regarded as
relative, as distances between sensible objects or events, an absolute space and time, true and mathematical. These are infinite,
homogeneous, continuous entities, entirely independent of any
sensible object or motion by which we try to measure them. Time
flowing from eternity to eternity, space existing all at once in
infinite immovability. By observation and experiment we can do
no more than approximate either of these two absolute, true and
mathematical entities."[32] Absolute space and absolute time were
clearly the two fundamental metaphysical principles of natural
philosophy. Attraction and order happened in God, in absolute
space, whose existence was implicitly proved through the mathematical demonstration of the law of inertia. Newton did not
recognize the contradictions inherent in the simultaneous acceptance of absolute and relative motions. The reason was, evidently, the crucial religious significance of absolute space and
time in his cosmology.

Many important architects of the late eighteenth century tried
to reconcile, as far as it was possible, the geometrical space of
Newtonian philosophy with a perception of the real world. Their
objective was to transform the infinite and empty ideal space into
a human place of dwelling. The Newtonian synthesis helped to

Symbolic Geometry in French Architecture

reinforce the old belief among architects regarding the simplicity and mathematical order of nature. Once reason could question the mythical justifications of traditional forms, however, the metaphysical principles of natural philosophy became more explicit. The symbolic connotations of the vast internal space of Newton's cenotaph could not be more evident. Boullée's architecture presented to perception the absolutely empty, infinite, and autonomous space of God.

Boullée's megalomaniacal concerns, evident in most of his theoretical projects, were part of this obsession to give physical form to infinite space. Referring to his design for a Metropolitan Basilica, he criticized all previous churches as lacking in "character." In his opinion, "temples" should inspire a profound religious respect as well as awe and admiration. These structures should appear "inconceivable" and overpowering. Boullée adopted in this case the Neoclassical preference for trabeated architecture. His own project owed much to Soufflot's Ste.-Geneviève, but it was the *immensity* of its internal space that gave the Metropolitan Basilica its true character: "A temple erected in the honor of divinity should always be vast. [It] should offer the greatest and most astounding image of existing things [and] if possible, it should resemble the universe."[33]

Not surprisingly, Boullée criticized the handling of scale and proportion in St. Peter's Basilica in Rome, which made the church appear smaller than it actually was. Grandeur was what Boullée advocated, and even horrendous images (for example, a volcano vomiting fire and death) excited, in his opinion, our admiration. "Wandering in an abyss of extension, [man] became deeply humbled by the extraordinary spectacle of an inconceivable space."[34] Greatness therefore must necessarily be allied to beauty. The immensity of nature was imposed upon man, reminding him of his limitations while revealing a transcendent presence. Consequently, anything that "appeared large" in architecture suggested superiority.

In the Metropolitan Basilica, everything contributed to the image of immensity. The dome, painted like the sky, descended over the back wall. The enormous colonnades receded in perspective, emphasizing the building's depth. Borrowing from Gothic architecture, the basilica's supporting members were hidden, so that it appeared to be held up by supernatural powers. Boullée's use of light, which he believed to be his greatest innovation, complemented the scene. Indirect light, coming from an occult source,

Boullée's project for a Metropolitan Basilica. Internal perspective view *au temps de la Fête-Dieu* (Bibliothèque Nationale).

shone intensely on the surface of the dome. The evidence of its mysterious origin thus produced "magical and surprising" effects, evoking "the most miraculous images of Nature."[35] The enigmatic essence of this light symbolized its affinity to the Masonic god of reason, whose presence was eloquent in Boullée's own drawings.

The notion of infinity went hand in hand with that of eternity in Newtonian cosmology. Boullée's great interest in funerary architecture and his use of ancient models of this type in many of his projects was therefore hardly a coincidence. By the late eighteenth century, posterity was conceived as a form of eternity in man's world and believed by many to be the only reward for virtue. This, of course, replaced the traditional faith in an afterlife.[36] Inspired by the pyramids and mausoleums of pre-Christian antiquity, Boullée's monuments symbolized the age's preoccupation with posterity, albeit the posterity of a brief heroic age: the rational eternity of post-Christian Deism.

The monuments of Boullée and his disciples reveal an acute concern with eschatological themes—a clear sign of the crisis of belief that would become widespread in the nineteenth century. Their projects, however, still represented a desperate attempt to reconcile human rationality with the finite dimension of life in a universe where God had not yet been expelled from epistemology.[37]

Boullée's "architecture of shadows" and "buried architecture" were his two genres of funerary architecture: pale geometrical solids in the dimness of moonlight or as parts of larger monuments interred by time. This architecture, he thought, demanded more than any other the implementation of poetry. Thus the pyramid, one of his most important prototypes, becomes "the sad image of barren mountains and immutability."[38] Because it was the most ancient and primordial of classical forms, the pyramid was conceived by Boullée as a quasi-natural model. The most elemental of bodies in a Platonic cosmology and fully endorsed by the aesthetics of sensualism, it suited Boullée as an appropriate symbol of eternity.

Boullée was not without his detractors. Jean-Louis Viel de Saint-Maux criticized Boullée's projects in his *Lettres*. Referring particularly to Newton's cenotaph, he contended that this type of "astrological" building did not represent a true innovation since it had often appeared in primitive cultures.[39] Boullée defended his originality in the *Essai*, claiming that although the means used in the precedents cited by Viel might be equal to his own, the

Geometry and Architectural Meaning

Internal perspective view of the Metropolitan Basilica *au temps des Ténèbres* (Bibliothèque Nationale).

Boullée's design for a pyramidal cenotaph (Bibliothèque Nationale; by courtesy of the University of St. Thomas, Houston).

Symbolic Geometry in French Architecture

"effect" was completely different. "I have discovered," he wrote, "the way to put nature to work." Boullée had a point, but Viel was not altogether mistaken in considering Boullée's architecture in the ancient tradition of cosmological building. Placed between the end of Vitruvianism and the beginning of positivism, Boullée's projects attest to the symbolic sense of elemental geometry inherent in primitive architecture's mythical horizon. This obviously is pre-Greek and consequently antedates *theoria*. The symbolic connotations that he attributes to the pyramid, for example, contrast with the cool objectivity of Quatremère de Quincy's article in the *Dictionnaire Historique de l'Architecture* (1832). Unable to comprehend the primeval meaning of this form, Quatremère filled long pages with historical descriptions and discussions of numerous buildings, concluding finally that it was impossible to incorporate pyramids in modern architecture.

Viel de Saint-Maux's *Lettres*, along with Boullée's writings, reveal an interest in unveiling the symbolic sense of architecture. They are indicative of the period of transition, when the true symbolic richness of architectural form, necessarily grounded in the coherence of everyday life, began to deteriorate. Symbolization remained possible only so long as epistemology accepted the ambiguous, irreducible, and enigmatic character of human life. With the increasing irrelevance of metaphysical speculation in science, rationalized symbols became allegories. Boullée's disciples covered the facades of their buildings with emblems and inscriptions, while their master was still confident in the effective symbolic nature of his elemental geometrical bodies.

| Ledoux and *Architecture Parlante* | The work of Claude-Nicolas Ledoux has always been difficult to evaluate.[40] The two large and opulent volumes of his work *L'Architecture Considérée sous le Rapport de l'Art, des Moeurs et de la Législation* were published in 1804 and 1846 (although Ledoux claimed that his projects antedated the French Revolution), and elicited both praise and condemnation. It is fair to assume, with Emil Kaufmann, that while Boullée was concerned mainly with the elucidation of the principles of architecture, Ledoux endeavored to apply these principles to all types of projects. His theory always made use of examples. He believed that this method, instead of a "cold and lethargic" rational discourse, was the only appropriate way to teach. |

Ledoux ran a successful practice, and many of his buildings are still standing. But, like Boullée, he believed that his architectural intentions were best embodied in his theory and in the theoretical projects that illustrated it. His impassioned text echoes familiar themes. He desires to discover, through reason, the basic elements of architectural beauty, whose fundamental principles are then to be revealed through his projects. These principles originate in Nature, whose "preponderant harmony is the *only* absolute and constant thing."[41] Ledoux maintained that nature and art were related in such an intimate and exact manner that they deceived even the most educated men.

After acknowledging the vacillations in taste throughout history and the existence of periods marked by a decadent architecture, Ledoux argues for the reality and effectiveness of immutable laws. Like Boullée, he refused to admit the relativism that he read in Perrault's theory: "Taste is invariable, independent of fashion. . . . It is not, as previously believed, something attached to the fugitive wings of the arbitrary, nor is it founded on conventions propitiated by imagination (*conventions fantastiques*); it is the product of an exquisite judgment passed by those brains that have been favored by nature."[42] Instead of accepting custom as a positive force, Ledoux warned architects against its dangers. Habit was, in Ledoux's opinion, capable of altering even the way in which mankind should perceive the divine. Avoid fashion, he admonished. Use only absolute, elemental, and natural principles.

Architecture was, for Ledoux, one of the wonders of the world, a part of the "divine breath" that enlivened and beautified the surface of the globe. Its absolute principles, however, could not be reduced to the traditional Greek orders. Although their beauty could not be denied, Ledoux argued that it was a mistake to consider them universal rules, applicable in all places or any country; for example, the acanthus of the Corinthian Order was not appropriate to northern climates. Only the sober and simple Doric Order, which he himself often used, was considered adequate to the French temperament and geography. This preference aside, Ledoux maintained that a knowledge of the *pentamètre* (five measurements, the five orders) was insufficient. True harmony could not be learned from the traditional masters. It consisted in the knowledgeable use of the *notes*, that is, the basic elements of form. This harmony, Ledoux stressed, was best exemplified in his projects: "Such are the combinations of art, bringing together all that which is divine; it is a mutual and independent accord that takes over the soul's affections, an irresistible impulse toward beauty, so well concerted that the gods have never given mankind anything more perfect."[43]

Unhappy with the designs of his contemporaries, Ledoux criticized those architects who had gone to Italy with the sole purpose of copying antique monuments. Ledoux detested erudition, though he recognized that a familiarity with historical precedents was necessary. Erudition alone, however, rarely produced exciting innovative architecture. The problem was, once again, the devaluation of architectural meaning. Ledoux believed in the existence of primordial forms, forms that had been ill represented and distorted through history. He propounded that these original forms could be recovered by architects endowed with a rich sensibility. A new architecture, simple and founded on nature, was indeed possible. "Man", explained Ledoux, "attained perfection through his own sensations."[44] An artist of genius could therefore recover all that which the preceding centuries had lost.

Ledoux remarked on the differences between architecture and construction. Architecture was sublime, transcendent poetry, possessing "the dramatic enthusiasm of the craft, of which we can only speak but in an exalted mood."[45] Architecture is to masonry what poetry is to literature. Design determines the form, which in turn provides charm and vitality to every production. Ledoux was convinced that the poet's genius is a divine gift. The Supreme Being had created the world for man, making available to him "all possible provocations by the attraction of moving powers and divine purpose."[46] God gave the poet a delicate sensibility to admire His work. Why then should not the architect join his knowledge to the wisdom of the great poets?

The architect, wrote Ledoux, places the spectator under the spell of the marvelous. Like Boullée, Ledoux employed the notion of architectural poetry, meaning by it the necessity to express emphatically the "character" of diverse buildings. This poetry is obviously not concerned with the invention of unequivocal signs, but with the discovery of meaning in everyday life. Referring to his project for a *Pacifère* (Temple of Peace), Ledoux writes, "If artists were disposed to follow the symbolic system that characterizes each production, they would acquire as much glory as the poets. . . . Every single stone would speak. . . . It could be said about Architecture that which Boileau stated about poetry: In it, all takes on a body, a soul, a mind, a face."[47]

With respect to architectural materials, Ledoux also believed that the role of the artist was to reveal their inherent meaning, concretizing their expressive potential. It is significant that both Boullée and Ledoux proclaimed that "to be an architect one should begin by being a painter."[48] No one had ever said this before. The *imitative* character of architecture was thereby emphasized, and with it the origin of its meaning in reality, the transcendent Nature of the eighteenth century. Ledoux remarked that in order to reveal the life of materials, an architect should, like a painter, discover the infinite variety of textures on the surfaces of walls.

According to Ledoux, the architect should have the freedom to imitate God's creation, which contained an infinite number of landscapes drawn from a few unique principles. Like a painter, the architect had access to "ideal beauty," presenting him with a "colossal power" to create a nature within Nature. Moreover, the realm of the architect was the totality of the heavens and earth; nothing should constrain the artist's grandiose conceptions. The architect is a creator.

Unlike earlier architectural theorists, whose works convey autonomy and a tranquil sense of assurance, Ledoux constantly invoked God to guarantee meaning in architecture. "God of harmony," he exclaimed, "free my voice from all measure! Ideal beauty is over and beyond the laws of man."[49] The architect should reconcile the powers of heaven with the conceptions that customarily fulfilled the needs of everyday life. Although Ledoux recognized the architect's power to dominate nature, he wished to reconcile this potential with the designs of divinity, an agonizing task that at this point in history was already counter to the prevailing trend of ideas and attitudes.

His interests in economy and hygiene should thus be understood as genuinely philanthropic and not merely as compliance with the new relations of production of the industrial world. The architectural projects that fill his *Architecture* were still true microcosmic structures, symbolizing a hierarchical universe, presided over by God. Here is how Ledoux expounds the virtues of architecture as part of his commentary on a project for the caretakers' house at the source of the Loue River: "True and transparent mirror of the Creator! My weak voice should learn to sing your marvels! You bring life to vulgar darkness . . . giving brilliance to mountains and trees, and evoking the happiness of the world." Architecture brought beauty to form; each project was like a new star, "its glittering light falling upon the earth and beautifying the universe."[50]

Ledoux pointed out that all nations, in spite of their differences, recognized the existence "of a remunerating God that fills the

Symbolic Geometry in French Architecture

Perspective view of Ledoux's project for the care-
takers' house at the source of the Loue River from
*L'Architecture Considerée sous le Rapport de L'Art, des
Moeurs et de la Législation.*

Geometry and Architectural Meaning

universe."[51] He criticized Gothic and classical "temples" and declared his preference for primitive rituals that occur out-of-doors, in a mysterious and overpowering nature, identified with the gods themselves. A truly eloquent modern temple should go beyond prosaic reality and capture through imagination the qualities of divinity: *"She comprises an immense space*; the vaults of her temple are the heavens; her dwelling cannot be built with perishable materials; time has not preceded her nor could it destroy her; she is eternal and almighty; *she is an intelligent Nature* whose contemplation is all light; it is in her that the soul finds the source of its immortality."[52] Once again, any modern sacred space must embody the two fundamental concepts of Newtonian metaphysics: absolute space, absolute time.[53]

Ledoux reproached God for not having enlightened architecture with the means by which He has "shown His designs to other high sciences," privileging them with the important destiny of applying natural principles. Architecture had, unfortunately, "wandered away from the paths of Nature." This is why he recommended that all young architects study the great book of nature and meditate about the great events of life. He believed that the world constituted a unity, intimately related to artistic production, and that it was *"governed by an immutable intelligence,"* which could only abet the architect's powers.[54]

In Ledoux's *Architecture*, Nature was not only the good and the beautiful, a source of health and the final justification of all human institutions; it was ultimately "the house of the poor." But the poor were miserable only superficially, since all men "occupy but a small space." Regardless of his station in life, each individual was responsible for his personal reconciliation with Nature.

Ledoux's god was the god of Newton and Voltaire, the Great Architect of the Masonic universe. Interpreting in his own way the Platonic myth of creation, he wrote that the Author of Nature had composed the universe through "atoms;" then "chaos" developed and provided the world with "space". God countered with the force of attraction, organized the celestial vault, and excavated the depths of the sea. God was identified with not only the immensity of space but also light.[55]

It should come as no surprise that Ledoux was a Freemason since the idea of a God geometrician, which was part of the mythical history of Freemasonry, coincided with his own beliefs.[56] As has already been mentioned, the fundamental ideals of Free-

Symbolic Geometry in French Architecture

Ledoux's House of the Poor, nature under the protection of divinity, from *L'Architecture*.

masonry fell in line with the more enlightened collective aims during the late eighteenth century. Its explicit deism and philanthropic concerns were widespread among architects, scientists, and philosophers. And particularly significant is the intimate relation between Newton's natural philosophy and the principles of Masonic doctrine. This connection was alluded to by several important Masons. J. T. Désaguilliers, a founder of speculative Masonry in the early eighteenth century, was a member of the Royal Society of London and author of several works on experimental physics. He was also the author of a famous allegorical poem, *The Newtonian System of the World, the Best Model of Government* (1728), in which he speculates that gravity and not God extended its blessing upon the Realm.[57] A. M. Ramsay, whose conception of history was mentioned in relation to Langley, published *The Philosophical Principles of Natural and Revealed Religion* (1748). In this book, he tried to prove that the great principles of "natural religion" were founded upon indisputable evidence and that, reciprocally, the essential doctrines of "revealed religion" were perfectly in accordance with reason. Once natural truth was established as equivalent to revealed truth, Masonic "religion" could fully adopt the metaphysical principles of Newtonianism.

To create a symbolic order in this context, Ledoux recommended that architects use simple geometrical solids and figures.[58] He accepted the importance of proportion as a source of beauty and of such traditional "immutable rules" as prudence, convenience, and economy. His theory is less consistent in this respect than Boullée's, but his fundamental principles are perfectly coherent with the transcendental harmony of the Platonic world in which he believed. The geometrical figures and bodies epitomized "ideal beauty" and were the elemental "notes" of architectural composition.

Ledoux believed that all forms derived from nature and could be classified in two large groups: those whose integrity assured the production of decisive effects and those that were only the product of an unbridled imagination.[59] The elemental forms, accessible through perception, were inspired by the geometrical purity of natural phenomena. These "letters of the architectural alphabet": the sphere, pyramid, circle, and square, were related to the image of the world, "where man dwells and fights." In Nature could be discerned the "fascination of the circle": the shape of fruit, the line of the horizon, the undulations on the surface of the water after being disturbed. The geometrical elements used in architecture could therefore become symbols of human values that were themselves implicit in Nature, thereby relating the reality of everyday life with the meanings of institutions. A simple and geometrical architecture was not only beautiful but good, propitiating the moral virtues with which Ledoux and his contemporaries were so concerned. It would embody *agathon* and yet be undisputedly perceived in Nature.

This perception of geometry in nature was reinforced at a different level by modes of representation such as the popular aerial and distant perspectives. The classical orders lost their detail, and, according to Ledoux, even trees were perceived as round or pyramidal from a distance. Aerial perspective had become popular with many architects of this generation, who had first learned the technique around the middle of the eighteenth century from Jean-Louis Legeay. It is interesting to observe how perspective treatises of the same period often contained plates in which the geometrical orders were reduced to their essential geometrical configurations. The influence of these images must not be underestimated. It should be remembered that the inception of *perspectiva artificialis* necessarily implied the geometrization of its contents. John Kirby, author of *The Perspective of Architecture* (1761), had written that compared to the infinite number of shapes in nature, those used in architecture were very few: the triangle, the square, and the circle. The classical orders were, in his opinion, nothing other than a series of horizontal square and circular planes.[60]

The buildings of Ledoux's *architecture parlante* were invariably composed of simple geometrical elements combined in different degrees of complexity. They were intended to be part of a new city built around the salt works of Chaux. Some of the industrial structures were built and are still standing.[61] The city itself was designed as an oval; its plan was meant to imitate the orbit of the sun, "the supreme source of life."[62]

Some historians have considered this city as a precedent of the utopian urban centers designed by Fourier and Saint-Simon. Although Ledoux did formulate his proposals in social, ethical, and economic terms, Chaux can still only be regarded as the culmination of a tradition of ideal cities extending back to the Renaissance. The city of Chaux was not an anticipation of technological utopias; it was still somewhere rather than *u-topos*. In Ledoux's projects and descriptions, the ideal is still grounded in reality; the Platonic cosmology of the city and its concomitant magical rec-

Geometry and Architectural Meaning

onciliation with everyday life are elucidated through the transformation of enlightened reason into poetry.

Ledoux attached great importance to "work" in his industrial city and created a series of unconventional buildings for communal life. His main concern, however, was not production efficiency but rather the creation of a physical environment where man could find true happiness. "Man," wrote Ledoux, "should not despise the benefits of Nature in order to search, in an imaginary emptiness, for the products of industry."[63] Only a humble attitude in the face of nature could lead to emotional stability. Ledoux would thus start his projects from a careful consideration of the site's natural qualities. His buildings were to derive their character from the qualities of a place rather than to impose a priori meanings or a universal geometry upon the world. Ledoux normally avoided the description of the physical character of his buildings. Only once, in referring to his project for a school of morals, did he attach a timid footnote providing a more literal, historical justification for his choice of a cube as symbol of immutability.[64] He obviously believed in the eloquence of his images. In the universe of discourse, he was interested only in the poetical sense of human dwelling, that is, in the activities to take place within the propitious framework of his buildings. The comments that he added to clarify the intentions of each project were, fundamentally, imaginative depictions of everyday life. The symbolism of each building was to emerge from life itself and its context, not from a formal style whose elements might possess univocal and aprioristic meanings.

The city of Chaux contained a number of peculiar social institutions and private houses. Among the institutions there was a Temple to the Supreme Being, dedicated to the God of Deism, whose model was Soufflot's Pantheon. (This was also, as you will remember, the model for Boullée's Metropolitan Basilica.) Ceremonies held in the building were to have equal civil and religious importance and were to stress the significant events of life: birth, marriage, and death. A great number of buildings were devoted to such moral virtues as devotion, conciliation, and union. Ledoux's obsession to give a visible form to all human activities through institutions that embodied their meanings is highly significant. His juxtapositions—for example, a Palace of Concord, devoted to solving family problems, and a Temple of Love, where man could satisfy his sensual appetites—betray a genuine need to legitimate human life, life that is being increasingly deprived of religious meaning while remaining within the context of a traditional cosmology.

Aerial view of Ledoux's design for the city of Chaux,
from *L'Architecture*.

Perspective view of a project for the House of Education, from Ledoux's *L'Architecture*.

Geometry and Architectural Meaning

Perhaps the most interesting of his projects is the cemetery, whose inspiration was the image of the sphere of the earth.[65] Half of the sphere was buried. Its internal space is depicted as horrible and mysterious, a dark labyrinth of galleries surrounding the immense, cavernous sphere, empty and pierced by a single beam of light coming in through the oculus. Corpses would be placed in niches along the galleries. Nature and particularly sunlight were intentionally excluded, so that the overwhelming darkness could convey an image of nothingness, without relief. Outside the austere and immense dome, man would recoil at its appearance.

As part of his design, Ledoux included an engraving showing the earth surrounded by the moon and other planets, floating in a space full of clouds and sunlight. Referring to the planets in his "elevation" of the cemetery, Ledoux asked these "insensitive atoms" and "masses in motion" to pay tribute to the "eternal, universal soul" who had prescribed their order with so much wisdom. "God impressed upon the face of the stars man's gratitude."[66] Rhetorically, Ledoux inquired what mortal would be incapable of perceiving all that the Creator had done for him. Had not the Creator "separated the elements", and is He not responsible for all physical phenomena?

It has been pointed out that the presence of God was necessary for Newton's epistemology. In Ledoux's interpretation, moreover, the participation of divinity in the cosmological drama is dominant. Any human act in nature would be senseless if such participation were ignored. Hence the cosmos, itself an infinite and eternal cemetery, of greater value than any tomb built with materials prone to decay, becomes, in Ledoux's words, "the sepulchre of Copernicus, Kepler, Tycho Brahe, Descartes, and Newton . . . confidants of the heavenly secrets," and also of "artists, poets, and geniuses of all sorts."[67] It is not by coincidence that the eternal cemetery was devoted mainly to scientists and artists. Science and art were not only reconcilable but complementary in the eighteenth-century universe. And incorporating both reason and myth, they provided man with justification for his being.

The reference to Newton's cosmology was most explicit in the funerary architecture of Boullée and Ledoux. The cemetery became a structure symbolizing the reconciliation between life and death—the ultimate, ineffable enigma of the human condition. This in itself is significant. All else was soon to be explained by logical reason. Ledoux emphasized, not without anguish, the presence

Plan and section of Ledoux's project for the cemetery at Chaux, from *L'Architecture*.

Elevation of the cemetery of the city of Chaux, from
L'Architecture.

Geometry and Architectural Meaning

of the Supreme Being via the contrast of an empty geometrical space within his dome and the "elevation," which represented the cosmos immersed in a luminous ether; the two paradoxical secret essences of Newtonian science became here symbols of divinity and potential life.

| **Boullée, Ledoux, and the Origin of Theoretical Projects** | In the architecture of Boullée and Ledoux, geometry "recovered" its symbolic connotations. And yet their use of simple solids and geometrical plans has been thought by some as an immediate precedent of the most common formal preferences of machine-age architects. This is an assertion that on close examination does not hold up. |

During the eighteenth century, the notion of progress was admitted in architectural theory. Differences of opinion and taste were recognized. And to the degree that reason was increasingly used, the possibilities for speculative metaphysics diminished. In his *Oeuvres d'Architecture*, Peyre stated that there was nothing to add concerning the principles of architecture.[68] J. L. Viel de Saint-Maux, in a more radical vein, openly questioned the authority of Vitruvius and the importance of proportions. In his *Lettres*, Viel de Saint-Maux stated that there was not a single existing book of real value for modern architecture. Vitruvius, in his opinion, had only described the monuments of his own time in relation to their dimensions; his reputation rested simply on his supposed antiquity. Furthermore, Viel de Saint-Maux claimed that no one had written how to produce "that enthusiasm that stirs and charms the soul of the spectator of admirable monuments."[69] Ultimately, however, eighteenth-century architecture required some kind of general principles (*grands principes*) to confer meaning on architecture. The theme sketched by Viel de Saint-Maux in 1787 was precisely the one that obsessed Le Camus de Mezières, Boullée, and Ledoux: the transformation of architectural meaning into an intellectual problem—meaning that could no longer simply be taken from tradition.

Eventually, the classical orders and proportion were replaced by the Euclidean solids, which possessed mainly qualities of scale and symmetry. But even the use of these solids was motivated by a symbolic intention. The geometrical bodies were considered to be the most appropriate vehicle for reconciling man and his institutions with an external Nature. This geometry was not a method or operation. The figures were used because they were

Symbolic Geometry in French Architecture

believed to be the fundamental constitutive and visible elements of Nature. This is a Platonic symbolism that could only exist through the Aristotelian perception of the world that had been perpetuated by empiricism. It should be remembered that for most of the eighteenth century, space was primarily the hierarchical, qualitatively differentiated structure of places given to perception. The continuous, infinite, and homogeneous space that became an absolute locational framework for phenomena was ultimately a concept of natural philosophy. During the Enlightenment, however, this conceptual dimension never became a substitute of physical reality; Euclidean geometry was not functionalized.

Boullée and Ledoux emphasized the differences between the "scientific" and "artistic" dimensions of architecture. Imagination, which had always been integrated with rationality, was postulated toward the end of the century as the basic means of producing truly meaningful buildings. Previous theory, always rational, was qualified by Boullée as science, concerned merely with construction. True art, on the other hand, was believed to consist in the conception of rhetorical images. A fragile equilibrium existed between the spheres of reason and perception within the framework of eighteenth-century epistemology. Only in view of this context is it possible to understand the genuine metaphysical concerns of Boullée and Ledoux's architectural theory.

Boullée and Ledoux wrote at a moment when positive science was about to exclude metaphysical speculation from "legitimate" thinking. As a response to this peculiar situation, both architects transformed theory into poetry. Indeed, their writings contrast with the cold analytical rationalism of architectural treatises written since the Renaissance, in which metaphysical justifications were more or less implicit. Once the necessity of a metaphysical justification in architecture became explicit, the poetic transformation of the universe of theoretical discourse was inevitable. Thus the scientific and artistic dimensions of architecture could still be, if only in intention, ultimately reconciled.

Ledoux, Boullée, and Lodoli (of whom more will be said later) recognized very early on the possibility of using the traditional Vitruvian categories as a metaphor to generate architectural form. The use or purpose to which a building was destined and the mathematics and geometry that endorsed its stability and permanence were treated poetically in the *architecture parlante*. The "character" of the building was meant to derive from these categories. But this did not mean that "form followed function." This direct mathematical relation would only be postulated by the disciples of Boullée and Ledoux. It is also significant that the symbolic intentionality of these two architects could no longer be embodied in three-dimensional buildings. Their practice—their actual buildings—did not conform to the ideas and drawings that most clearly represented their intentions. Thus for the first time in the history of European architecture—apart from the rather fragmentary precedent of Piranesi's *Carceri*—architectural intentions had to be expressed almost exclusively through theoretical projects that obviously did not fit into the new, essentially prosaic world of industrial society.

The theoretical projects of Boullée and Ledoux, which coherently synthesized the dimensions of *mythos* and *logos* in a context where traditional speculative metaphysics was no longer valid, and which took into account the a priori of the world and the ambiguous nature of symbolization, were unfortunately disregarded or misinterpreted by their successors.[70] Their position in a period of rapid change inevitably resulted in confusion about their work. For example, Bodin, in his funerary discourse in Boullée's honor, pointed to the great importance of his buildings and praised the late architect's ability to determine precise cost estimates. Boullée's theoretical projects and merits as an educator were hardly mentioned.[71]

The Platonic dimension of Galileo's scientific revolution eventually became the main source for technology's dominance in architecture. That famous phrase by Du Fourny, cited earlier, about the importance of geometry in architecture could thus be interpreted by nineteenth-century architects as an invitation to use geometrical operations, devoid of symbolic intentionality, in order to fulfill in design, structural analysis, and other building techniques the technological aims of the industrial economy and its demand for efficiency in production.

Symbolic Geometry in French Architecture

III

GEOMETRY AND NUMBER AS
TECHNICAL INSTRUMENTS IN
EARLY MODERN ARCHITECTURE

5

PERSPECTIVE, GARDENING, AND ARCHITECTURAL EDUCATION

In medieval and Renaissance Europe, the order of things and the social hierarchy were prescribed through revelation. The Galilean revolution represented the end of an understanding by which man had always held a privileged position, while at the same time being subordinated to the discipline of the cosmos as a whole. After the seventeenth century, the notion of system, or a whole made of coordinated parts (the prototype of all rationality), was taken from astronomy and utilized as the model for the science and philosophy of the sublunar world.[1]

The epistemological revolution implied a radical transformation of the human condition. Medieval Christianity did not question the inveterate cosmological tradition in which the astral domain was perceived as the prototype of truths and values existing in the sublunar regions. But when the new science rejected the superiority of the heavens, the universe was transformed into a whole comprised of common elements and governed by universal laws. Earth became the "field" of an exact science, as precise as the one that studied the motions of the stars. Modern physics thus originated in the application of exact, immutable notions of an abstract order (*mathemata*) to the sphere of reality.

Modern seventeenth-century philosophy faced for the first time the problem of defining the relation between a perceiving subject and the object of his attention. Man was no longer an integral, nondifferentiated part of the hierarchical totality; he was isolated from the world and other individuals. His attitude vis-à-vis the world had to be modified, and two options were given to him: either dominate and possess the physical universe or effect, through mathematical reason, a new form of reconciliation. The first of these options would become during the early nineteenth century the task of modern technology. It is important to stress that the presupposition of a mathematical structure of reality was impossible to justify ontologically. In order to impose itself, it necessarily had to be proved through experimentation. Hence the importance of clarifying the sources and implications of this presupposition at the earliest stages of modern technological intentionality.

Galileo simultaneously desecrated the heavens and humanized science. He postulated a field of unified knowledge that opposed the ancient hierarchical scheme in which the exactness of the heavens regressed to the confusion of earthly life.[2] By connecting mathematics to experience, Galileo founded modern quantitative science.[3] His overall achievement was much more than a sum of

Geometry and Number as Technical Instruments

isolated scientific discoveries. He presented to the world a new ideal of intelligibility, one that would eventually encompass the totality of human knowledge. One can discern this as early as 1671 in W. Petty's *Political Arithmetic*. It would be difficult to overestimate Galileo's contribution. The epistemological revolution he ushered in would one day wear the mantle of positivism and, later, scientism.

The new philosophy rejected the texts of Aristotle and instead adopted "the book of nature"; its "text" became the immutable geometrical figures and numbers. Galileo presupposed that the laws of nature were mathematical. Believing that the real incarnated the mathematical, he was incapable of recognizing the distance between geometrical theories and experience. This illusion lay at the heart of all modern quantitative science, particularly of mechanics, which became almost immediately the model for all intellectual endeavours.[4]

The idea of nature, which in antiquity was associated with the idea of life (*physis*), could become an independent entity, and the correspondence between microcosm and macrocosm could be questioned. Thus the notion of a harmonic cosmos, full of anthropomorphic connotations, decipherable by astrology, could be replaced by the transparent universe of astronomy. Motion, once considered a manifestation of life, became a state of material bodies. In the context of a harmonic cosmological order, contemplation was given more value than action; and techniques did not have immanent value. It would have been sacrilegious to imagine that the world, a living and divine being, could be improved by human actions. Consequently, one's intent was never to modify the world's order but rather to discover and celebrate its harmonies. This traditional humility was indeed very difficult to overcome. The fact is that in one way or another, it was perpetuated through Newtonianism and was not subverted until the end of the eighteenth century.[5] But once the tools of physico-mathematical intelligibility were forged, science became the dominant ethos until subsumed by technology during the early nineteenth century.

Modern science implied, therefore, a distance between objects and mind, so that the latter could affirm its right of jurisdiction over the materiality of the former. This relation started to appear during the second half of the sixteenth century in the writings of philosophers, craftsmen, and mathematicians.[6] During the seventeenth century, the idea of dominating the physical world was explicit in the work of Francis Bacon and become a fundamental premise for research at France's Royal Academy of Science and England's Royal Society.[7] In both institutions, technical and experimental investigations held the same importance as scientific speculation. This was indicative of the role assigned to the new epistemology, that is, the joining of the practical and theoretical dimensions of knowledge, transforming the previously contemplative *orbis doctrinae* into an instrument of power.

Implicit in the geometrization of the epistemological universe was the possibility of transforming architectural theory into an instrument for technological domination. This situation, however, as should be evident from previous chapters, was never free of ambiguity. Geometrical science throughout the seventeenth century retained powerful symbolic connotations. Consequently, the use of geometry to modify God's work, that is, the technical actions of man in the world, was frequently shaded with the colors of traditional magic.

Magic and Technique

Bernard Palissy, a well-known craftsman, gardener, and architect, was one of the late-sixteenth-century authors who considered practical knowledge more important than any exclusively theoretical speculation derived from Aristotelian contemplation. He was a fascinating figure who became very popular in Paris between 1575 and 1584 through a series of public lectures illustrated by physical demonstrations and natural objects from his own collection, which included minerals, plants, and animals. Modern biographers have overemphasized the liberal, scientific, and antimedieval spirit of this man who spent long years of his life trying to discover procedures for clay enameling. This rendering of his intentions is simplistic, however.[8]

Palissy was concerned with a variety of themes, all referring essentially to the transformation or configuration of the human world. The first section of his *Recepte Véritable* (1563) is devoted to agriculture and reveals the mythical dimension underlying the conception of a geometrical garden. This symbolic program, to be modified and enriched, remained the basis for the majestic creations of Baroque gardening. It drew its authority from the meaning of Euclidean geometry and its necessary reference to intuition. The book is organized as a dialogue in which the author responds to questions and objections from an imaginary interlocutor. After describing his garden as "the most useful and delightful that has ever been conceived," Palissy explained that his source of inspiration had been Psalm 104, in which a garden was described as a place of refuge for persecuted Christians.[9] Then "confused with admiration" and inspired by the wisdom of the prophet and the good will of God, Palissy "imagined the figure" of a garden whose excellent beauty and ornament corresponded, at least in part, to the biblical description.[10] He declared that it was not his intention simply to emulate his predecessors, who had worked without *theory*. Only those who have "acted correctly according to the order of God" should be imitated. Palissy perceived "so great abuses and ignorance in all the arts" that it seemed all order had been corrupted; laborers worked on the earth with no philosophy, blindly following the routines and customs of their predecessors, ignorant of the "main causes" and nature of agriculture.

Palissy's interlocutor could not believe his ears. What need had a laborer for philosophy? Palissy replied that there was no art in the world that needed so much philosophy as agriculture. Although Saint Paul had warned men against false philosophers, his admonition concerned those thinkers who pretended to attain divine knowledge. Palissy, however, regarded his philosophy not of this speculative kind but rather as a collection of observations derived from experience. Thus Palissy avoided the dangers that, for a traditional order, were implicit in his recognition of the value of technique. Paradoxically, he achieved his objective through an incipient dissociation of the domains of religion and science.

Palissy provided some practical advice, referring to the four traditional Aristotelian elements: air, water, fire, and earth, always conscious of their mythical significance. He then described his garden. The site was to be located near water: a river or a fountain. This also implied the proximity of mountains. After having found such a place, he intended to design a garden of "incomparable ingenuity," the most beautiful under the sky after Eden. First, he would determine the "squaring" of the garden, its width and breadth, in relation to the topography and the location of the source. He would then divide the whole into four equal parts and separate them by great avenues. In the four corners of the crossing, there would be amphitheatres, and at the endings of the avenues and the corners of the perimeter, eight "marvelous cabinets" would be built, all different and "of a kind such as has never been seen before." Palissy stressed that his conception was inspired by Psalm 104, "where the prophet described the excellent and marvelous works of God and, contemplating them, humbled himself in His presence and commanded his soul to praise the Lord."[11]

Each extraordinary cabinet, containing a variety of fountains and mechanical inventions, was described separately. The mysterious iridescence of the enameled surfaces that were to cover the walls and vaults of these grottoes was intended to be their most prominent feature. Palissy seemed fascinated by the reflectiveness of enamel, a property traditionally associated with the symbolic value of gems and precious metals. He managed to achieve the same effect with clay brick through an artificial process and described his accomplishments as true acts of white magic. The different colors, melted by fire, combined to produce evocative figures, while hiding the joints of the brick construction, so that everything appeared as one piece. The walls, polished like precious stones, could be left uncovered, their beautiful surfaces reflecting the fountains and automata. Each cabinet would also exhibit a clearly visible phrase praising human knowledge, emphasizing its transcendent value: for example, "Without wisdom it is impossible to please God," and "Wisdom is our guide to the eternal Kingdom."[12]

In the mythical universe adhered to by Palissy, his technical interest was totally explicit, and yet his concern was always to establish contact between God and man through the actions of the latter. Accordingly, he devoted himself to the clarification of technical operations. His "philosophy" was meant to guide human action, but only within the established order. Scientific knowledge, that is, geometry, mechanics, and alchemy, was motivated by reconciliatory objectives. Palissy's geometry and mechanics dominated nature, an early declaration of their autonomy from theological speculation. In the end, however, this domination was a form of magic, and the empirical philosophy of agriculture drew meaning from its own power of transcendence.

It is interesting to note that Palissy's attitude actually led him to anticipate some of the principles of eighteenth-century architectural theory. For example, the cabinets at the ends of both avenues were to be completely natural. Branches of trees would constitute architraves, friezes, and pediments, while the trunks would act as columns. The interlocutor of the *Recepte Véritable* pointed out that all famous architects had provided fixed proportions for their buildings and questioned Palissy's solution with the fact that the proportions of the cabinets would have to change with the growth of the trees. The answer was simply that the model was better than any copies. Palissy maintained that the architects of antiquity had copied in stone the forms of trees and the human body, and therefore the "columns of the First Architect" had priority. The bases and capitals were to be formed by making incisions and allowing the sap to harden. The growth of the branches would be controlled through "geometry and architectural rules."

Palissy was frequently accused of sorcery. In the eyes of his contemporaries, he possessed certain recipes that allowed him to control nature. His technical operations were still viewed as tampering with God's order at a time when the line between white magic and black magic was becoming increasingly more difficult to draw. (Intoxicated by his freedom from religious determinism, man would eventually transform black magic into technology.) But the mechanical arts, which had been given a new status during the early modern era, particularly architecture and gardening, were intended as white, reconciliatory magic; Palissy's primitive natural philosophy was only a means of showing respect and following God's will in the best possible way.

During the first half of the seventeenth century, the meaning of *techné* was not substantially modified. An excellent testimonial to this is provided by the writings of Salomon de Caus, a brilliant gardener and mathematician with interests in mechanics, architecture, music, and anamorphosis. His *Les Raisons des Forces Mouvantes* (1615) is basically a collection of illustrations that, apart from a few elementary machines, such as levers, pulleys, and gears, demonstrate the workings of marvelous fountains and complex automata invented by the author. De Caus did not distinguish between toys and useful machines. Moreover, he was interested particularly in those machines that embellished his gardens and inspired awe and fascination. His work also included garden designs that combined anthropomorphic and geometrical schemes. As with Palissy, the act of giving form to nature was for De Caus a meaningful *poesis*.[13]

In the preface of *La Perspective avec la Raison des Ombres et Miroirs* (1612), De Caus proposes to produce a useful work for architects, engineers, and painters, as well as to enjoy the pleasures of speculation. He was very interested in perspective, believing that it was the only "part of mathematics" capable of providing pleasure to the sight.[14] The first attempts to structure a mathematical theory of perspective date back to the last two decades of the sixteenth century. Mathematicians such as Federico Com-

Perspective, Gardening, and Architectural Education

Design for a grotto of Neptune, showing the mechanism of the fountain, from Salomon de Caus's *Raisons des Forces Mouvantes*.

Geometry and Number as Technical Instruments

Anthropomorphic garden, design by Salomon de Caus, from his *Raisons des Forces Mouvantes.*

The garden of Heidelberg Castle as originally designed by Salomon des Caus, from his *Hortus Palatinus* (1620).

Perspective, Gardening, and Architectural Education

mandino, Simon Stevin of Bruges, and Guido Ubaldo del Monte wrote texts of great complexity, which were impossible to apply in practice. Only during the seventeenth century did the use of methods of *perspectiva artificialis* become truly popular with artists.[15]

The problem of perspective is not easily reducible. Perspective became strictly possible only when man began to view himself as a subject and external reality as a collection of objects. The development of perspective theory is intimately connected with the epistemological revolution and, associated with this revolution, the fundamental dissociation between man and world, between body and mind. Cartesian philosophy postulated perspective as a model for human knowledge. But it was not until the nineteenth century that perspectivism became a true form of subjectivism and was adopted as a universal prototype of knowledge. Only then did man actually believe in the isolation of his mind from other minds and the world, thereby rejecting the fundamental intersubjective reality given to embodied perception. And this, of course, led him to accept no objectivity other than the evidence of mathematical logic. Even today it is difficult to admit that our embodied perception of the world is not equivalent to perspective representation. The images of the photographic camera are taken to be the only true representation of reality.[16] Perspective, of course, is only one way of seeing, corresponding initially to Cartesianism and implying the imposition of a geometrical scheme on reality in order to establish a relation between *res cogitans* and *res extensa*.

During the seventeenth century, art, gardening, and architecture—disciplines responsible for the configuration of man's world—were necessarily concerned with the fundamental problem of philosophy; the reconciliation between subject and object. In order to endorse the meaning of human life, the arts had to confirm mankind's relation to the sphere of absolute values. Hence the use of perspective as an ideal organization of external reality. The transformation of cities, gardens, and internal spaces implicitly demonstrated the belief in the transcendent nature of the new geometrical knowledge. But Baroque perspective, in marked contrast to nineteenth-century perspectivism, was a symbolic configuration, which allowed reality to keep the qualities of traditional perception in an essentially Aristotelian world. The great vistas at Versailles are not equivalent to Haussmann's boulevards. Although by its very nature a geometrical operation, perspective

Geometry and Number as Technical Instruments

made it possible for seventeenth-century artists to transform their physical environment into a symbolic reality. In this way, it also embodied a symbolic operation that, perceived through sensuous experience, evoked ideal truth and excellence. In seventeenth-century Versailles, color, smell, light, water games, fireworks, and, indeed, the full richness of mythology played a major role. The meaning of the place as the seat of government and the dwelling of the Sun King derived from a synthesis of the power of geometry and its potential to enhance sensuality. The intention was not to express "absolute domination" but rather to make manifest a truly human order.

The theory of perspective could very readily abandon its intimate ties to perceived reality to become pure geometry. This became apparent in the examination of Desargues's work (see chapter 3), which, because it was so exceptional in its disregard of traditional practice and symbolism, was rejected by artists. As a rule, however, the architects of the seventeenth century managed to synthesize the dimensions of qualitative, preconceptual spatiality and geometrical conceptual space. Since *spatium mundanum* was identified with the *ens rationis* of geometry, the possibility of a conceptual space appeared for the first time in the sciences and the arts. But Baroque space also retained its qualities, its character as place. It was always a *plenum*, never an odorless or colorless vacuum. The infinity and geometrical characteristics of Baroque space required the sensual qualities of materials and their plastic representation. Baroque architecture emphasized the presence of space in the world of man, reestablishing a meaningful relation between the subject and external reality.

Baroque architecture conveyed the almost tactile presence of a space filled with life and light, with angels and mythological figures. This contrasted vividly with the empty and homogeneous spaces suggested by Boullée and Ledoux. Descartes, Galileo, and Leibniz rejected the existence of the vacuum. Descartes even recognized a difference between the *indéfinition* of geometrical human space and infinity, which was the exclusive attribute of God.[17] Perspective only made visible the geometrical infinity in the world of man. This was, in effect, a pregnant infinity, full of symbolic connotations, which established a hierarchy with reference to the temporal power of the king or the spiritual power of the church. The paradigm of the seventeenth century was to allow infinity to appear *in reality*. The late eighteenth century, on the other hand, wished to create a new nature in which the infinite and eternal void would be evident.

Perspective view of the stables and the courtyard of
Versailles. Engraving of the view from the palace by
Pérelle.

View of Schönbrun Palace and Vienna in the back-
ground, from the *gloriette* in the garden. Project by
J. B. Fischer von Erlach and Ferdinand von
Hohenberg.

Geometry and Number as Technical Instruments

Stage-set design by G. Galli-Bibiena, from his *Archi-tetture e Prospettive* (1740).

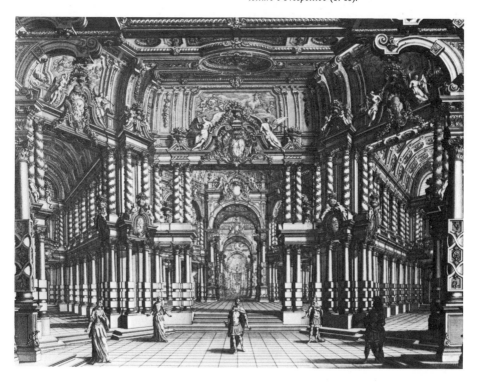

Perspective, Gardening, and Architectural Education

The theory of perspective allowed man to control and dominate his external, physical reality. Like other mechanical techniques in their implementation of mathematics, however, this formal control of the traditional hierarchy of qualitative places by the rules of geometrical perspective was always an act of reconciliation. The famous frescoes of *quadratturisti* like Andrea Pozzo were supposed to be seen from one predetermined point of view, permanently marked on the pavement of a church. This revealed a true hierarchical and transcendental vision that appeared only when man occupied his place in the geometrical structure of the Creation. Another type of perspective projection, anamorphosis, involved the *distortion* of the reality it represented. Here a geometrical theory clearly dominated and subjected normal perception to its own wishes by placing the point of view in unexpected places, generally on the surface of the drawing or painting.[18] These "tricks" revealed the artificial character of perspective and showed the extent to which theory could become autonomous and control practice. Although these projections had been used sporadically during the late Renaissance,[19] they became extremely popular during the first half of the seventeenth century, when the theory of anamorphosis was being written. Once it had been clearly formulated, it became a scientific curiosity, a form that could be imposed on any content. Reality as presence and reality as appearance were not only intentionally disjointed, but the primacy of undistorted presence was replaced by the primacy of distorted appearance.[20]

During the earlier part of the century, however, anamorphosis had other connotations. The architect J. F. Niceron devoted a whole book to the study of this "curious perspective or artificial magic of marvelous effects."[21] His *Perspective Curieuse* (1638) employs the tone of a scientific work but develops in an atmosphere of fantasy and myth. Niceron understood the importance of applied mathematics and praised Archimedes for having reputedly used this science in the resolution of technical problems. He believed that mathematics possessed many wonderful qualities. It provided the means for the execution of projects, was useful for the delight and recreation of our senses, established rules of order and symmetry in architecture, and indicated how to build machines.

Niceron rejected all "useless speculation." His theory seemed to be concerned only with mathematics as it applied to the transformation of reality. The results of this application had, in his view, a *miraculous* character. And perspective was important be-

View of the vault in the *Jesuitenkirche* of Vienna.
The dome is a fresco by Andrea Pozzo, an example
of the *quadrattura* method.

Perspective, Gardening, and Architectural Education

Jean-François Niceron, engraving by Michel Lasne,
showing S. Trinità dei Monti in the background,
from *Thaumaturgus Opticus* (1646).

Geometry and Number as Technical Instruments

cause it was identified with the "miraculous productions" of mechanics, hydraulics, and pneumatics. It was his opinion that perspective was indispensable to architecture, lending to it order and symmetry.[22] Explaining the title of his work, he wrote that "curious perspectives" were not only useful, like normal perspective, but delightful as well. Calling it artificial magic did not imply any illicit practice or communication with "the enemies of our health." In fact, "natural magic" was not only permissible but constituted the "optimal degree of perfection of all sciences."[23] Niceron identified magic with the technical inventions that had their origin in mathematical science. The beautiful and marvelous effects of "the sphere of Poseidonius," which explained the configuration of the heavens; Archimedes's mirrors and war machines; and the "automata of Daedalus" were to him the highest examples of art and industry. Thus "true magic or the perfection of the sciences consists in perspective, allowing us to know and discern more perfectly the beautiful works of nature and art."[24]

The dual nature of Baroque perspective is evident in Niceron's work. By geometrizing the world, man gained access to the truth. Perspective both revealed the truth of reality and reflected man's power to modify it; that is, it was a form of magic. It is significant that the more ambitious applications of anamorphosis to fresco painting appeared in the convents of the Minimes, where some of the most advanced ideas of the time were being discussed. This was the order entered by Niceron and also by M. Mersenne, the well-known author of a treatise on universal harmony, whose letters provided an important link among scientists and philosophers of the early seventeenth century.

In the epistemological framework of the first half of the seventeenth century, technical action could never be free from magic or symbolism. This is attested to by the various texts written at the time, which addressed the transformation of human reality. Due to the nonspecialized character of the traditional epistemological universe, this transformation, in any of its forms, was always relevant to architecture. It should come as no surprise, then, to note the great interest architects had in fireworks and other similar machines "for war and recreation"[25] or their concern for ephemeral structures, like canvas triumphal arches, facades, and perspective stage designs framing processions and state or religious celebrations: transformations that sought to realize the symbolic potential of public space.

In 1652 C. Mollet published a book on astrology and *Theatre des Plans et Jardinages*, a treatise on gardening.[26] After some prac-

Perspective, Gardening, and Architectural Education

Geometry and Number as Technical Instruments

John the Apostle at Patmos. Details from the execution method of a fresco in anamorphosis by Niceron.
Works like this, executed in the monasteries of the
Minimes at Rome and Paris, would be intelligible
when viewed close to the wall plane, but hidden in
conventional frontal perception. Illustration from
Thaumaturgus Opticus.

Perspective, Gardening, and Architectural Education

tical advice, Mollet described the Aristotelian heavenly spheres and showed how to avoid evil influences from the stars. *Praxis*, for Mollet, was intimately linked to the conceptions of a hierarchical and animistic cosmos. Reality was perceived as the place where man was in close contact with God. The gardener's life thus follows the pattern of cosmic time: praying to God in the mornings, living the day in peaceful harmony, and receiving His blessing every evening. Mollet thought that this was the incorruptible model to be followed by young people seeking knowledge in gardening.

Stipulating a similar universe, J. Boyceau's *Traité du Jardinage* (1638) describes the four Aristotelian elements as a reconciliation of opposites.[27] Boyceau declared that the earth had been placed by God in the center of the universe, receiving from Him the power to beget and support life. The gardener should have some technical knowledge, including geometry, arithmetic, architecture, and mechanics. But ultimately, the traditional *poesis* of gardening, which connects man to the earth (his womb and sepulchre), was the dominant theme. Gardening and agriculture still did not take place in a universe of precision. Its object was never merely to dominate nature or to increase the productivity of crops.

After the seventeenth century, God began to retire from the world. This was an unavoidable consequence of the epistemological revolution and the generalization of mechanistic intelligibility.[28] In 1693 B. Bekker published an important work that shows the great transformation that had occurred between the seventeenth century and the Enlightenment. *The Enchanted World*, described the substitution of supernatural revelation by nature. Bekker did not stop at revealed truth. Since God had given man reason, it should be used in our interpretation of the Bible. Sacred authority could be criticized through the natural knowledge of God that man possessed. Bekker expelled angels and demons from the world, and miracles and sorcery he considered illusions. God was now revealed through the still inexplicable marvels of nature, open to the perceptions of the enlightened man.

During the eighteenth century, craftsmen still operated with care; they respected the natural order and were conscious of the transcendent humility of action. The sacred nature of reality did not encourage mindless exploitation. Throughout the century, there was a genuine fascination with technical achievements that reproduced the wonders of nature. For example, C. C. Scaletti, in his *Scuola Mecanico-Speculativo-Practica* (1711), extolled mathematics as the true cause of mechanical, hydraulic, and optical

Geometry and Number as Technical Instruments

phenomena.[29] He rejected explanations based on "occult qualities" and adopted an experimental method. Nonetheless, he described the operator of "practical mechanics" as a magician with miraculous powers. Instead of concentrating on pragmatic applications of mechanics, he was more interested in describing such marvelous toys as a walking silver cup or a mechanical fly that had belonged to Charles V. And the architect Pierre Patte listed, among the other arts and sciences that had advanced significantly during the reign of Louis XV, the manufacture of automata.[30] He was especially impressed by the mechanical flutist five and a half feet tall designed and built by Vaucanson.

It is unquestionable, however, that toward the end of the seventeenth century and coinciding with the cultural transformations represented by Bekker's work, occult qualities were removed from technical operations. The foundation of the academies, which replaced the traditional guilds, and the institutionalizing of the *Corps du Génie Militaire* and the *Corps des Ponts et Chaussées*, were events indicative of this first exorcism of *techné*.

In his role as *historiographe des bâtimens du Roi*, André Felibien attended the first deliberations of the Royal Academy of Architecture. He was also appointed *inspecteur du devis*, and was in charge of reviewing and approving the designs for the roads and bridges of France. In his *Des Principes de l'Architecture, de la Sculpture, de la Peinture* (1699), his interest was mainly linguistic. He was concerned with the prevailing confusion of concepts and names given to tools or elements, and his work was an attempt to define the parts and instruments of the different arts and crafts.

In his section on architecture, he praised Perrault's translation of Vitruvius and then pointed out that his own intention was not to write another treatise. He noted that there were a great number of existing books on the orders, but only a few authors like Philibert de l'Orme, Derand, Desargues, Jousse de la Fleche, and Bosse said anything about stone- and woodcutting or the trades of locksmith and engraver. Felibien believed that these few attempts to elucidate the techniques of architecture did not present a complete theoretical discussion. He was convinced that technique was a most important aspect of architecture and wrote his *Principes* to explain the techniques and tools of the trades: masonry, carpentry, plumbing, windowmaking, blacksmithing, locksmithing, and so forth. He maintained that it was important to have direct contact with craftsmen, to visit their workshops and to examine their machines. But it was at this point that he began to encounter problems. He could not find "reasonable" workers: These "ignorant and strange people" pretended not to know what he was talking about; they "invented ridiculous stories" and hid the most common utensils.[31] The tension between traditional craftsmanship (with its secrets and mythical frame of reference) and the new scientific attitude of academic architects and engineers could hardly be more explicit. This tension only ended after the Industrial Revolution, when the transformation of the long-established relation of production actually took place. Felibien's new attitude to technical operations is nevertheless revealing. He associated his work directly with the academy, presenting it as the result of a common enterprise that reflected the interest of the most distinguished European architects.[32]

Intellectuals of the late seventeenth century also manifested interest in technical and practical problems. John Locke declared a preference for practical knowledge over the manipulation of abstractions in *De Arte Medica*.[33] Leibniz believed it was important to describe the procedures employed by technicians and craftsmen, a task made necessary and possible because "practice is only a more particular and compounded theory."[34] The traditional values of intellectual contemplation, still present in the Baroque period, were superseded in the eighteenth century by values derived from human action and man's eagerness to transform the world. In his article on art for the *Encyclopédie*, Diderot complained about the "harmful consequences" resulting from the traditional distinction between liberal and mechanical arts, which had produced great numbers of vain and useless intellectuals.[35]

The Galilean revolution continued into the eighteenth century in the guise of axiological reform,[36] and the cosmic reason of the seventeenth century became truly human. Once the a priori universality of reason was questioned, human rationality became a pressing invitation to action; the systematization of knowledge was deemed indispensable. Renouncing contemplation for its own sake, Enlightened reason strove to join technical theory with practice, and was often frustrated by the failures of the former to influence the latter.

These transformations are apparent in eighteenth-century treatises on gardening and differ markedly from the ideas expressed in the works of Mollet and Boyceau. Batty Langley, who recommended the "non-stiff" type of garden in his *New Principles of Gardening* (1728), criticized the "abominable mathematical regularity" of some French gardens. His own method, however, also took as its starting point a detailed exposition of geometrical rules.

Geometry and Number as Technical Instruments

The blacksmith's workshop, from Felibien's *Des Principes de l'Architecture.*

Perspective, Gardening, and Architectural Education

But it should be obvious by now that this is not a real paradox. For although Langley considered this science "the basis of any layout,"[37] he was not capable of understanding the symbolic implications of a geometry that imposed its form on nature in the manner of the Baroque gardens. For Langley, geometry was a tool, albeit one of great importance.[38] When applied to gardening, geometry was supposed to reproduce the way in which nature itself "strikes with astonishment upon man," surprising him with unexpected "Harmonious Objects."

In 1711 A. J. Dezalliers d'Argenville published his *Théorie et Pratique du Jardinage*. Although it comes rather late in the Baroque period, it represents the first and last systematic exposition of the principles of French Baroque gardens. This is in itself significant. The geometry of the seventeenth-century garden hardly needed elucidation; its symbolic horizon was totally transparent. Dezalliers already cautioned against the use of extravagant features, pointing out that a garden should derive from nature more than from art. He thought it incorrect to sacrifice variety for symmetry.[39] He included general rules, methods, and proportions and added a section on practice, "which is but a consequence of the certainties of theory." This, he thought, had never been previously provided to the public. The description of practice contained instructions on tracing all sorts of figures using geometrical methods, both on paper and in the field.

Dezalliers was conscious of the fact that to trace a layout on the field, actual experience and continuous practice was more important than "profound science." He nevertheless insisted on the importance of his prescriptive methods. The gardener should be able to produce scaled drawings, and Dezalliers provided step-by-step instructions for this craft. In contrast to seventeenth-century texts, his theoretical discourse is a mere *ars fabricandi*, lacking references to the transcendent justifications of technical action. It is significant that in this late work, the geometry of the Baroque garden is already identified with the practical geometry of the surveyor.

Later in the century, as might be expected, natural philosophy exerted its influence on gardening. The two volumes by R. Schabol, *La Pratique du Jardinage* and *La Théorie du Jardinage*, published posthumously in 1770 and 1771, bear witness to this. Schabol believed that gardening was the most noble part of agriculture[40] and that the gardener always "reflects on what he is to do and never acts without a method founded on rules and principles."[41]

Geometry and Number as Technical Instruments

Nor should he fail to consult Nature if he desires to be in harmony with it. Moreover, the gardener is likened to the astronomer, as one who observes phenomena in order to fully comprehend them: "The gardener . . . contemplates Nature in the dark sanctuary of the earth's womb, or in the mechanism of plants."[42] Consequently, Schabol rejected speculative methods and contended that "experimental and instrumental physics" were indispensable for the clarification of phenomena in nature. He realized that nature often confronted man with insurmountable difficulties and enigmas and that the diversity of phenomena was often astounding and disconcerting—thereby forcing man to accept the humility of his intelligence. In spite of this, Schabol believed he could explain some of the "effects" he had observed in plants. It was not a matter of presenting solutions or demonstrations but of suggesting "probabilities founded on conjectures and presumptions derived from facts."[43]

Thus nature, while retaining its evocative mysteries, became a book open to scientific discovery. Schabol, for example, could not understand why plants and animals, composed of internal parts whose "functions" were very similar, were nevertheless very different. In view of all that remained mysterious, the gardener should simply admire and follow the laws of the "Author of Nature," whose will hides from us the causes. But because God had attributed "particular actions" to each one of the different species of plants in the Creation, the gardener should not be discouraged. He should always respect and praise the Lord's design.

Schabol's work thus demonstrates the epistemological humility of the eighteenth century. His understanding of *mathemata* contrasts sharply with that of nineteenth-century biology, for which the identity of functions and structural similarities became the dominant feature, leading eventually to a godless theory of evolution and providing a formal model of classification that had a deep and long-lasting influence on architectural history and theory.[44] Schabol, however, also believed that theory, understood as a technical set of rules, should be applied to practice in order to increase production. In his *Théorie*, he complained because primitive intuitive methods were still being used. Earlier authors had not combined experimental physics with a knowledge of the mechanism of plants, but Schabol thought this union was essential: "Theory and practice need one another; their success depends on their correspondence."[45]

Perspective, Gardening, and Architectural Education

This ambiguity was present in all technical disciplines during the Enlightenment since practice retained its traditional character. Building techniques, in particular, did not change much. Around midcentury, the famous engineer Jean-Rodolphe Perronet received some rather striking reports about the talents and abilities of members of the *Corps des Ponts et Chaussées*, the most distinguished civil engineers in Europe: Picard, for example, knew practically no geometry, mechanics, or hydraulics; he had some idea about mensuration but encountered great difficulties determining cost estimates or architectural details. Also, he had no education and found it difficult to design, to read, or to do mathematics.[46] At Soissons, the engineer Loyseau confessed that science, art, and architecture were as foreign to builders as Greek.

Transformations in theory of perspective also revealed the exorcism of the technical dimension. Around the middle of the seventeenth century, there was a famous dispute between Desargues and Du Breuil concerning the significance of anamorphosis. In 1653 Bosse published a work entitled *Moyen Universelle de Pratiquer la Perspective sur les Tableaux ou Surfaces Irregulières*, a treatise that examined all sorts of strange projections. In contrast to the traditional implications of these "tricks," which were generally recognized in the early seventeenth century and appeared in Niceron's work, Bosse emphasized the universality and simplicity of his methods while ignoring the qualitative difference between normal perspective and distortions. He made no allusion to occult or magical characteristics; to him any projection was merely the result of applying a common set of geometrical rules.

In his *Manière Universelle pour Pratiquer la Perspective* (1648), Desargues showed a precocious prototechnological turn of mind. He unequivocally declared his dislike for studying and doing research in physics or geometry "unless these sciences prove truly useful to the intellect" and can be "reduced" to effective action.[47] Thus the same author who discovered the theoretical principles of projective geometry[48] and who took the first step toward a true functionalization of reality also denied the value of speculative geometry unless it became an effective technique for practice in all the arts.

Toward the end of the seventeenth century, the mathematician Ozanam also wrote about anamorphosis as a simple scientific curiosity.[49] In his work on perspective, Ozanam denied the magical or symbolic attributes of perspective, emphasizing that this art simply represented visible objects as they appeared to the human

Geometry and Number as Technical Instruments

eye.[50] This is the conception of perspective, popularized initially by Andrea Pozzo's treatise, that would become common in the eighteenth century. It is significant that the closest identification between perspective, architecture, and stage design also occurred around this time in Ferdinando Galli-Bibiena's *Architettura Civile* (1711). This work touched upon geometry and mechanics, whose synthesis was epitomized by Bibiena's own "invention," the *scena per angolo*. In this method of stage design, the introduction of oblique vanishing points created an impression of reality that had not been possible using only one-point perspectives. The identification of the stage and the city was also evident in the customs and dress of the eighteenth century, especially in Paris.[51] The city became a stage for the play-acting of roles, that is, the representation of individuals' stations in life. In a world where the absolute value of conventions could be questioned, the traditional public (social) order, framed by the architect's design, was still perceived as indispensable for human freedom and cultural coherence.

As the seventeenth century drew to a close, geometry increasingly lost its claims to transcendence in science and philosophy. In his *Studies in a Geometry of Situation* (1679), Leibniz proposed a science of extension that, unlike Cartesian analytic geometry, would be integral and not reducible to algebraic equations. But this project of a "descriptive geometry" more universal than algebra could still magically describe the infinite qualitative variety of natural things. This transcendental geometry was part of Leibniz's lifelong dream to postulate a universal science, called by him at various times *lingua universalis, scientia universalis, calculus philosophicus*, and *calculus universalis*. From all the disciplines of human knowledge, he tried to extrapolate the most simple constitutive elements in order to establish the rules of relation by which to organize the whole epistemological field into a "calculus of concepts."[52] The elemental *characteristicae generales* were to be necessarily transcendental, referring to the specificity of things in the world of everyday life. Hence, his "monad," the differential of his calculus, was not a quantitative atom, but necessarily possessed qualities.

Leibniz draws upon Euclidean geometry to explain his *characteristicae*. For example, a circle on a piece of paper is not a true circle, but one of the "universal characters," a vehicle for geometrical truths. It would simply be impossible to reason if these characters did not exist. Leibniz believed that there was not only a similarity between characters and the things they represented,

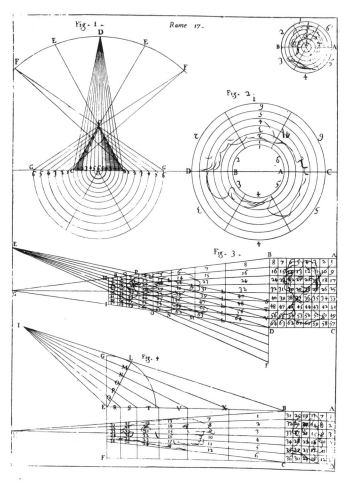

Anamorphosis as a scientific curiosity, from F. Galli-Bibiena's *Architettura Civile*.

An example of F. Galli-Bibiena's *scena per angolo*, from his own *Architettura Civile*.

Rame 22.

Perspective, Gardening, and Architectural Education

but that the order of characters corresponded to the order of things.[53] Hence discovering the appropriate characters in every field of knowledge makes it possible to achieve a complete systematization of the universe, thus forging "a new crucial instrument for the practical objectives of humanity."[54]

Leibniz's science of combinations was the last great metaphysical system; it was, in fact, the culmination of a long tradition of conceptual structures founded on the belief that it was possible to reflect the absolute order of the cosmos. It was a set of rules formulated with the intention of rendering all possible combinations among the primary elements of things, thus making possible the "calculation" of their origins and destinies—an intention similar to that of medieval cabalists and seventeenth-century Pansophists. Leibniz's dream of an encyclopedia related to a universal language, however, was also not unlike the systematization of knowledge postulated by d'Alembert; although it retained a classical ontology, the work of Leibniz represented the moment of transformation of philosophy into a general epistemology—an epistemology not grounded in the traditional notions of theology or metaphysics. His vision of the consequences of systematization was, indeed, a prophecy of technology.

Early in the eighteenth century, Fontenelle, the famous historian of the Royal Academy of Science, denied the transcendental dimension of Leibniz's calculus. In his *Eléments de la Géometrié de l'Infini* (1727), he asserted that geometry was purely intellectual, and independent of the immediate description and existence of the figures whose properties it discovered.[55] He emphasized that infinity, whose existence it was possible to demonstrate in geometry, was only a number, much like the finite spaces that it determined. This infinity had nothing to do with the limitless extension that was usually imagined in association with the word; "metaphysical infinity" could not be applied to numbers or extension, where it has always caused confusion.

Fontenelle was responsible for the establishment of the program to systematize knowledge at the Royal Academy of Science.[56] Aware of the limitations of the traditional seventeenth-century ontological systems that "knew it all in advance," he believed that knowledge should derive from quantitative observation and experimentation. Without ever accepting Newton's philosophy, Fontenelle endorsed the existence of a general geometrical space in which all phenomena were contained. If all nature "consisted of innumerable combinations among figures and motions," then

Geometry and Number as Technical Instruments

geometry, being the only science capable of determining figures and calculating motions, was absolutely indispensable in physics.[57] Only geometry appeared evident in astronomy, optics, and mechanics. Other phenomena, such as the illness of animals or the fermentation of liquids, although they could not be conceived with the same clarity "due to the great complexity of their motions and figures," were also, in Fontenelle's opinion, dominated by geometry. Thus was postulated the mathematical imperialism of modern science. Fontenelle's general geometry, at the level of technical action and mechanics, was without symbolic implication.

It could be said that after Leibniz, the human intellect lost its immanent power of transcendence. Correlatively, geometry and number became mere formal entities, instruments of technique. The Baroque synthesis was subverted at its very roots. And although Euclidean geometry maintained during the Enlightenment a residual symbolic dimension, the freedom and autonomy of geometrical applications in technical disciplines was firmly and irrevocably established. This transformation propitiated the development of statics and strength of materials, as well as the great interest in technical problems that would characterize eighteenth-century architecture.

Education: Civil Architecture and Engineering

The Royal Academy of Architecture was founded in 1671 to elucidate the beauty of buildings and to provide a means for the instruction of young architects.[58] The best architects in France would convene once a week to discuss their ideas, and the rules emerging from these discussions would be taught in public courses two days a week.[59] The academy's first formally appointed professor was François Blondel, who stressed the importance of mathematical disciplines, geometry, perspective, stonecutting, and mechanics, all within a Baroque framework. But in 1687 he was replaced by P. de la Hire, a well-known geometrician and architect, a member also of the Academy of Sciences and a disciple of Desargues. Thereafter, the weekly deliberations were mostly addressed to problems of statics, stereotomy, surveying, and mensuration.[60]

De la Hire introduced in the academy questions concerning the equilibrium of arches and provided solutions based on Galilean mechanics.[61] He broached the possibility of applying practical geometry to the technical problems of architecture apart from symbolic or aesthetic considerations.[62] In 1711 the academy devoted many sessions to examine de la Hire's theory about the thrust of vaults, and it was generally agreed that his rules were founded on sound geometrical principles. But because these rules were based on a hypothesis of infinitely polished voussoirs, the architects realized it could not be applied in practice.[63] The distance between the theory of statics and the actual behavior of materials would be a problem throughout the eighteenth century. Still, the early detection of this issue is significant, for it implied a general perception of a very different nature than what was presented in the Baroque synthesis. Geometry could now be regarded as a simple tool capable of determining the dimensions of structural components in relation to the laws of mechanics (with all the problems of true effectiveness that this involved).

André Felibien, Pierre Bullet, and Antoine Desgodetz also presented a great number of papers on technical problems to the academy during the early eighteenth century. Between 1719 and 1728, the period in which Desgodetz was the holder of the professorship, the weekly sessions were devoted almost exclusively to the discussion of legal problems and to the establishment of precise methods of mensuration.[64] In 1730 abbé Camus, also a member of the Royal Academy of Sciences, began to teach mathematics to the architects at their academy.

After 1750 the architects' interest in mathematics and geometrical methods generally flagged, while their concerns with the more specifically technical problems heightened. The discussions now centered on, among other things, recently invented machines, techniques for producing better glass, methods for centering, and the quality of building materials. Perronet, Régemorte, and Soufflot presented papers based on the results of quantitative experiments pertaining to the strength of materials. In his work on the origins of architecture, read at the academy in 1745, G. D'Isle—while crediting Vitruvius's mythical account—argued that geometry's role was purely practical. He thought it sharpened the intellect and was useful for surveying, leveling, mensuration, and the drawing of plans and maps.[65]

In a letter addressed to J. A. Gabriel, read at the academy in February 1776, D'Angiviller, *directeur general des bâtimens*, expressed his dissatisfaction with the lack of positive results produced by the institution. He reminded architects that the academy had been established "to maintain and perfect" their art. He emphasized that teaching and criticism were not enough. Discussions on taste, physics, and the exact sciences provided, in his opinion, more than enough material for research. And yet architects seemed to be uncommitted, and their work was not at the level of "other academic institutions that every year enrich Europe with their discoveries."[66] The identification of architecture with the ideals of science could hardly be more explicit. The rationalization of traditional practice and the establishment of truly effective rules and precepts were always important concerns of the academic program, but they would only become exclusive interests in nineteenth-century academicism.

Indeed, it should be remembered that the Royal Academy of Architecture, until its functions were suspended in 1793, always managed to reconcile reason and progress with tradition and a belief in the necessity of absolute rules. Discussions centered around good taste, the meaning of the great Renaissance treatises, and the significance of ancient buildings—all of which indicated a general belief in the transcendent character of *mathemata*. This belief accounts for the profound differences, often disregarded by historians, between the eighteenth-century academy and the *École des Beaux Arts* after the French Revolution. Having accepted art as a synonym of formal manipulation, contemporary architects have often misinterpreted the meaning of the apparent reaction of the *Beaux Arts* against technology and its pedagogical programs. It is important to emphasize that academicism, that is, the reduction of practice to a rational theory, together with the application of positive reason to planning (composition) and style (decoration), became dominant only in nineteenth-century architectural education, after Durand's theory was published and taught at the *École Polytechnique* (see chapter 9). During the eighteenth century, the academy provided lectures on mathematical subjects, but the architect was still fundamentally apprenticed as a builder. The objective was to teach young architects how their work could embody taste, that is, a meaningful order, rather than how to implement rules of formal logic.

The Royal Academy of Architecture was the only institution in Europe offering instruction in architecture until Jacques-François Blondel started to teach his own independent course in 1742. He thought of it as similar to other public lectures on physics, geometry, and perspective, which had been offered by Camus, Le Clerc, and Nollet.[67] Thus architecture became an important part of the Enlightenment's program of knowledge.

Blondel offered an elementary course on good taste and two electives: one for architects, concentrating on theory and pro-

Perspective, Gardening, and Architectural Education

portions; and one for builders that was totally devoted to practical geometry and the mechanical arts. Blondel believed that architects should not only know perspective, mensuration, human proportions, surveying, the properties of the conic sections for stonecutting or how to elaborate precise cost estimates; they should be able to apply all these sciences to practice.[68] Indeed, after emphasizing in his *Cours* the knowledge common to architects and engineers, Blondel complained because the former, although usually knowledgeable in theory, "ignored the laws of proportion in their facades" as well as the rules of geometry and trigonometry in surveying. His dream of seeing students apply theory directly, without first having to undergo traditional practice and apprenticeship, constituted a fundamental *raison d'être* for the foundation of his school and is still the basis of most modern architectural institutions.

Only after midcentury did the fields of professional action of architects and civil and military engineers become more clearly defined. Specialization in bridge construction was, indeed, a relatively late phenomenon. Not until 1688 was official certification required for this type of work. And until the end of the seventeenth century, the title of *ingenieur du Roi* was granted indiscriminately to engineers, masons, and architects.[69] Although the *Corps de Ponts et Chaussées* was founded in 1715, the need to unify surveying and design-presentation methods and to improve the training of young engineers did not become truly evident until 1745. Finally, in 1747, Jean-Rodolphe Perronet was called to Paris and appointed head of a new official institution: the *Bureau des Dessinateurs*.

Perronet divided his office into three "classes"; each class was based on the individual's knowledge of practical geometry and its applications to design, stereotomy, mechanics, hydraulics, cost estimates, surveying, and mensuration. In 1756 the *École des Ponts et Chaussées* replaced the previous institution and almost immediately acquired enormous prestige in France and the rest of Europe. In his biography of Perronet, Riche de Prony emphasized the importance of this first school of civil engineering. Perronet had instituted a system of mutual teaching, so that the most advanced students became tutors of their less knowledgeable colleagues. Previously, the members of the *Corps de Ponts et Chaussées* did not have a full curriculum and a sound theoretical background. Riche de Prony thought this problem had been finally solved after Perronet founded his school.[70]

Geometry and Number as Technical Instruments

The curriculum of the institution did not remain constant, but normally it included algebra, analytic and Euclidean geometries, the properties of the conic sections, mechanics, hydraulics, and stereotomy. Infinitesimal calculus was sometimes taught, but was never mandatory. Physics, construction methods, mensuration, and natural history had to be taken elsewhere. The engineers were also required to learn artistic drawing and graphic design, courses usually taught by such architects as Blondel. After the French Revolution, the *École des Ponts et Chaussées* was transformed into a school of specialization for students who had already finished their preparation at the *École Polytechnique*.

Education:
Military
Architecture

The "universal men" of the Renaissance were the first to concern themselves with military architecture, that is, the geometrical determination of the elements of fortification. They considered this science to be a liberal art. During the seventeenth century, military engineers were recruited at random among old officers, builders, and architects. In spite of the great number of treatises on fortification that were published throughout Europe during this century, engineers always learned their craft from their predecessors. Until Sebastien Le Prestre de Vauban instituted a compulsory entrance examination in 1697, the French *Corps du Génie* did not have a defined structure.[71]

The first official examiners were J. Sauveur and F. Chevallier, two geometricians of the Royal Academy of Science. The *marquis* D'Asfeld, *directeur général des fortifications* (1715–1743), wrote to Chevallier stipulating the type of knowledge that should be required to pass the examination. The new officers had to be capable in drawing and mensuration of fortifications, estimating costs, and setting up construction schedules. They had to be familiar with arithmetic, geometry, leveling, and some basic aspects of mechanics and hydraulics, and they had to know how to draw maps. He recommended three theoretical works: Frezier's treatise on stereotomy and Forest de Bélidor's *Science des Ingenieurs* and *Architecture Hydraulique*.[72]

In 1720 the king founded five schools to prepare officers for the *Corps d'Artillerie*; the curricula were based on common mathematical disciplines.[73] But only in 1744 did a royal *arrêt* provide the *Corps du Génie* with a general organization and statutes.[74] In 1748 the *École Royale du Génie* was founded at Meziéres, with the abbé Camus as official examiner. In 1755 his functions were extended to cover the artillery schools, and for three years both *corps* worked together. Their textbook was Camus's *Cours de Mathématiques*. This work, published between 1749 and 1752, discussed arithmetic, geometry, the use of proportions, and the basic tenets of statics and mechanics. It was a rather elementary book based on Camus's lessons to the architects of the academy.

As early as 1753, C. Bossut, a member of the Academy of Sciences and "free associate" of the Academy of Architecture, who had been appointed professor of mathematics at Mezières, tried to introduce perspective, calculus, and dynamics into the curriculum, but the customary examination of Camus was not immediately modified. During the second half of the century, more emphasis was given to experimental physics and practical applications. The abbé Nollet taught physics at Mezières, and a new director, Ramsault, sought permission from the minister to substitute Bossut's course for Camus's. Ramsault felt that in order to improve the quality of the school, the engineers should learn algebra, analytic geometry, and calculus. Only then would they be capable of solving problems of mechanics, strength of materials, retaining walls, and hydraulics. But he also believed that these sciences were too complicated for the majority of students. Therefore he recommended that these subjects be taught in private only to the qualified few.[75] This undoubtedly epitomizes the age's ambivalent attitude toward the possibility of solving technical problems through an *effective* implementation of theory.

Bossut wrote numerous treatises from a truly protopositivistic vantage point, insisting on the uselessness of compiling empirical data without a theory or hypothesis to relate them.[76] His works, which appeared after 1772, were conceived as part of a grand scheme for a mathematical curriculum that was to include, apart from the traditional subjects, analytic geometry, algebra, hydrodynamics, and calculus. His *Traité Elémentaire de Géométrie et de la Manière d'Appliquer l'Algebre à la Géométrie* (1777), regards algebra as "purely intellectual," using signs to represent general relations, while geometry is considered "less abstract" and capable of treating extension only in the figurative sense. Geometry, then, "necessarily [implies] the participation of sight and touch" in establishing relations among lines, surfaces, and bodies. The text also contained such curious problems as the tracing of arches using analytic geometry so that their configurations could follow the determinate equation of a conic section.

Geometry and Number as Technical Instruments

Bossut's attempts to clarify the relations between geometry and algebra and to find practical applications of analytic geometry in building constitute two important contributions to the process of functionalization of geometry. His work surely stimulated his young assistant Gaspard Monge, whose descriptive geometry would eventually have enormous repercussions for architecture. When Bossut was finally appointed official examiner of the school in 1770, Monge took over as professor of mathematics. After 1772 a new curriculum gave greater importance to the teaching of geometrical projections and perspective. Both subjects were now considered tools of precision, indispensable to the military engineer. Geometrical drawing was studied "to find the configuration of any piece of stone or wood" in an architectural element and to trace the five orders, as well as the plans, sections, and elevations of civil and military buildings. Perspective was taught not only "to determine geometrically the shadows of drawing or watercolor" but because it was believed essential for a *true* perception of reality. The study of the rules of perspective "is necessary to educate the eye for the drawing of detailed maps in military operations."[77]

This last curriculum, which thereafter did not change much, also included Nollet's course on experimental physics, natural science, and visits to various industries. The vitality of the school now began to decline, and finally, in 1794 it closed down.[78] Like the *École des Ponts et Chaussées*, this institution was an immediate predecessor of the *École Polytechnique*. The effort to link scientific theory with technical knowledge had a long history, and after 1770, at Mezières, this ideal came close to its realization. Most members of the original academic staff of the world's first truly technological school had received their education in the *École du Génie*.

6

FORTIFICATION, MENSURATION, AND STEREOTOMY

Treatises on fortification published during the second half of the sixteenth century utilized rules of practical geometry to determine the configurations of polygonal plans and their elements. Girolamo Cataneo's *Dell'Arte Militare* (1559) falls within this category. His work, however, was not systematic. Unconcerned with the implications of the geometrical order, he merely described a still meaningful craft.[1] In Simon Stevin's *Oeuvres Mathématiques*, first published in Flemish in 1584, fortification was discussed alongside perspective, statics, and mensuration. This was perhaps the first universal mathematical encyclopedia, a forerunner of the many popular works of this type published in the seventeenth century. The section on fortification was similar to Cataneo's, teaching the tracing of polygonal plans through geometrical operations.[2]

A great number of treatises on military architecture were published in Europe during the seventeenth century. Practically all of them included a description of the geometrical operations necessary to trace the polygonal plans of fortifications. S. Marolois's book on practical geometry, *Géometrie . . . Necessaire à la Fortification* (1628), explained the use of the compass in surveying and many other operations.[3] Also described were methods of calculating the volumes of material necessary to build different parts of a fortification. In another book, *Fortification ou Architecture Militaire* (1628), Marolois used trigonometry to calculate the angles and dimensions of these parts.[4] Although fascinated by the precision of geometrical operations, he disregarded the problems and limitations of reality. Significantly, irregular fortifications, whose perimeters were not an ideal polygon, were hardly mentioned. Another treatise with the same interests was N. Goldman's *La Nouvelle Fortification* (1645). Goldman identified the art of fortification with geometry, claiming that the careful use of geometrical operations was imperative for this "liberal art" to fulfill its purposes.[5]

Milliet Dechales's *L'Art de Fortifier* (1677) betrayed an even greater interest in geometrical operations and regular polygons. All military problems were described in terms of lines and angles, and the text itself was written *more geometrico*.[6] But in the context of Dechales's *Cursus seu Mundus Mathematicus* (1674), the geometrical encyclopedia of knowledge that Guarini so admired as an example of absolute certainty, the symbolic intentionality inherent in these geometrical operations becomes immediately evident.

The underlying intentions of seventeenth-century treatises on fortification are perhaps best discerned in Bernard Palissy's *Recepte*

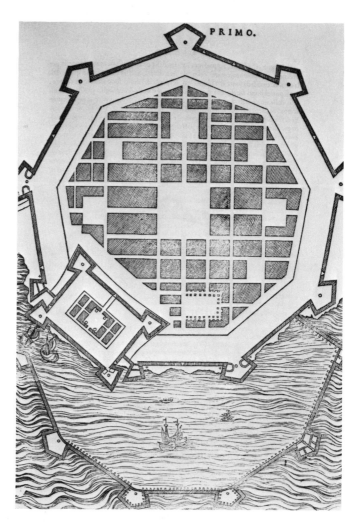

Plan of a nine-sided polygonal fortification, an example from the Renaissance treatise of P. Cataneo, *Architettura* (1554).

Fortification, Mensuration, and Stereotomy

Véritable. After confessing his ignorance of rhetoric, Greek, and Hebrew, this "humble craftsman" defended his design of a fortification against critics who accused him of lacking military experience. He thought that "military art" derived more from a natural sense than practice. Having received from God his ability to understand the art of the land, he could certainly design a fortified city, "consisting mainly of tracings and lines of geometry."[7]

Palissy believed that existing fortified towns failed because their protecting walls were not really part of the towns' architecture. He tried to find better ideas in the treatises of the old masters, but was sadly disappointed. In desperation, he turned to nature and after traversing woods, mountains, and valleys, he arrived at the sea. It was there that he observed "the miraculous protection of mollusks like oysters and snails."[8] God had given these weak animals the ability to build themselves homes, designed "with so much geometry and architecture that not even King Solomon, with all his wisdom, could have produced something similar."[9] Confronted with this marvelous discovery, he fell on his face and adored God, "Who had created all these things for the service and commodity of man."[10]

The sea snail was clearly the best prototype for a fortified city. In case of siege, the city's inhabitants would only have to give up one compartment at a time, making the city practically impregnable. The sections in a spiral plan would be not only beautiful but also useful as buttresses of the external wall, while in peacetime, the walls could be used for housing. Palissy was convinced that only places that God himself had fortified in nature could be better than this model. He praised the "Sovereign Architect" for his inspiration, which should, he believed, guide the "art of geometry and architecture."

This geometry, which God had given to nature, was reproduced by Palissy and others in their own technical endeavours in order to assure the meaning of their works. Jacques Perret de Chambéry's folio of plates (1594) illustrated polygonal and star-shaped fortifications that were surrounded by inscriptions taken from the Psalms of the New Testament.[11] Perret even thanked God for having allowed him to conceive so many marvelous war machines. And war itself, signifying man's obsession to dominate, was perceived in a transcendent light, as a ritual whose goal was to establish order. Military architecture could thus represent an order in which "all nations may praise the Lord" and "live according to His Holy Laws."

Geometry and Number as Technical Instruments

In some early-seventeenth-century treatises, the magical and naturalistic aspects of geometry often appeared to be mere re-statements of older Renaissance notions. Such is the case in P. A. Barca's *Avertimenti e Regole* (1620), which recommended the use of square, pentagonal, or hexagonal fortifications since these figures were symbols of the relation between the human body and the cosmos. God, the divine architect, had created the heavens and earth "with weight, number and measurement," conforming everything to the circle, the most perfect figure. Man, on the other hand, "is a small world. . . . His flesh is the earth, his bones are mountains, his veins are rivers, and his stomach is the sea."[12] Similarly, P. Sardi's *Couronne Imperiale de l'Architecture Militaire* (1623) described regular fortifications using the human body as a metaphor. It also stressed the importance of images in teaching the operations of practical geometry.[13]

Gabrielo Busca's *Architettura Militare* (1619) showed less concern for practical geometry. Busca was more interested in the history of military buildings, the significance of their geographical locations, and the relations between rulers and citizens. He was especially concerned with the rituals of foundation deriving from ancient tradition considered necessary for the effectiveness of fortification. These ceremonies involved the tracing of orthogonal paths that divided the city into four parts (the Roman *quadrattura*), which corresponded to the four regions of the sky, thus emulating the cosmic order.[14] Similar concerns can be detected in *L'Architecture Militaire Moderne* (1648) by Mathias Dögen.[15] Although Dögen was more typical in his belief concerning the crucial role of geometrical operations in fortification, he gave equal importance to the description of the heroic deeds that took place in these buildings. He included long sections in which he provided detailed instructions on how to conquer cities, taken from the "laws" established in the Holy Scriptures.

A few exceptional early treatises showed a more pragmatic understanding of military engineering. Jean-Errard de Bar-le-Duc's *Fortification* (1594)[16] advocates that individuals responsible for the fortification or defense of a city should not only be experienced soldiers with military authority but also good geometricians. This would enable them to invent useful machines and to understand how the proper use of proportion can save unnecessary expenses. Consequently, a military engineer also had to be knowledgeable in some aspects of architecture and masonry.[17] Errard believed that the art of fortification consisted in determining the slope and angles of the foundations of walls. But although he included geometrical methods for describing regular polygons, he devoted most of his work to the explanation of irregular fortifications. This was the logical extension of Errard's belief that location and practical considerations had to be taken into account before designing a fortified city. Simply imposing an arbitrary geometrical figure upon a terrain was insufficient; it was imperative to consider its topography and other particularities. Also, Bonaiuto Lorini's *Delle Fortificazioni* (1597) distinguished between the points and lines of the mathematician and the true problems encountered by the "practical mechanic," whose ability consists in knowing how to foresee the difficulties characteristic of the diverse materials with which he must work.[18]

Whatever the limitations of these early discussions on the importance of an effective technical knowledge, which were often motivated (as it became clear in relation to Palissy's work) by an implicit recognition of the transcendent dimension of human action, they do contrast with the seventeenth century's obsession with regular polygons and geometrical methods. Count Pagan, for example, could recognize in 1645 that the "science of fortifications" was not "purely geometrical."[19] Because the objective was "material" and drew its inspiration from experience, "its most essential postulates depend only upon conjecture." Yet Pagan did nothing more than to provide simple recipes for tracing "small, medium, or large" polygonal fortifications, and he included in his treatise only a brief section on irregular fortification. His typically Baroque identification of geometry with reality appeared in two other books, published in 1647 and 1649. In his *Théorie des Planètes*, Pagan adopted the Copernican planetary system. The second work, however, was devoted to astrology; its intent was "to found this science on geometrical and natural principles"— the same principles that lay at the heart of astronomy. The reader may remember how the synthesis between technical and symbolic intentions that motivated the use of geometrical operations during the Baroque period was most prominent in the work of G. Guarini. His *Trattato di Fortificatione* (1676) appears to have been the last book on military architecture that explicitly assigns geometry symbolic or magical significance.

Inevitably, the epistemological revolution influenced the reduction of military architecture into *ars fabricandi*, which is to say in this case, the rules of practical geometry. During the second half of the century, authors like François Blondel and A. Tacquett wrote about "methods" of fortification and discussed their dif-

Geometry and Number as Technical Instruments

Hexagonal fortification, plan and details from Felibien's *Principes* (1699).

Fortification, Mensuration, and Stereotomy

ferences.[20] And Ozanam's *Traité de Fortification* (1694) took a significant step beyond the Baroque world. Although Ozanam did not discuss ballistics or statics, and while he still believed that regular fortification epitomized the totality of military science, his exposition of the subject was thoroughly systematic. Every problem was solved through a geometrical operation, and nothing was left to chance or personal experience. He included a careful comparative analysis of all existing methods of fortification, including those of Errard, Pagan, Bombelle, Blondel, Sardi, and even Vauban. In his *Cours de Mathématiques . . . Necessaires à un Homme de Guerre* (1699), Ozanam affirmed the priority of mathematics over other sciences, praising its potential to provide absolute certainty. In this and in his works on perspective and anamorphosis, this contemporary of Perrault already perceived mathematics as a merely formal science. He emphasized that, unlike poetry, it did not "provide delicate pleasures" to our "spiritual voluptuousness," its objective being "to prepare men for more solid things."[21]

However, it was the brilliant French Marshall Sebastien Le Prestre de Vauban who first understood the consequences of the Galilean revolution and effectively applied the new science to transform military architecture. Vauban was born in 1633 and was an important figure in the consolidation of France under Louis XIV.[22] He was appointed *commissaire général des fortifications* by Colbert, taking over from a man who apparently had known very little about fortification and who had recommended Renaissance methods, for example, building bastions perpendicular to the walls.[23]

Vauban was responsible for numerous inventions and technical innovations. Generally, however, he retained all the elements of sixteenth-century fortification, developing only Pagan's notion of "defense in depth," which gave greater importance to the "external works"—those parts outside the main wall. Vauban's real contribution took the form of a fundamentally different attitude to the problem. He believed the art of fortification *did not* consist in the application of rules or conceptual geometrical systems, but that it had to derive from experience and common sense.[24] Empirical reality and practical adaptability had to balance geometrical rules.

Significantly, Vauban rejected the idea of writing a book on fortifications.[25] He was convinced that dogmatic systems were totally useless when applied to different situations. For Vauban

Geometry and Number as Technical Instruments

SEBAST. LE PRESTRE, DE VAUBAN
Marêchal de France
Né le 12 Mai 1633. Mort à Paris le 30 Mars 1707.

Sebastien Le Prestre de Vauban, engraving by
Dupuis.

Fortification, Mensuration, and Stereotomy

the geographical and topographical particularities of a place were of paramount importance. Only late in his life did he write a formal treatise on attack, defense, and entrenched camps, in which he summarized his experience and conclusions. He also emphasized that to understand his work, no knowledge of geometry was necessary;[26] reality was more important in war than any conceptual knowledge. In order to besiege a city it was not enough to have its plans. These, he said, could be bought in any bookstore. What truly mattered was a first-hand knowledge of the terrain and the city.

These apparently straightforward remarks are very significant in light of the epistemological revolution and Vauban's special interest in mathematics. His use of the mathematical sciences was clearly devoid of symbolic intent. Vauban constantly employed arithmetic as a tool for cost estimates and statistics; his treatise is full of tables for determining, for example, the amounts of gunpowder, food, infantry, and cavalry that should be available in relation to the number of bastions in a fortification.

Vauban wrote extensively on diverse subjects, but one concern was preeminent: quantitative rational planning.[27] In a paper calling for the reestablishment of the Edict of Nântes, he utilized statistics to argue for the end of the deportation of Protestants, thereby avoiding moral discussions and reducing the problem to a question of political economy.[28] In his study of Vezelay's census, he used ethnic and demographic statistics to devise a method establishing a more equitable taxation law. In 1699 he wrote a report on the French colonies in America, concentrating on the potential of Canada, and described the way to settle new towns through carefully planned stages.[29] There was no trace here of the myths and rituals of foundation evident earlier in the century. For Vauban, only rational quantitative considerations were to determine the choice of a site for a new city. No thought was spent on the traditional question of the place's "meaning."

The precision, order, and clarity of Vauban's own projects, including his specifications and cost estimates, were novel and remarkable. The reports he prepared for each one of his fortifications always contained four parts: (1) general precedents of the work; (2) a detailed description of the constituent parts with reference to the drawings; (3) cost estimates after a careful calculation of volumes of materials used; and (4) special features or advantages of the work. His concern for economy and efficiency in building could also be seen in an earlier work that listed 143 observations on such subjects as foundations, masonry, plan distributions, carpentry, and construction of doors and windows.[30] In a paper on the functions of officers in charge of fortification, he attributed the high cost of these works to the lack of organization in their construction.[31] His method for the presentation of projects and reports was in itself an attempt to overcome these problems through rationalization of the whole building process.

In the same paper, Vauban also provided a profile of a good military engineer. Young men willing to enter the *corps* should have some knowledge of mathematics, geometry, trigonometry, surveying, geography, civil architecture, and drawing. He believed that an examination to test candidates' abilities was necessary and that it alone should be considered in granting appointments. After 1699 such an examination became institutionalized. That same year Vauban was voted an honorary member of the Royal Academy of Science. After his death in 1707, Fontenelle eulogized the late *marechal de France*,[32] pointing out that he had brought mathematics from heaven to solve the needs of man. This statement alone, equating Vauban's achievements to Galileo's, would be sufficient to postulate the *marechal* as the first modern engineer. Fontenelle also emphasized the importance of Vauban's rejection of the older systems of fortification. Vauban had proved through his practice that there was no universal manner applicable to all situations. The difficult problems of military art could not be solved by fixed rules, but required the natural resources of genius.

Vauban was also the first to apply a different sort of fixed rules—those of mechanics—to determine the necessary thickness of fortification walls. His contribution represented the first true application of statics to military engineering.[33] Vauban also successfully modified the shape and disposition of bastions in relation to the lines and properties of artillery fire. This was an old concern expressed by the architects of the Renaissance. Vauban's seemingly minimal adjustments were so effective, however, that they were copied throughout Europe during the eighteenth and nineteenth centuries. With Vauban, geometry in fortification became a truly efficient instrument for determining the configuration of elements in relation to the location of artillery, topography, and the physical characteristics of cities. His work and methods were totally different from those of his predecessors and contemporaries, for whom the regular geometrical shape of fortifications was an end in itself, full of symbolic connotations, constituting both the most important part of the process and its ultimate justification.

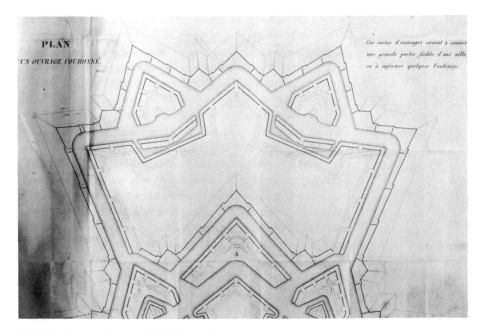

Detail for the external works of a fortification, from
Vauban's *Défense des Places*.

By the end of the seventeenth century, Vauban was already famous in Europe. Even before his death, various authors tried to work his contributions into a "system," which only revealed how difficult it was for his contemporaries to understand his thought and the transformations it implied. Such was the case in treatises published between 1669 and 1713 by Cambray, Pfeffinger, Sturm, and even Christian Wolff, who reproduced Vauban's "system" in his *Cours de Mathématiques*.[34] In the eighteenth century, various publications still compared Vauban's system to some others, and as late as 1861 Prevost de Vernoist defended Vauban's method as the best.[35] All this notwithstanding, the number of treatises on fortification published during the Enlightenment decreased conspicuously. Especially after the second decade of the eighteenth century, fortification was no longer the dominant theme of military engineering.

The engineers of the eighteenth century, educated in the new technical schools, came to realize that the determination of the polygonal plan of a fortification was only a minor problem compared to the questions of mechanics or hydraulics, which had to be resolved in order to build adequately and efficiently. This new scientific interest was manifested initially in the works of Bernard Forest de Bélidor, professor of mathematics in the artillery schools and author of three influential texts. Bélidor was a member of the scientific societies of London and Prussia and a *membre correspondant* of the Parisian Academy of Science.

In his most important book, *La Science des Ingénieurs* (1729), he coherently outlined the discoveries and contributions of Vauban. Bélidor, better than most, could appreciate Vauban's achievement. As the author of the first truly scientific work on military architecture,[36] he criticized sixteenth- and seventeenth-century treatises for having merely taught how to trace polygons and the names of parts without having dealt with the real problems of construction. Likewise, he rejected Pagan's book and, significantly, all those treatises that pretended to disclose Vauban's "system," works which, he remarked, the *marechal* himself had disowned.

La Science des Ingénieurs went into many editions, including two in the nineteenth century annotated by Navier, the famous professor of structural design at the *École Polytechnique*. The book was divided into six chapters whose contents and objectives explained the "science" of the engineer. The first chapter was dedicated to the determination of dimensions in masonry retaining walls (that is, the external walls of fortifications) in relation to the thrust of the earth and the spacing between buttresses. In the second chapter, Bélidor examined the thrust of vaults and determined general laws by which to find the dimensions of vertical structural elements with regard to vaults' shapes and uses in civil and military buildings. The third chapter analyzed the quality of materials and their appropriate uses, describing the building procedure for the most important parts of a fortification, "from the tracing of the project to its complete execution."[37] The fourth and fifth chapters, significantly, concentrated on civil architecture. They dealt with technical problems, providing some practical rules for buildings, and included a long section on the five classical orders. The final chapter was an example of *devis*: the application of the science to one specific project; this entailed the precise elaboration of specifications and cost estimates in the manner of Vauban's report for Neuf-Brisach.

A conflict between a theory intentionally postulated as *ars fabricandi* and an eminently traditional practice is explicit from the very first pages. Bélidor believed that mathematics was finally capable of perfecting the arts, but that very few people understood its power.[38] Artists and craftsmen retained greater faith in practice to solve technical problems. This prejudice, thought Bélidor, had to be overcome. Reason must elucidate experience; otherwise, knowledge was imperfect: "In *architecture*, for example, no progress can be observed with regard to certain essential points that constitute its basis, in spite of the fact that this art has been cultivated for a very long time."[39] Bélidor declared that with the exception of a few rules about "convenience and taste for decoration," architecture did not have precise and exact principles with respect to "all its other parts" (for example, principles of statics for determining the dimensions of structural elements and avoiding the use of superfluous material).

Bélidor stressed that architecture, having always depended on proportions, should by definition be subject to mathematics. Architects of the past, "lacking any knowledge of mechanics or algebra," had always created excessively expensive works; they had been incapable of saving material since they were unsure about the stability of their buildings. Young architects, admitted Bélidor, learn through experience, but they should not waste their lives repeating what had already been done. He thought it was possible to replace experience by an *ars fabricandi* based on geometry and mathematics: "This knowledge will be as instructive as their own practice."[40]

Geometry and Number as Technical Instruments

Bélidor's treatise constitutes the first methodical attempt to solve the problems of construction in engineering and architecture through the application of geometrical rules founded on statics. In his *Nouveau Cours de Mathématique* (1725) for the artillery schools, he refused to deal with useless mathematical knowledge. Instead, he applied the laws of dynamics to "the art of throwing bombs," summarized Varignon's book on mechanics, and rejected the merely geometrical rules of late-Gothic ancestry that had been often used to determine the dimensions of the vertical supporting elements of arches and vaults (rules popularized by Derand and F. Blondel during the seventeenth century).[41]

Some interesting comments, from the perspective of the early nineteenth century, were added by Navier to *La Science*. Navier asserted that the hypothesis in Bélidor's solution to the problem of retaining walls was false, that it was not "in accordance with the phenomenon as it occurs in nature."[42] Bélidor considered the walls as solid pieces, disregarding the true composition of masonry. Nevertheless, Navier justified Bélidor's hypothesis by pointing out that in the early eighteenth century, the solution had to appear as absolutely certain in order to convince skeptical practitioners. In the second chapter, Bélidor applied De la Hire's mechanical hypothesis about the behavior of vaults. Navier added a note in a similar vein, stating that De la Hire's hypothesis had been generally accepted until, after much systematic observation, a new theory was established late in the eighteenth century that actually considered "natural effects." The implications of Navier's different standpoint will become clear in a later chapter. It is important to emphasize here, however, the great significance of Bélidor's treatise, which was considered by Navier as the point of departure for effective scientific engineering, and which in spite of its "mistakes" demonstrated technological interest.

In chapter 4, Bélidor focuses on the problem of distribution and the general characteristics of fortified cities and military buildings. Like most French writers on architecture during the eighteenth century, he considered "convenience" a fundamental value. Consequently, he wished to provide general rules for building derived from common sense, but which also posited a relation between physical proportions in general and convenience. Although engineers could not pretend to be first-rate architects, they should appreciate the proportions necessary for a building to be "comfortable and graceful." After Bélidor's description of building details and construction systems, Navier added a note indicating that anything missing could be found in Rondelet's

Art de Bâtir (1802). The relation established between Bélidor's *Science* and the first truly effective textbook on construction is, once again, highly revealing.[43]

The theme of the sixth chapter would also receive its definitive formulation toward the beginning of the nineteenth century in Rondelet's book. This was the elaboration of *devis*, or the description of comprehensive programs for the planning of building operations that included, at a conceptual level, considerations that had been previously taken into account only through practice. Bélidor stressed that these programs were the most important part of engineering theory since they discussed detailed specifications, the order in which the work must proceed, exact dimensions of even the smallest parts, and "all circumstances of construction" that might help to prevent accidents.[44] These programs were already attempts to *reduce* practice to a preconceived rational plan. Bélidor took the idea from Vauban and perhaps also from Pierre Bullet, an architect of the academy who, also late in the seventeenth century, had shown the importance of *devis* in architecture. But in his *Science*, Bélidor defined precisely the objectives of such programs, asserting their crucial importance for scientific building.

Now we come to what might appear as the odd chapter from the standpoint of nineteenth- and twentieth-century engineering. For Bélidor, an engineer should be as capable of building a palace as a fortification, and chapter 5 betrays his traditional concern with decoration. Significantly, he also criticized in this context Baroque treatises that had ignored the rules of "Vitruvius, Palladio, Vignola or Scamozzi" and taught instead only methods for tracing polygons.[45] Bélidor was also critical of "the confusion of Gothic architecture" and the exaggerations of Baroque artists like Guarini.[46] He obviously rejected all magical and symbolic implications of Baroque geometrical operations, but he believed instead that the rules of the classical orders were extremely important for engineers. So rather than trying to improve upon the "science" of proportions, which "had already attained a high degree of perfection," he chose to reproduce Vignola's rules "for the simplicity of [Vignola's] recommended measurements."[47]

After repeating the Vitruvian myth on the origin of the orders, Bélidor devoted more than seventy pages to their rules. He then set down some maxims on the problem of "distribution"—in his opinion, the most essential part of architecture because it dealt with the efficient use of available land.[48] Bélidor's "wise appreciation" of this problem won the approval of Navier, who pointed

Geometry and Number as Technical Instruments

Plate showing the parts of the Tuscan and the Doric orders, from Bélidor's *Science des Ingénieurs*.

Fortification, Mensuration, and Stereotomy

out that these maxims had been consecrated and developed by Durand in his *Précis des Leçons* and were "treasured" by the students of the *École Polytechnique*. Navier added, however, that other aspects of this chapter were not as important as Bélidor had imagined. For example, the rules of the classical orders were useful but not fundamental. "The architect," wrote Navier, "should know them like a writer grasps the use of language. With this knowledge, however, one can still produce very bad works."[49]

For Navier, the rules of the orders were already a formal system, which was not necessarily meaningful in itself. In his opinion, only Durand had been capable of truly overcoming old prejudices by placing architecture on solid and positive grounds that recognized convenience as a unique and exclusive principle: "a perfect relation established between the disposition of a building and the use to which it is destined."[50] Navier emphasized that design was nothing more than "the resolution of a problem whose data are found in the conditions of *solidity, economy,* and *utility* that the work must fulfill."[51] Durand had shown how this principle of convenience, far from contradicting decoration, was the only sure guide to providing building with true character and beauty.[52]

The similarities and differences that Navier observed between Bélidor and Durand are significant and illuminate the immense distance between them. Bélidor clearly attached great importance to traditional architectural theory and imagined it as part of the science of the engineer, perceiving no contradictions between the two fields. To his way of thinking, the time-honored Vitruvian categories of decoration, distribution, and solidity of construction were not independent values, but arose from more fundamental, unstated and irreducible symbolic intentions.

In this respect, it is interesting to note how Vauban defended his projects to beautify the gateways of his fortifications from official criticism. While Louvois cared only to save the money and effort involved in this task, Vauban insisted upon the importance of entry and its meaning. The presence of this residual symbolism, perhaps not suprising in Bélidor's teacher, appeared even more explicitly after 1750. The engineer Joseph de Fallois published in 1768 a work entitled *L'École de la Fortification*, whose stated objective was to enlarge upon Bélidor's *Science*.[53] It might be expected that this work would develop the scientific principles and technological interests found in Bélidor's book. Instead, De Fallois emphasized the importance of geometrical methods for tracing the plans of polygonal fortifications; he also reproduced Coëhorn and Vauban's "systems" and repeated some of the same

Geometry and Number as Technical Instruments

rules concerning the resolution of problems in mechanics that had been in use fifty years earlier. Even more revealing was De Fallois's attempt to establish the fundamental and general principles of military building. Following a train of thought very similar to Laugier's, and obsessed like so many of his contemporaries with finding the natural origin of his activity, De Fallois drew up fifteen basic principles that could be derived from the original character of primitive fortification: man's need to defend himself from animals and other men. This mythical history clearly acted as a metaphysical justification for established principles. This was perhaps the last work on military engineering in which a myth constituted the ultimate foundation of practice and such speculation was intended to ensure the transcendence of military building.

Mensuration

At this point, it is important to examine the applications of practical geometry and arithmetic to mensuration, surveying, and other aspects of the building craft. In Bernard Palissy's *Recepte Véritable*, the symbolic content of practical geometry used in the configuration of the physical world is made evident by its inclusion in the traditional anthropocosmological structure. This is brought out in an imaginary midnight dialogue among his instruments.[54] The compass, the ruler, the plummet, the level, the astrolabe, and a fixed and an adjustable triangle discuss their respective attributes, stating the roles they play in construction and the metaphors they embody. The compass, for example, demands a place of honor among the others, being in charge of "conducting the measure of all things. . . . Men without compass are admonished and asked to live according to the compass." The ruler describes its merits in these terms: "I conduct all things directly. . . . Of an individual of dissolute customs, one says he leads an unruly life. . . . Without me he cannot live rightly." And the triangle claims, "I determine the perpendicular angles of corners. . . . No building could stand without my help." The astrolabe then points out that it has the greatest merit because its domain is beyond the clouds and it determines the weather, the seasons, fertility, and sterility. Finally intervening in the noisy dispute, Palissy tells his instruments that the true place of honor belongs to man, who gave them all form.

The use of practical geometry for the tracing of walls and foundations (in order to ensure verticality or symmetry) is obviously as old as the building craft itself. Only toward the end of the Renaissance, however, did concerns with mensuration and to-

Fortification, Mensuration, and Stereotomy

pography become more dominant, as the theoretical universe of these sciences acquired greater specificity. The initial attempt to systematize the processes of measurement appeared in Leone Battista Alberti's *Ludi Matematici*,[55] while the first of a long series of books on the subject appears to have been Cosimo Bartoli's *Del Modo de Misurare le Distantie* (1564), which was followed in 1565 by Silvio Belli's *Libro del Misurar con la Vista*. Belli taught how to measure distances using an instrument, the *quadrato geometrico*, that employed the law of similar triangles.[56]

The military engineer G. Cataneo also published a book on mensuration in 1584.[57] His work was unsystematic and practically impossible to apply. But the fundamental purpose of measuring all sorts of areas and volumes and providing methods for surveying was already evident and would be discussed in similar treatises for the next hundred years. Simon Stevin included a section on practical geometry in his *Oeuvres Mathématiques*.[58] Stevin stressed the importance of this science, explaining the special "communion" that existed between extension and number: "What can be done to one, it is also possible to do to the other."[59] He dealt with problems of mensuration in terms of addition, subtraction, multiplication, or division of lines, areas, and volumes. His "arithmetic geometry" was not only a forerunner of Descartes's analytic geometry but also showed how difficult it was to conceive mathematics as an abstract science, devoid of figure and apart from reality.

In the new intellectual atmosphere of the Baroque period, treatises on practical geometry proliferated and were simplified. But the authors of these works never seemed particularly interested in the effective applicability of their theories. The geometry of the seventeenth century, even on this level, basked in an aura of transcendental abstraction. Some texts, as in Stevin's case, were part of universal geometrical systems. Milliet Dechales included in his *Cursus seu Mundus Mathematicus* (1674) a dissertation on practical geometry that was mindful of trigonometry and stereometry.[60] Other authors described specific instruments of measurement; for example, Casati's "proportional compass" and Ozanam's universal "geometrical square," which was capable "of solving all the problems of practical geometry without the use of calculations."[61] Ozanam also wrote in 1684 a comprehensive treatise on practical geometry in which the methods for determining areas and volumes were precise and easily applicable. But this was still not the main concern of his book. Avoiding the exposition

Geometry and Number as Technical Instruments

of theoretical principles, he revealed a fascination with geometrical exercises. We need only remember here Guarini's reduction of all architectural elements to geometrical figures in his *Modo de Misurare le Fabriche*.[62] All construction techniques were subsumed in a transcendental and universal geometrical science.

Only toward the end of the seventeenth century did treatises on practical geometry begin to reveal an interest to relate it directly and effectively to actual problems of building. Coinciding with the epistemological transformations of this time, the use of geometry and mathematics to solve problems of construction assumed an unprecedented importance—thereafter becoming essential for the success of any building task. Geometry and mensuration ceased to be an end in themselves, but began to be applied as mere tools for the elaboration of construction programs and cost estimates. This transformation was evident initially in the works of Pierre Bullet (1639–1716), one of the first elected members to the Royal Academy of Architecture. His name was frequently associated in the minutes with discussions on technical problems.[63] In 1675 he published *Traité de l'Usage du Pantomètre*, which illustrated the use of an instrument for determining all sorts of topographic angles and accessible and inaccessible distances; and in 1688 he published *Traité du Nivellement*, which provided the theory and practice of another leveling instrument he had invented. Following in the steps of De la Hire, Bullet saw the possibilities in applying the laws of mechanics to architecture and wrote a few papers on the subject.[64]

Bullet's most important work, however, was his *Architecture Pratique*, published initially in 1691 and then quite often during the eighteenth century. This was the first book to provide a concrete application of mathematics to the problems of mensuration and the determination of volumes in all types of building operations.[65] Bullet claimed he had been shocked when he realized that there were no treatises on a subject that was "an absolutely indispensable science for determining with precision the cost of a building." Bullet was familiar with earlier works by Du Cerceau and Louis Savot, which included measurements on the buildings they illustrated and some notions about the determination of volumes of materials, but these were unsystematic operations without a true method.[66]

Bullet acknowledged that the theory of architecture included the principles of proportion (necessary to harmony and decorum), good judgment, drawing, the reading of important authors, the

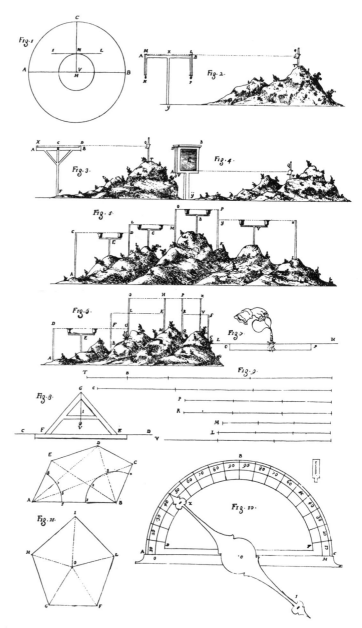

Surveying operations, from Guarini's *Architettura Civile*.

Geometry and Number as Technical Instruments

study of ancient and modern buildings, and mathematics (mainly geometry).[67] But he also insisted that to be an architect, practice was indispensable; it did not suffice to be an *homme des lettres.*[68]

Bullet's *Architecture* started with a general introduction to practical geometry, followed by a careful description of the construction of the typical parts of a building by way of explaining the operations of measurement. A rule based on mechanics was put forward for determining the thickness of a retaining wall in relation to its height and the thrust of the earth. (This was the same problem that had concerned Vauban and whose solution would be reproduced later by Bélidor.) Bullet also considered methods for determining a wooden beam's dimensions and provided a series of rules for finding its depth in relation to the load. But he concluded that due to the infinite qualitative differences among types of wood, such rules could not be absolute.[69] He then provided detailed methods for determining exact quantities of material necessary in each of the building trades: carpentry, masonry, plumbing, glazing, locksmithing, paving, roofing, and so forth. Bullet discussed legal problems, explained building regulations, and finished his book with an illustration of *devis*, that is, detailed specifications and cost estimates for one specific example.

Bullet's architectural intentions were essentially identical to Vauban's and Bélidor's concerns in military engineering. The implications of this reduction of practice to a conceptual program should be apparent. *Architecture Pratique* represented the first attempt to teach methods leading to the establishment of precise construction programs based on quantitative data, including costs, general and particular specifications, and building systems.

In the area of civil engineering, H. Gautier in his *Traité des Ponts* (1714) voiced similar interests. Precision in the design and a comprehensive *devis* were considered extremely important for the successful construction of bridges.[70] The reader may recall how this concern in fact prompted the foundation of Perronet's office.[71] During the second half of the century, Perronet's own projects were considered exemplary for their exactness and for taking into account many and diverse factors.

During the Enlightenment, mathematics was seen only as a practical tool in texts concerned with building techniques, and its instrumental value in construction programs was recognized by most French architects. The general interest in technical problems and the quantitative methods needed to solve these problems increased considerably throughout the eighteenth century. The

Fortification, Mensuration, and Stereotomy

works by Frezier, Patte, and Potain, and also D'Aviler's *Cours d'Architecture* (1696), Jacques-François Blondel's *De La Distribution des Maisons* (1737), Jambert's *Architecture Moderne* (1764), and another book of the same title attributed to Briseux (1728), are only a few among the many treatises on civil architecture that were concerned with the quality of building materials, foundations, specifications, building systems, or structural soundness and efficiency.[72] Many articles touching upon the building trades appeared in Diderot's *Encyclopédie*, and the Academy of Science continued a systematic study of the crafts that it had begun in the late seventeenth century.

It should be noted that practical geometry and mathematics were not used in the same way in systematic construction programs outside France. Geometrical operations always retained some measure of symbolic power.[73] New treatises on surveying and mensuration, very similar in spirit and content to books of the Baroque period, were published in Italy throughout the eighteenth century.[74] And though G. A. Alberti dealt with more complex problems in his *Trattato della Misura delle Fabbriche* (1757),[75] his lack of interest in the applicability of theory to the solution of real technical problems was nevertheless conspicuous. In many of these books, the traditional connotations of geometry still appeared, often incoherently. G. F. Cristiani, for example, published a text on "the usefulness and delight" of models in military architecture. After mentioning Bélidor, Galileo, Leibniz, Descartes, and the virtues of geometrical calculations and physical experiments, Cristiani emphasized (as did Ricatti) the harmonic structure of perception and the human body. Hence he opted for the "necessity" of employing scale models in fortification.[76]

In England, William Halfpenny used geometrical projections to determine the configuration of all sorts of arches and vaults in his *Art of Sound Building* (1725).[77] He complained about the constant mistakes incessantly committed in practice and provided a careful explanation of brick construction. In *The Modern Builder's Assistant* (1757), he included a catalog with a detailed description of projects, but his cost estimates were very general, not unlike those produced by Du Cerceau in the sixteenth century.[78]

During the second half of the eighteenth century more empirical subjects, such as the application of appropriate methods of measurement and a more precise determination of the areas and volumes of geometry, began to be taught in the French technical schools. This led to the production of eminently quantitative *devis*, which became increasingly effective instruments of technical domination in architecture and engineering. Eventually, the rational planning and programming of construction became the basis of building operations in the industrialized world. The culmination of this process, however, would only take place during the early nineteenth century when the science of measurement and geometrical drawing, the two disciplines that could implement the reduction of the reality of building practice to two dimensions, had become sufficiently systematized.

Stereotomy

Stereotomy, the use of geometric projections in determining the shape and dimensions of stone or wooden elements in arches, vaults, trusses, stairs, and domes, was specifically a French concern. It was initially incorporated in Philibert de l'Orme's *Architecture* (1567), the first original architectural treatise published in that country to show a Renaissance influence. De l'Orme devoted several chapters of his book to illustrate the use of horizontal and vertical projections in determining in two dimensions the precise configuration of complex parts of buildings. This method of simultaneous projections was never used before the Renaissance. Dürer used similar techniques in his studies on the human body in 1528 and in his research on conic sections in 1525.[79] Generally, however, stereotomy was not an effective technical method during the sixteenth century. Of the problems studied by De l'Orme, for example, the solutions were so specific that it is impossible to understand them at a merely conceptual level. The fundamental dimension was still the Gothic craftsmen's experience. Without it theory was useless, and even with such experience, theory was practically irrelevant to technique. The plates illustrating the use of projections in De l'Orme's *Architecture* did not constitute a method; they did not derive from a general geometrical theory capable of generalizing specific solutions of specific problems.

Several works on stereotomy were written during the seventeenth century. In 1642, Mathurin Jousse published *Le Secret de l'Architecture*, in which he claimed that although he admired the buildings of antiquity, many of them failed to fulfill one's expectations because they were built by craftsmen who ignored the necessary geometrical tracings for stonecutting.[80] He was aware that neither Vitruvius nor Renaissance authors had written on the subject and believed that De l'Orme's two chapters were too complicated for craftsmen. His own work was therefore intentionally simple, reducing to the minimum the elements of each problem and the lines of projection. But in his attempt to provide a strictly useful technical instrument for carpenters and stone-cutters, he produced, in fact, a work that was incapable of coming to terms with the real complexity of the problems.

In accordance with his interest in technical problems related to construction, Jousse encouraged young architects to study arithmetic, geometry, dynamics, and statics. In his *L'Art de la Charpenterie*, he provided geometrical descriptions of all sorts of trusses, centering, and roofing and a complete catalog of all known elements for wood construction. Although there were no explicit symbolic intentions in Jousse's use of practical geometry, he referred to carpentry as the art of original architectural ornament; and above all, he believed that the exposition of the craftsman's geometry was like the revelation of a transcendent secret: the essential *modus operandi* of architecture. These echoes of the late medieval world were obviously in perfect accord with the implications of the Baroque geometrization of the cosmos.

The Jesuit François Derand published in 1643 *L'Architecture des Voûtes*. Much more extensive, specialized, and ambitious than the works of his predecessors, this treatise was intended both for architects and craftsmen. Derand maintained that to learn stereotomy, practice was indispensable. It was not sufficient only to read about it because in the mechanical arts, "practice is not invariably linked to the laws of rigorous geometry."[81] His book included tracings for all sorts of masonry works and their geometric projections. Derand used a more specific technical language than previous authors. An understanding of his work demanded a knowledge of geometry, careful and systematic reading, and constant practice. The solutions of the problems were, nevertheless, very similar to those proposed by De l'Orme, whose *Architecture* Derand frequently cited.

Dechales also included stereotomy in his *Cursus seu Mundus Mathematicus*, as one more discipline subject to the transcendent order of a universal geometry.[82] A considerable section on this science was an important part of Guarini's *Architettura Civile* and was taken fundamentally from Derand's treatise. The symbolic concern underlying Guarini's interest in stereotomy is now evident. Also, François Blondel included problems of stereotomy among the "principal" and most difficult in architecture.[83]

During the seventeenth century, there were no autonomous techniques claiming to derive their value from efficiency or applying their specific parameters to decision making in architecture.

The geometry implicit in vault construction and other stereotomic marvels constituted, like the mathematical order of a fugue, both the structure of the work and the ultimate source of its meaning. The description of geometrical projections in treatises was the elucidation of an eminently symbolic (that is, poetic) operation.

The great exception to this rule appeared, perhaps not surprisingly, in the work so far ahead of its time of G. Desargues. Stereotomy was one of the disciplines for which his universal geometrical method would serve as the foundation. He established the theoretical principles of his "universal manner" in the *Brouillon-Project*, a small pamphlet published in 1640. This was followed by a more extensive treatise on stonecutting published by Bosse in 1643.[84]

While Derand's *Architecture des Voûtes* was still being published in 1743 and 1755, Desargues's *Brouillon-Project*, containing the basic postulates of projective geometry, remained unknown until the nineteenth century. It is clear that masons and architects could not comprehend Desargues's attempt to replace practice by an all-embracing general theory. In *La Pratique du Trait... pour la Coupe des Pierres*, Desargues indicated that "the means to do something" were an essential part of any art. Theory, in his opinion, had to include an explanation of these technical means and not only an elucidation of the art's objectives. These technical means could be "exact, developed through reason," or imprecise, deriving from approximation and the intuition of craftsmen. Desargues was the first to argue so strongly for the need to implement exact technical means.

He believed that in order to invent the rules of any art, one should know its "reasons," but it was not always necessary to be a craftsman. This assertion contrasts sharply with the commonplace acceptance of the role of practice as propounded by Jousse or Derand. Desargues recognized three aspects in any activity, all important, but ordered hierarchically: first, the theory— a framework in which to invent and establish the rules of practice; second, the rules themselves, derived directly from theory; and third, practice—the execution of these rules, somehow inferior, obliged to follow strictly the prescriptions of theory.

Desargues was conscious of the fact that no one before him had reduced the art of stonecutting to a set of methical and universal principles. He pointed out that other treatises had only solved specific problems relating to the times in which they were written. Alluding to Jousse, Desargues reminded his readers that not long ago each projection and tracing was "considered a secret

Fortification, Mensuration, and Stereotomy

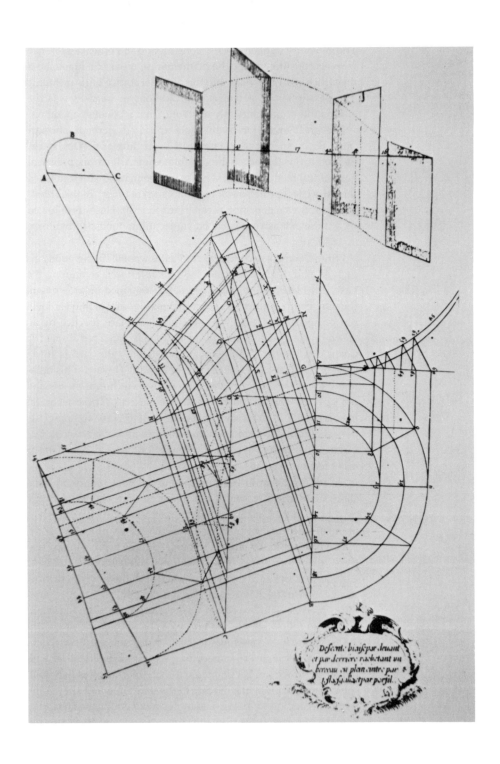

Descente biaisé par deuant
et par derriere rachetant vn
berceau ou plan entre par
s flasfoillis par porfil.

Geometry and Number as Technical Instruments

Geometric projections applied to the stereotomic description of a vault, from F. Derand's *L'Architecture des Voûtes* (1643).

Stereotomic virtuosity in the vaulting of the *orangerie* in the Palace of Versailles, designed by J. H. Mansart (1681–1686).

Fortification, Mensuration, and Stereotomy

that had to be learned by heart. . . ."[85] He proposed instead a simple and unique method that could be used to solve *any* problem. It sufficed to follow a set of step-by-step rules, regardless of the operator's firsthand knowledge of the craft. Desargues thought that the architect should provide the craftsmen with precise stereotomic tracings to cut every piece of stone, just as he provided plans, sections, and elevations. Architects should never allow the masons to invent these tracings since they had nothing more to go on than their own experience.

During the last decade of the seventeenth century and the beginning of the eighteenth century, there were some discussions about stereotomy in the academy.[86] But generally speaking, the architects of the Enlightenment, in contrast to their Baroque predecessors, were not interested in geometrical projections. The only important work on stereotomy written during the eighteenth century was Amédée-François Frezier's *La Théorie et la Pratique de la Coupe des Pierres et des Bois* (1737). Frezier was a highly regarded military engineer and in 1712 was made responsible for the construction of several French fortifications in Europe. His was one of the textbooks recommended by D'Asfeld to the students at Mezières.

Frezier wrote his book believing that theory was the "soul" of both the arts and the sciences. His interest was to elucidate the "geometrical reasons of tracings used in architecture" because this dealt with the most difficult part of practice, namely, the "exactness, solidity, and propriety" of all types of vaults.[87] Three preliminary dissertations preceded this voluminous work. In the first, Frezier proved the "usefulness of theory in the arts related to architecture" by arguments very similar to those used by Bélidor in his *Science*. He emphasized the importance of theory as a technical instrument and its effectiveness in practice—something denied by most of his contemporaries. Frezier stressed that we should not wait for practice to teach us and that reflection and theory hastened the way to the solution of problems. His objective was to provide a different route from that of other authors, who had considered stereotomy from a standpoint "too close" to practice.

Unlike seventeenth-century architects, Frezier felt that he had to *justify* his interest in geometry, citing examples drawn from *mechanics*. Frezier claimed that before geometry and mechanics had been applied to architecture, the structural soundness of vaults was not assured; they lasted only a short time and had to be demolished, were not pleasant to behold, or, because the di-

Geometry and Number as Technical Instruments

mensions of their supports were exaggerated, were unnecessarily expensive.[88] With regard to construction, Frezier adopted De la Hire's hypothesis, thereby showing that he understood how statics could be applied to architecture and engineering. He rejected seventeenth-century geometrical methods for determining the dimensions of piers and emphasized the importance of mechanics as an example of a truly effective and indispensable theory of architecture. The associations established by Frezier between a theory conceived as *ars fabricandi* and the geometrical theories of statics underscore his comprehension of mechanics as the paradigmatic modern science. His interest in geometry arose from his perception of mechanics as an instrument capable of controlling matter—not, as had been the case among his predecessors, from a belief in the immanent symbolic attributes of geometrical operations.

Frezier stressed that military engineers should be cognizant of geometry, mechanics, and hydraulics when planning their attacks or building fortifications. Stereotomy was indispensable not only for them but for architects as well. He criticized earlier treatises for not being sufficiently methodical and, with the exception of Derand's book, for presenting the subject matter only to craftsmen. What was needed was a book for architects and engineers who already knew something about geometry. Significantly, Frezier had to conclude his first dissertation with the admission that the "natural geometry" of the craftsman was usually enough to solve most problems of stone- or woodcutting. His theoretical *tour de force* was therefore rendered ineffective by a traditional practice that was for the most part still successful. Indeed, this was the paradox faced by most eighteenth-century theoreticians. Nevertheless, Frezier believed in the importance of providing a method that would allow the architect to solve any stereotomic problem, regardless of its complexity. This, once again, attests to the architect's interest in technological control, which originally was motivated by the epistemological revolution, and which appeared in the sphere of theory long before its effective implementation during the nineteenth century.

Frezier's intention, therefore, was to postulate a general theory of stonecutting as an autonomous technique that could direct the craftsman's work in the execution of any structural element of a building capable of being treated as an aggregate of smaller pieces. And its principles are necessarily derived from geometry, mechanics, and statics. Frezier's first volume was devoted to geo-

The uses of geometry, an allegory on the cover page
of Frezier's treatise on stereotomy (by courtesy of
Daidalos, Berlin).

Geometry and Number as Technical Instruments

metrical theory and discussed conic sections, intersections of solid bodies, properties of all types of curves, projections on flat and spheric surfaces of arches and vaults, and a method for finding the voussoir's angles. The text, full of neologisms and technical terms, often criticized the absence of principles in previous works on the subject. It is important to note, however, that Frezier only referred briefly to Bosse's *La Pratique du Trait* as "a totally different system" that had been derived from Desargues's and that had never become popular.[89]

In fact, two full volumes of Frezier's treatise were devoted to practical applications. But in spite of his intentions, his theory was not truly systematic and universal; it never went beyond Euclidean geometry and was therefore limited to specifics. Each example ultimately depended on intuition and the particular properties of the figures or bodies involved. The complexity of the operations involved in treating these figures and bodies within the framework of Euclidean geometry amounted to a dead end. And because the exercises were hardly related to the much more simple problems of conventional practice, his book was not used by architects, engineers, or craftsmen. The editor of the 1760s version of D'Aviler's popular *Cours d'Architecture* included a small section on stereotomy in which he criticized Desargues, "who hid all that he wanted to teach," and Frezier, whose book he found extremely complicated. He recommended instead Derand's *Architecture des Voûtes* because in stonecutting, "practice is preferable to theory."[90]

Frezier's book seemed to be addressed to some imaginary *virtuosi* who might find pleasure in mathematical complexity. In any case, it is clear from Frezier's interest in proportion and the classical orders, and from the polemic in which he supported Patte's criticism of Soufflot's mathematical determinism, that he still perceived *mathemata* not only as a source of stability or durability but also, however ambiguously, as the ultimate origin of beauty.[91] It could be concluded, therefore, that with the exception of Desargues's work, the relation between the theory and practice of stereotomy did not effectively change during the seventeenth and eighteenth centuries. The problems of projection were indeed solved in different ways by different authors, each of whom employed manifold graphic systems. But these techniques were not capable of sufficient precision; and the reduction of three-dimensional reality to the plane was never really thorough enough to provide an effective, rational control over stone- or woodcutting operations.

7

STATICS AND STRENGTH OF MATERIALS

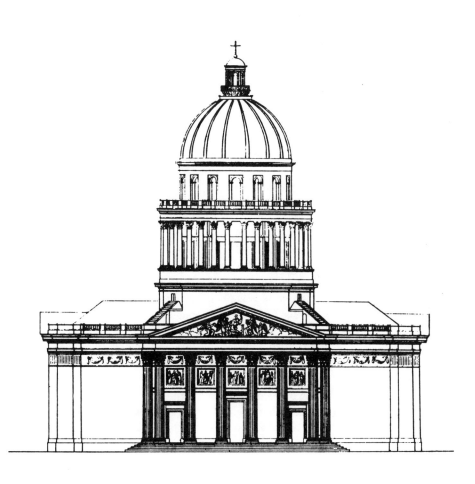

The reorganization of the heavens by Copernicus and Galileo brought about not only a transformation of Western man's intellectual sensibility but also a dislocation of his place in relation to reality. The most fundamental presuppositions of mental space were reversed. Simple events of everyday life, particularly motion, began to be conceived as much more complex phenomena. Robert Boyle defined nature as "the inventory of bodies which constitute the world in their present state, considered as a principle by virtue of which they are active or passive, according to the laws of movement prescribed by the Author of all things."[1] For Leibniz, the world was also a *Horologium Dei*.[2] The degree to which mechanics became the essential discipline for a knowledge of nature affected the necessity of divine intervention in epistemology. And it was precisely in the field of mechanics—defined by Boyle as "the application of mathematics to produce or modify movement in the bodies"—that number conceived as a technical instrument merged with natural science, thereby producing the first functionalization of reality, and endowing the human mind with an effective power to dominate matter.[3]

Mechanics, as is well known, is comprised not only of dynamics but also (and of greater interest for architecture) statics: the analysis of bodies in a state of rest or equilibrium. Apart from the rare speculations of Leonardo da Vinci about forces acting on structural members, Simon Stevin was the first to try to understand, geometrically, some basic problems of mechanical equilibrium. A chapter on statics in his *Oeuvres Mathématiques* (1584) analyzes the forces acting upon a body on an inclined plane. Stevin declared that this science was incapable of considering such factors as friction or cohesion. The force needed to move a cart was obviously greater than that which resulted from a theoretical calculation. But the discrepancy, according to Stevin, was not the fault of science. Like Kepler, Stevin accepted the traditional distance between geometry and reality. His application of this science to the sublunar world was obviously an innovation, but his work was still an elucidation of the geometrical behavior of reality. Stevin did not believe that a connection between geometrical hypothesis and the mutable world of reality was necessary; even less necessary was a reduction of the latter to mathematical operations.

Only Galileo formulated clearly the problems of statics and strength of materials as part of the total geometrization of human space: To determine, by means of a geometrical hypothesis, the dimensions of structural elements in relation to the weights they had to carry and the quantitative properties of the building materials. The application of geometry to mechanics thus revealed from the very beginning an intention of technical control. As the world was transformed into *res extensa* (number and figure), man discovered the power of his rational mind to control and exploit nature.

During the seventeenth century, mechanics was essentially the concern of philosophers, scientists, and geometricians, particularly after the foundation of the scientific academies in the 1660s. In a historical introduction to a treatise on strength of materials published in 1798, P. S. Girard attributed the first quantitative experiments in this science to a Swede, P. Wurtzius. He said that he had obtained this information from a letter that Wurtzius had addressed to François Blondel in 1657. Girard referred to a work by Blondel entitled *Galilaeus Promotus* and indicated that the French architect had been the second to write on the subject after Galileo.

This interest on the part of the founder and first professor of the Royal Academy of Architecture is in itself significant. Blondel's observations on Galileo's hypothesis appeared in the fourth of his "principal" problems of architecture, which provided a geometrical method for determining the dimensions of beams.[4] In the same problem, however, he also discussed the errors of Pappus on harmonic proportion. Blondel's geometrical tracing to determine the dimensions of the piers and buttresses of an arch or vault was taken from Derand's *Architecture des Voûtes* and, although this tracing was concerned with the configuration of the arch in question, it was not based on a mechanical hypothesis.[5] It should be remembered that Blondel's geometry was still, fundamentally, a Baroque universal science.

In this respect, it is interesting to consider *Il Tempio Vaticano e sua Origine*, a book published in 1694 by the successful architect Carlo Fontana.[6] Fontana was convinced that the only way to ensure the stability of domes was to determine their sections by means of complex and precise geometrical tracings. Discussing the structural problems of St. Peter's dome, Fontana superimposed on the section his ideal geometrical tracing to "prove" the dome's soundness. Similar tracings were also used for his designs of doors and frontispieces. This geometry obeyed not the logic of mechanics, but the orders of the architect's imagination, which ensured the meaning of the work: its beauty *and* solidity. This discovery of the geometry "implicit" in St. Peter's design still had

Statics and Strength of Materials

The principle of the cantilever, from Galileo's *Discorsi Intorno à Due Nuove Scienze* (1638).

Geometry and Number as Technical Instruments

the character of divine revelation; it endorsed the value of the most important church of Catholicism, whose legendary origin Fontana also disclosed.

Although much of the theory of statics had been developed by scientists and geometricians in the seventeenth century,[7] it was not until the 1680s that there appeared the first true applications of statics to architecture and engineering. I have mentioned the attempts of Vauban and Bullet to determine the dimensions of retaining walls, as well as De la Hire's presentation of these problems in the discussions of the Academy of Architecture after 1688. Bearing this in mind, it should be noted here that De la Hire was the first in a long tradition of architect-geometricians who tried to apply Varignon's general theory of the resolution of forces to the fundamental problem of stability of arches and vaults.[8] It was De la Hire who actually postulated the first truly mechanical hypothesis concerning this problem.

In contrast to prior works on mechanics and automata (for example, De Caus's *Raisons des Forces Mouvantes*), De la Hire's *Traité de Mecanique* (1695) praised the discoveries of Galileo and avoided all allusions to the magical or occult qualities of mechanical effects. De la Hire realized that physical reality did not behave with all the rigor of geometry. Nonetheless, he emphasized that all the arts needed the science of mechanics to assure their success.[9] Concerning arches, he advocated a geometrical method for determining the load that should be taken on by each voussoir in order to fulfill the conditions of equilibrium, assuming no friction between the surfaces of the pieces. This was obviously derived from Varignon's solution to the problem of equilibrium in solid bodies through the resolution of vectors, independently of cohesion or other external factors. De la Hire presented his hypothesis to the architects of the academy in 1712, outlining a concise geometrical method for quantifying the stress produced by the thrust of an arch. Taking into account the height of the piers and the radius, maximum height, and weight of the arch,[10] these calculations would determine the necessary dimensions of the supporting piers.

Although De la Hire believed that geometry was indispensable for all sorts of operations in architecture, not even his position was free from ambiguity. For example, he publicly recommended Ouvrard's treatise on harmonic proportion and in 1702 presented a paper to the Academy of Science in which he tried to prove that many arches used intuitively by architects were in fact pa-

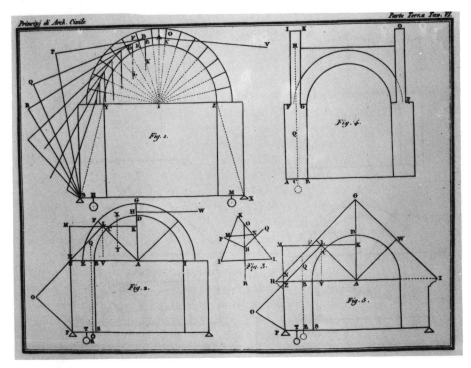

Illustration of De la Hire's hypothesis applied to diverse problems in the design of arches, from F. Milizia's *Architettura Civile* (1781).

Geometry and Number as Technical Instruments

rabolas, more agreeable in their proportions than sections of circles or ellipses.[11] (Editing this paper, Fontenelle remarked how geometry, although in itself "boring and dry," had corrected an "invention" whose only purpose was to please the eye.)

Similar ambiguities appeared in Pitot's paper *Sur la Force des Cintres*, which was presented to the Academy of Science in 1726. Making use of data on the resistance of wood and Varignon's theory, Pitot found the corresponding stresses in the parts of a wooden scaffold and was able to determine their thicknesses given their angles. His intention was to quantify the "correct proportions," reduce the number of members, and improve their connections. And yet Pitot too believed that the geometry of statics also produced a disposition that was sometimes more agreeable to the sight.[12]

H. Gautier, an "architect, engineer, and inspector" of the recently formed *Corps des Ponts et Chaussées*, was the author of the first specialized treatise on bridges written by a "professional." The first part was traditional; it listed and compared famous old and existing structures and the models proposed by Alberti or Palladio. His advice was generally empirical. There was an explanation of technical terms and of the regulations of the *Corps des Ponts et Chaussées*, an example of *devis*, and the rules of Vauban for determining the dimensions of retaining walls.[13] But in the dissertation on the piers, voussoirs, and thrusts of bridges added to the second edition of his *Traité* (1727), he discussed problems of statics and strength of materials.[14] Familiar with recent contributions in this field, Gautier tried to apply them to bridge construction. He believed that the arts, particularly architecture, were "founded on mechanics," which, being a part of mathematics, was liable to rigorous demonstration. Regardless of its origin, proportion was, in Gautier's opinion, the most difficult part of architecture, on which a consensus was still lacking. Although he recognized that mechanics was needed to establish definitive rules of proportion in architecture, he openly rejected De la Hire's hypothesis, considering it too complex and divorced from practice. Instead, he applied the simple geometrical tracings of Derand and Blondel to determine the dimensions of piers in bridges. He also emphasized the need of quantitative experiments in strength of materials, but was seemingly unable to distinguish between geometrical methods and truly mechanical hypotheses. He obviously considered the seventeenth-century tracings more practical for craftsmen and, indeed, more in keeping with traditional practice.

Statics and Strength of Materials

Most French engineers and architects of the Enlightenment, however, did accept De la Hire's theory with a greater or lesser awareness of the problems resulting from the distance between geometrical hypotheses and real phenomena. And De la Hire's fundamental intention was in fact shared by all. Bélidor and Frezier used his hypothesis in their texts on building and stereotomy, while scientists like Parent and Couplet incorporated it in papers on the equilibrium of vaults during the first thirty years of the century.[15]

The first half of the eighteenth century also witnessed the beginning of systematic experiments on the strength of materials. Following in the steps of Mariotte, who had reported some isolated tests in the previous century, Parent presented a paper to the Academy of Science on the strength of wood in 1707; and in 1711 Reaumur read a piece on the resistance of steel wire.[16] Bélidor's treatise was the first book on construction to include the quantitative results of experiments on the strength of the wood normally used for beams. Inspired by the new empirical method of Newton, Musschonbrek published in 1729 *Physicae Experimentales et Geometricae*, which included several machines of his own invention for testing stresses in various materials. The text reveals that he was much more methodical and precise than his predecessors. Similarly, Buffon tested wooden beams of all sizes, including full-scale specimens. According to Girard, Buffon was the first to consider all the important factors affecting the strength of wood (for example, the way a tree had been felled or its humidity content). Such systematic observations took on a greater significance for architecture and engineering during the second half of the century.

Around 1750 the quantitative results of experiments seemed to have taken priority over geometrical hypotheses in the minds of those architects and engineers who were concerned with structural problems. The work of Jean-Rodolphe Perronet, founder of the *École des Ponts et Chaussées* is highly significant in this respect. His quantitative observations regarding the structural behavior of bridges and his systematization of construction methods had a great influence on his contemporaries and became absolutely indispensable toward the end of the eighteenth century in correcting the old theories on statics. His own bridge projects were the first in which a consideration of the materials' mechanical behavior was attempted. In *Description des Projects* (1782), a splendid collection documenting some of his works, he described in great detail and with precise engravings the construction of

Geometry and Number as Technical Instruments

the famous bridge at Neuilly. The project was in fact an engineering masterpiece. Nothing was left to chance; every building stage was carefully planned, including the specific quality of materials, special machinery, the dimensions of each detail, and even the number of workers to be employed at each phase.

Perronet clearly attached great importance to observation and adopted the empirical method of natural science to engineering. Therefore it is almost paradoxical that Perronet's general advice to his students appears to be more conservative than that of his predecessors'. Following upon his comprehensive discussions, he finally decided that his own experience was more valuable than the results of calculations. Theory, he wrote, is insufficient; a successful practice is the surest guide.[17]

Perronet's *Description des Projects* was not an analytical treatise on bridge construction. It was essentially an attempt to teach by examples, and in this it was not unlike the didactic methods used at the *École des Ponts et Chaussées*. The text was an amalgam of the author's experiences and quantitative data organized systematically. It is perhaps significant to note how limited Perronet's contributions were to the Royal Academy of Science.[18] For although Perronet demonstrated a full understanding of mechanical effects—such as the role of piers as buttresses, the advantages of reducing the mass of such piers to allow a freer flow of water and save material, and the greater thrust of lower basket arches—his well-known preference for this latter type of arch over the traditional semicircular one was justified only in terms of common sense.[19] And while he acknowledged the results of experiments on the strength of stone, "such as those realized by Soufflot at Saillancourt," which suggested the possibility of considerably reducing the dimensions of the piers—traditionally one fifth of the span—Perronet did not provide geometrical methods or equations to apply in actuality the quantitative data derived from experiments to structural design. On the contrary, he believed that his rules, based on his own experience, were far superior. Thus in spite of "the great strength of the stone," he advised his students to continue using simple arithmetic proportions to determine the dimensions of all parts of a bridge—a method reminiscent of the most traditional Renaissance rules of thumb.[20]

Perronet stressed the importance of quantitative experiments in other academic papers.[21] With regard to methods of laying a foundation, he mentioned the experiments of Musschonbrek, Buffon, Parent, and Gautier, but finished by providing simple recipes in terms of the duplication, triplication, or division of the diameter

Statics and Strength of Materials

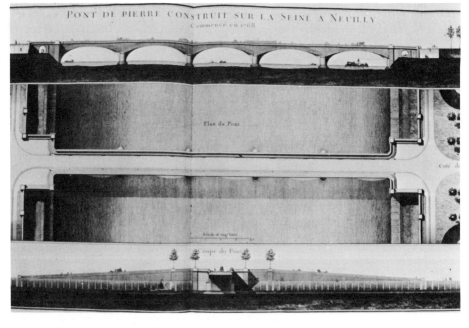

Plan and elevation of Perronet's bridge at Neuilly,
from *Description des Projets*.

Geometry and Number as Technical Instruments

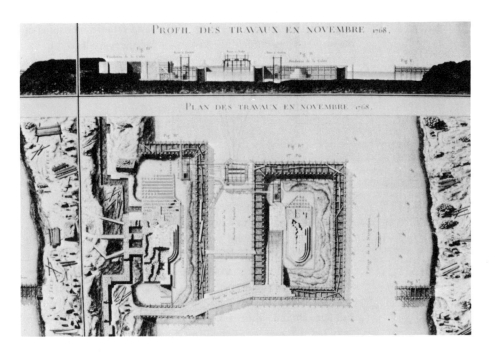

PROFIL DES TRAVAUX EN NOVEMBRE 1768.

PLAN DES TRAVAUX EN NOVEMBRE 1768.

Année 1770   Pl. 11

IIᵉ. VUE DES TRAVAUX DU PONT DE NEUILLY.

Levage d'un Centre de Charpente.

A. 1ʳᵉ Ferme déja assemblée   D. Culée du côté de Courbevoye.
B. 2ᵐᵉ Ferme assemblée à moitié   E. Mont Valérien.

One of many plates showing the process of construction at Neuilly. In November 1768 the foundations and preliminary operations were evident. From
Description des Projets.

View of the scaffolding for one of the arches of the
bridge at Neuilly during 1770, from *Description des
Projets.*

of piles, according to their own weight and other dimensions of the structure. Although his recommendations were linked to experimental observations, the quantitative results were not translated into mathematical analysis. Everyhing was summarized in a conventional discourse in which the experimental results were subsidiary to his own experience in building.

Tradition and Mechanics in Italian Architecture	The application of statics by French scientists, architects, and engineers in the early eighteenth century did not go unnoticed by the rest of Europe. Particularly in Italy, there appeared original interpretations that merit attention. In 1748 Giovanni Poleni published his famous work in which he recapitulated the debate concerning the structural problems of St. Peter's Basilica in the Vatican.[22] The dome had been deteriorating for some time, as Fontana had already pointed out. But the cracks became more dramatic after 1742, and many mathematicians, architects, and engineers wrote papers in an attempt to diagnose and solve the problem. Poleni, after providing a history of the church, then unfolded his own ideas about mechanics.

He declared that the application of mechanics to architecture was impossible without mathematics and that it presented the greatest difficulty when focused on the building of arches and domes. Mentioning the "geometrical methods" of Derand and Blondel and the "occult geometrical rules" of Fontana, he dismissed their contributions "for not being adapted to the mechanical properties of building materials."[23] Thus Poleni distinguished between the traditional use of geometry as it appeared in seventeenth-century treatises and its potential as a technical instrument in mechanical hypotheses. Also mentioned were the contributions of De la Hire, Parent, and Couplet, as well as Gregory's analysis of the catenary, which had been published in Britain in 1697. Gregory's work was based on Robert Hooke's discovery about this curve's properties of ideal stability and additionally assumed a direct transmission of forces among frictionless voussoirs. The shape of a freely suspended chain would then be the ideal configuration for a masonry vault or arch, and Poleni superimposed one on a section of St. Peter's dome, believing that because the tracing fell within the mass of the structure, the dome's stability was guaranteed.[24]

Poleni described the structural problems of other well-known domes before going on to discuss reports and analyses by various

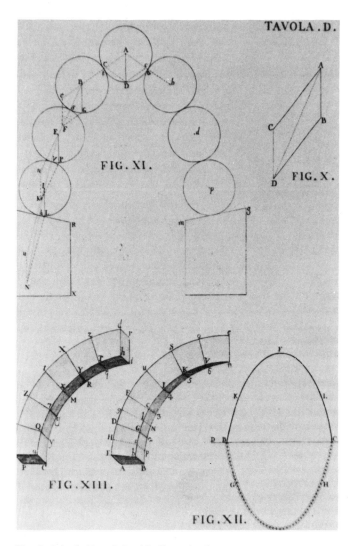

Plate in Poleni's *Memorie Istoriche* illustrating the catenary hypothesis.

Statics and Strength of Materials

authors. Of particular interest are his deliberations concerning the ideas of the mathematicians Le Seur, Jacquier, and Boscowitch.[25] These authors had applied a geometrical hypothesis to the problem of determining the lateral thrusts of the dome of St. Peter's Basilica, thereby obtaining a very high value, which, according to Poleni, was obviously false. Poleni believed that since the dome had been created by Michelangelo without the aid of mechanics or mathematics, then it should be possible to solve its problems without these sciences.[26] While Poleni explained that he was fond of mathematics and agreed with the anonymous Venetian philosopher who said that they could be useful to architecture, he did not think that mathematics should have priority in the architect's decisions: "Although excellent in themselves," they should not be abused in their application.[27]

Poleni criticized the solution proposed by the three mathematicians because it was excessively theoretical. He attributed the problems of the structure to "internal" and "external" natural causes. These were the aspects that always tended to undermine the solidity of buildings, and they did not result from errors in design or a lack of structural analysis. Among the factors Poleni cited were the quality of materials, their defective manufacturing or inappropriate use in construction, heat, humidity, the differences in pressure caused by several forces acting simultaneously, wind, thunder, and earthquakes. Poleni was also interested in experiments on strength of materials. He mentioned Musschonbrek's *machina divulsoria* and reported the results of his own experiments on the resistance of steel. He referred to these results in his final recommendation: Use steel reinforcing rings to relieve the tensile stresses on St. Peter's dome; this will help to avoid any further deterioration.[28] In the end, Poleni had greater confidence in his own empirical observations than in any geometrical theory of statics. Wherever he referred to theories or even to his own quantitative results, his conclusions were modified by the experience contained in traditional practice.

As in the case of other technical subjects, the tension between a theory that could be transformed into an instrument for the domination of the physical world and a practice still justified in relation to a metaphysical framework was much more evident in eighteenth-century Italian texts. In his *Dialoghi sopra le Tre Arti del Disegno*, Giovani Bottari envisioned a debate between two knowledgeable personalities of the previous century: Pietro Bellori and Carlo Maratta.[29] Bellori affirmed that to design solid and stable buildings, the architect required much practice. Maratta replied that the study of particular cases was not sufficient since this was useless when circumstances changed. Maratta stressed the necessity of establishing universal rules that would guide the actions of young architects by teaching them how to measure the stresses in arches and vaults and the resistance of walls. He believed that such knowledge could only be gleaned from geometry and was to be found in treatises on mensuration, strength of materials, and mechanics. Bellori tried to refute this argument by emphasizing the virtues of the great monuments of the past, all of which were created without the use of geometrical hypotheses. The discussion was inconclusive, but it was perhaps significant that in the end, Maratta also praised the artistic achievements of the Renaissance and called for a new synthesis of the arts in the persons of universal men, equally able as painters, sculptors, and architects.

Ermenegildo Pini explored the same issue in his *Dell'Architettura, Dialogi* (1770), in which fictional students of mathematics discussed the difficulties involved in applying geometrical theories to architecture and construction. The first student propounded the need to know rules in order to determine thrusts and structural stresses (rules derived from "the universal mathematics of Newton," the theories of Leibniz, and the calculations of Bernoulli).[30] But he admitted there were great difficulties involved in the application of these rules to practice due to the irregularities of vaults and the diversity of forces acting upon them. A second student added that the greatest architects had never applied mechanics to their buildings. In his opinion, it was more important to have relevant knowledge of the quality of materials; algebraic equations and the subtleties of theoretical mechanics and calculus were unable to ensure the stability of buildings. His conclusion was, surprisingly, that architects should design simple buildings so that they could be easily understood and analyzed by means of the geometrical rules of statics. Such buildings would be not only structurally sound but also beautiful "according to the law of continuity in nature." Such an assertion, alluding to Newton's universal empiricism, obviously brings to mind the projects of late Neoclassical architecture in France and clearly points at the ambiguous role of geometry and number in eighteenth-century architectural theory and design.

Francesco Ricatti wrote about "the science of proportions" in his *Dissertazione intorno l'Architettura Civile* of 1761. As a liberal

Statics and Strength of Materials

art, architecture should, in his opinion, possess true and positive rules, capable of guaranteeing the solidity and stability of buildings without offending their proportions and beauty.[31] Ricatti stressed that architects should use optics for their projections, geometry to combine in one structure arches of different dimensions, and "music together with analysis" (!) to solve the problem of the harmonic mean, thereby producing a stable and universal law.

This same "confusion" appeared in Nicola Carletti's work. Influenced by Christian Wolff, Carletti postulated an architectural theory *more geometrico* and devoted a chapter of his *Istituzioni d'Architettura Civile* (1772) to the traditional notions about proportion and the determination of the dimensions of piers "taking into account" the strength of materials.[32] After enumerating the different types of columns, walls, and piers used in architecture, he described his "experiences" with statics, mentioning the weight of materials and a rule for determining the thickness of walls. But then Carletti immediately returned to the traditional notion of the human body as a prototype of proportion, stating that this "postulate" could be demonstrated through "experiments." The ambiguity created by the simultaneous presence of a geometry with symbolic resonances and the mathematics of technology is even more evident in the final scholium, where Carletti (repeating an assertion by Wolff) declares that if the rules of statics or geometry did not coincide with the "institutions of architecture," then experience should have priority over reason.

In his eclectic *Principi di Architettura Civile* (1781), Francesco Milizia maintained that proportions were of fundamental importance for architecture, but that no one had as yet found satisfying rules. Referring to previous opinions by Frezier and Patte, he remarked that architectural proportions were not "arithmetic, geometric or harmonic," but were derived a posteriori from the observation of nature and were intimately related to the stability and solidity that they provided.[33] In the third part of his *Principi*, Milizia argued that architects had to know something of experimental physics and mathematics. It was essential for practice to bear in mind the precepts of theory in order to "reflect, observe, confront, and even experiment," thereby establishing certain rules and contributing to the progress of art.[34] Milizia displayed a thorough knowledge of the works of French architects and geometricians and included in his book tables, rules, and experimental results. He cited the works of Musschonbrek, Bélidor, De la Hire, Frezier, and Camus, among others. However, he also thought there were limitations involved in the application of statics to construction, and in the end, if he thought geometry and mathematics were indispensable to architecture, it was because he also recognized their importance as symbols. Milizia stressed that above and beyond its technical applications, geometry was necessary "to understand correctly the important doctrine of proportions."[35] Thus, like their predecessors, eighteenth-century architects held, however incoherently, that geometry and numerical proportion endorsed the relation between aesthetic values and solidity, stability, and durability.

The *Rigoristti*: Structural Function as Metaphor

The most original Italian interpretation of this paradigmatic problem of Neoclassical architecture is to be found among the *Rigoristti*, the disciples of Carlo Lodoli, the Venetian "Socrates of architecture." Historians who have studied Lodoli's devastating criticism of Vitruvian authority and the classical orders have called him a true "modern." Recently, however, this perception has been qualified.[36] In many respects, Lodoli's understanding of architecture and history appears to be more profound than even that of most nineteenth- and twentieth-century theoreticians. This was probably due to his friendship with Giambattista Vico, the exceptional Neapolitan philosopher whose work anticipated certain insights of contemporary phenomenological hermeneutics.

Lodoli's writings have not survived, and like Socrates's teachings, his thought had to be set down by his students. In the first chapter of the *Elementi di Architettura Lodoliana* (1786), the most reliable of extant sources published after Lodoli's death, Andrea Memmo felt the need to justify the importance of Lodoli's theory, reminding the reader of the frequent failure of buildings due to structural unsoundness—failure that involved economic catastrophe.[37] A large part of this unusual treatise consisted of chapters on historical criticism in which Memmo discussed in the same enlightened mood Greek and Roman architecture, the theories of Vitruvius, and Renaissance and modern authors. Memmo then ventured a conclusion supported by his historical research: Although Vitruvius had defined architecture as a science, this art still lacked fixed and immutable principles. It was not even necessary to discuss this point. It was sufficient to recognize the great diversity of existing ideas about the essence of architecture to be convinced that "we are still in darkness." And since the most famous authors did not share one single clear idea, "we should at least have the courage to doubt."[38]

The fundamental criticism by the *Rigoristti* of all previous theories had already appeared in Francesco Algarotti's *Saggio sull'Architettura* (1753).[39] The argument was based on the notion that architecture should be consistent with the essence or nature of the materials used in building. Nothing could be more absurd than to use a certain material to *represent* another. Algarotti affirmed that falsehood was the greatest abuse of all. Architectural forms should therefore be compatible with the individual qualities of their materials, their rigidity, flexibility, or "resisting strengths." The "original" mistake of classical architecture, unconditionally accepted by modern imitators, was in fact the transposition of primitive wooden forms into stone or marble. Memmo emphasized that this diversity in materials, regardless of their various specific properties, made it impossible to establish definitive and absolute rules of proportion.[40]

Memmo pointed out that only two Italian authors, Milizia and Lamberti, had written about the problem of solidity and stability of buildings.[41] Lodoli, in his opinion, would have considered a knowledge of statics, strength of materials, and construction as essential for architecture. Vitruvius and other authors had written in the past *de re aedificatoria*, but had not thought to quantify the strength of materials or to calculate loads and stresses.[42] After demonstrating his familiarity with works on these subjects by the best-known French architects and geometricians, Memmo tells us that Lodoli himself had spent much time and effort in the elaboration of tables that summarized the results of his own experiments on the strength of wood, stone, marble, and other materials.

Also, Memmo refuted the validity of harmonic proportion, criticized the writings of Vitruvius on this subject, and showed how the Greeks themselves had not respected the original dimensions of the orders. These dimensions, he claimed, did not derive from a "beautiful nature," the human body, "which is unalterable," or the trees, as some others had suggested, but were the products of custom and a blind belief in the authority of the ancients. Memmo concluded by stressing that Vitruvius and his followers had been incapable of establishing a correct theory of proportions because they had disregarded the differences among building materials, particularly in relation to their "greater or lesser internal cohesion."[43]

Unlike most French architects of the Enlightenment, Memmo was capable of questioning not only Vitruvianism but *also* the myth of a transcendental nature. Nonetheless, we should not forget that the experiments on strength of materials and the ideas about the geometrical behavior of matter were not, for the *Rigoristti*, simple instruments of technology. On the contrary, these concerns were integrated into their interest in discovering the phenomenic essence of building materials. The new architecture was to be visibly true and was to represent the intrinsic properties of matter through the formal configuration of buildings. This is precisely the meaning of Lodoli's own work in San Francesco della Vigna; it is best illustrated by the famous windows with lintels shaped like catenary curves and by the "corollaries" that synthesized his teaching (which have been interpreted, paradoxically, as an early formulation of nineteenth- and twentieth-century functionalism).[44] Even Lodoli's contemporaries, including Algarotti, misinterpreted his thought as an absolute rejection of all ornament in architecture.[45]

Memmo wrote, "the straight function and representation are the two final scientific objectives of civil architecture."[46] These objectives he thought were equivalent: "Solidity, analogy and commodity are the essential properties of representation. . . . Ornament is not essential." The new vision of history that the *Rigoristti* shared with Vico enabled them to apprehend the synthetic and irreducible character of architectural value. In Vico's thought, history was postulated as the true science of man, a "new science," qualitatively different from natural science and capable of elucidating the origins of humanity.[47] The Vitruvian *firmitas, commoditas,* and *venustas* could not be conceived as independent, reified abstractions. Making use of historical criticism, Memmo could then question the traditional Vitruvian myths, but only to reveal the absolute primacy of man's original mythical structure. This phenomenological a priori, which embraced the idea of the "invariable body," had to be reflected in architecture in order to produce a truly meaningful human world. Meaning also became an explicit problem for the *Rigoristti*, as it was for the late-eighteenth-century French theoreticians. But Vico had emphasized that the humanity of man depended on his poetic being. Primitive man first dwelled in the world by implementing his poetic powers; he was initially a poet, not a scientist. And a fundamental form of *poesis* was, originally, building.

Hence, Memmo argued that although architectural value should derive from an appropriate use of materials, taking into consideration both their intrinsic properties or essences (precisely represented by mathematics and geometry) and the singular architectural program, the relations between form and matter had to be metaphoric and imaginative, not merely rational. This is far indeed from nineteenth-century structural determinism or the reductionistic obsessions of functionalism. Function, for the *Rigoristti*, retained the ambiguous dual connotation of abstract mathematics (number) and visible representation (quality). It could therefore be a symbol of human order. Memmo himself wrote that representation was "the individual and total expression that resulted when matter had been disposed with geometrical-arithmetical-optical reason;" this was done in order to fulfill a given architectural objective.

It should be remembered that ornament had never been perceived as superfluous by Renaissance or Baroque architects.[48] Regardless of theoretical discussions about the specificity of structure and ornament, the latter was always perceived as an integral part of a building's *meaning*. The problem of reconciling disjointed structure and ornament became explicit after the epistemological transformation of the late seventeenth century and was reflected in Perrault's work, the advent of Rococo, and by the autonomy of the technical dimension. Lodoli's attempt to reconcile ornament and structure in his "corollary" was already *beyond* Alberti's initial distinction, which had obviously relied on the traditional belief in the absolute value of the classical orders.

Inspired by Vico's understanding of history as the archetypal human science, Lodoli could produce his early criticism of Vitruvian theory, while simultaneously postulating the necessity of a symbolic intentionality in architecture. Perceiving the meaning of architecture as primaeval ritual building, a privileged form of reconciliation between man and external reality, he rejected the use of the classical orders because they were unsuited to masonry construction. Architecture as building had to respond to the poetic potential of the materials. This amounted to a rejection of a rational theory of architecture based on the models of natural science and mathematical logic, such as was prevalent in Europe during the eighteenth century. Like Vico, Lodoli rejected rational reductionism and put forward an early form of hermeneutic criticism as the most appropriate method for architectural theory. He could thus understand what Renaissance architecture had "lost" through the inception of theory and the division between design and building. The architect's fundamental role was to make poetry, not designs. Lodoli's theory was obviously overwhelmed by the new processes of production after the Industrial Revolution, and his profound criticism remained misunderstood by practitioners who took it to be simply a rejection of ornament. His reconciliation of ornament and structure is indeed so advanced that it is still an adequate criticism of simplistic "postmodernism."

Perhaps the only architect to understand fully the sense of Lodoli's theory was Giovanni Battista Piranesi. Recognizing the limitations of *disegno* once it involved the reduction of building through the implementation of structural analysis and systematization, Piranesi became aware of the increasing meaninglessness of conventional architectural practice. Piranesi's architecture, for the first time in history, is fully embodied in his drawings and "visions" (and not in his very limited practice). His depictions of ruins and of a mythical Roman past are desperate attempts to reveal the meaning of an architecture that could no longer be built. This concern with meaning is, of course, parallel to that already examined in connection with late-eighteenth-century French architects, resulting in theoretical projects attempting to recover the meaning in the world. Piranesi's passionate interest in construction and his preference for the Roman "builders" over the Greek "designers" is, therefore, coherent with his other concerns. The Romans seemed to understand the poetic properties of stone, instead of merely translating, like the Greeks, the idealized forms of wooden temples. Piranesi believed that Roman architecture, deriving from the Egyptian and the Etruscan, was closer to mythical building, in the sense of the *Rigoristti*. But it was not enough to reproduce Roman buildings. Piranesi's "Roman" architecture was immense and overwhelming, often buried, mysterious, and prone to decay. Meaning could not be attained through conventional classical buildings or the implementation of a geometry that imitated nature; the drawing or engraving was the embodiment of the symbolic intention. Geometry or conventional forms would obviously be devalued if the represented buildings were placed in the context of the industrial world, in a city that denied the symbolic, intersubjective dimension of architecture.

In the famous *Carceri* etchings, Piranesi tried to understand the phenomenic essences of stone and wood architecture. This essential architecture occurs in a space that is already beyond perspective reductionism. Piranesi dominated the methods of perspective representation and the *scena per angolo* of the Galli-Bibienas. But his *Carceri* etchings are not illusionistic in a Baroque sense. He was not interested in producing the image of a building

Statics and Strength of Materials

whose reality would be realized beyond the drawing itself. If the city had become a prosaic stage in perspective, and perspective was identified with reality, he used geometrical methods to create an intentionally ambiguous reality, an architecture where man would be confronted with the absurdity of his own powers of abstraction. His *Carceri* are an anticipation of cubism and surrealism; through the appearance of perspective they deny perspective reductionism and confirm the primacy of embodied perception. But all this is achieved not in the usual way, through a three-dimensional building, but through the reality of the drawing itself. The drawing is no longer the symbol of an intention that would be fulfilled in the surreality of the building, as in Baroque architecture; but the drawing itself becomes an architecture of geometrical essences, consciously avoiding the external world where mathematics was being transformed into a tool of technology.

| Soufflot, Patte, and the Piers of Ste.-Geneviève | The most significant discussion concerning the application of statics to a building project occurred in Paris between Jacques-Germain Soufflot and Pierre Patte during the second half of the eighteenth century. The debate concerned the dimensions of the piers supporting Ste.-Geneviève's dome and clearly reveals the tensions and ambiguities that marked the architecture of the Enlightenment. |

Belief in the empirical method as the only access to truth encouraged the accumulation of a sufficient quantity of data eventually to transform the geometrical theories of statics into an effective structural analysis. Yet this same empiricism was also responsible for those architectural positions that appear traditional in comparison to the intentions expressed in theoretical and scientific texts during the first half of the eighteenth century.

I have shown how Patte, by adopting an empirical method in relation to the problem of the classical orders and their proportions, rejected the relativism of values attributed to Perrault's theory. In 1770 he published a *Mémoire sur la Construction de la Coupole Projectée de ... Sainte-Geneviève* in which he argued that the dimensions proposed by Soufflot for the piers were not adequate to support the great weight of the dome.[49] Clearly, both architects were very interested in technical problems. Soufflot kept up with advances in geology and with experimental physics and chemistry and was himself involved in industry. And Patte believed that "the most important aspects of architecture (aside from the classical

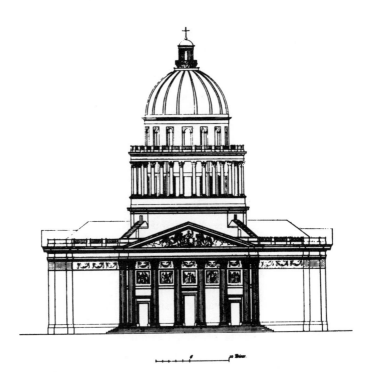

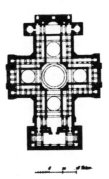

J. G. Soufflot's Ste.-Geneviève. Schematic plan and
elevation showing the large mass of the dome and
drum in relation to the rest of the building, from
Quatremère de Quincy's *Histoire de la Vie et des
Ouvrages* (1830).

orders) were technical problems of construction such as determining cubic volumes, cost estimates and specifications, and the building of sound foundations or entablatures reinforced with iron rods."[50]

Both men were aware of their predecessors' work in the field of statics and strength of materials. Patte's *Mémoires* mention Bullet, Frezier, De la Hire, and Bélidor, and Patte was actually the author of the two last volumes of J. F. Blondel's *Cours*, which dealt with technical problems.[51] The proportions he recommended for the classical orders were to be derived not from optical considerations, but from a determination of the loads they had to support.[52] Like Soufflot, he admired the lightness of Gothic structures,[53] and thus praised the synthesis of that quality with the nobility of trabeated classical architecture that characterized Ste.-Geneviève and Contant's project for La Madelaine.[54] The aesthetic norms of both architects were ultimately determined by a belief in an intersubjective taste and the power of numerical proportion to ensure positive beauty.

The differences between Patte and Soufflot should, therefore, be examined carefully. It has been pointed out that Patte represented a traditional and empirical approach to the problem of statics, while Soufflot and his supporters (Perronet, Rondelet, Bossut, and Gauthey) tried to implement a true theory of structures based on experiment and calculation. Although this view is not altogether false, it should be qualified. In his *Mémoire*, Patte invoked the aid of mathematics and mechanics, which in his opinion were indispensable to the progress of science. But after citing the works of Parent, Couplet, and De la Hire, he decided that the strictly geometrical rules proposed by Carlo Fontana in his *Tempio Vaticano* (1694) were the best means for determining the proportions of domes. In fact, what Patte could not accept was Soufflot's belief in the absolute infallibility of mathematical formulas and quantitative data derived from tests on the resistance of building materials to fracture. Instead, Patte thought that design decisions should correspond to the experience of everyday practice. He compared the dimensions proposed by Soufflot with those used under similar conditions by the great architects of the past: for St. Peter at the Vatican, St. Paul in London, and the churches of La Sorbonne, Les Invalides and Val-de-Grace in Paris. From this he concluded that the piers of Ste.-Geneviève were too slender and, if built as designed, would fail due to the load of the dome.

Patte might be called traditional because of his adoption of Fontana's simple geometrical rules, which lacked a mechanical

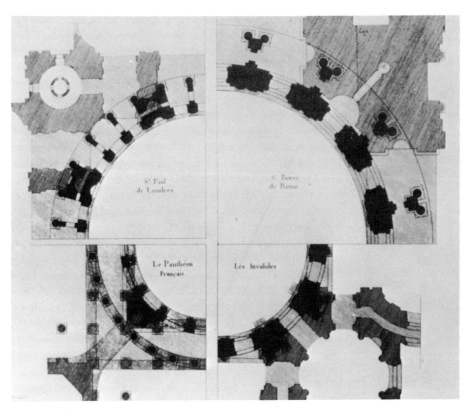

Comparison of the dimensions of the piers supporting large domed structures in Europe with those of
Ste.-Geneviève, after Patte's *Mémoire* (1770).

Statics and Strength of Materials

or physical foundation and whose validity, he believed, was endorsed by the survival of ancient masterworks. On the other hand, Patte was conscious of the limitations on the applicability of mathematics and geometry to physical problems—limitations that Soufflot tended to overlook. In contrast with the ideas of Frezier or Bélidor, Patte emphasized the importance of practice in solving problems of structural mechanics. In volume six of J. F. Blondel's *Cours*, Patte affirmed that practice had always preceded theory and that the art of construction had in fact made great progress before the intervention of theory; admirable buildings had been constructed through simple routines and experience, not only during "centuries of ignorance" but also in his own time, when craftsmen executed difficult works based only on comparisons with similar buildings of the past.[55]

Unlike many of his contemporaries, who were obsessed with the potential of structural analysis, Patte was not surprised by the success of traditional buildings, which had been erected without the aid of mechanical theories. Construction, after all, was simply the art of elevating bodies over other bodies, fashioning their verticality and position by means of diverse combinations and relations based on a small number of rules of statics—rules that were part of everyday experience and thus an extension of common sense. For example, the weak must be supported by the strong, and a slope is essential for the stability of piled objects. Deceptively simple, such knowledge had to be gleaned from experience and practice. Only in his way could the architect determine the appropriate dimensions of his structures without endangering their stability while also avoiding a wasteful use of materials.[56]

The great success of historical monuments demonstrated, according to Patte, that the rules established through routine and practice should not be ignored. He did not object to architects' and geometricians' recent applications of a mechanical theory to construction since, he felt, this amounted to substituting routine with fixed principles founded on the development of the "eternal laws of weight and equilibrium."[57] He believed that the discovery of these absolute geometrical laws was important, but he stressed that such laws should always be able to take into account the real problems of practice. Scientists often encountered insurmountable obstacles when dealing only with simple problems of the thrust of vaults, and due to their lack of practical knowledge, for which there was no substitute,[58] they could only contribute minimally to the advancement of construction. This state of affairs had precipitated, in Patte's opinion, "the invention of principles and hypotheses" not in accordance with the facts: "In a word, only the reunion of practice and theory can allow for a profound treatment of the subjects concerning construction."[59]

The synthesis of theory and practice was obviously not equivalent to a simple rejection of statics by a conservative practitioner. Patte was familiar with the empirical methods of science and recognized their potential to provide fixed quantitative results through experimentation. In his *Mémoires*, he cited Buffon's tests on the resistance of steel,[60] and in the *Cours*, he emphasized that the precise knowledge of the loads that different types of stones could support was very useful.[61] He also complained that architects often determined the dimensions of their buildings only through approximation and not through the application of the laws of equilibrium.[62] He distinguished between De la Hire's mechanical hypothesis about the thrust of vaults (which he praised) and seventeenth-century rules of a merely geometrical character. In fact, he believed that De la Hire and Frezier represented the culmination of the possible applications of mathematics to construction: "The limits of this art seem to have been fixed because educated people are now capable of appreciating and calculating in advance that which can or cannot be executed; there are no more enigmas in this respect but for the ignorant."[63]

It is likely, then, that Patte's criticism of the project for Ste.-Geneviève was motivated by conflicting considerations, which were reconciled only in the eighteenth century. On the one hand, guided by the strict rationality of empirical science, Patte revealed the distance that still existed between the geometrical theories of statics and the real problems of practice. On the other hand, he retained a traditional understanding of architectural value, which was legitimized by the metaphysical dimension implicit in his empirical method. Thus he believed, like Soufflot, that the same mathematical rules provided for stability and beauty. But these rules were derived, in Patte's case, from *both* empirical observation and historical precedents, that is, from the totality of the architect's personal experience, which he felt had priority over ideal calculations as the origin of meaningful design.

The polemic continued for thirty years. In time the piers of Ste.-Geneviève failed due to the normal deficiencies of building procedures, which Soufflot had disregarded in basing his calculations only on the experimental resistance of the stone. The

Statics and Strength of Materials

alarming cracks in the piers kept the discussion alive long after Soufflot's death, and in 1798 Patte was still writing critical *mémoires* on the subject.[64]

Emiland Gauthey, a brilliant *architect et ingénieur des ponts et chaussées*, took it upon himself to defend Soufflot. His name has been mentioned as the author of a text incorporating Laugier's theory and as the inventor of a machine to test the strength of stone. In 1771 he published a paper accusing Patte of having mistakenly used De la Hire's hypothesis of frictionless voussoirs in his calculations while ignoring the adhesive force of mortar.[65] Patte admitted in one of his letters that some of his calculations were indeed based on the theory that Soufflot had used, but that his own results were always tested by practice and historical precedents.[66] Gauthey criticized Patte's reverence for old monuments, his approval of Frezier's theory, and especially his adoption of Fontana's principles. In the end, Gauthey also applied De la Hire's hypothesis to the problem, but his conclusion was just the opposite of Patte's; in his opinion, the piers projected by Soufflot could support an even larger and heavier dome.[67]

Gauthey shared Soufflot's faith in the possibility of applying geometrical hypotheses to the resolution of practical problems of construction. It is perhaps significant that Charles-François Viel, an early-nineteenth-century architect and critic (of whom more will be said later) blamed Gauthey and Bossut for causing Soufflot to abandon the rules of traditional building, which were still observed by most of his contemporaries. Such disregard had brought about, in Viel's opinion, ominous consequences for architecture as a whole.[68]

Throughout the eighteenth century, architects, engineers, and geometricans, impatient to see Galileo's dream come true, applied the theory of statics to certain specific structural problems. Some, like Patte, were more cautious and recognized the limitations of such applications vis-à-vis traditional building methods. But while they shared the same curiosity and passion for technical problems, their enthusiasm was modulated by the implications of the empirical method. Furthermore, the residual symbolic character of numbers and geometric figures impeded the application of infinitesimal calculus to the realm of human action. The survival of Euclidean geometry constituted the most fundamental obstacle to the establishment of a universal theory; its unchallenged presence as the only form of geometrical science served to stall the final reduction of building operations into a generalized technological process until the end of the century.

Geometry and Number as Technical Instruments

After 1770, however, several scientists and engineers—for example, Prony and Carnot, future professors at the École Polytechnique, and Bossut and Coulomb, from the École du Génie—began to perceive the need to revise the old theories of statics.[69] The eighteenth century had produced two types of scientists: those who, like Musschonbrek and Buffon, were mainly interested in experimental physics, and others, like Euler, whose interest in geometry and applied mechanics was frequently motivated by hidden metaphysical concerns, so that their scientific involvement was merely to demonstrate the power of mathematics. In spite of architects' and engineers' wish to join theory and practice in technical problems, the definitive mathematization of the principal factors of physical reality, the mathematization of sufficient precision to provide analytical solutions of structural problems, did not come about until 1773, when Charles-Auguste Coulomb presented to the Royal Academy of Science his paper "On the Application of the Rules of Maximums and Minimums to Some Problems of Statics Relative to Architecture."[70]

Following a successful career as a military engineer, Coulomb studied at Mezières and then turned to science. He proposed a method of algebraic analysis that allowed for the consideration of the effects of friction and cohesion in structural problems, the two fundamental aspects that had either been ignored in previous theories or merely observed experimentally. Coulomb was the first to propose a truly scientific method for solving structural problems, effectively taking into account essential practical requirements. In the first part of his work, he provided a full discussion of the original problem of Galilean mechanics: the forces acting upon a typical cross section of a cantilever beam. In the second part, he examined the two most popular structural problems of the eighteenth century. Unhappy with the theories about retaining walls that appeared in books by Bullet and Bélidor, and which were based on a strictly geometrical conception of statics, Coulomb was finally in a position to reduce the physical properties of the retained earth and of the wall's masonry to the conceptual level of mathematics. His equation for the design of retaining walls is still useful today.

With regard to the problem of stability of arches and vaults, Coulomb overcame the difficulties that had impeded the effective application of De la Hire's theory to practice. His method of analysis took in the quantitative values of friction and cohesion as well as the fact that fracture did not always occur at the crown.

As Poncelet wrote in 1852, "Concerning the equilibrium of arches, before Coulomb, one possessed only mathematical considerations or very imperfect empirical rules based on limited hypotheses, the majority lacking that character of precision and certainty that alone can recommend them to the confidence of enlightened engineers."[71]

Coulomb's paper was not presented in a way that allowed for an easy application of his discoveries to architectural and engineering practice. This would still take a few decades. Nonetheless, it is significant that in the first history of statics ever written, an introductory chapter to P. S. Girard's *Traité Analytique de la Resistance des Solides* (1798), Coulomb's theory was referred to as the culmination of a development that had started with Galileo.[72] Girard thought that Coulomb's contributions constituted a true *fil d'Ariadne*, guiding practitioners through the labyrinth to truth. Girard used Coulomb's discoveries as the premise of his own work, producing the first truly analytic treatise on the science of strength of materials as we know it.

Girard explained that although motion in the theory of statics could be conceived in terms of absolutely rigid levers, this supposition was inadmissible when statics was applied to the calculation of real machines or construction. Nature had not created substances whose parts might not be severed. There were, therefore, two types of equilibrium: one is between two opposing forces in balance (for example, a lever), the other is between a certain function of these forces and the internal cohesion of the constituent parts. The conditions of the first kind of equilibrium could be determined rigorously, but those of the second only approximately.[73] Girard quoted d'Alembert's remark that experience should be used not only to prove a theoretical insight but to provide new truths that theory alone would be incapable of discovering.

Girard's work represented the first successful integration of experimental observations on the strength of materials into the mathematical structure of theory. Experimental data, which normally referred to fracture loads, had been considered in a more or less arbitrary fashion and never became, during the eighteenth century, a true vehicle for reconciling geometrical hypotheses with empirical reality. In Girard's *Traité*, quantitative observations became mathematical coefficients. His theory is truly *analytical*, avoiding the use of Euclidean geometry. Finally, architectural reality could be truly functionalized, allowing for an effective substitution of mathematical rules for the experience derived from building practice. Building practice could now be effectively controlled and dominated by "theory." The *Institut National*, founded after the Revolution, "solemnly" adopted the conclusions of Girard's work in a report signed by Coulomb and Prony.

IV

GEOMETRY, NUMBER, AND
TECHNOLOGY

8

POSITIVISM, DESCRIPTIVE
GEOMETRY, AND SCIENTIFIC
BUILDING

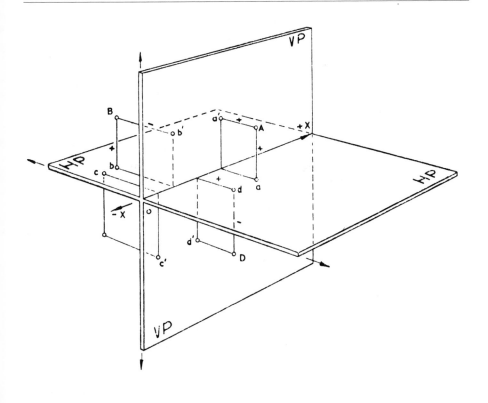

Voltaire wrote in his *Éléments de la Philosophie de Newton* (1738) that the whole philosophy of Newton leads of necessity to the knowledge of a Supreme Being who had created everything and arranged all the universe in accordance to His own free will: "If matter gravitates . . . it received its gravitation from God." This cosmology provided the backdrop for the intellectual accomplishments of the Enlightenment. The achievements of absolute reason were always endorsed by a series of deeply rooted metaphysical assumptions. Geometry, the science of the immutable par excellence, still maintained its intimate and inveterate relation with the world of embodied perception, retaining its potential as a source of symbols. But Voltaire was mistaken in thinking that Newtonian metaphysics could arrest the atheism that had begun to dominate epistemology. During the last two decades of the century, the poetic and metaphorical representations of reality were rejected in favor of the successful interpretations of logical reason. Scientists like Lagrange and Laplace began to offer natural explanations for the apparent irregularities observed in physical phenomena, particularly in astronomy, showing how they were part of larger regular systems that had not been adequately understood. It became evident that the totality of the universe, including the sublunar world, behaved more in accordance with perfect mathematical laws than had so far been imagined. Thus if everything could be explained by means of mathematical equations accessible to the human mind, the notion of God becomes dispensable.

The epistemological revolution ushered in by Galileo and Descartes was irreversible, and reason effectively became the master of human destiny, disregarding concerns beyond its control. Laplace wrote in his *Essai Philosophique sur les Probabilités* (1814) that all events, including those so small that they did not seem to be subject to the great laws of nature, depended upon these laws as much as the sun's revolutions. Only a lack of knowledge about their relation to the "total system of the universe" made them seem to depend on final causes or chance. Laplace was certain that these "imaginary causes," which were nothing but the expressions of human ignorance, would recede and eventually disappear completely under the light of a "positive philosophy."[1]

Hence the mission of the philosopher was to discover the mathematical laws that governed all phenomena and their possible causal interrelations. The cosmos was losing its mystery, for nothing was bound to remain enigmatic when it could be scrutinized

Geometry, Number, and Technology

logically. Laplace described the character of objective reason like this: The present state of the universe should be conceived as the effect of its previous state and as the cause of its future one. An intelligence capable of knowing, at a certain instant, all the forces animating nature and the respective positions of beings, and also able to subject these data to mathematical analysis, would be capable of incorporating in *one formula* the motions of the largest bodies and the lightest atoms. Laplace emphasized that nothing would be uncertain for such an intelligence; it would be powerful enough to know, and thus be in a position to control, past and future.

Laplace thus formulated the basic principles of positivism— the philosophy that lay behind the noisy explosion of technology and industrialization during the nineteenth century. Positivism created the illusion of the infinite capacity of human reason to control, dominate, and put to work the forces of nature that had so far intimidated man. Thus inspired, man could think (and perhaps still does) that there would come a day when nothing in his life or his world would remain hidden to reason. To the degree that the fluid, mutable, and necessarily ambiguous reality of everyday life was *reduced* to the mathematical clarity of the ideal realm, *values* were also divorced from the *Lebenswelt*.

Laplace believed that human knowledge should emulate the model of mathematical astronomy, where discoveries in the fields of mechanics and geometry had allowed for an understanding of "the past and future states of the system of the world" through analytical formulas. This regularity was present in all phenomena, enabling human intelligence to deduce the general laws that govern them and even to predict such phenomena.[2] Laplace reminded his readers that not so long ago extraordinary phenomena such as a violent storm, a drought, a solar eclipse, or a comet were considered signs of divine anger. But today man no longer invoked the heavens, having realized, through observation, that prayer was useless.[3]

The criticism of Newton's metaphysics in Laplace's *Mécanique Celeste* is highly significant. Here astronomy was finally purified of traditional mythical connotations. Newton had written (according to Laplace) that the regularity of the motion of planets and satellites did not have mechanical causes, but that this "admirable concert" was the work of an intelligent and powerful being. To this Laplace responded with a rhetorical question: Could it not be possible that this disposition of the planets was itself

Positivism, Descriptive Geometry, and Scientific Building

an effect of the law of motion, and that Newton's "Supreme Intelligence" had been replaced by a more general phenomenon?[4] After reading *Mécanique Celeste*, Napoleon I allegedly asked Laplace why he had not mentioned God in his work about the universe. To which the author is supposed to have replied: "Because I have no need of such a hypothesis."

This new epistemological framework also brought about the unconditional acceptance of relativism. The fundamental paradox of the modern world is derived from a simultaneous belief in reason (with its infinite capacity to discover absolutely certain mathematical truths) and the belief in the radical subjectivity of each human being, condemned to his own partial perspective of the world (providing only a limited access to "objective" reality). This characteristic ambiguity of modern Western culture became critical when scientists and philosophers of the early nineteenth century declared that all intellectual operations outside mathematical reason were illegitimate. The necessary mythical dimension, the sphere of dreams, poetry, and imagination, which had allowed for the reconciliation of man with the world, was eliminated from scientific thought. Truth and knowing were finally severed, with the former assuming priority over the latter. The traditional primacy of an intersubjective world given with meaning to perception was rejected. And the individual searching for orientation in order to make an existential decision was thereby condemned to rely solely on formal logic.

Long before Einstein's theory of relativity, the absolute time and space of Newton was questioned by Laplace: "A body appears to us to be in motion when it changes its situation relative to a system of bodies which we suppose at rest; but as all bodies, even those which seem to be in a state of the most absolute rest, *may be in motion*, we conceive a space, boundless, immovable and penetrable to matter: It is to the parts of this *real or ideal* space that we by imagination refer the situation of bodies."[5] Later Auguste Comte would assert that there was nothing good and nothing bad, absolutely speaking: "Everything is relative, and this is the only absolute statement."

At this point, it is important to remember that the concept of infinity in calculus, in spite of Fontenelle's commentary on Leibniz's discovery did not become during the eighteenth century "a number like any other." Geometrical infinity could never avoid a certain "metaphysical contamination" during the Enlightenment. As long as philosophical speculation remained an integral part of mathematical thinking, the problem of transition between the infinitely large and the infinitely small (one identical abstract number), appeared as an unsolvable dilemma, irreconcilable with the pristine notion of a transcendent and static infinity. In fact, most eighteenth-century mathematicians decided to return to more simple notions of arithmetic and algebra.[6] D'Alembert, for example, introduced the idea of "limit." Infinity in calculus thus became the limit of the finite: the term toward which it tends without ever arriving. In 1772 Lagrange insisted that the new methods of calculus based on functions could be simplified, and in 1797 he published a work containing the principles of differential calculus that were viewed "apart from any consideration of the infinitely small, of evanescent elements, limits or fluxions;" in short, they had been reduced to the algebraic analysis of finite quantities.[7] That same year Lazare Carnot published his *Réflexions sur la Métaphysique du Calcul Infinitesimal*, demonstrating that infinitesimal calculus did not need to prove its own truth, that its real and only value was to be an efficient tool for the solving of technical problems. That a serious scientist would write a book on this topic so late in the century is in itself significant. For it was only at around this time that scientific research became truly autonomous from philosophical speculation, transforming itself into a specialized compartment of knowledge, immune to ethical, aesthetic, or metaphysical controversy. At this point, man's technical actions were divorced from human values, becoming a blind technological intentionality determined by abstract, utopian parameters.

Hence calculus could now be effectively applied to practice in any discipline. Laplace's *Mécanique Celeste* represented the first successful application of this science to the "system of the world," depicting a universe that was, for the first time, no longer a hierarchical cosmos. The first analytical mechanics of the sublunar world was postulated by Lagrange in his *Mécanique Analytique* (1788). The difference between his work and previous treatises on mechanics (like De la Hire's) was that he intended to reduce the theory of this science and the art of solving its specific problems to general formulas, whose simple development would provide all the necessary equations for the solution of each particular problem. Lagrange synthesized under a single premise the known mechanical principles, while increasing their precision and applicability. His work was the first coherent reduction of mechanics to pure algebraic analysis, *avoiding* the use of geometrical figures.

Positivism, Descriptive Geometry, and Scientific Building

Lagrange stressed that only algebraic operations were needed in physics and discarded "constructions or geometrical reasonings."[8]

The reduction of phenomena to mathematical laws was to become the obsession of nineteenth-century thought. The physical and human sciences had to be reduced to a small number of truths that, although obtained initially through observation, could be combined and handled exclusively through reason.[9] The inherently problematical model of an atheistic Newtonianism, that is, mathematical astronomy and mechanics, thus dictated the character of positivistic thought, providing the epistemological framework for the new specialized nineteenth-century sciences. Or as Auguste Comte put it: Astronomy had preceded sociology as the cause of the great intellectual revolutions of humanity.[10] In the preface of the first edition of the *Critique of Pure Reason* (1781), Kant wrote that human reason was overwhelmed by questions it could not solve. In the name of experimental philosophy, he condemned speculative metaphysics. The philosophy of the future had to respond to a different model of truth based on geometry and mathematics. Kant's own work was an attempt to transform traditional metaphysics and bring about a revolution in philosophy, following in the footsteps of physicists and geometricians.[11] Comte expressed a similar intention more than eighty years later in his *Cours de Philosophie Positive*. The main thrust of positivistic philosophy was the notion that phenomena were subjected to invariable natural laws. All intellectual enterprises were to have as their objective the precise determination of such laws and their reduction to the least possible number in each discipline.[12]

I have shown how most of these ideas and intentions were in some way evident in Europe since the seventeenth century. But it was only after the French Revolution, when "serious" scientific thinking excluded metaphysical speculation, that the intention of technological domination became effective in the realm of the physical world. Positivism was then openly extended to the social sciences without a sense of guilt; later, by rejecting symbolization as a basic form of knowledge, it particularly hampered man's understanding of the true nature and importance of poetry and art.

In 1810 Delambre published his *Rapport Historique sur les Progrès des Sciences Mathématiques depuis 1789*. This text represents the first attempt at a history of science by means of a simple collection of facts, without a philosophical standpoint to shape it.[13] Its positivistic program effected a clear division of knowledge. Each particular discipline now possessed its own autonomous history, apart from a world view; each was seen as an accumulation of positive experience, as a linear progression that excluded "failures" or "irrelevant speculations." This model had a profound impact upon all historical disciplines of the nineteenth century. Such a conception of history, still popular today, creates many misunderstandings and reinforces the illusion that meaningful intellectual achievement necessarily has to occur within specialized compartments of knowledge.

According to Saint-Simon, the aristocracy of the nineteenth century was to be composed of specialized scientists and technicians; *applied* science would determine the future of humanity.[14] Only in the Napoleonic university was an independent faculty of science created, institutionalizing the distinction between objective sciences and subjective humanities (*lettres*). The first few years of the nineteenth century also witnessed the emergence of a new intellectual leader: the arrogant and self-sufficient technical specialist. Such individuals received their education at the *École Polytechnique* in Paris, an institution founded by the revolutionary *Convention* that became a model of progressive education around the world. The technical specialist unquestionably has been the most influential figure in Western culture for the last two centuries. With an infinite faith in mathematical reason and believing himself educated because he had passed through difficult schools, he had little or no knowledge of society, its history and problems, and despised the humanities because their content was always ambiguous and practically impossible to formulate with mathematical certainty.[15]

According to Fourcy, who wrote the first history of the *École Polytechnique* in 1828, more than half of the members of the physics, chemistry, and mathematics sections of the *Institut*, as well as the best engineers in the country, were graduates from the school. The most illustrious names in all scientific and technical fields during the early nineteenth century were associated with the institution: Lagrange, Laplace, Monge, Fourier, Prony, Poinsot, Lamblardie, Navier, Berthollet, Poisson, Ampère, Gay-Lussac, and of course, J. N. L. Durand in the area of architectural theory and design.[16] The *École Polytechnique* prepared equally scientists and technicians, both of whom were obsessed with the illusion of a technological utopia. Evaluating the impact of the school, Cournot wrote that by giving the physical sciences their mathematical precision (thus transforming the art of the engineer), the *École* produced a revolution in industry, influencing current ideas and even encouraging French nationalism.[17]

Fourcy had considered the *École du Génie de Mezières* and the *École des Ponts et Chaussées* as the immediate forerunners of the new institution. Nevertheless, at the *École Polytechnique* teaching methods were quite different. All students had to fulfill a series of strict admission requirements, including a written examination. Once in the school, they followed a mandatory curriculum designed to provide everyone with general methods of universal applicability. Unlike the atmosphere of apprenticeship, which had been geared to solving specific problems in the technical schools of the eighteenth century, the *École Polytechnique* advocated impersonal lectures and the notion of required subjects, which everyone had to master before specializing. This became the dominant pedagogical idea in professional education thereafter.

Indeed, the school was created to provide a "solid and vigorous" mathematical and scientific foundation for individuals who wished to go on to one of several *Écoles d'Application* before entering public service. The general statutes of the school stated that the institution would also provide a basic knowledge of chemistry and the graphic arts.[18] Having fulfilled its requirements, a student would be in a position to enter services as diverse as artillery, the navy, civil construction, shipbuilding, mining, or geographical engineering. Students had to learn not only basic mathematics and algebra but the infinitesimal calculus necessary for rational mechanics. Apart from physics and chemistry, the other basic subject was descriptive geometry, which could be applied to civil engineering, fortifications, architecture, mines, machinery, and naval construction.

In the "first notebook" of the *Journal Polytechnique*, architecture was defined as the art of designing and building works of earth, masonry, or wood, utilizing established principles and proportions.[19] "Civil architecture" was divided into two courses. Interestingly, Baltard wrote only a one-page introduction to architecture, which was full of vague and uncertain notions.[20] Lamblardie, however, wrote ten pages about civil engineering and provided a detailed program of his course.

Within the new school, architecture became almost a subprofessional discipline, with no coordinated *École d'Application* for graduates seeking further academic specialization. Little time was devoted to courses on design and architectural theory. In the "third notebook," a revised curriculum was proposed in which architecture was not even an independent subject, but part of the course on civil works. The obvious reason was eventually revealed by Durand in his *Précis des Leçons* (1809). He pointed out that not only were all types of engineers capable of doing architecture; they were also afforded more opportunities to undertake large commissions.[21]

Once the rational part of building was identified with the objectives of the new positivistic civil engineering, the specific character of architecture was reduced to decoration. And decoration, in the new epistemological context, was bound to be considered a frivolous, expensive, and relatively useless occupation. It should be remembered that Napoleon, as opposed to his predecessors, despised architecture and accused it of ruining the state and its citizens through excessive expenditure. This, of course, was sinful in an industrial society whose values were based on economics. The Emperor mainly used engineers in his building enterprises; architects were only invited to participate when decoration was called for. Ornament became a value commodity, a consumer's product added to the work of architecture, which otherwise was essentially the result of a simple technological process.

| The Functionalization of Euclidean Geometry | The last decade of the eighteenth century also witnessed the appearance of a mathematical discipline in which Euclidean geometry became truly functionalized, that is, reduced to the realm of algebraic analysis. This was Gaspard Monge's *Géométrie Descriptive* (1795), which was studied by the students of the *École Polytechnique* and which represented the first possibility of an effective and precise mathematical description of reality. |

Although the use of geometrical projections had been present in architectural design and other building techniques since the sixteenth century, the theories of geometricians before Monge were always concerned with specifics. They lacked the independence and coherence that make descriptive geometry a true science, one capable of functioning abstractly and thus applicable to a wide range of problems.[22] With the exception of Desargues's *manière universelle*—which was still too theoretical and never postulated in a sufficiently systematic way to include all techniques—Monge's method was the first to provide a truly synthetic system that could be universally applied to all arts and crafts, that is, to the totality of human action. Descriptive geometry thus constituted "a complete theory and practice of the operations that result from the combination of lines, planes, and surfaces in space."[23] Consequently, it concerned not only stonecutting, carpentry, fortification, and perspective but all those parts of pure or applied mathematics in which three-dimensional space figured. Delambre stressed that Euclidean geometry could only measure areas and volumes "in two dimensions," while descriptive geometry was able to consider space itself mathematically.

Descriptive geometry is a mathematical discipline whose fundamental principles can be proven analytically. It is a tool for reducing systematically and with absolute precision three-dimensional objects into "two-dimensional space." Monge believed that there was no construction in descriptive geometry that could not be translated into algebra. In his opinion, both sciences should be learned together, with emphasis on their interrelations.

In *Géométrie Descriptive*, practical and theoretical considerations were systematized and subsumed to a clear technological intentionality. To attain truth, mathematical precision was necessary in all disciplines. Monge also believed that a popularization of scientific methods and outlook was imperative for the advancement of industry. This would finally dispel the mystery concerning many manufacturing processes. He perceived his own work as a basis for the new *ars fabricandi* of technology, the "theory" of the new breed of engineers, whose only purpose was to make production more efficient.[24]

Hence Monge stressed that "everyone should know the theory and applications of descriptive geometry," whose objectives were twofold. First, it should effect the exact representation, through drawings in two dimensions, of three-dimensional objects that lend themselves to rigorous definition. From this standpoint, it was a "necessary language for all those men of genius" in charge of either conceiving or executing a project and for all the craftsmen that participated in its construction. The second objective was to deduce outcomes from the exact description of bodies and their positions (that is, their mathematical relations). In this sense, descriptive geometry becomes a means of acquiring the truth, offering "perpetual models" of the passage of the known to the unknown. Monge claimed that his discipline should be included in a plan of national education since the implementation of descriptive geometry was bound to accelerate the progress of industry.[25]

The invention of descriptive geometry was a crucial step in achieving a systematic mathematization of *praxis*; it subjected the

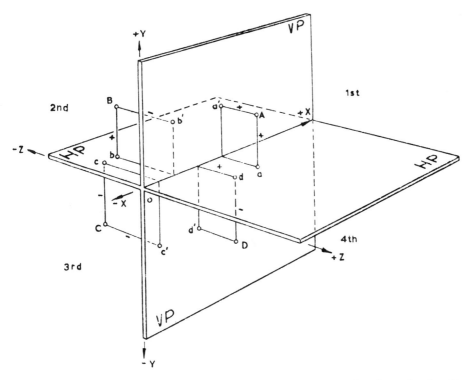

The orthogonal planes and quadrants of modern descriptive geometry, which allow for the reduction of three-dimensional reality to a system of coordinates and for their manipulation and transformation independently from intuition, from R. G. Robertson's *Descriptive Geometry* (by courtesy of Sir Issac Pitman and Sons Ltd.).

Positivism, Descriptive Geometry, and Scientific Building

arts and crafts to the goals of technology and was instrumental in the genesis and development of industrialism and rational building during the nineteenth century. It is necessary to stress that the geometry of the new architects and engineers graduating from the *École Polytechnique* (and of most practicing architects ever since) was the geometry invented by Monge. It was "the only conception," wrote Comte, capable of providing a precise idea of the characteristic doctrines that constituted the essence of engineering.[26]

In his article on the teaching of geometry that appeared in *Journal Polytechnique*, Gayvernon asserted that only after having studied the application of descriptive geometry to the different arts and crafts could the architect be in a position to determine the exact form and composition of his buildings and their parts.[27] In a different volume of the same journal, Monge pointed out that descriptive geometry provided a knowledge of forms of the different parts involved in all sorts of buildings, which were relative not only to the buildings' stability but also to their "decoration."[28]

One of Monge's disciples, M. Chasles, devoted many pages of his *Aperçu Historique sur l'Origine et Développment des Méthods en Géométrie* (1837) to descriptive geometry. He referred to Monge's achievement as "the first contribution in geometrical science for nearly a century, being a necessary complement of Descartes's analytic geometry."[29] Descriptive geometry "initiated a new era" in the history of the science of extension and had immense repercussions. In Chasles's words, this beautiful creation was destined originally to transform practical geometry and all the arts that depended upon it. It was, in fact, "a true general *theory*, having reduced to a small number of abstract and invariable principles and to a few easy and certain constructions all the geometrical operations that might be necessary in stonecutting, carpentry, perspective, fortification, the tracing of solar clocks, and other techniques that previously were only executed through incoherent, uncertain, and not very rigorous procedures."[30]

Chasles also recognized other profound implications of Monge's functionalization of three-dimensional reality. As a graphic translation of rational geometry, it prompted considerable advances in the field of analytic geometry, effecting a greater familiarity with the shapes of bodies and their ideal conceptions. The tools of research in geometry were doubled. Considered as a geometrical doctrine, Monge's science became an effective means of demonstration, rigorously relating three-dimensional objects to figures on a plane. According to Chasles, descriptive geometry provided the methods for solving a priori certain questions that Descartes's geometry could not solve, being restricted by the limits of algebra itself.[31] He explained that traditional Euclidean geometry was beset with complicated figures and that lacking general and abstract principles, it was forced to deal with each question in its concreteness, to discover the necessary elements for a solution or demonstration of a problem in the figure itself. Chasles stressed that this limitation was extremely inconvenient because of the complications inherent in the construction of figures, particularly in three dimensions. Relating algebraic formulations with visible objects whose parts were connected, descriptive geometry contributed enormously to the progress of algebraic analysis. Monge, according to Chasles, was thus "capable of doing algebra with geometry."[32]

The secret of algebra is the "mechanism of transformations," allowing it to achieve a high degree of generality. Chasles explained that Monge's great merit was to have applied this mechanism to geometry, discovering a "principle of continuity" between the volume and the plane. However, it remained for Monge's disciples, particularly General Jean-Victor Poncelet in his *Traité des Propriétés Projectives des Figures*, to discuss openly this principle of continuity, which had been tacit in descriptive geometry.[33] The difficulties involved in expressing a principle that, in effect, legalized the functionalization of the *Lebenswelt* were enormous; the overcoming of such difficulties amounted to the acceptance of the most fundamental epistemological transformation since the discovery of theory in Greece.

General Poncelet was probably Monge's most brilliant disciple. He studied at the *École Polytechnique* and in 1822 published a treatise that, according to his biographers, was instrumental in the shaping of industrial mechanics.[34] His projective geometry held that there were certain relations of position in geometrical figures that remained invariable before and after they were subjected to a perspective projection.[35] Some of the universal principles postulated by Poncelet had already been discovered by Pascal and Desargues, but were conceived as independent propositions and never became part of a methodical geometrical theory.

Poncelet wished to increase the generality of theories in the mathematical sciences, so that their realm of action could remain under the control of the intellect.[36] A small number of fruitful truths could be the abbreviated expression of a great variety of particular facts. Poncelet's main objective was to provide ordinary geometry with the "character of extension" that had made algebra so fecund. Euclidean geometry not only lacked generality but, in his opinion, it also did not have a direct and uniform method by which to search for truth; it was forced to use arithmetic proportions with excessive frequency. In contrast, descriptive geometry possessed the quality of a true doctrine whose few principles were linked in a necessary manner. "It is easy to realize," wrote Poncelet, "that these characteristics derived exclusively from the use of projections."[37]

The "projective properties"—those that remain constant before and after a projection—constituted the true nature of figures. These metric or descriptive properties or relations would necessarily have the greatest possible generality and indetermination since they would be independent of any absolute dimension.[38] Like Monge, Poncelet sought to "increase the resources of simple geometry," generalizing its conceptions and restricted language, assimilating it into analytic geometry. His main contribution was to provide adequate general means for demonstrating and discovering easily the projective properties possessed by figures, when considered in a purely abstract manner, apart from their real determinate dimensions.[39]

Applying the principle of continuity, Poncelet was able to establish a synthetic geometry with universal methods. Figures, which in Euclidean geometry were treated as qualitatively different entities, became members of a "family," with a potential for reciprocal transformation. Now figures consisted of the constant relations among their parts. Henceforth, purely formal considerations would define the essence of all geometrical figures, ignoring their primordial relation to the visible world. From this point of view, projective geometry became a prototype of Western nineteenth-and twentieth-century thought, and its appearance marked the beginning of the crisis of European science.

In Euclidean science, a diverse interpretation and deduction corresponded to each difference in sensuous appearance. For Poncelet, however, each individual form was to be examined not in itself but as part of the system to which it belonged and as an expression of the totality of forms into which it could be transformed.[40] Desargues had already noticed the similarity between an infinite straight line and a circle. But Poncelet declared that all the points projected to infinity on a plane could also be ideally considered as being part of a single straight line itself placed at

Geometry, Number, and Technology

infinity. Poncelet was the first to establish clearly the homology between two-dimensional planes and three-dimensional space, showing the way toward multidimensional, non-Euclidean geometries. This implied, in fact, the power to *substitute* the ideal for the real. This power of substitution is at the very root of the crisis of Western science; it has been the source of man's profound disorientation. It is also the paradigmatic problem of modern art; space became increasingly more flat toward the end of the eighteenth century, to the point of allowing, in anticipation of cubism, the disappearance of Euclidean relations among depicted objects.[41]

After Poncelet, geometry became an independent syntactic system, capable even of dispensing with algebra. It was a discipline that no longer needed to place its problems in the context of the perceived world-as-lived. It could avoid imagination, achieving instead a perfect logical coherence that made it ideal for technological applications. Projective geometry could now be employed effectively in the resolution of problems of statics and strength of materials. This was proved in the methods of Culmann and Cremona, which appeared in 1866 and 1872, respectively.

Building Science   Around the beginning of the nineteenth century, technology became the *modus vivendi* of man; human action (the traditional techniques) became totally "serious," rejecting its traditional dimension of existential play. It might be said that at this point external reality lost its divine character and was reduced to matter, and thus it finally came to be dominated by mankind. The arrogance, anguish, and correlative responsibility of architects, engineers, and technicians of the nineteenth century contrasted with the general tranquility and self-confidence of their predecessors. Also, the intention to reduce architectural theory to a simple set of fixed rules, whose primary objective was a more efficient and economical practice, was finally brought to fruition in the early nineteenth century. With the development of the new geometries and their application to military engineering, stereotomy, carpentry, and working drawings in general, sufficient precision was achieved to guarantee the success of these theories in practical problems.

The work of Jean Rondelet represents an excellent example of this transformation of theory into a technological tool. He had been commissioned by Soufflot to finish the Pantheon, after defending the projected dimensions of the building against the objections of Patte. In his *Mémoire Historique sur le Dôme du Panthéon Français* (1797), Rondelet expressed the same interests and technical knowledge found in the works of his contemporaries. He assumed an approach similar to Gauthey's, giving greater importance to the quantitative results of experiments made with a device of his own invention—apparently the first device actually capable of providing sufficiently precise results.[42] Rondelet's objective was the solution of structural problems by means of a scientific method, one that would eschew intuitive considerations. In his description of Soufflot's building, he dealt almost exclusively with materials and building procedures. The mathematization of the theory of construction obviously implied in his thought a greater and more effective control of diverse techniques. Rondelet taught stereotomy in the new *École Speciale d'Architecture*, which was founded after the suppression of the Royal Academy. Between 1794 and 1795 he also participated in the *Direction de Travaux Publics*. And in 1789 he presented a paper that was responsible for the formation of the *École Centrale de Travaux Publics*, which would later become the *École Polytechnique*.[43]

Rondelet's extensive *Traité Théorique et Pratique de l'Art de Bâtir* (1802), which provided methods for solving all sorts of practical problems through the application of easy, step-by-step rules, was the first truly effective textbook on building science. It became extremely popular and went into many editions. In his introduction, Rondelet provided a historical account tracing the "progress" of the building craft. His interest was exclusively *firmitas*—the solidity, stability, and durability of buildings—and only from this point of view did he pronounce judgment on the different periods in a history of architecture that he conceived of as a linear process, as the evolution of rational construction. From this unprecedented vantage point that would become the basis of nineteenth-century architectural history, he criticized, for example, Egyptian architecture for having been concerned only with "immutable solidity" and because once it had reached this objective ("mainly through instinct"), it had never gone beyond it.[44]

Like the *Rigoristti*, Rondelet rejected Greek architecture, criticizing the transposition into marble of forms derived from wood. In contrast to Lodoli, however, Rondelet considered solidity not only as a totally independent value but as the only essential value in architecture, in opposition to any other.[45] After expressing his admiration for the development of building techniques attained during the Roman Empire and for the great Gothic structures (which had been determined by structural necessity, convenience, and an appropriateness of use), he deplored the fact that great modern masters like Palladio or Serlio, "captivated by the art of drawing," had only perpetuated the classical orders in their treatises, dealing with proportions but providing no guide with respect to the science of construction.[46]

Rondelet observed that only during the eighteenth century were these "difficult abstract questions" considered. After Poleni's discussion of St. Peter's dome and Gauthey's commentary on the French Pantheon, it became increasingly clear that "the essential objective [of architecture] was, above all, the construction of solid buildings, using a just amount of selected materials with art and economy."[47] Rondelet claimed that the perfection deriving from the art of construction "excited our admiration" and that it embodied "the first degree of beauty in a building" by simply being a guarantee of its longer endurance. He defined the art of building as "a happy application of the exact sciences to the properties of matter. Construction becomes an art once theoretical knowledge is joined with that of practice to regulate equally all its operations."[48]

Theory, for Rondelet, was the result of experience and reasoning, founded on the principles of mathematics and physics. Through the application of theory, a good builder should be able to determine the correct form and dimensions of any part of a building by its situation and the load it has to support. Rondelet stressed that only such buildings would be well proportioned, solid, and economical. Only through theory could a builder explain the necessary procedures for the execution of a certain work. But, as Rondelet emphasized, the knowledge of principles and experience should be joined with the knowledge of practical operations and the nature of materials in order to be effective. His treatise was written with this in mind: to put forward a theory conceived as a powerful and universal instrument for the thorough domination of the building craft. Within a positivistic framework, myth and nonscientific speculation were unacceptable. For the first time in a book on building, the transcendent justification of architecture no longer mattered. Intended meaning was perceived as irrelevant. If it appeared at all, it would be as a result of a technological process.

The encyclopedic content of Rondelet's treatise was indeed impressive. In detail and range alone, it was far superior to other books on construction. It provided long descriptions of the major building materials, enumerating different types of marble or stone, discussing their geological and geographical origin, their properties and appropriate uses based on the results of experiments on their resistance under diverse conditions. It included detailed accounts of masonry construction methods, conspicuously adopting geometry and physics from the start while rejecting the traditional notions that had always surrounded the act of building. The objectivity and rationality of the text is truly astounding; nothing is left to chance or intuition. The problems were always formulated mathematically, and precise working drawings were usually added. Numerous, often superflous details betrayed Rondelet's obsession with matter and its subleties. Architecture, or at least its "fundamental part," was thus transformed into an exact science. Rondelet, who obviously considered modern building science far superior to all past technical methods, also emphasized that the road to progress was open. His writing lacked the absolute and definitive tone that had characterized previous works on architectural theory, even those concerned particularly with building techniques. Rondelet had every confidence in mathematical evidence; but in a truly positivistic vein, he believed in the utopian potential of reason and thought that further discoveries would necessarily lead to better theories.

The first application of the new descriptive geometry to problems of building appeared in the third, fifth, and sixth chapters of the treatise. All imaginable propositions of stereotomy, carpentry and cabinetmaking were solved through the systematic use of projections and the a priori graphic determination of the precise configurations and dimensions of all building elements in arches, trusses, stairs, vaults, ornamental details, and even furniture. Once the architect familiarized himself with the universal method, he could conceive with unprecedented detail and precision any solid element; the illustrative plates accompanying such texts lose their apparent complexity and become totally transparent to mathematical reason, directly translating real space onto the intelligible space of the plane. Rondelet's plates represented the first *effective* graphic solutions to questions of building technology.

With this transformation of architectural drawing, represented images lost their symbolic dimension and became prosaic signs of a material reality. This was not a disturbing outcome to the architects, who in this positivistic world were generally prepared to disregard the value of symbolic knowledge. It is significant in this regard how descriptive geometry was readily accepted by modern architecture as a neutral tool, an acceptance whose implications are made apparent today when design projects are conceived or criticized as buildings rather than as irreducible symbols of an intention. The univocal character and absolute clarity of descriptive geometry responded perfectly to the most basic intentions of nineteenth- and twentieth-century architects.

Descriptive geometry provided the means for overcoming, with a considerable degree of success, the limitations endemic to a lack of practical, immediate knowledge of building techniques. The architect could now dictate to the carpenter or mason, even if his familiarity with the crafts was practically nil. Thus he could specialize in design. The significance of the application of descriptive geometry to building science cannot be overemphasized for it precipitated the reduction of building to a mere technological process. Bearing this in mind, we can see that only after the French Revolution could an architect or engineer be considered qualified to practice once he had undergone an extensive curriculum, examinations, and theoretical tests, though he might never have had any real involvement with actual building practice.

The tenth chapter of Rondelet's *Art de Bâtir* was devoted to the quantitative evaluation of buildings. In a sense, it represented a culmination of all those texts on mensuration, cost estimates, and specifications that first appeared in the late seventeenth century. Rondelet, however, was exclusively concerned with the technological values of efficiency and economy. He criticized Renaissance and Baroque architects for having disregarded these values and for spending their time imagining "capricious, sumptuous, or gigantic projects."[49] He maintained that the excellence of an architect consisted not only in his capacity to choose forms and orders in a more or less happy way but that his integrity and reputation rested on those building operations conceived in mature consideration and executed in an orderly and economical manner.[50] Rondelet was representative of the new technological mentality, for which the elaboration of precise comprehensive projects and construction programs of easy execution became a fundamental operation. These all-encompassing projects or *devis* were believed capable of anticipating and controlling building operations in their entirety. Rondelet also helped establish the normalized decimal system; the simplicity and precision of measurements using decimal units were obviously superior to those based on measuring units that were not only imprecise but changed from country to country, region to region. The introduction of the decimal metric system along with precise working drawings using the methods of descriptive geometry transformed the *devis* into an effective tool.

Rondelet placed a great deal of importance on the methodical elaboration of *devis*. He criticized his predecessors who had shared the same intention, but always failed in fulfilling it. The production of these comprehensive projects (yielding a precise cost estimate) became the most important task for architects and engineers. And by the early nineteenth century, there were already attempts to institutionalize them.

In 1805 Rondelet was invited to write a set of regulations concerning cost estimates, which was to guide architects and builders in the emperor's service.[51] He stressed that a comprehensive project—one that took into account precise measurements, the specification of building procedures, quality of materials, and complete working drawings—was the necessary point of departure for building. He described the main aspects that had to be specified for each one of the building crafts and concluded that each process had to be accompanied by details. For Rondelet, it was extremely important to prevent the abuses and negligence of contractors and craftsmen; in this way one could construct buildings "ornamented with the virtues of solidity and economy."[52]

The elaboration of truly efficient *devis* required a comprehensive knowledge of the scientific theory of building and its practical applications. Conscious of this, Rondelet's treatise included a compendium of mechanics and strength of materials under the general subtitle "Theory of Construction." He explained that while the rest of the treatise was devoted to particular considerations of the diverse types of construction from a material standpoint, the objectives of the theory of construction considered which forms and dimensions should be given to different parts of a building, to ensure its solidity and stability.[53] Rondelet believed that mechanics and strength of materials should determine not only the dimensions but also the *form* of architectural elements, thus anticipating some of the more prosaic types of determinism that would become prevalent in architecture toward the midnineteenth century.

Drawing upon his own understanding of theory, Rondelet refuted the difficulties that had traditionally been associated with the division between theoretical and practical knowledge. Theory was often rejected by practitioners as "abstract reasoning," while theoreticians criticized practice as "blind routine." Rondelet argued

Geometry, Number, and Technology

that such a conflict was the product of a misunderstanding and did not actually exist. Indeed, from the point of view of a technological theory, that is, a truly effective *ars fabricandi*, theory and practice had to be intellectually united. The necessary ambiguity, implicit in the traditional relation between thinking and doing, was no longer acceptable.

Rondelet understood the importance as well as the limitations of calculations, hypotheses, and general formulas derived from geometry and mechanics. For an adequate theory of construction, experience and observation were equally important. He realized that theoretical results are conditional solutions and that they may have to be adapted to material circumstances. Without repeating the mistakes of his predecessors, he tried to combine an extremely acute empiricism with absolute mathematical solutions in order to work out particular problems. Although he refrained from applying the analytical method developed by Coulomb, he studied and evaluated all the past and present geometrical and algebraic solutions that he could find for each specific problem of statics. With great patience, he compared the results of other methods against those of his own theories and quantitative tests. From a positivistic standpoint, the question was to abide by the most adequate mathematical formulation until science should discover *definitive* solutions.

| **Structural Analysis** | The first few years of the nineteenth century witnessed the implementation of effective analytical methods that finally provided adequate solutions to those fundamental problems of statics and strength of materials that had concerned architects and engineers for over a hundred years. In the works of Gauthey, Mayniel, and Navier, the discoveries of Coulomb were translated into practical methods for structural design. Through the use of infinitesimal calculus, building reality could be mathematized. Such aspects as friction and cohesion, which had to be ignored in De la Hire's theory, or which were considered only experimentally by Denizy and Rondelet, could finally be incorporated within the universe of algebraic analysis. |

In marked contrast to the important role of Euclidean science in eighteenth-century statics and mechanics, the new solutions avoided the use of classical geometry. Mechanics became a purely analytical discipline and remained so until the second half of the nineteenth century, when Culmann and Cremona formulated their

Positivism, Descriptive Geometry, and Scientific Building

graphic alternatives, which, utilizing projective geometry, could compete with the precision and reliability of algebra.

The name of Emiland-Marie Gauthey, an architect and inspector of *Ponts et Chaussées*, has already been mentioned in connection with the dispute between Patte and Soufflot. According to his anonymous biographer (probably Navier), Gauthey had rejected in his *Dissertation sur les Degradations Survenues aux Piliers du Dôme du Panthéon François* De la Hire's hypothesis of the behavior of vaults.[54] Writing in 1809, the biographer declared that "today, this theory has been replaced." Although Gauthey did use, in the end, De la Hire's geometrical hypothesis, he was obviously aware of its fallacies and the complexities of the problem, which put him in a similar position to that of Rondelet.[55]

Gauthey was the uncle and teacher of Louis-Marie-Henri Navier, and the relation between them appeared to be quite close. Between 1809 and 1813 Navier completed and published Gauthey's most important work, the *Traité de la Construction des Ponts*. In an editorial preface, Navier stressed the originality of Gauthey's treatment. The famous engineers of the Enlightenment—Perronet and De Regemorte—had only offered "applications" in their texts. Gauthey, however, outlined the *principles* of bridge design and construction in a coherent body of doctrines, adding the necessary elements for a complete theory.[56]

In his own introduction, Gauthey explained that most architects had been concerned mainly with decoration; they had said very little about construction in general or the particular problems of bridges. These buildings, he thought, did not lend themselves to decoration and presented perhaps the greatest difficulties of execution. The only real objective of bridge building was, in his opinion, a faultless solidity and stability. True economy in public works consisted in ensuring the greatest endurance possible, while avoiding superfluous expenditure.[57] The bridge was no longer a "place"; it was a piece of traffic engineering; and decoration, traditionally enhancing a bridge's symbolic power, was now irrelevant.

Gauthey regretfully noted that aside from Alberti, Serlio, and Palladio, who had discussed some rules and proportions for bridges, the subject had practically been bypassed by architects prior to the eighteenth century. Referring to Perronet's great book on the bridge at Neuilly, Gauthey praised the instructive descriptions of the building procedures, but deplored the expense and minimal number of such publications, which put them beyond the reach of most architects. A far worse failing on the part of

Geometry, Number, and Technology

eighteenth-century works was that they provided "examples on the application of rules," but never a methodically ordered exposition and discussion of the rules themselves. Gauthey appreciated the earlier *Traité des Ponts* by Gautier, who had intended to establish general rules for bridge construction. But this treatise was full of mistakes and contradictions arising from a lack of practical experience.[58]

The first chapter of Gauthey's book provided a historical catalog of ancient and modern stone bridges all drawn to the same scale (the method used by Durand in his own history of architecture, of which more will be said later). The third chapter was devoted to scaffolding, and the fourth to building details. The fourth chapter also dealt with the fundamental question of estimating costs and its ramifications.

But it was in the second chapter that Gauthey outlined his "general principles for the establishment of bridges." Significantly, he began by condemning the great expense involved in eighteenth-century bridges, which had hindered the construction of other, perhaps less magnificent structures, but that would have benefited commercial expansion. Again we see a radical transformation concerning the essence of architectural value. Gauthey bitterly criticized Perronet's bridges, particularly their low arches "of difficult execution and elevated price," whose configurations were still ultimately determined by a symbolic intentionality.

Unlike even his immediate predecessors, Gauthey believed that no consideration in the design of a bridge should be arbitrary or outside mathematical reason. All factors contributing to the determination of form and dimensions were to be subjected to mathematical rules. The resulting design would thus be a function of all these mathematical variables. Five fundamental aspects were to be taken into account: (1) choice of site; (2) volume of water; (3) form of the arches; (4) dimensions of the arches; and (5) width of the bridge. Each of these aspects was determined through fixed rules, in relation to specific circumstances. In order to produce a final comprehensive project (one that should be strictly followed by the builders, leaving no place for improvisation), all these interrelated conditions had to be united in the intellect. This was, in fact, the first clear formulation of a functionalist attitude with regard to a problem of construction. Never before had the diverse factors that determined the design of a building been separated from a traditional, necessarily ambiguous, and hierarchical embodied structure, becoming in the process simple homogeneous "variables" in a mathematical formula.[59]

Gauthey examined how best to determine scientifically the dimensions of piers. He rejected the theories of De la Hire, Prony, and Bossut (all of which hinged upon the hypothesis of frictionless voussoirs), concluding that their results were not feasible. Instead, Gauthey opted for Coulomb's solution, which, as we have seen, was the first to synthesize successfully analytical statics with the physical qualities of materials expressed in quantitative terms.

Throughout his treatise, Gauthey provided mathematical formulas for quantifying all the aspects and conditions of building reality that had to be considered: for example, the speed of water, the type of soil, and the efficiency of workers. In contrast to Perronet's work, Gauthey's observations and quantitative experiments were no longer applied arbitrarily (as part of an indefinable personal and practical experience). Instead, they were transformed into coefficients and became part of a formula. Finally, the structure of mathematical analysis *replaced* experience, becoming the basis of a successful scientific method for the design of bridges.

Significantly, several other engineers applied Coulomb's method to building problems toward the beginning of the nineteenth century. L. C. Boistard, an engineer of *Ponts et Chaussées*, arrived at similar conclusions on the behavior of vaults, after having done many experiments.[60] The military engineer K. Mayniel published in 1808 his *Traité Expérimental, Analytique et Pratique de la Poussée des Terres et des Murs de Revêtement*, in which he objectively examined the existing theories on retaining walls. He explained that Bullet's theory, the first by an architect interested in establishing mechanically based principles on the thrust of the earth, did not coincide with experimental results. In fact, only Coulomb's solution had considered "all the physical circumstances" of the problem.[61] Mayniel's book provided a method based on Coulomb's theory that could now be easily applied in practice and that allowed for the mathematical determination of all the dimensions of retaining walls.

Riche de Prony, another engineer of *Ponts et Chaussées* and a disciple of Perronet, was the first to teach a course on analytic mechanics in the *École Polytechnique*. The course reviewed the theories of Euler, Lagrange, Laplace, Bossut, and Coulomb. In his *Mécanique Philosophique* (1801), Prony formulated a methodical table with the algebraic solutions to the main problems of mechanics, thereby avoiding any intermediary deduction of equations and speculations.[62] This synthesis was an ideal tool for the new generation of architects and engineers. It is significant that this work, in spite of its deliberate title, did not consider the objectives of mechanics in light of human existence or refer to its historical development. Prony believed that he was providing "the philosophical part of mechanics." This was not a careless use of words. "Philosophy" meant precisely the set of rules that allowed for the control and domination of matter; it became an instrument for fulfilling the designs of technology (applied science), avoiding all speculation about the meaning of technical action. Like Rondelet, Riche de Prony denied the value of both "blind routine" and "sterile speculation." The intellectual *juste milieu* of technology would now replace the delicate and ambiguous balance between theory and practice and would demand a concomitant mathematization of knowledge and its immediate domination of *praxis*. Geometry, pure science, and speculation would have no other *raison d'être* than the facilitation of all types of technological processes.

The work of Navier represents an appropriate culmination of this trend. Universally considered as the father of modern structural analysis, he gave coherent form to all previous discoveries, providing a theory that was much easier to learn and was universally applicable. In the course he taught at the *École des Ponts et Chaussées*, published in 1826, Navier showed how to apply principles to practice, postulating simple methods for determining analytically the forms and dimensions of structures in general.

Many of the formulas still used in structural analysis were first worked out by Navier. Unlike the engineers of the eighteenth century, whose experimentation was concerned only with the determination of fracture loads, Navier deduced his formulas within the elastic limits of materials. This radically simplified the problem of distance between mathematical theory and the real behavior of matter. He stressed that previous works on statics were based on false geometrical hypotheses and had been more useful to the progress of mathematics than to the advancement of the art of construction (see his commentaries on Bélidor's *Science des Ingénieurs*). In spite of the many theoretical works then available, he emphasized that during the Enlightenment, architects and engineers still determined the dimensions of their structures solely through personal experience.[63] Navier's objective was nothing less than the formulation of a general and prototypical method for structural analysis. It is therefore almost pathetically ironic that one of the first rigorously calculated bridges by Navier failed structurally—an early paradox of technology that immediately betrayed the limitations of mathematical reductionism.

Positivism, Descriptive Geometry, and Scientific Building

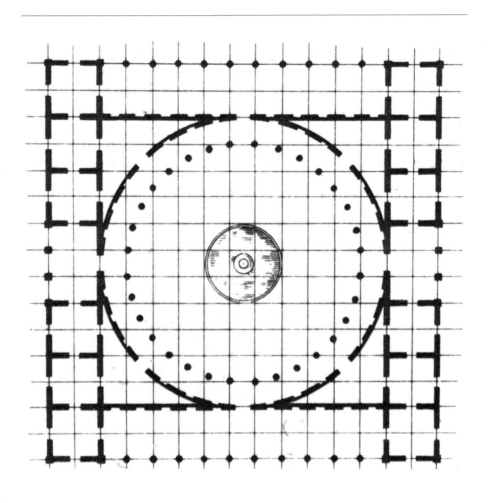

In the area of architectural theory and design, the stage at which *theoria* was transformed into a self-referential instrument for the control of *praxis* is best exemplified by the writings of Jacques-Nicolas-Louis Durand. Durand (1760–1834) was the most important of Boullée's disciples. The two enjoyed a close personal relation, and this, together with similar formal preferences, have caused historians to group them together under the "revolutionary" label and to fabricate misleading connections between them. While it is true that Durand admired Boullée, he represented in essence a different world; it is significant that the pyramidal monument that Durand built to honor the memory of his master was at the same time dedicated to the achievements of Gaspard Monge. In glancing at the project that initially made him famous, the Temple de la Felicité Publique, it is already possible to discern the differences between master and disciple. Form had become more emblematic than symbolic, and the piers that sustained Happiness were also engraved with the virtues championed by the French Revolution: alongside Wisdom, Concord, and Courage, there stood also Economy and Work. This attitude was already an anticipation of Labrouste's *neo-Grèc* approach to the problem of architectural meaning—a "legible" ornament added to a rational structure and clothing an otherwise inexpressive building.

Durand's most important contribution was his two theoretical works: the *Recueil et Parallèle des Edifices de Tout Genre, Anciens et Modernes* (1801), a vast collection of famous, less known, and even imaginary buildings, drawn at the same scale; and the *Précis des Leçons d'Architecture* (1802), which summarized the content of his courses at the *École Polytechnique*.

In the *Précis*, Durand defined architecture simply as the art of composing and executing all private and public buildings.[1] And because architecture was the most expensive of all the arts, it should not be whimsical or guided by prejudice or routine. In order to avoid wasteful expense, architectural design had to follow closely totally rational and immutable rules. In a sense, its elevated cost was consistent with its fundamental purpose: to sustain human life. After all, was it not the most advantageous of all the arts, the art to which man owed his conservation, society its existence, and the arts and crafts their inception and development? Without architecture, the human species, faced with the rigors of nature and lacking the means to protect itself against the elements, would not have enjoyed the rewards of society and might have perhaps disappeared from the earth. Hence "architecture had no other objective than private and public usefulness, the conservation and happiness of individuals, families and society."[2]

In contrast to previous architectural theory, Durand stressed the irrelevance of any transcendental justification. Architecture should merely be assured of its usefulness in a material world ruled by pragmatic values. There was no need to look for explanations outside the field of the new theory, a theory of architecture postulated for the first time as autonomous, self-sufficient, and specialized, composed exclusively of truths evident to mathematical reason. Durand thought that the means by which architecture reached its objectives were "no longer difficult to identify"; architecture, created by men for mankind, could find these means "within its own way of being."

In one rather terrifying paragraph, Durand summarized the basic precepts of his value system: In all times and all places, the totality of man's thoughts and actions were generated by two principles: love of well-being and aversion to pain.[3] This materialistic premise became the basis of the ethics and aesthetics of technology, and it still underlies the most popular historical and ideological conceptions inherited from the nineteenth century. Only after Durand would it become important for architecture to provide "pleasure" or that it be "nice" rather than truly meaningful.

Buildings were to be convenient and economical. Durand believed that these attributes were the "natural means" of architecture, the true source of its principles, which had always, in all times and all places, guided reasonable men in the construction of buildings. For building to be convenient, it had to be, above all, solid, healthy, and comfortable. To be solid, it had to be built with materials of high quality and proportioned with intelligence. To be healthy, it had to be placed on a well-chosen site. And to be comfortable, the forms and dimensions of its parts had to be "in the most precise possible relation," considering the use for which the building was designed.[4] With regard to economy, Durand explained that simple and symmetrical geometrical forms should be used in architectural design. Although these forms were very similar in appearance to those employed by the architects of the late eighteenth century, their presence was advocated from a standpoint totally different from the one expressed in the texts of Boullée or Ledoux. Durand recommends the use of a circular instead of a square or rectangular plan, for the simple reason that its perimeter is less. The more symmetrical, regular, and simple a building is, the less costly it will be. Economy thus prescribed the manner and means of buildings, forbidding all that which was not strictly "necessary."[5]

Durand opposed what was in his opinion a belief that had always been widely accepted: The fundamental objective of architecture is to be pleasant to the sight through decoration and imitation. He pointed out that architecture could not cause pleasure through imitation because, unlike the other arts, nature was not its model. Consequently, Durand rejected the traditional Vitruvian explanation of the anthropomorphic origin of the classical orders and Laugier's theory of the primitive hut, published only some fifty years earlier. In the light of positivistic reason, both hypotheses seemed nothing less than ridiculous. There was obviously no relation between a human body, whose width kept changing, and the cylinder of a column, and human proportions could not be the basis for the proportions of the classical orders. Durand no longer had, like his eighteenth-century predecessors, the capacity to accept at least the necessity of myth as a fundamental complement of the *logos* in architectural theory. For him, the imitation of nature was, for the first time, no longer *mimesis*. He could only understand it in a *literal* sense, as two terms of an equation, not as a metaphorical relation.

The mathematical reason of positivism rejected metaphor as a serious and legitimate form of knowledge, and this exclusion was what Durand brought to architecture. Traditional theories were, to his way of thinking, nothing but imaginary tales lacking scientific value; their sole purpose was to prove that the objective of architecture, being an art of imitation, was to please the eye. This "obvious" assumption, however, was a mistake. For Durand was unable to realize that the mythical dimension was actually the realm where the transcendent justification of architecture had to be found. It was only in the context of the new positivistic world that "reactionary" architects who questioned the power of reason could be considered mere decorators.

After showing how the primitive hut was not a natural object, nor the human body a model for architecture, Durand explained that the classical orders imitated neither the hut nor the body and could not therefore be considered as the essence of architecture. He stressed that the pleasure one might expect from their use and from decoration in general was nil. Decoration, he wrote, is nothing but a chimera, the cause of foolish expenditure.[6] This was diametrically opposed to the traditional attempt to reconcile ornament and structure which had prevailed even during the Age of Reason.

Elsewhere in the *Précis*, Durand explained that there were three kinds of forms and proportions in architecture: (1) those derived from the nature of the materials and from the use of the objects in whose construction they were employed; (2) the forms dictated by custom, like those found in ancient buildings; and (3) the simple and well-defined shapes that were preferred because they could be easily apprehended. In Durand's opinion, only the first type was essential—determined by the laws of mechanics and utility. But because those were not absolutely defined "by the nature of things," forms from the other two categories could be added to buildings. The rules of the classical orders belonged to the second variety and in Durand's theory were devoid of symbolic value.

Although Durand provided simple recipes for determining the proportions of the orders, he emphasized that these numerical relations had nothing to do with beauty. However rational the orders and their rules, the human eye simply could not apprehend objective proportions; the dimensions changed with each different point of view. Hence it was evident that "these proportions had very little influence on the pleasure produced by an aspect of a building."[7] The reader may recall that even for Perrault, proportions were ultimately indispensable to ensure a building's "arbitrary beauty" because dimensions, according to him, were indeed perceived directly by the human mind and were thus associated with "positive beauty. " François Blondel and other traditional architects solved the problem of perspective distortions through intuitive "optical corrections." But for Durand, the problem of perspectivism became insurmountable, and this led him to relativism; objective proportions became irrelevant as a norm of value since all individuals perceived them differently from their subjective points of view. In Durand's architectural theory, the possibility of reconciliation between the objective and the subjective was finally excluded.

Although both logic and history revealed that neither pleasure nor decoration were the true objectives of architecture, Durand acknowledged that some buildings were more "pleasant" than others. In fact, Durand believed that it was impossible for architecture not to be pleasant when derived from true principles. Since man's most intense pleasures resulted from the satisfaction of his most pressing needs, it was hardly surprising that an art that satisfied a great number of our needs also gave us much pleasure.[8]

The system of values underlying Durand's theory was, indeed, radically different from those of his predecessors. The value of architecture was no longer defined by a complete, irreducible set of categories that depended on a transcendental intention for their hierarchical organization. By now architecture had ceased to be a metaphorical image of the cosmic order. True, the new self-contained and necessarily prosaic architecture seemed to be ruled by similar categories; but the categories were now totally autonomous, and their structure was logical, not symbolic. Failing to recognize this issue, architectural historians have misinterpreted nineteenth-century historicism, and consequently, the most relevant questions concerning modern architecture have eluded them. Using Durand as a springboard, later architects would conceive the Vitruvian categories—stability or durability, beauty, and convenience—as independent entities, to be realized separately in accordance with mathematical reason, and which at best could be integrated like the terms of an equation, in order to achieve the greatest pleasure and the least pain.

Swerving away from Boullée and Ledoux's *architecture parlante*, Durand emphasized that the "character" of buildings, their meaning, was not a specific problem. In his opinion, it was enough to solve adequately the "disposition" of a plan (based on the work's intended use) in order to produce buildings that would be perceptibly different from those designed with another program.[9] Durand was incapable of understanding the problem of character in its symbolic sense, the way it was viewed by even his immediate predecessors. To his way of thinking, character was nothing but a sign, or the result of a direct mathematical relation postulated between the final form of a building and the organization of its plan. The architect's only concern should be to achieve the most appropriate (useful) combination of the different parts of his building in plan. No architectural decoration would be pleasant, stressed Durand, unless it sprang from the most convenient and economical "disposition." Here is the direct precedent of twentieth-century functionalism, which is still present today in explicit and disguised forms. With Durand, the "disposition" of the plan becomes the prototypical problem for architecture.

From this vantage point, the talent of the architect is reduced to his ability to solve two problems: (1) the design and construction of the most convenient building with a given amount of money,

Geometry, Number, and Technology

as in the case of private commissions; and (2) the most economical construction of a building whose details are already given, as in the case of public institutions.[10] For Durand, economy and efficiency were not a limitation, but sources of inspiration. They became the *only* acceptable values of architecture. And as long as the work fulfilled its program. it would be pleasant. The idea of efficiency is a functional relation: to achieve a *maximum* result with a *minimum* effort, with maximum economy. The system of values in architecture was thus reduced to a scale between pleasure and pain. Value could be "measured" as it approached ideal efficiency and maximum pleasure. The ethics of the new architecture of positivism was, then, nothing but a transposition of the law of maximums and minimums—the same law that had allowed Coulomb to solve the classical problems of structural mechanics. This system of values lies at the origin of the still prevalent emphasis on comfort over meaning in contemporary architecture.

In this theoretical context, the simple geometrical solids used as prototypes in architectural projects lost their symbolic connotations; they became signs of the new values, the "formal language" of technology. Durand was convinced that simple forms that were easy to perceive produced some pleasure in the observer. But this was not the crucial issue. Such forms were to be used because they corresponded essentially to those conceptions already shaped by the rules of economy. This notion was underscored in Durand's criticism of Soufflot's Pantheon. He wrote that if Soufflot had adhered to the rules of economy instead of using forms in search of effects and "movement," his building would not have resulted in a "complex Greek-cross plan," but would have been a simple circular temple surrounded by a colonnade. This "disposition" would have not only saved half of the money but truly increased the building's magnificence and grandeur.

Obviously, Durand's lessons were consistent with his pragmatic intentions. In the first part of the *Précis*, he analyzes the elements of buildings, such as columns, walls, openings, foundations, roofs, vaults, trusses, and terraces, which are considered from two different standpoints: in relation to the materials used in their construction; and according to the forms and proportions that they should naturally possess. In the second part, Durand explains how to combine these elements, which are for architecture "like words in language or notes in music." Through these combinations, which comprise, in his opinion, the essential aspect of the architect's work, diverse parts of buildings are formed: vestibules, rooms, porticoes, atriums, and so forth. Once these parts are well formulated, he explains how to combine them to compose whole structures. And in the third part, he examines the properties of different types of buildings.

Thus architectural design as a whole was reduced in Durand's theory to a formal game of combinations, devoid of transcendental intentions. Meaning was to be derived from *within* the system. Architecture became a language whose possible meaning depended entirely on syntax, and absolute semantic relations were obviously beyond positivistic reason. This *ars combinatoria*, unlike traditional ones, was in essence outside reality, obeying only those rules accommodated by mathematical reason, not by the logic of everyday life. While even the *distribution* of J. F. Blondel managed to become a metaphor of reality, Durand's methodology excluded this possibility. Durand believed that his method alone constituted the proper study of architecture, a method whereby a small number of fruitful ideas, elements, and simple combinations could achieve results that would be as rich and varied as language itself. This succinct theory was actually intended as nothing more than a useful tool to aid students in speedily designing any building, "even those of which they have never heard before."[11] Finally, with Durand, architecture did become understood as formal language or style. And in this we discern the source of the most banal formalist approaches, still popular today in many schools and offices of the Western world.

To repeat: The objective of all theory, for Durand, was to ensure the efficiency and economy of operations. In order to achieve this and to simplify architectural design, Durand taught his students the *mécanisme de la composition*, which consisted in the use of a grid to solve the fundamental problem of disposition, or arrangement of the elements in plan. Columns were to be placed at the intersections, walls on the axes, and openings at the centers of the modules. Durand showed how to apply this method to all parts of a building, and these parts would then be combined in a specific project. Although the solution of the plan was always the primary concern, the application of combinations to facades, general volumetric studies, roofing, and *parti* generation was also taught. Combinations were the means by which any architectural problem could be solved, which is another way of saying that the method *was* the theory.

The use of the grid in design was, of course, not Durand's invention. In Cesariano's edition of Vitruvius (1521), the famous

Geometry, Number, and Technology

Plate in the *Précis* comparing Soufflot's Ste.-Geneviève with Durand's proposal.

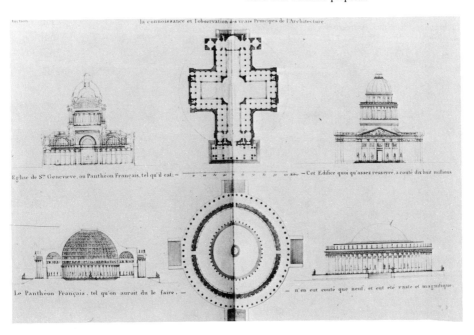

Durand and Functionalism

Durand's geometrical method for the composition of
plans, applicable to all types of buildings, from his
Précis.

Combination of vertical elements for the composition of facades, from Durand's *Précis*.

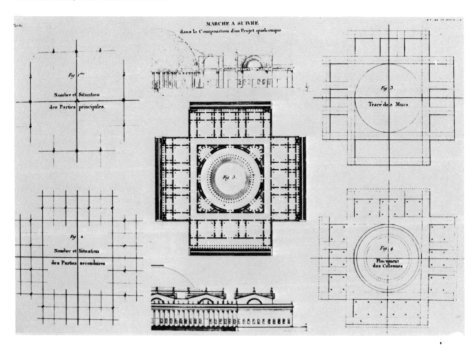

Geometry, Number, and Technology

Vitruvian man was superimposed on a grid, and later Philibert de l'Orme used it in his system of Divine Proportion.[12] In all these instances, however, and even in those more ambiguous applications that we encountered in eighteenth-century treatises, the grid's character as an instrument of design was secondary to the symbolic value of the order it denoted. Only in the case of Durand's *mécanisme* did the grid become an instrument whose *sole* value was as a tool in a technological process. This grid represented lived space finally transformed into a concept—a notion that nineteenth and twentieth-century architects would become very fond of, which eventually came to be taken for granted, abused in architectural education, and even mistakenly applied in interpreting other periods in the history of architecture.[13] Essentially, Durand's grid as a generator of the plan was already the reticulation recommended by Le Corbusier, founded on the misconception that man inhabits not qualitative places, but a homogeneous and universal geometrical space.

The methodology of descriptive geometry was used by Durand and his disciples to simplify the expression of architectural ideas and to make the relation between the projects and the physical reality of the buildings as immediate as possible. Durand thought that drawing was "the natural language of architecture"; in order to fulfill its objective, architecture should be in harmony with the ideas of which it is an expression. Simple architecture, which avoided the useless and unnatural, should reflect a type of drawing free of ostentation and difficulty. Any other drawings, in Durand's opinion, would be detrimental to the project, a bother to the hand and a hindrance to the imagination, and would even lead to false judgments. Plan, section, and elevation were considered the only drawings necessary for communicating a complete idea of a building; it was highly recommended to include them on a single sheet of paper as corresponding projections.[14]

Drawing upon Monge's method, Durand and his disciples always presented their projects as two dimensional. In fact, this characterized all the designs included in Durand's *Précis*. In contrast with the drawings and watercolors of Boullée and Ledoux, Durand's projects consisted of perfectly sharp plans, sections, and elevations, traced with a very thin and precise line. He eschewed the use of atmospheric effects or perspectives, avoided shading, and explicitly rejected watercolor, which was "employed only by those who believed that the objective of architecture was to please the eye."[15] While Ledoux was still able to write that an architect

Geometry, Number, and Technology

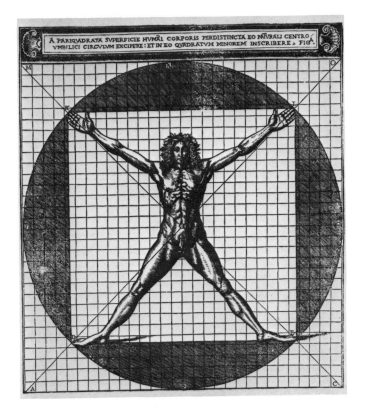

The Vitruvian man on a grid, from Cesariano's edition of the *Ten Books* (1521).

Durand and Functionalism

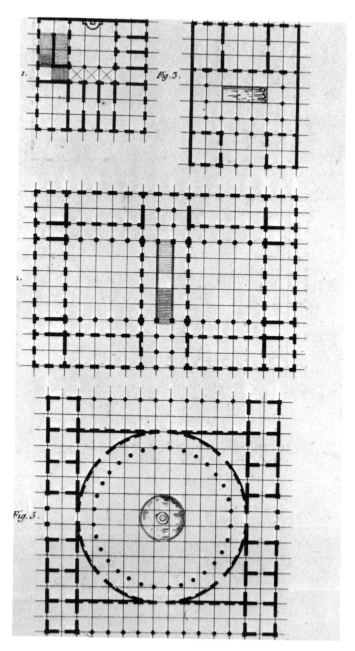

Detail of a plate showing the *mécanisme de la composition*, from Durand's *Précis*.

Geometry, Number, and Technology

should start by being a painter (Boullée even used Corregio's "And I am also a painter" as the epigraph to his *Essai*), Durand and his students at the *École Polytechnique*, proud of their new scientific and specialized architecture, took pains to emphasize the *differences* between their own eminently rational profession and the other fine arts, which were ruled by intuition. For them, architectural drawing was no more and no less than an instrument for precisely representing a building. For the first time in the history of architecture, drawing became a means and was perceived devoid of value in itself. Presupposing the continuity between three-dimensional space and drawing, the figure was no longer a symbol of the building, but its mechanical reduction to the plane.

In Durand's theory, number and geometry finally discarded their symbolic connotations. From now on, proportional systems would have the character of technical instruments, and the geometry applied to design would act merely as a vehicle for ensuring its efficiency. Geometrical forms lost their cosmological reverberations; they were uprooted from the *Lebenswelt* and their traditional symbolic horizon, and they became instead signs of technological values. This in turn led to the geometry of the Bauhaus, the International Style, and the Modern Movement, which was essentially the undifferentiated product of a technological world view. As part of a theory that cast off metaphysical speculation, the simple and anonymous geometry of most contemporary architecture speaks only to a technological process, not to the world of man.

An understanding of the crisis of European science brings about the possibility of overcoming it. Now that the circle of Western philosophy seems to have been completed, and as man witnesses the eclipse of reason, he can grasp again the primordial meaning of geometry and use it in theoretical projects to create a new metaphorical architecture. Meanwhile, however, the dominant geometry of our impersonal cities remains the one implemented by Durand.

The architecture of the Industrial Revolution owed to Durand the first coherent articulation of its fundamental principles and intentions. The influence of his theory on nineteenth-century European architecture, and indirectly upon all architects who have accepted the utopian objectives of technology, has been enormous. His books were translated into many languages, and students of the *École Polytechnique* were quick to spread the new ideas, which

Durand and Functionalism

indeed seemed indisputable. L. A. Dubut, for example, an old student of Ledoux's, adopted Durand's principles in his *Architecture Civile* (1803). The book was primarily a catalog of houses, any one of which, according to Dubut, could be built without knowing about architecture. It was possible to adopt a general *parti*, changing its distribution or even eliminating porticoes and colonnades, for reasons of taste or economy. As long as the house protected the occupant from the elements, all else was superfluous. Dubut used a thin and precise line in all his projects. His plans were always symmetrical, and his volumes almost invariably cubical, made up of a simple combination of modular elements.[16] The continuing publication of books like Dubut's, which implicitly adopted the values put forward by Durand, betrayed an increasing lack of clarity concerning the architect's role in society as well as a misunderstanding of the very essence of architecture itself.

Louis Lebrun was another graduate of the *École Polytechnique* who adopted Durand's ideas. His interest in *Théorie de l'Architecture Grecque et Romaine* (1807) was to determine scientifically the true source of pleasure in architecture. His analysis led him to conclude that pleasure derived from the structural stability of buildings.[17] Finding immutable, mathematical rules would become an obsession of the new rational architecture, shared even by those architects concerned with the "less important" aspect of decoration.

Decoration was not, in fact, as irrelevant as some of the more radical architectural engineers liked to believe; witness the creation of the *École des Beaux Arts* from the ashes of the old academy. Even with all his technology, man still has to face the ambiguities of his personal existence, the necessity of reconciliation in the here and now, and not in some utopian future. Such necessity demands a symbolic order in the environment that man builds for himself. Buildings therefore cannot be simply reduced to prosaic construction or structure. Often a need is felt for the building to speak to something else, apart from the technological process that produced it. For example, the engineer Brunel reluctantly asked the architect Wyatt to decorate Paddington Railway Station in London. This contradictory situation of the purely functional versus the purely decorative has created a profound tension in architecture since the beginning of the nineteenth century. Even Durand himself was not able to escape this inherent ambivalence. His *Recueil et Parallèle* (1801) is actually devoted to the elucidation of formal problems, being a compilation of plans and elevations of the great buildings of the past drawn to the same scale, without discriminating between cultures or historical periods. Supposedly this information would enable the architect to compare the different monuments and to establish or verify his own taste and judgment.[18]

It is particularly illuminating to compare Durand's *Recueil* with the first history of universal architecture, published in 1721. The famous *Entwurff Einer Historischen Architectur* by the Austrian architect J. B. Fischer von Erlach was also a product of that protopositivism that I discussed in relation to Perrault's work and that preceded the popularization of Newtonian philosophy. Fischer was highly regarded in scientific circles. He was a friend of Leibniz and Hüyghens, and his decision to write a comparative history of architecture *instead* of a treatise was significant. Like Perrault, Fischer acknowledged the relativity of taste, shaped by different cultures, places, and times. But Fischer also recognized the necessity for absolute principles—principles that he believed were derived from the mythical Temple of Solomon in Jerusalem and that had been brought to fruition in the precepts of Roman imperial architecture.[19]

Fischer seems to have been the first architect capable of isolating architectural forms that possessed specific horizons of meaning: obelisks, pyramids, triumphal columns, and so forth, and combining them through juxtaposition in his projects. This mode of operation was very different from Renaissance or Baroque "composition." Fischer's projects were ongoing syntheses composed of elements whose meaning depended on the explicit histories of these elements rather than on their ordering by geometry or proportion. Fischer's advocacy of a mythical history had a profound influence on Neoclassical architecture, playing an important role in the conceptions of Boullée and Ledoux. By identifying the natural with the primitive, for example, Boullée and other eighteenth-century theoreticians regarded history as a means of reconciling the facts of reality with a series of a priori beliefs, whose principles were always explicit and merely corroborated by history. Moreover, Ledoux conceived historical time as a corruptor and spoiler of the primitive purity of principles and forms.

The positivistic conception of history was fundamentally different from Neoclassical *mythistoire*. Transformed into science, history could be viewed as a progressive linear accumulation of experience and data, from which it might be possible to *derive* fixed principles: precepts for human conduct or solutions to the

Durand and Functionalism

problems of a certain discipline. Durand's *Recueil* was the first history of architecture that entertained such a viewpoint. It purported to summarize the experience necessary for an architect in order for him to arrive at the most correct rules, or the appropriate style. It should be stressed, however, that Durand did not simply intend to prove the relativity of taste through the formal expressions of different cultures; that is, he did not favor a merely eclectic attitude. On the contrary, Durand and the more serious architects and theoreticians who succeeded him genuinely wished to transform history into an objective science, one that was based only on material evidence, repudiating the acts of imaginative interpretation that had always characterized the profession. Once archaeological excavations and precise topographic methods made the monuments of the past more accessible, theoreticians, sharing in the illusion of a positivistic history, became convinced that it was possible to find a rational and definitive solution to the problem of decoration through the analysis of formal styles.

The influence of Durand's ideas during the nineteenth century is a complex affair, deriving from simultaneous beliefs in the possibility of obtaining rational and fixed solutions to all aspects of human knowledge *and* the subjectivity of human perceptions, whose outcome is relativism. Not surprisingly, certain basic contradictions in the theory of architecture emerged during the nineteenth and twentieth centuries. There has been an acute and unprecedented division between science and art, reason and poetry, architecture and engineering. Architects have opted for the extreme expressions of rationalism or romanticism, formulating design decisions from either positivistic reason or intuition. For the last two centuries, a reconciliation of the spheres of *logos* and *mythos* has been, explicitly or implicitly, deemed impossible. Ultimately, these contradictions must be seen as a result of the technological world view, the condition described in the introduction (after Husserl) as the crisis of European science, with its consecration of the Cartesian split between objective truth and subjective opinion, between mind and body, and its rejection of myth, poetry, and art as legitimate and primary forms of knowledge.

Viel's Critique   In examining the problems confronted by Durand, Monge, and Rondelet through the critical standpoint of a colleague who did not share their technological obsessions, one can discern that profound division of attitudes in architecture regarding reason and intuition, functionalism and decoration. The theoretical work of Charles-François Viel (1745–1819), a practically unknown architect, was until recently confused with that of his brother Jean-Louis Viel de Saint-Maux.[20] Viel's buildings, unlike those of his contemporaries, were not at all "revolutionary." His designs reflected the eternal value of classical forms, rejecting all megalomaniacal or unconventional imagery. Some historians have interpreted Viel's criticism of the excessive imagination, which motivated the projects of Boullée, Ledoux, and their disciples, as the expression of an academic reaction, voiced by the conservative faction during the years preceding the Revolution of 1789. Actually, Viel's vast literary production published during the first two decades of the nineteenth century has not been properly studied by architects and historians, who have either ignored or rejected all so-called reactionary theories from the standpoint of a triumphant rational architecture.

Viel's critical position has much deeper ramifications than one might expect to find in a simple conservative theory. His writings, were, in fact, the first to recognize and reject the evils brought about by the transformation of architectural theory into an instrument of technological domination that excluded metaphysics. Viel claimed that late-eighteenth-century French architecture was essentially decadent and devoted himself to proving this. In his *Principes de l'Ordonnance et de la Construction des Bâtimens* (1797), he stressed that the relation between the traditional theory of the classical orders and building practice should be intimate. He refused to entertain the distinction between theory and practice, which was increasingly postulated as a basic premise by contemporary architects, engineers, and geometricians. This "distance" between the art of design and buildings was, in his opinion, the main cause of architectural decadence.[21] Viel believed that a fundamental continuity existed between theory and practice. These terms, however, had specific connotations for Viel, quite different from contemporary usage. He was referring to a phenomenological synthesis, to be achieved through the architect's embodied being, which recognized the necessary ambiguity between thought and action, mind and body, intellectual and motor intentionalities.

Theory, for Viel, was not synonymous with a book of recipes, a book written by some disembodied and almighty reason, dictated by rules of mathematical logic. Theory was first of all a rational justification of architectural work, but one necessarily related to a mythical frame of reference. And practice was not simply a highly efficient process devoid of clear objectives; building was poetic, essentially meaningful, that is, more than a mere act of technological domination. This radical continuity, acknowledging the ambiguity between two independent universes of discourse ultimately linked in the very articulation of existence, had been universally accepted during the preceding centuries. The act of reconciliation was thus an implicit and personal task of the architect; he necessarily brought it to each individual project in relation to a world view. True, after the transformation of architecture into a liberal art, some architects began to give greater importance to theory. During the eighteenth century, many architects stressed the importance of theory to ensure the success of construction. But it was only in Viel's time that the relation between theory and building became truly critical, when the meanings of both terms were actually transformed.

Viel admired Buffon and Batteux and believed that absolute principles could derive from the patient observation of nature— a nature pregnant with traditional myths and poetic connotations.[22] He advised both artists and amateurs to become familiar with the canons of art through perception or "sentiment" rather than the dry study of theoretical principles. Viel accepted the usual belief that the human body was the origin and prototype of beauty, harmony, and proportions; and although he admitted that science could cast light on many aspects of art, he stressed that theoretical principles, once acquired, should be modified by observations and comparisons, or else they would only leave a weak impression on the mind.[23] Viel's position was obviously grounded in the "transcendental empiricism" that was the model of Enlightened reason. He thought architects who followed a "blind routine" lacked a true knowledge of principles. But he distinguished between the architectural theory gained from trips, books, and meditation and the kind acquired through practice. It was this latter theory that architects should employ in their projects.[24]

Viel declared that the two fundamental principles of architecture were proportion and eurythmy. These traditional premises even led him to criticize Perrault's use of paired columns in the facade of the Louvre because he thought (with François Blondel) that they contradicted the authority of the ancients.[25] Nature was not only the origin of the basic elements of architecture but also, in his opinion, the source of the principles of construction.[26] Although these rules could be learned from observing nature, they could, in a more immediate way, be derived from the manner in which they were applied to examples of ancient and modern building—buildings that should therefore be profoundly respected. Only to his own contemporaries did these basic principles seem to have no relevance. Viel attributed this failing to the abuse of geometry as it was applied to building.

Although Viel conceded that the algebraic formulas discovered and applied by De la Hire, Parent, Frezier, and Bélidor effected a better understanding of traditional building practice, he also believed that "the immoderate application of these new procedures became a great calamity, affecting the composition of some architectural works."[27] In fact, Viel had nothing against a careful application of geometry in stonecutting or of algebra to determine the point at which a structure was no longer stable, but he also believed that these geometrical exercises did not provide absolute results. True stability (*firmitas*) could only be attained through the establishment of correct proportions between the points of support, their foundations, and the supported masses. Such dimensional relations had to be derived from a correct distribution of solids and voids, which, in turn, could be found within the traditional proportions of the classical orders. And this "admirable correspondence," as he pointed out, was what had been used by great masters of the past.[28]

Viel bitterly criticized architects who were competent in the mathematical sciences but ignorant of beautiful proportions and who lacked genius and taste. Such individuals were attempting to apply mathematics directly to construction and were coming up with extremely poor results. In order to illustrate this thesis, Viel compared "Perronet's new bridge" with Du Cerceau's Pont Neuf, and Soufflot's Pantheon with Mansart's church of Les Invalides. In both cases, he found the eighteenth-century buildings less beautiful and ridden with structural problems. Because Viel was writing at a time when theory had finally become capable of effectively solving practical structural problems (especially in the works utilizing Coulomb's discoveries), his intense criticism takes on additional significance. To still argue that symmetry and eurythmy, qualities intimately associated with the use of the traditional proportions of the classical orders, were the only means to achieve beautiful *and* structurally sound buildings was, to say the least, much more than the expression of a conservative theory.

Viel was obsessed with this theme, which he developed in four different publications. In *De l'Impuissance des Mathématiques pour*

Assurer la Solidité des Bâtimens (1805), he examined the limitations of geometrical hypotheses in statics. This problem had been recognized since the early eighteenth century, but it was not crucial in the context of traditional practice. Only Viel stressed the critical nature of those limitations vis-à-vis the successful application of mathematics to practical problems of construction. He acknowledged the usefulness and precision of mathematics in solving mental or ideal problems, but did not think that they were infallible when applied to physical quantities whose attributes were indeterminate, that is, infinitely diverse.[29]

Viel also emphasized that all aspects of an art were intimately related and that this was "the fundamental theorem from which derive all the truths that constitute the art of building." Thus the perfection of architecture could only be attained by imitating the great buildings of the past, which were universally accepted precisely because they simultaneously embodied *all* the rules. A partial knowledge of mathematics, mechanics, or statics was insufficient to produce good architecture. Through numerous examples, including Soufflot's Pantheon, he tried to prove that statics, which, in his opinion, replaced real acting forces with "totally abstract," indirect components, produced results that were never in accordance with reality.[30]

As for quantitative experiments concerning the strength of materials, Viel did not think such experiments sufficient to form critieria about the materials' potential use in buildings. He pointed out that the quality of materials (that is, what they revealed to perception and experience) was more important for architecture. In his *Dissertations sur les Projects de Coupoles* (1809), he wrote that a stone's density could not set limits on the height in a project or the span of a vault.[31] The thickness of a vault had to be established in relation to the module of the building and the walls, not through the function of the quantitative resistance of the stone. He was therefore very critical of the testing machines used by Perronet, Soufflot, and Rondelet, which he thought fostered dangerous illusions.

Viel understood that construction consisted in the determination and use of the appropriate volumes of materials. Such an assessment could not be accomplished through abstract mathematical calculations, however, but had to be deduced from the harmonic proportions chosen by an experienced architect: "True solidity always results from eurythmy. . . ."[32] He refuted the notion then popular that "to be an architect one should necessarily first be a geometrician." On the contrary, he claimed that to design a building of merit, a geometrician first had to be an architect.[33] Moreover, knowledge and study were not sufficient; he believed that "one [was] born an architect," possessed of a delicate and sensitive spirit capable of discovering the mysteries of construction through the observation of exemplary structures.[34]

It is significant, although perhaps not surprising, that Viel bemoaned the fact that his modern colleagues were not more like François Blondel, who had been *both* an architect and a mathematician. Yet he seemed to realize that such a synthesis was no longer possible; the use of a symbolic geometry as contained in Blondel's works could not be passed along to eighteenth-century architects since geometry had by then lost its transcendental power in philosophy and science. Viel resented this loss of meaning and rejected the use of geometry in architecture once it had been reduced to a technical tool. According to him, this sort of geometry, which had seen its culmination in Monge's science, actually *precluded* the possibility of a synthesis between mathematical theory and the reality of practice.

In his *Dissertations*, Viel maintained that the construction of vaults depended essentially on the excellence of the plan. The virtues of a good floor plan resulted from the relation invented by the architect's genius, which, in turn, was inspired by the dimensions of the orders.[35] In another publication, *De la Solidité des Bâtimens, Puissé dans les Proportions des Ordres d'Architecture* (1806), Viel attempted to establish the rules by which sound buildings could be designed. He devoted over thirty pages to show how this method could be applied in specific examples. His rules, however, did not consist in providing a table of dimensions or a formula that anyone could use to design a building. Not without some sarcasm, he wrote that he preferred to leave the production of such "harmful" books to others, and that he would not be party to "indigested and arguable compilations," which tended to simplify great matters.[36] Viel thought that his own method, even with rules, still demanded much study of the classical orders and an immediate understanding of building procedures. The orders, after all, were "the basic principles of composition and construction," which, like stars in the sky, illuminated the way for the architect in search of harmony and solidity.[37]

Viel's rejection of a theory that had been reduced to the condition of *ars fabricandi* could not have been more explicit. In his *Dissertations*, he wrote that in his own time the ideas upon which

Durand and Functionalism

the science of construction was founded were so confused that professors, who believed themselves to be teaching fundamental principles to young architects, were in reality only discussing the theory and practice of techniques like masonry, stonecutting, and carpentry.[38] Viel was the first of his contemporaries to realize that the theoretical framework of architecture lacked *real principles*.

Never before had an architect openly complained about the loss of the metaphysical dimension of theory. Around 1800 the theory of architecture was being transformed into a collection of precise and highly efficient instructions, which disregarded theory's function as a transcendent justification of practice. This is what makes Viel's perception of the problem so extraordinary; he was writing precisely at the time when metaphysical speculation had become suspect, and when physics, unconcerned with final causes, had become the prototype of nineteenth-century science.

Viel also criticized comprehensive projects of the type recommended by Rondelet. Such projects, he thought, hindered the artist's genius, altering his first ideas and causing him to lose sight of perfection.[39] He stressed that these *devis*, generally considered in his own time to be the most crucial aspect of any architectural or engineering undertaking, had only a didactic value and were not, in fact, more economical since they failed to generate better buildings. He deemed it impossible to reduce the process of building to a purely conceptual operation and pointed out that contemporary architects would do better to imitate their ancient predecessors, who never endangered their structures by following false building systems or miserable economic requirements.[40]

Not surprisingly, Viel also criticized the new tendencies in architectural education. He was concerned because he felt that aspiring architects were not being taught the true principles of art. To teach them, one had to be an architect, not a geometrician capable only of training students in such techniques as stereotomy.[41] He regarded treatises on descriptive geometry as misrepresentations of architectural meaning.[42] After all, it was not so difficult to learn mathematics; even ordinary students could appear to be geniuses after a few years of training. This opinion seemed to be borne out by the "great number of candidates" who performed extraordinarily well at the École Polytechnique. And even after these graduates visited Italy, they never fulfilled the hopes that the general public had placed in them. Viel pronounced them to be incompetent both in design and construction.[43]

After defending in *Des Anciennes Études d'Architecture* (1807), the traditional methods of architectural education, Viel criticized

Geometry, Number, and Technology

the new methods adopted by the *École Polytechnique.* Avoiding the true principles of composition, these teachings allowed each architect the freedom to modify the proportions of the orders. Now if all the possibilities of composition were equally pleasant and beautiful, so long as they produced a useful disposition of the elements in plan, it would make it impossible to recognize a good building from a bad one.[44] Viel could not accept the relativization of architectural values that resulted from placing architecture among the positive sciences. Architectural meaning existed in history and had always transcended reason. Exasperated by the contradictions resulting from the new theories, he exclaimed, "What a delirium of perfection has taken hold of this physicomathematical faction, composed of different sects, some accepting and others refusing the existence of universal principles in architectural design, all devoted exclusively to the exact sciences!"[45]

Convinced that students were now learning only geometry and drawing, Viel thought that "the study of architecture was being reduced to the elaboration of projects." This in turn led young architects to abuse their imaginations, to ignore the principles of their art, and to design without good taste. All they could produce then were terrible exercises, often simple images that could not be built.[46] Viel was contemptuous of Durand's notion that efficiency in design was the main objective of architecture. He could not accept the immense buildings designed by his contemporaries in a few weeks. The conception of an important building had to take a long time; it was the result of a synthesis between a fruitful and vast imagination and an eminently sensible mind. Speed in the process of design created the illusion that architecture was an easy discipline, when in fact the true talent of an architect could only be measured through the execution of buildings.[47]

Although several historians have commented on Viel's criticism of this "fantastic architecture," the product of a "licentious imagination," they could not account for the fact that Viel disapproved of not only the megalomaniac conceptions of Boullée and Ledoux but also the "inheritors of Perronet," the engineers at the *École Polytechnique.* This dual criticism, aimed at both design and construction, lay partly in Viel's inability to appreciate the desperate symbolic intentionality that still motivated the theoretical projects of Boullée and Ledoux. For Viel, the separation between conception and execution at all levels was a reason of concern. He simply could not accept the greater emphasis given to imaginative conceptions at the expense of real possibilities of execution.

In *Décadence de l'Architecture à la Fin du XVIIIème Siècle* (1800), Viel refers (but not by name) to two popular architects who appeared toward the end of the eighteenth century. He characterized one by the extension of his ruinous enterprises, and the other by the great number of his excessively imaginative designs. M. Petzet has speculated that these two architects were Soufflot and Ledoux. Viel's severe criticism of these two architects summarized his fundamental thesis: *Architectural composition could not be reduced to the art of designing, nor construction to mathematical formulas.* It was not sufficient to possess imagination or to study the theory of construction; only a synthesis of theory and practice would allow architecture to fulfill its transcendental objectives.[48]

Viel's work was ignored by his contemporaries and successors, and the reasons for this are now obvious. His thought, based on the traditional eighteenth-century models, was seen as reactionary in a world devoted to the consumption of technological ideologies and obsessed with the works of Navier, Durand, and Rondelet. It was only his exegesis of style that proved him to be even more "modern" than his contemporaries. The three chapters of his *Principes*, which are devoted to style, represents the first explicit formulation of this issue in an architectural treatise.[49] Viel stressed that "purity of style" should be rigorously observed in architectural design. Although the notion of style as a closed and independent formal system also appeared in Durand's *Recueil* and in Legrand's introduction to Durand's 1809 edition, Viel's text was the first to understand style as a formal language whose coherence might be a problem within architectural theory. Thus any application of this nineteenth-century notion to the architecture of previous times in terms of "polemical styles" already constituted a fundamental misunderstanding, one that has been all too often shared by twentieth-century architectural history.

Architectural theory during the nineteenth century would be founded on the belief that all the variables of the real world can be reduced to the conceptual realm and that the resultant of any architectural problem is a direct "function" of the combination of these variables. Viel's perceptive writings, then, reflected the moment at which a functionalized theory could operate successfully upon architectural reality. Unwilling to accept the disintegration of values implicit in architectural theory after 1800, he questioned the intention of transforming and reducing the theoretical dimension into an instrument of technological domination. In effect, Viel doubted the success, that is, the meaning, of any building operation for which everything had been planned beforehand. Could one, in fact, effectively reduce to a conceptual scheme all sorts of aesthetic, human, and technical requirements? In Viel, we see the first critic of the rationalist doctrines upon which modern architecture was to be generally based.

<table>
<tr><td>Theoretical
Sequel</td><td>Two hundred years after Galileo and Descartes, architecture lost its metaphysical dimension, and the relation between theory and practice reached a critical state. After Durand and Viel, architecture could no longer be a privileged form of reconciliation between man and his world, between the fluidity and evanescence of everyday life and the immutable and eternal dimension of ideas. An architecture subjected to utopian ideas, to a technological process whose objectives had been uprooted from the reality of everyday life, would necessarily lose its essential symbolic dimension; it would become mere prosaic construction.</td></tr>
</table>

But symbolization is a profound human need and is indispensable for the perpetuation of culture. Man's humanity depends on nothing less than his ability to come to terms with the infinite in terms of the finite, precisely through symbols, whether totems or magnificent churches. Symbols are part of the visible world, but are also outside the world. Goethe wrote that they made visible the invisible and expressed the inexpressible. Like human knowledge and perception itself, symbols are ambiguous; they possess an eternal, ahistorical dimension and a dimension determined by a specific cultural context. Positive science obviously distrusted symbols and tried replacing them during the nineteenth century with a belief in mathematical signs as the epitome of meaning. In spite of the popularization of this attitude, however, a reaction against the rationalist positions in architecture was almost immediate, contradicting the fundamental intentions of the later Modern Movement.

Fortunately, modern historians have recently begun to reevaluate the romantic dreams of Lequeu, Gaudi's "edible architecture," Kiesler's surrealism, and movements like Art Nouveau and expressionism. But truly meaningful architecture has been, by necessity, the exception rather than the rule over the last two centuries. The architecture of our sterile industrial cities has been subjected to the parameters of technology, and no added ornament or formal virtuosity can restore its meaning. Symbolic intentions are thoroughly rejected in a prosaic world, where only the pragmatic values of efficient building are considered "real." The reconciliation between a necessarily rational structure and a necessarily mythical world view is extremely difficult, if not impossible, as has been shown by the frustrated efforts of the best architects after Labrouste. The *École des Beaux Arts* could not simply "restore" what had been lost at the *École Polytechnique*. To think in such terms is simplistic, but is the fundamental dilemma of contemporary architectural education. The real split between design and building cannot be repaired by beautiful rendering and a superficial reintegration of architecture and the fine arts. The academic rules of classical composition as stated initially by Quatremère de Quincy may seem to derive from principles similar to those of Laugier, but they are in fact guided by Durand's positive reason, not by myth. All nineteenth- and twentieth-century formalisms partake of the same contradiction.

In view of this, some contemporary critics have started to recognize the vital importance of theoretical projects from Piranesi to the present. It is in these theoretical projects, rather than in buildings, that symbolic intentionality has been best embodied after the Industrial Revolution. These projects become a critique of technological or reductionistic design and construction, and question implicitly the possibility of realizing their poetry in a prosaic world.

Today, practicing architects and their clients are also becoming aware of the limitations of functionalism and formalism, of the impossibility of reducing architecture to decoration, sociology, or psychology. So far, powerful computers, methodologies, and geometrical strategies have failed to provide a mathematical solution to urban and architectural problems. Thus Viel's critique, in spite of transformations in the means of production, should be taken seriously by architects who are concerned with meaning.

The misleading division between rational and intuitive architecture, between scientific and artistic architects, between functionalism, typological methodologies or formalism, and all types of expressionisms, has marked, as I have endeavoured to show, only the last two centuries of architecture. This profound rift was the inevitable outcome of a world view that posited the absolute separation of the objective and subjective realms of human reality. In fact, before the late eighteenth century, architects did not have to choose between two irreconcilable options. It was only with the work of Durand that architects began to perceive the dilemma that still engages them today.

Even the contemporary "schools" of capitalist formalism and Marxist rationalism fall into the same trap, believing that one can separate structure from meaning. Capitalist formalism emphasizes the possibility of architecture as a hermetic, elitist manipulation of forms, with no intended culturally based meanings. Marxist rationalism pretends that art is not individual expression and that architecture is a craft, a direct result of typological analysis, pure ahistorical content, for which form is irrelevant. Both positions obviously fall short of the truth. There are no structures without meaning; perception is the body's, not merely the mind's. Buildings may be identical typologically (urban and rural "hotels," or Early Christian and Renaissance basilicas), but their *meaning* is, indeed, very different. Furthermore, art is necessarily personal expression, much more so than science and language (which are, nonetheless, also forms of interpretation). On the other hand, architecture cannot be a private game of combinations, a "formal language" invented a priori (architecture for architects), or a question of merely decorating technological structures with arbitrary historical quotations; the necessarily transcendental (semantic) dimension of meaning cannot be disregarded.

Only contemporary phenomenology, with its rediscovery of the primacy of perception, where structure or *mathesis* is given and yet embodied in the mutable and specific, has been capable of overcoming the fundamental dilemma that modern philosophy inherited from Descartes. By revealing the limitations of mathematical reason, phenomenology has indicated that technological theory alone cannot come to terms with the fundamental problems of architecture. Contemporary architecture, disillusioned with rational utopias, now strives to go beyond positivistic prejudices to find a new metaphysical justification in the human world; its point of departure is once again the sphere of perception, the ultimate origin of existential meaning.

The reconciliatory mission of the architect is poetic. This is necessarily an individual task, encompassing personal expression *and* reference to the totality. There is no meaningful logic without acknowledging the intersubjective world, best revealed in dreams and myths. Even in the eighteenth century, poetic wisdom was not without its supporters. Giambattista Vico was perhaps the first to speak up for the primordial knowledge of all people, a knowledge that stemmed not from reason but from imagination. Today Heidegger has given new validity to this idea; we may be condemned to live in the absence of gods, but the void is evident.

The ever present enigma of the human condition is only denied by the foolish. And it is this mystery that architecture must address. Part of our human condition is the inevitable yearning to capture reality through metaphors. Such is true knowledge, ambiguous yet ultimately more relevant than scientific truth. And architecture, no matter how much it resists the idea, cannot renounce its origin in intuition. While construction as a technological process is prosaic—deriving directly from a mathematical equation, a functional diagram, or a rule of formal combinations—architecture is poetic, necessarily an abstract order but in itself a metaphor emerging from a vision of the world and Being.

NOTES

Introduction

1. In connection with the primacy of perception and the limitations of intellectual reductionism, see Maurice Merleau-Ponty, *Phenomenology of Perception*, and *The Primacy of Perception*. See also Mikel Dufrenne, *The Notion of the A Priori*, and John Bannan, *The Philosophy of Merleau-Ponty*. Reality appears meaningfully in embodied perception. It is in the sense of Merleau-Ponty's phenomenology that I use the notion of perception in this book.

2. The distinction between technology and technique, between how and why, is set forth by Jacques Ellul in *The Technological Society*. Technology has become a dominating force in the last two centuries, one that has radically determined both thought and action. Its purpose is to subjugate external reality to interests of efficiency, thereby postponing indefinitely the human need for reconciliation. Traditional knowledge and technique, in contrast, have always ultimately been concerned with the most fundamental existential problems. This view is shared in good measure by Martin Heidegger in his late philosophy. See Vincent Vycinas, *Earth and Gods. An Introduction to the Philosophy of Martin Heidegger*, and Jürgen Habermas, *Toward a Rational Society*, chapter 6.

3. Edmund Husserl, *The Crisis of European Sciences and Transcendental Phenomenology*, and *Phenomenology and the Crisis of Philosophy*.

4. I use "idea" and "everyday life" also with a horizon of meaning taken from phenomenology. Idea implies figure even in the case of the most abstract notions, while the specific perceptions of everyday life are given a priori in a framework of categories. See Merleau-Ponty, *Phenomenology*, and Stuart Spicker, *The Philosophy*

Notes to Page 2

of the Body, pp. 334ff. I use "symbol" as does Alfred Schutz in *Collected Papers I: The Problem of Social Reality*, part III.

5. This notion has been a common point of departure for existential phenomenology. See A. de Waelhens, *La Philosophie de Martin Heidegger*, or William Luijpen, *Existential Phenomenology*.

6. See also José Ortega y Gasset, *En Torno a Galileo*, translated as *Man in Crisis*, and Oswald Spengler, *The Decline of the West*, originally published in Munich in 1918.

7. Edmund Husserl, *L'Origine de la Géométrie*; Leon Brunschvicg, *Les Étapes de la Philosophie Mathématique*; and José Ortega y Gasset, *La Idea de Principio en Leibniz*.

8. Mikel Dufrenne, *Le Poétique*. I use this term in its widest sense as "metaphorical reference," relating it to not only the realm of written poetry but primarily art and myth. See also Paul Ricoeur, *The Rule of Metaphor*.

9. Habermas, *Toward a Rational-Society*, and Theodore Roszak, *Where the Wasteland Ends*.

10. Edmund Husserl, *Formale und Transzendentale Logik* (1929), French translation 1957. See Herbert Spiegelberg, *The Phenomenological Movement*, vol. 1, pp. 91ff. See also Ernest Nagel and James Newman, *Gödel's Proof*.

11. The *logos* has excluded the *mythos* only during the last 180 years of Western history. This is one more symptom of the crisis described by Husserl.

12. I use "reality" also in the phenomenological sense, as the realm of intentionality existing between our embodied selves and the outside world.

13. The precondition of a true symbol is the acceptance of the transcendental dimension of human existence. Thus symbolization becomes a problem, that is, a private language of the genius in art and architecture, only after the crisis has begun.

14. Gottfried Semper's explicit formulation was first brought to my attention by Dalibor Vesely.

15. See, for example, Christopher Alexander, *Notes on the Synthesis of Form*, and Nicholas Negroponte, *The Architecture Machine*.

16. In his *Collected Papers*, Schutz defines "symbol" as an "appresentational" pair that relates the finite and mutable with the immutable and eternal, lived reality with ideas. Symbolization is

thus the most fundamental operation constituting meaning in human existence, the basis for the perpetuation of culture.

17. See Merleau-Ponty, *Phenomenology of Perception*, pp. 3–63.

18. In the text, I generally use "metaphysics" as does José Ortega y Gasset, *Unas Lecciones de Metafísica*, translated as *Some Lessons on Metaphysics* (1974). Ortega defines metaphysics as a radical coming to terms with the fundamental problems of human life (reality as it appears in the field of intentions); it is a basic orientation that allows man's thoughts and actions to be ordered in a meaningful hierarchy. Although it implies the intention to address the question of being, it is not necessarily synonymous with the speculative metaphysics of seventeenth-century philosophy. One of the issues that I shall touch upon in this book is precisely how the metaphysical question was taken up in the natural philosophy of the eighteenth century and the manner in which it was finally excluded from nineteenth-century science, coinciding with Kant's final rejection of legitimate speculative metaphysics. Today it seems that the question of metaphysics cannot be addressed through a still more sophisticated conceptual system. The failure of Husserl's "philosophy as a rigorous science" opened the way for the insights of later philosophers who have placed the question in the realm of mythopoesis, implying an "unthinking" of issues (Ortega), a return to the *"Lebenswelt"* (Merleau-Ponty). See also Georges Gusdorf, *Mythe et Métaphysique*. It is Gusdorf who refers to the possible philosophy of today as "mythopoesis," a term that seeks to recover the lost connection between thinking and doing, which the Greek notion of *poesis* still involved. This "second mythology" is not "an architecture of concepts, but a justification of real existence in the plenitude of its lived years."

19. See Georges Gusdorf, *Les Origines des Sciences Humaines*, and Alexandre Koyré, "Les Étapes de la Cosmologie Scientifique," *Revue de Synthèse* (1951–1952): 11. I owe much of my understanding of science and its implications in a wider cultural context to Gusdorf's fascinating (untranslated) history of the human sciences. The work, whose general title is *Les Sciences Humaines et la Pensée Occidentale*, is already eight volumes long. It concentrates on the seventeenth and eighteenth centuries.

20. Elsewhere in the text I use the terms "Galilean" and "epistemological revolution" to describe a fundamental transformation that took place during the last decades of the sixteenth century and the beginning of the seventeenth. The terminology and its implications are taken from Georges Gusdorf, *La Revolution Gal-*

iléenne, 2 vols. Keeping in mind that intentionality, understood phenomenologically, covers the span from thought to action, what is in question is a transformation of the world picture, not only as the articulation of beliefs and ideas (although it certainly started at that level; thus the term "epistemological"), but as the given historical context of human life, art, and architecture. The new relation between man and his external reality was best understood in the seventeenth century by Galileo; it only became accepted at a popular level 200 years later with the "success" of the Industrial Revolution. The Galilean revolution obviously is not the cause of the phenomena that I shall be describing and analyzing. It should be understood as a metaphor for a radical change in the order of the world and the cosmos in which these phenomena originate.

21. For a discussion of "spatiality" and "intellectual space," see Merleau-Ponty, *Phenomenology of Perception*, pp. 98–147.

22. I use "technological intentionality" in the sense of Habermas (see note 2).

23. It should be emphasized that the notions of intention and intentionality are often used in the text with their precise phenomenological connotations. See Joseph Kockelmans, *Phenomenology*, pp. 118–149.

24. I use "epistemological context" not in reference to the theory of knowledge as understood by idealist nineteenth-century philosophy, but in its wider etymological sense as that which constitutes the sphere of nonspecialized knowledge and embodied consciousness. Architectural intentions appearing in theoretical writings are, therefore, examined in their epistemological context in an attempt to approach this problem hermeneutically.

25. Hans-Georg Gadamer, *Truth and Method*, and *Philosophical Hermeneutics*.

Chapter 1

1. See Joseph Rykwert, *The First Moderns*, chapters 1 and 2.

2. For the Middle Ages, truth was contained in the Bible and Aristotle. The problem consisted merely in their interpretation. During the Renaissance, the number of texts used as sources increased greatly. In the sixteenth century, philosophers and mathematicians such as Stevin, Barbaro, and Ramus seemed to realize that no science arrived at perfection through the work of a single individual. But Renaissance science consisted of a closed universe of knowledge, founded on the veneration of a mythical

past. See Georges Gusdorf, *De l'Histoire des Sciences à l'Histoire de la Pensée*, and Paolo Rossi, *Philosophy, Technology and the Arts in the Early Modern Era*.

3. See Gusdorf, *La Révolution Galiléenne*, vol. 1, part II, chapter 1.

4. See Rossi, *Philosophy, Technology and the Arts*, chapter 2.

5. Descartes, for example, seemed to have been associated in some way with the Rosicrucian movement. See Frances Yates, *The Rosicrucian Enlightenment*. Galileo was defended by Tomasso Campanella, the famous Renaissance *magus* who had a propitiatory session with Pope Urban VIII in the Vatican. Perhaps the best example of how the traditional and mechanistic cosmos are integrated appears in the work of the amazing polymath Athanasius Kircher. For a rather superficial but recent survey of his work, see Joscelyn Godwin, *Athanasius Kircher*. Frances Yates refers to Kircher and his intellectual predecessors in *Giordano Bruno and the Hermetic Tradition*. Also Marin Mersenne, the well-known correspondent of the greatest scientists, philosophers, and mathematicians of the seventeenth century, falls in this category. In his *Harmonie Universelle* (Paris, 1636–1637), he seems capable of distinguishing positive science from cosmobiological explanations. And yet he could write, "Music is in God, and if we knew the harmonic ratios that he used when building the world . . . our concerts and motets would attain perfection."

6. See, for example, Pierre Gassendi, *Exercitationes Paradoxicas Adversus Aristoteleos* (Amsterdam, 1649). Gassendi writes, "We should not only follow the masters; liberty of spirit is more precious than gold. We should not despise ourselves and consider the ancients as giants."

7. J. L. F. Bertrand, *L'Académie des Sciences 1666–1793* (Paris, 1869). For a good account of Perrault's life and work and a discussion of his *Ordonnance*, see Wolfgang Herrmann, *The Theory of Claude Perrault*.

8. Antoine Adam, *Grandeur and Illusion*, pp. 158–164.

9. Charles Perrault, *Parallèle des Anciens et Modernes* (Paris, 1692–1696), 2nd ed.

10. Descartes's biography appears in Charles Perrault, *Les Hommes Illustres Qui Ont Paru en France pendant ce Siècle* (Paris, 1696). His criticism is most explicit in *Parallèle*, vol. 1, p. 47.

11. René Descartes, *Les Principes de la Philosophie* (Paris, 1681).

12. Ibid., p. 53.

13. Gusdorf, *La Révolution*, vol. 1, part I, chapter 3.

14. Robert Boyle also believed that the obsession to write systems, "thinking that one must either keep quiet or write a complete body," was a great obstacle for the progress of physics. See M. Boas, "La Méthode Scientifique de Robert Boyle," *Revue d'Histoire des Sciences* (1956).

15. C. Perrault, *Parallèle*, vol. 4, pp. 46–59.

16. Sorcery and the belief in miracles clearly declined toward the end of the seventeenth century, coinciding with the increasing empiricism in natural philosophy. The perception of angels and demons was a "true illusion" in the traditional cosmos, where every aspect of reality was related to a transcendental order. Magic and sorcery were linked to the essence of religious life. The witch craze was clearly related to the most critical period of transition between the old cosmobiological order and the new mechanistic world picture.

17. This belief was also shared by Bernard de Fontenelle, the long-lived and famous historian of the Royal Academy of Science. Fontenelle's rejection of both Cartesian metaphysics and Newton's natural philosophy is a clear indication of the protopositivistic epistemology of the period. See Fontenelle, "Disgression sur les Anciens et les Modernes," *Oeuvres*, vol. 4 (1767), pp. 170 and 190.

18. Claude and Nicolas Perrault, *Oeuvres Diverses de Physique et de Méchanique* (Leyden, 1721).

19. Ibid., 1, p. 60.

20. See Paolo Rossi, *Clavis Universalis*. Rossi's brilliant study traces the influence of this notion from Raymond Lull to Leibniz. During the seventeenth century, logic was indeed understood as a "key" to universal reality. The Pansophic ideal of the century depended upon this key, which allowed a direct reading of the geometrical essence of reality. The real world and the world of knowledge appeared linked by a substantive identity of structure.

21. This corresponds to the concept of system as it was understood generally in the discussions of the Royal Academy of Science and the Royal Society of London.

22. C. and N. Perrault, *Oeuvres*, p. 60.

23. Ibid., p. 62.

24. C. Perrault, *Mémoires pour Servir à l'Histoire Naturelle des Animaux* (Paris, 1671), preface.

25. C. and N. Perrault, *Oeuvres*, p. 513.

26. See Rykwert, *The First Moderns*, chapter 2, and Herrmann, *The Theory of Claude Perrault*, pp. 130ff.

27. Claude Perrault, ed., *Les Dix Livres de l'Architecture de Vitruve* (Paris, 1684), 2nd ed., and *Ordonnance des Cinq Espèces de Colonnes selon la Méthode des Anciens* (Paris, 1683).

28. C. Perrault, *Les Dix Livres*, note 16, pp. 78–79.

29. Ibid.

30. C. Perrault, *Ordonnance*, p. XXIV.

31. Perrault's name appears in the minutes of important sessions, and it is known that he was officially a member, but no direct contributions are credited to him in the *procès-verbaux* published by H. Lemonnier (1911–1929).

32. See D. Mahon, *Studies in Seicento Art and Theory.*

33. Perrault, *Ordonnance*, pp. XIII–XIV.

34. Ibid.

35. Roland Freart de Chambray, *Parallèle de l'Architecture Antique et de la Moderne* (Paris, 1711). The first edition was published in 1650.

36. Perrault, *Ordonnance*, p. XIV.

37. Ibid.

38. Ibid., p. XX.

39. Ibid., p. XIX.

40. Ibid., p. VII.

41. Ibid., p. X.

42. Charles Perrault, *Parallèle*, vol. 1, p. 132.

43. C. and N. Perrault, *Oeuvres*, pp. 295ff.

44. See Erwin Panofsky, *La Perspective comme Forme Symbolique*, and William Ivins, Jr., *Art and Geometry.*

45. Claude Perrault, *Ordonnance*, p. XIV.

46. Ibid., pp. XVI–XVII.

47. For an excellent account of the interest in the Gothic during this period, particularly in France, see Robin Middleton, "The Abbé de Cordemoy and the Graeco-Gothic Ideal," *Journal of the Warburg and the Courtauld Institutes* 25 (1962), 26 (1963).

48. Charles Perrault, *Parallèle*, vol. 1, pp. 128–129.

49. Ibid.

50. Ibid., p. 132.

51. Charles believed that the excellence of his contemporaries was such that there would not be many things to envy in times to come. Ibid., pp. 98–99.

52. C. Perrault, *Les Dix Livres*, preface.

53. In Perrault's time, the only translation of Vitruvius available was that by Martin and Goujon (1547), whose text and illustrations are very inaccurate.

54. Perrault, *Les Dix Livres*, preface.

55. Ibid.

56. Ibid.

57. Ibid.

58. Perrault, *Ordonnance*, p. XII.

59. Ibid.

60. Perrault, *Les Dix Livres*, note 16, pp. 78–79.

61. Ibid.

62. One such response is to be found in Isaac Ware's *Complete Body of Architecture* (London, 1756).

63. See Alexandre Koyré, *Metaphysics and Measurement*, chapters 2 and 3.

64. Erwin Panofsky, *Galileo as a Critic of the Arts*.

65. Galileo believed that only circular motion was natural. Consequently, he rejected Kepler's elliptical planetary orbits and was never in a position to postulate in its definitive form the law of inertia. Kepler accepted the sphericity of the universe and the perfection of the circle. His cosmos was completely traditional, full of animistic and astrological implications. But being a more strict Platonist, Kepler was able to distinguish between ideal and mechanical action, between the intelligible idea of a circle and the actual path of the planets.

66. The power that images still possessed in seventeenth-century epistemology is particularly difficult for our modern world of mechanical reproduction to understand. It might be remembered that Pansophy, the ideal science of John Comenius, appreciated by the most illustrious philosophers of the century, depended on images as the means of establishing true knowledge. A logic or universal language could only be conceived on the basis of intuition. See P. Rossi, *Clavis Universalis*.

67. François Blondel, *Cours d'Architecture Enseigné dans l'Académie Royale d'Architecture* (Paris, 1698), 2nd ed., preface.

68. Ibid.

69. Ibid., pp. 714ff.

70. Ibid., p. 722.

71. François Blondel, *Résolution des Quatre Principaux Problèmes de l'Architecture*, introduction. This text was published as part of the series Recueil de Plusieurs Traitez de Mathématiques de l'Académie Royale des Sciences (Paris, 1676). The idea had been expressed previously by the Jesuit C. F. Milliet Deschales in his *Cursus seu Mundus Mathematicus* (Lyons, 1674) and would be taken up by Guarini. See chapter 4 in the present work.

72. The first problem concerns the geometrical tracing of the entasis or diminution of columns. The next two concern methods for describing the curves of arches with different springing heights. The last problem involves determining the width and depth of wooden beams in order to achieve their optimal resistance.

73. Blondel, *Cours*, preface.

74. François Blondel, *Nouvelle Manière de Fortifier les Places* (The Hague, 1694).

75. He probably took this method from F. Derand, *L'Architecture des Voûtes* (Paris, 1643). It is purely geometrical and is not derived from statics; see chapter 7 in the present work.

76. Blondel, *Cours*, pp. 168–173.

77. Ibid.

78. In the *Résolution*, he described the great joy that overwhelmed him every time he could ascertain a new discovery in architecture.

79. Blondel, *Cours*, pp. 168–173.

80. Ibid., *Livre Cinquième*, chapter 5.

81. Ibid., pp. 731–736.

82. Ibid., pp. 761–764.

83. Ibid.

84. Ibid., p. 774.

85. Ibid., p. 766.

86. Ibid., p. 768.

87. Ibid.

88. Ibid., p. 771.

89. Perrault, *Ordonnance*, p. XV.

Chapter 2

1. See Henri Lemmonier, *Procès-Verbaux de l'Académie Royale d'Architecture* (Paris, 1911–1913), vols. 1–3. Also see part III in the present work.

2. Michel de Fremin, *Mémoires Critiques d'Architecture* (Paris, 1702), p. 22.

3. Ibid., pp. 6–7.

4. Ibid., pp. 18–29.

5. See chapter 9 in the present work.

6. Abbé de Cordemoy, *Nouveau Traité de Toute l'Architecture* (Paris, 1706). I used the second edition of 1714.

7. Ibid., p. 1.

8. Ibid., p. 2.

9. Ibid.

10. Ibid., p. 260.

11. Sebastien Le Clerc, *Géométrie Pratique* (Paris, 1669), *Nouveau Système du Monde Conforme à l'Escriture Sainte* (Paris, 1719), *Système de la Vision Fondé sur des Nouveaux Principes* (Paris, 1719).

12. Le Clerc, *Traité d'Architecture* (Paris, 1714), *au lecteur*.

13. Ibid., p. 16.

14. Ibid.

15. Ibid., p. 39.

16. Ibid., p. 16.

17. See chapter 6 in the present work.

18. He opposed both Cordemoy and Laugier. Later in his life he also sided with Pierre Patte in the latter's dispute with Soufflot.

19. Amédée-François Frezier, *Dissertation sur les Ordres d'Architecture* (Strasbourg, 1738), pp. 5ff.

20. Ibid., p. 4.

21. Ibid.

22. Ibid., pp. 7–8.

23. Ibid., p. 14.

24. Ibid., p. 16.

25. Ibid., p. 17.

26. Ibid., p. 18.

27. Ibid.

28. Ibid., p. 17.

29. Ibid., p. 35.

30. This declaration, which appeared in one of his articles for *Mércure de France* (July 1754), is cited by Herrmann, *Laugier*, p. 146.

31. Père André, *Essai sur le Beau où l'on Examine en Quoi Consiste Précisément le Beau dans le Physique, dans le Moral, dans les Ouvrages d'Esprit et dans la Musique* (Paris, 1741). Later editions appeared in 1759, 1762, 1770, and 1827.

32. Charles Etienne Briseux, *Traité du Beau Essentiel dans les Arts, Appliqué Particulièrement à l'Architecture et Démontré Physiquement et par l'Experience* (Paris, 1752), 2 vols., vol. 1, p. 1.

33. See Rykwert, *The First Moderns*, chapter 5.

34. Briseux has been usually considered the author of another book published in 1728, *Architecture Moderne ou l'Art de Bien Bâtir*. However, Wolfgang Herrmann has pointed out that there are problems of authorship in "The Author of the 'Architecture Moderne' of 1728," *Journal of the Society of Architectural Historians* 18 (1959): 60–62. This book is much closer to the spirit of the treatises that I have discussed in the earlier part of the chapter. It is not concerned with the orders and deals mainly with problems of construction, including methods for writing specifications, applying geometry to mensuration, and producing cost estimates.

It also includes a catalog of plans showing imaginative combinations of rooms for private dwellings, in small houses and palaces, each one with sections and precise elevations. It is one of the earliest instances of the French eighteenth-century interest in *distribution*. See part III in the present work.

35. Briseux, *Traité*, vol. 1, pp. 7–8.

36. Ibid., chapter 1.

37. Ibid., pp. 34–36.

38. Ibid., p. 45.

39. Ibid., part III, chapter 2, pp. 45–55.

40. Ibid. Briseux also examined the internal workings of the human body and concluded that its fibers and organs were also governed by proportions. He admired Plato for having stated that the harmony of the universe was to be found in the human intellect.

41. Some remarks in his text seem to indicate this. See *Traité*, vol. 1, p. 10.

42. Briseux, *Traité*, p. 65.

43. Germain Boffrand, *Livre d'Architecture* (Paris, 1745), p. 1.

44. Ibid., p. 16.

45. For a good biography and a study of Laugier's *Essai*, see Wolfgang Herrmann, *Laugier and Eighteenth-Century French Theory*.

46. Abbé Laugier, *Essai sur l'Architecture* (Paris, 1755), preface, pp. XXXIII–XXXIV.

47. Ibid., p. XXXVIII.

48. Ibid., p. XL.

49. See Herrmann, *Laugier*, chapter 1. Laugier delivered a famous sermon in the chapel at Versailles in February 1754. In it he openly criticized the king and his government, espousing points of view closer to parliamentary democracy.

50. See, for example, Joseph Rykwert's study on Alberti's understanding of ornament in *Architectural Design Profiles* 21, pp. 2ff.

51. See Herrmann, *Laugier*. This book, however, is not concerned with Laugier's *Observations* or with the role of proportion in relation to the rest of his theory.

52. Laugier, *Observations*, p. 3.

53. Ibid., p. 4.

54. The abbé Du Bos, author of the popular *Réflexions Critiques sur la Poésie et sur la Peinture* (Paris, 1719), stated that judgment in art belongs not to the province of reason, but to that of feeling or sentiment.

55. Nicolas-Marie Potain, *Traité des Ordres d'Architecture, Première Partie: de la Proportion des Cinq Ordres où l'On a Tenté de les Rapprocher de Leur Origine en les Établissant sur un Principe Commun* (Paris, 1767).

56. Leonard Euler, *Lettres à une Princesse d'Allemagne* (Saint Petersburg, 1770).

57. Jacques-François Blondel, *Discours sur la Nécessité de l'Étude de l'Architecture* (Paris, 1752).

58. See chapter 5 in the present work.

59. The king offered scholarships to the best students in Blondel's school, enabling them to become *ingenieurs du Roi*.

60. J. F. Blondel, *Cours d'Architecture ou Traité de la Decoration, Distribution et Construction des Bâtiments* (Paris, 1771), 9 vols., vol. 3, pp. LXXXIff.

61. On Gauthey, see chapter 7 in the present work. His views on architecture are given in his *Mémoires sur les Règles d'Architecture*, quoted by Dartein, *Les Ponts Français*, vol. 4.

62. J. F. Blondel, *Cours*, vol. 1, pp. 448ff.

63. J. F. Blondel, *Discours*.

64. J. F. Blondel, *Cours*, vol. 3, p. 10.

65. J. F. Blondel, *Architecture Françoise* (Paris, 1752), p. 318.

66. Ibid.

67. J. F. Blondel, *Cours*, vol. 1, p. 376.

68. Ibid., vol. 3, p. 4.

69. J. F. Blondel, *Architecture Françoise*, p. 318.

70. Jean Monval, *Soufflot: Sa Vie, Son Oeuvre, Son Esthétique* (Paris, 1918), appendix, pp. 523–542.

71. See Lemmonier, *Procès-Verbaux*, vol. 8.

72. His daring proposals drew considerable criticism from Pierre Patte. See chapter 7 in the present work.

73. Jacques-Germain Soufflot, *Mémoire Lu à l'Académie de Lyon le 9 septembre, 1744*, reproduced in Monval, *Soufflot*, pp. 492–497.

74. J. G. Soufflot, *Mémoire sur les Proportions d'Architecture*, 1739, reproduced by M. Petzet, *Soufflots Sainte-Geneviève*, pp. 131–135.

75. The best monograph on Patte is still M. Mathieu, *Pierre Patte. Sa Vie et Son Oeuvre* (Paris, 1934).

76. Pierre Patte, *Discours sur l'Architecture* (Paris, 1754), pp. 9ff.

77. P. Patte, *Mémoires sur les Objets les Plus Importans de l'Architecture* (Paris, 1769), chapter 2, pp. 71ff.

78. Ibid., p. 82.

79. Nicolas Le Camus de Mezières, *Le Génie de l'Architecture* (Paris, 1780), p. 45.

80. Ibid., p. 54.

81. Ibid., pp. 7–8.

82. Ibid., pp. 7–14.

83. Ibid., pp. 13–14.

84. René Ouvrard, *Architecture Harmonique ou Application de la Doctrine des Proportions de la Musique à l'Architecture* (Paris, 1677), and Jerónimo Prado and Juan Bautista Villalpando, *In Ezechielem Explanationes* (Rome, 1595–1602).

85. L. B. Castel, *L'Optique des Couleurs, Fondée sur les Simples Observations, et Tournée Sur-Tout à la Pratique de la Peinture, de la Teinture et des Autres Arts Coloristes* (Paris, 1740).

86. Le Camus, *Le Génie*, p. 10. In this connection, see Marjorie Nicolson, *Newton Demands the Muse*.

87. This reconciliation between *mythos* and *logos* would become impossible in the nineteenth century, particularly after Kant's *Prolegomena to Any Future Metaphysics*, first edition 1783.

88. See A. Koyré, *Newtonian Studies*, chapter 2.

89. Isaac Newton, *Principes Mathematiques de la Philosophie Naturelle* (Paris, 1759), second edition of Châtelet's translation, vol. 1, p. 7, and vol. 2, pp. 179, 201.

90. See Y. Belaval, "La Crise de la Geometrisation de l'Univers dans la Philosophie des Lumières," *Revue Internationale de Phi-*

losophie (1952); E. Burtt, *The Metaphysical Foundations of Modern Physical Science*, pp. 208–211; and L. Brunschvicg, *Les Étapes de la Philosophie Mathematique*, chapter 11.

91. E. Burtt, *The Metaphysical Foundations*, chapter 7.

92. See Frances Yates, *The Rosicrucian Enlightenment*, chapter 14.

93. I. Newton, *The Mathematical Principles of Natural Philosophy* (London, 1803), translated from the Latin by Motte, 2 vols., vol. 1, pp. 6ff, and vol. 2, pp. 311ff.

94. I. Newton, *Unpublished Scientific Papers*, p. 103; quoted by A. Koyré, *Newtonian Studies*, p. 89. In comparing Cartesian with Newtonian physics, Koyré shows that world and time are indissolubly united for Descartes, as they were for Aristotle. But for Newton, space and time were not essentially connected with the world or with matter. The world is obviously in space as it is in time, but if there were no world, there would still be time and space. It is true that absolute space is not directly given to us in perception; we only perceive bodies, and it is in relation to these bodies that we determine our spaces. Still, Newton believed it was an error not to recognize that our relative, movable spaces were only possible in one immovable space, the space of God. See *Newtonian Studies*, chapter 3.

95. The origins of modern speculative Masonry are also related to the foundation of the Royal Society of London. See F. Yates, *The Rosicrucian Enlightenment*, chapter 14.

96. See Anthony Vidler, "The Architecture of the Lodges", *Oppositions* 5 (1976):75ff, and J. Rykwert, *The First Moderns*, particularly chapters 6 and 8.

97. C. Batteux, *Les Beaux Arts Réduits à un Même Principe* (Paris, 1746), pp. 56ff.

98. In this respect, I find misleading Peter Collins's *Changing Ideals in Modern Architecture (1750–1950)*, and Emil Kaufmann's *Architecture in the Age of Reason*.

Chapter 3   1. The titles of Guarini's works are *La Pietà Trionfante* (Messina, 1660), *Placita Philosophica* (Paris, 1665), *Euclides Adauctus et Methodicus* (Turin, 1671), *Modo di Misurare le Fabbriche* (Turin, 1674), *Compendio della Sfera Celeste* (Turin, 1675), *Leges Temporum et Planetarum* (Turin, 1678), *Coelestis Mathematicae* (Milan, 1683), *Disegni d'Architettura Civile ed Eclesiastica* (Turin, 1686), *Architettura Civile* (Turin, 1737), and *Tratatto di Fortificazione* (Turin, 1676).

2. The philosophical position of Guarini has been discussed by B. Tavasi La Greca in "La Posizione del Guarini in Rapporto alla Cultura Filosofica del Tempo," an appendix of the modern edition of *Architettura Civile*. See also Giulio Carlo Argan, *L'Architettura Barocca in Italia*, and A. del Noce, *Il Problema del Ateismo*. Compare Nicolas Malebranche, *De la Recherche de la Verité* (Paris, 1674–1675), vols. 2 and 3, and *Entretiens sur la Métaphysique* (Paris, 1688), vol. 1, with Guarino Guarini, *Placita Philosophica*.

3. See M. Nasti, "Il Sistema del Mondo di Guarino Guarini," a paper in the collection *Guarino Guarini e l'Internazionalità del Barocco*, 2 vols., vol. 2, pp. 559ff.

4. Guarini, *Placita*, p. 179.

5. Ibid., p. 833.

6. Malebranche, *De la Recherche*, part VI, chapter 1.

7. See Paolo Rossi, *Clavis Universalis*, particularly chapters 5–7.

8. M. Fagiolo, "La Geosofia del Guarini," in *Guarino Guarini e l'Internazionalità*, vol. 2, pp. 179ff. Fagiolo has shown how geometry was not for Guarini a branch of science, but a *Weltanschauung*: a world view, a pure idea, the matrix of all things.

9. Guarini, *Architettura Civile* (Milan, 1968), p. 10.

10. Ibid., pp. 19–20.

11. Ibid., p. 5.

12. Guarini, *Euclides Adauctus*, epigraph.

13. Carlo Cesare Osio, *Architettura Civile Demostrativamente Proportionata* (Milan and Lyons, 1684).

14. Guarini, *Architettura*, p. 129.

15. Compare Rudolf Wittkower, "Introduzione al Guarini," with Henry Millon, "La Geometria nel Linguaggio Architettonico del Guarini"; both articles are in *Guarino Guarini e l'Internazionalità*, vol. 1, pp. 19ff., and vol. 2, pp. 35ff.

16. W. Müller argues precisely this point in "Guarini e la Stereotomia," *Guarino Guarini e l'Internazionalità*, vol. 1, p. 531.

17. See chapter 6 in the present work.

18. See E. Battisti, "Schemata del Guarini," in *Guarino Guarini e l'Internazionalità*, vol. 2, pp. 107ff.

19. Abraham Bosse, *Manière Universelle de M. Desargues pour Pratiquer la Perspective par Petit-Pied comme le Géométral* (Paris, 1648), *La Pratique du Trait à Preuves, de M. Desargues Lyonnois pour la Coupe des Pierres en l'Architecture* (Paris, 1643), and *Moyen Universelle de Pratiquer la Perspective sur les Tableaux ou Surfaces Irregulières* (Paris, 1653).

20. This dimension of his thought appears most explicitly in his writings on stereotomy; it is examined together with other books on the subject in chapter 6 of the present work.

21. See Maurice Merleau-Ponty, *Phenomenology of Perception*, part I, chapters 1–3.

22. See José Ortega y Gasset, *Idea de Principio en Leibniz*, 2 vols., vol. 1, chapters 17 and 18.

23. M. Chasles, *Aperçu Historique sur l'Origine et Developpement des Méthodes en Géométrie* (Brussels, 1837), p. 83. More techically: If the lines joining corresponding vertices of two triangles are concurrent, the corresponding sides intersect in collinear points (from *McGraw-Hill Encyclopedia of Science and Technology*, vol. 2, p. 3).

24. G. Saccheri, *Euclides ab Omni Naevo Vindicatus* (London, 1920), in an English translation by G. B. Halsted.

25. Andrea Pozzo, *Rules and Examples of Perspective for Painters and Architects* (London, 1709).

26. See Georges Gusdorf, *Dieu, la Nature, l'Homme au Siècle des Lumières*, chapter 4.

27. Denis Diderot, "De l'Interpretation de la Nature" (1754), in *Oeuvres Philosophiques de Diderot*, pp. 180ff.

28. Diderot and Buffon could criticize the mathematical structure of Newton's discoveries. See Buffon, "De la Manière d'étudier et de Traiter l'Histoire Naturelle," in *Oeuvres Philosophiques de Buffon*, pp. 24ff. D'Alembert was also troubled by the "inconsiderate pretensions" of some geometricians who substituted mathematical hypotheses for experience. See d'Alembert, *Discours Préliminaire de l'Encyclopédie*, ed. Gonthier, p. 36.

29. There is a modern monograph on Vittone: Paolo Portoghesi, *Bernardo Vittone. Un Architetto tra Illuminismo e Rococco* (Rome: Officina ed., 1966).

30. See the collection of papers from the congress *Bernardo Vittone e la Disputa fra Classicismo e Barocco nel Settecento* (Turin: Ac-

cademia delle Scienze, 1972). See also Werner Oechslin, *Bildungsgut und Antikenrezeption des frühen Settecento in Rom.*

31. Francesco Algarotti, *Il Newtonianismo per le Dame, ovvero, Dialoghi sopra la Luce e i Colori* (Naples, 1737).

32. P. Portoghesi, *Bernardo Vittone*, pp. 12–14. See chapter 7 in the present work.

33. B. Vittone, *Istruzioni Diverse Concernenti l'Officio dell'Architetto Civile* (Lugano, 1766), title page.

34. Ibid., p. 123.

35. See chapter 9 in the present work for an analysis of the implications of Durand's use of the grid.

36. See Marjorie Nicholson, *Newton Demands the Muse.*

37. Vittone, *Istruzioni Diverse*, appendix 2, "Istruzioni Armoniche osia Breve Tratatto sopra la Natura del Suono del Signor G.G."

38. Ibid., p. 219. Hermes Trismegistus was the mythical *magus* who, during the Renaissance, was believed to be an ancient prophet of Christianity. His writings were translated by Ficino from the Greek. This supposed *prisca theologia*, actually a collection of gnostic writings from the Early Christian Era, was influential. Hermetic magic seems to have played a major role in the development of modern science. See Frances Yates, *Giordano Bruno and the Hermetic Tradition*; Wayne Shumaker, *The Occult Sciences in the Renaissance*; and D. P. Walker, *Spiritual and Demonic Magic from Ficino to Campanella.*

39. Vittone, *Istruzioni Diverse*, p. 235.

40. Ibid., p. 320.

41. Nicola Carletti, *Istruzioni d'Architettura Civile* (Naples, 1772), p. VII.

42. Ibid., p. VIII.

43. Ibid., p. 332. Etienne-Louis Boullée's architecture, discussed in the following chapter, represents the clearest embodiment of this vision.

44. See Elie Konigson, *L'Espace Théâtrale Médiéval* (Paris, 1975).

45. Christian Wolff, "Ratio Praelectionum Wolfianarum," in *Lebensbeschreibung* (Leipzig, 1841), pp. 135–136.

46. C. Wolff, *Vernünftige Gedanken von den Kräften des menslichen Verstandes* (Halle, 1742), p. 226.

47. C. Wolff, *Elementa Matheseos Universae* (Magdeburg, 1713), 2 vols., vol. 1, p. 937.

48. C. Wolff, *Cours de Mathématique* (Paris, 1747), 3 vols., vol. 2, p. 246.

49. Robert Morris, *Lectures on Architecture Consisting of Rules Founded upon Harmonick and Arithmetical Proportions in Building* (London, 1734), preface.

50. R. Morris, *An Essay in Defence of Ancient Architecture* (London, 1728), pp. 1ff.

51. Ibid.

52. R. Morris, *Lectures*, preface.

53. Ibid.

54. Ibid., pp. 74ff.

55. Ibid.

56. R. Morris, *An Essay Upon Harmony as It Relates Chiefly to Situation and Building* (London, 1739).

57. The speech is reproduced by Chevallier, *Les Ducs sous l'Acacia*, pp. 146–148.

58. This issue has been studied by various scholars. See René Taylor, "Architecture and Magic: Considerations on the Idea of the Escorial," in *Essays in the History of Architecture Presented to Rudolf Wittkower*, pp. 81ff, and J. Rykwert, *The First Moderns*, chapter 6.

59. Prado and Villalpando, *In Ezechielem Explanationes*.

60. Batty Langley, *The Builder's Compleat Assistant* (London, 1738), p. 61.

61. *Constitutions*, MS Cooke, British Museum, Ad. 23198. Reproduced in appendix A, John Harvey, *The Mediaeval Architect*, pp. 191–202.

Chapter 4

1. See Emil Kaufmann, "Three Revolutionary Architects: Boullé, Ledoux and Lequeu," *Transactions of the American Philosophical Society* 43(3) (1952); Helen Rosenau, *Boullée and Visionary Architecture*; and *Visionary Architects*, a catalog of an exhibition on the work of Boullée, Ledoux, and Lequeu.

2. See, in particular, Emil Kaufmann, *Architecture in the Age of Reason* (1st ed. 1955), and his *Von Ledoux bis Le Corbusier* (Vienna, 1933).

3. Louis Kahn wrote his twelve lines on the occasion of the exhibition of Boullée's and Ledoux's work in North America (1968). See *Visionary Architects*, p. 9.

4. See Hugh Honour, *Neo-Classicism*, particularly chapters 1 and 4.

5. J. F. Blondel, *Cours*, vol. 1, chapter 5.

6. Marie-Joseph Peyre, *Oeuvres d'Architecture* (Paris, 1765), p. 3.

7. Werner Oechslin, "Pyramide et Sphère," *Gazette de Beaux Arts* 77 (1971).

8. Robert Rosenblum, *Transformations in Late Eighteenth Century Art*, chapter 3.

9. Jean-Louis Viel de Saint-Maux, *Lettres sur l'Architecture des Anciens et Celle des Modernes dans Lesquelles se Trouve Développé le Génie Symbolique Qui Presida aux Monuments de l'Antiquité* (Paris, 1787).

10. The best recent monograph on Boullée is Jean-Marie Pérouse de Montclos, *Etienne-Louis Boullée*. There is an abridged English translation.

11. Pérouse de Montclos, *Boullée*, p. 253, for a complete inventory of his library.

12. I have used the edition by Pérouse de Montclos, *Essai sur l'Art* (Paris, 1968).

13. Boullée, *Essai sur l'Art*, p. 49.

14. The same peaceful coexistence between rules and genius is evident in the works on aesthetics by Dubos and Montesquieu.

15. Boullée, *Essai*, pp. 67–68.

16. Ibid., p. 69.

17. Ibid., pp. 51, 154.

18. Ibid., p. 61.

19. Ibid., p. 35.

20. Ibid., p. 63.

21. Ibid., pp. 47–48.

22. Lodoli achieved the same feat in Venice earlier in the century. But apart from some isolated building details, and Piranesi's *Carceri*, there was never an application of the principles of the *Rigoristti* to design. See J. Rykwert, *The First Moderns*, chapter 8; also see chapter 7 in the present work.

23. See Mikel Dufrenne, *Le Poétique*, book 3, pp. 199ff., and Paul Ricoeur, *The Rule of Metaphor*, study 1, pp. 9ff.

24. Boullée, *Essai*, pp. 75–76.

25. Pérouse de Montclos has pointed out that *fecondité, caractère, éloquence*, and *poèsie* are synonymous for Boullée; his use of these words was approximately equivalent to *convenance* in previous theoretical writings. The poetry of architecture was already for J. F. Blondel *anoncer ce qu'un édifice est* and was related to the notions of harmony and proportion. See Boullée, *Essai*, p. 112n79.

26. Boullée, *Essai*, p. 69.

27. Ibid., pp. 137–138.

28. Ibid.; see Pérouse de Montclos's commentary on the cenotaph.

29. M. A. Vogt, *Boullées Newton-Denkmal*.

30. Boullée, *Essai*, pp. 63–64.

31. Descartes and Leibniz conceived space as geometrical; and when the dimension of infinity was introduced (*indéfinition* as Descartes would have it), space was still never conceived as a void; it was always full of matter. Descartes wrote, "it is repugnant that there be a vacuum or a place where there would be absolutely no thing. . . . It is clear that vacuum in the philosophical sense, that is, a place in which there would be absolutely no substance, cannot exist because the extension of space, or internal place, does not differ from the extension of body." See R. Descartes, *Principia Philosophiae*, in *Oeuvres* (Paris, 1905), Tannery ed., vol. 8, part 16, p. 49. Leibniz believed that the existence of vacuum would be in contradiction to God's infinite perfection and implied a limitation of His power of creation. See *A Collection of Papers, which passed between the late learned Mr. Leibniz and Dr. Clarke* (London, 1717), third and fourth papers, pp. 57, 103ff.

32. I. Newton, *The Mathematical Principles of Natural Philosophy* (London, 1803), vol. 1, p. 6. For the influence of Henry More, the Cambridge Platonists, and Isaac Barrow, on Newton, see Max Jammer, *Concepts of Space*. Jammer points out that the idea that God is the place of the universe was derived from Jewish sources and was assimilated into European thought during the Middle Ages. It was used in the fifteenth century by magicians like Pico

and Agrippa and in the sixteenth century by Bruno and Campanella. An anti-Aristotelian notion, it was embraced by modern scientists like Gassendi and ultimately by Newton himself.

33. Boullée, *Essai*, pp. 81–82.

34. Ibid., p. 85.

35. Ibid., pp. 89, 94.

36. D. Diderot, "Oration," cited by H. Honour, *Neo-Classicism*, p. 153.

37. Interesting, in this connection, were the curious dogmas and forms of worship of the French people at the time of the Revolution; for example, their principle of Holy Equality and their *fêtes*. The Festival of Reason of November 1793 was, according to Becker, a tentative step in the effort to replace Christianity by a civic or secular religion of humanity. Robespierre, however, thought it too atheistic and decided to publish his famous decree of May 1794, which stated that "the French people recognize the existence of the Supreme Being and the immortality of the soul. . . . The worship due to Him is the practice of the duties of man. . . ." Cited by Carl Becker, *The Heavenly City of the 18th-Century Philosophers*, pp. 156ff.

38. Boullée, *Essai*, pp. 133–135.

39. J. L. Viel de Saint-Maux, *Lettres*, fifth letter.

40. The editor's opinion in the *avertissement* of volume 2 of Ledoux's theoretical work, *L'Architecture Considérée sous le Rapport de l'Art, des Moeurs et de la Legislation* (Paris, 1804 and 1847), 2 vols., clearly reveals this ambiguity. In his work on Ledoux, M. Raval points out the diverse opinions held of him between 1762 and 1944. Du Fresne, for example, wrote in 1789 that Ledoux was a very turbulent and dangerous man, while "L. G.," in *Annales du Musée et des Arts* (1803), complained about the destruction of some of Ledoux's *barrières* for the city of Paris. See M. Raval and J. C. Moreaux, *C. N. Ledoux*, and Y. Christ, *C. N. Ledoux, Projects et Divagations*. For Ledoux's work in Paris see Michel Gallet, *Ledoux et Paris*.

41. Claude-Nicolas Ledoux, *L'Architecture*, vol. 1, pp. 117, 123.

42. Ibid., pp. 10, 20.

43. Ibid., pp. 136–137.

44. Ibid., pp. 15, 20.

45. Ibid., p. 15.

46. Ibid., p. 149.

47. Ibid., p. 115.

48. Ibid., p. 113.

49. Ibid., p. 63.

50. Ibid., p. 150.

51. Ibid., p. 132.

52. Ibid., p. 142.

53. Boullée had also designed a Temple à Jour in which God could be venerated in the open fields. See Boullée, *Essai*, pp. 69–70.

54. Ledoux, *L'Architecture*, p. 180.

55. Ibid., pp. 142–143.

56. See Anthony Vidler, "The Architecture of the Lodges," *Oppositions* 5 (1976):75ff.

57. Désaguilliers's publications include *A System of Experimental Philosophy Prov'd by Mechanicks* (London, 1719) and *Physico-Mechanical Lectures* (London, 1717). See also D. Campbell Lee, *Désaguilliers of No. 4*, and J. Stokes and W. R. Hurst, *An Outline of the Career of J. T. Désaguilliers*.

58. Ledoux, *L'Architecture*, p. 140.

59. Ibid., p. 178.

60. J. Kirby, *The Perspective of Architecture in Two Parts* (London, 1761), introduction.

61. See Y. Christ, *Ledoux*, p. 167ff.

62. Ledoux, *L'Architecture*, p. 73.

63. Ibid., p. 174.

64. Ibid., p. 185n1.

65. Ibid., p. 194.

66. Ibid., p. 195.

67. Ibid., p. 196.

68. J. M. Peyre, *Oeuvres*, p. 3.

69. J. L. Viel de Saint-Maux, *Lettres*, p. 12.

70. In twentieth-century art, these concerns were epitomized by the surrealist movement. See Roger Shattuck's excellent account on the origins of modern art, *The Banquet Years*. In architecture, see the work of A. Kiesler and the recent projects by John Hejduk and Aldo Rossi. Intentional ambiguity and the recovery of architectural meaning are also evident in Daniel Libeskind's use of the abstract architectural universe of discourse in nonrepresentational theoretical projects, a pure architecture of essences that questions the conventional reductionism of contemporary practice. See Libeskind, "End Space," in *An Exhibition at the Architectural Association* (London, 1980); Dalibor Veseley, "The Drama of the Endgame," in the same catalog; and Libeskind's *Between Zero and Infinity*.

71. Baudin, *Funerailles du Citoyen Boullée* (Paris, 1799).

Chapter 5

1. See G. Gusdorf, *La Révolution Galiléenne*, vol. 1, chapter 1.

2. Gusdorf, *La Révolution Galiléenne*, vol. 1, chapter 2.

3. See Paolo Rossi, *Philosophy, Technology and the Arts in the Early Modern Era*, p. 116.

4. For this issue, see Gusdorf, *La Révolution Galiléenne*, 1, chapter 3.

5. Malebranche, for example, explained that technology could be positive because although God was never wrong, certain particular consequences of His acts could be harmful to humanity. Hence Malebranche excused man for taking measures for his own benefit, so long as they did not imply blasphemy or oppose divine wisdom. Malebranche, *Traité de Morale* (Paris, 1684), vol. 1, chapter 1.

6. See, for example, P. Ramus, "Actio Secunda pro Regia Mathematicae Professionis Cathedra" (1566), in *Collectanae* (Paris, 1577), pp. 536ff.

7. Thomas Sprat, *L'Histoire de la Societé Royale de Londres* (Paris, 1669), p. 490. This is a translation from the English original.

8. T. C. Allbut, *Palissy, Bacon and the Revival of Natural Science*.

9. Palissy, himself a Huguenot, had suffered considerably from the religious wars.

10. Bernard Palissy, *Recepte Véritable par Laquelle Tous les Hommes de la France Pourront Apprendre a Multiplier et Augmenter Leurs Thrésors* (La Rochelle, 1563). I shall quote from a modern edition in *Oeuvres* (Paris, 1880), p. 22.

11. Ibid., pp. 75–77.

Notes to Pages 161–170

12. Ibid., pp. 79–80.

13. Salomon de Caus, *Les Raisons des Forces Mouvantes avec Diverses Machines tant Utiles que Plaisantes, aus Quelles son Adjoints Plusieurs Desseigns de Grotes et Fontaines* (Frankfurt, 1615). De Caus worked in Heidelberg, where he designed the castle's garden and probably had connections with the Rosicrucian movement. See F. Yates, *The Rosicrucian Enlightenment*, chapter 2.

14. S. de Caus, *La Perspective avec la Raison des Ombres et Miroirs* (London, 1612), preface.

15. Simon Stevin of Bruges, *Oeuvres Mathématiques* (Leyden, 1634); Guido Ubaldo del Monte, *Perspectivae Libri Sex* (Pesaro, 1600). See L. Guerry, *Jean-Pelerin Viator*, and Decio Gioseffi's article "Perspective" in *Encyclopedia of World Art*, vol. 11 (1966).

16. See William Ivins, *On the Rationalization of Sight*, pp. 7–13.

17. A. Koyré, *From the Closed World to the Infinite Universe*, pp. 110ff.

18. See Jurgis Baltrušaitis, *Anamorphic Art*.

19. The best-known example is Holbein's *Ambassadors*, painted in 1533. See Baltrušaitis, *Anamorphic Art*, chapter 2.

20. I owe this formulation to Dalibor Vesely.

21. J. F. Niceron, *La Perspective Curieuse ou Magie Artificiele des Effets Marveilleux* (Paris, 1638), pp. 1–2.

22. Ibid.

23. Ibid., p. 5.

24. Ibid., p. 6.

25. This had been, indeed, a traditional concern. It is well known that Vitruvius made money trading in weapons. See H. Lorraine, *La Pyrotechnie ou Sont Representez les Plus Rares et Plus Apreuvez Secrets* (Paris, 1630).

26. C. Mollet, *Theatre des Plans et Jardinages Contenant des Secrets et des Inventions* (Paris, 1652).

27. J. Boyceau, *Traité du Jardinage Selon les Raisons de la Nature et de l'Art* (Paris, 1638).

28. In Pascal's philosophy, for example, God performed very few miracles, whereas Spinoza's God was identified with nature and consequently predetermined all that depended on Him. See Blaise Pascal, *Pensées*. A good general history of philosophy from Des-

cartes to Leibniz is Frederick Copleston, *A History of Philosophy*, vol. 4.

29. C. C. Scaletti, *Scuola Mecanico-Speculativo-Practica in Cui se Essamina la Proporzione, che hà la Potenza alla Resistenza del Corpo Grave* (Bologna, 1711), preface, pages not numbered.

30. Pierre Patte, *Monuments Érigés en France à la Gloire de Louis XV* (Paris, 1765), pp. 25ff.

31. Andre Felibien, *Des Principes de l'Architecture, de la Sculpture, de la Peinture, et des Autres qui en Dependent* (Paris, 1699), pp. 8–9.

32. Ibid., pp. 9–10.

33. John Locke, *De Arte Medica* (1689), cited by H. Marson, *J. Locke* (1878), p. 94.

34. Gottfried Wilhelm Leibniz, *Philosophischen Schriften*, vol. 2, p. 69, cited and translated by P. Rossi, *Philosophy, Technology and the Arts*, p. 130. There is also an English translation of Leibniz, *Philosophical Writings* (Totowa, NJ, 1973), including a good selection.

35. Denis Diderot and Jean d'Alembert, *Encyclopédie, ou Dictionnaire Raisonné des Sciences, des Arts, et des Métiers par une Société de Gens de Lettres* (Paris, 1751–1765), 17 vols.

36. See G. Gusdorf, *Les Principes de la Pensée*, pp. 249–256.

37. Batty Langley, *New Principles of Gardening* (London, 1728), preface.

38. See chapter 3 in the present work.

39. A. J. Dezalliers d'Argenville, *Théorie et Pratique du Jardinage* (The Hague, 1711).

40. R. Schabol, *La Pratique du Jardinage* (Paris, 1770), p. 1.

41. Ibid., pp. 2ff.

42. Ibid., p. 4.

43. Ibid., p. 30.

44. The theory of style, and particularly the work of Gottfried Semper, are nineteenth-century examples of such extrapolations. See chapter 9 in the present work.

45. R. Schabol, *La Théorie du Jardinage* (Paris, 1771), preface.

46. *École des Ponts et Chaussées*, ms. 2629 bis and 1926, reproduced by J. Petot, *Histoire de l'Administration des Ponts et Chaussées 1599-1815* (Paris, 1958), pp. 142-143.

47. A. Bosse, *Manière Universelle de M. Desargues pour Pratiquer la Perspective* (Paris, 1648), p. 1.

48. See chapter 3 in the present work.

49. J. Ozanam, *Récréations Mathématiques et Physiques* (Paris, 1696), preface.

50. Ozanam, *La Perspective Théorique et Pratique* (Paris, 1720), preface.

51. See Richard Sennett, *The Fall of Public Man*, part II, pp. 45ff.

52. G. W. Leibniz, *Protogea* (1693), in *Werke* (Stuttgart, 1949) vol. 1, p. 170.

53. Leibniz, *Dialogue on the Connection between Things and Words* (1677), translated by Leroy Loemker, *Philosophical Papers and Letters* (Chicago, 1956), pp. 278-282.

54. Leibniz, *On the General Characteristic* (Loemker), pp. 344-345.

55. Bernard de Fontenelle, *Éléments de la Géométrie de l'Infini, Suite des Mémoires de l'Académie Royale des Sciences* (Paris, 1727), preface.

56. Fontenelle, *Préface sur l'Utilité des Mathématiques et de la Physique et sur les Travaux de l'Académie de Sciences* (1699), in *Oeuvres* (1825), vol. 1, p. 59.

57. Fontenelle, *Préface de l'Histoire de l'Académie des Sciences depuis 1666 jusqu'à 1699*, in *Oeuvres*, vol. 1, pp. 15-16.

58. F. Blondel, *Cours d'Architecture* (Paris, 1698), pp. 2-4.

59. Ibid.

60. H. Lemonnier, *Procès-Verbaux*, vol. 3.

61. See chapter 7 in the present work.

62. Among De la Hire's many contributions are geometrical methods for tracing complex arches (1698), the resolution of problems of surveying, mensuration, and detailing (1698-1699), and many discussions about the dimensions of retaining walls (1707) and arches (1711) based on mechanical considerations.

63. Lemonnier, *Procès-Verbaux*, vol. 3, pp. 358-360.

Notes to Pages 190-196

64. Ibid., vols. 4 and 5.

65. Ibid., vol. 6.

66. Ibid., vol. 8, pp. 247–248.

67. See J. F. Blondel, *Discours sur la Nécessité de l'Étude de l'Architecture* (Paris, 1752).

68. J. F. Blondel, *Cours d'Architecture*, vol. 3, p. XXVIII.

69. See G. Serbos, "L'École Royale des Ponts et Chaussées," in the collection edited by R. Taton, *Enseignement et Diffusion des Sciences en France au 18ème. siècle*, pp. 356ff. See also E. Vignon, *Études Historiques sur l'Administration des Voies Publiques en France au 17ème. et 18ème. siècles* (Paris, 1862), and J. Petot, *Histoire de l'Administration des Ponts et Chaussées*.

70. Riche de Prony, *Notice Historique sur Jean-Rodolphe Perronet* (Paris, 1829).

71. See René Taton, "L'École Royale du Génie de Mezières," in *Enseignement et Diffusion des Sciences en France au 18ème. Siècle*.

72. A.M. Augoyat, *Aperçu Historique sur les Fortifications, les Ingenieurs et sur le Corps du Génie en France* (Paris, 1860–1864), vol. 1, pp. 253–254.

73. R. Hahn, "Les Écoles Militaires et d'Artillerie," in Taton, ed., *Enseignement et Diffusion des Sciences*. Bélidor pointed out that there were schools in Metz, Strasbourg, Grenoble, Perpignan, and La Fère. See Forest de Bélidor, *Nouveau Cours de Mathématique à l'Usage de l'Artillerie et du Génie* (Paris, 1725), preface.

74. R. Taton, "L'École Royale," chapter 3, pp. 559ff.

75. *Archives de l'Inspection du Génie*, box I, number 26; cited by Taton, "L'École Royale," p. 587.

76. C. Bossut, *Nouvelles Expériences sur la Resistance des Fluides* (Paris, 1777), preface.

77. *Archives*, cited by Taton, "L'École Royale," pp. 593–596.

78. Taton, "L'École Royale," pp. 596ff.

Chapter 6

1. Girolamo Cataneo, *Dell'Arte Militare Libri Cinque* (Brescia, 1584), 1st ed., 1559. A well-illustrated introduction to Renaissance fortification is J. R. Hale, *Renaissance Fortification. Art or Engineering?*

2. Simon Stevin, *Oeuvres Mathématiques* (Leyden, 1634). The French translation is by A. Girard.

3. S. Marolois, *Géométrie Contenant la Théorie et la Pratique d'Icelle, Necessaire à la Fortification* (Amsterdam, 1628).

4. S. Marolois, *Fortification ou Architecture Militatire tant Offensive que Defensive* (Leyden, 1628), translated into English in 1638.

5. N. Goldman, *La Nouvelle Fortification* (Leyden, 1645).

6. C. F. Milliet Dechales, *L'Art de Fortifier* (Paris, 1677).

7. B. Palissy, *Recepte Véritable*, pp. 12–13.

8. Ibid., p. 147.

9. Ibid.

10. Ibid.

11. J. Perret de Chambery, *Des Fortifications et Artifices, Architecture et Perspective* (Paris, 1594).

12. P. A. Barca, *Avertimenti e Regole circa l'Architettura Civile, Scultura, Pittura, Prospettiva et Architettura Militare* (Milano, 1620), introduction.

13. P. Sardi, *Couronne Imperiale de l'Architecture Militaire* (Frankfurt, 1623), introduction.

14. G. Busca, *L'Architettura Militare* (Milano, 1619). For a description of the history and importance of foundation rituals, see Joseph Rykwert, *The Idea of a Town*.

15. M. Dögen, *L'Architecture Militaire Moderne ou Fortification, Confirmées par Diverses Histoires tant Anciennes que Nouvelles* (Amsterdam, 1648).

16. Jean-Errard de Bar-le-Duc, *La Fortification Demonstrée et Reduite en Art* (Paris, 1619), *Premier Livre*, chapter 11. See also M. Parent and J. Vernoust, *Vauban*.

17. J. Errard de Bar-le-Duc, *La Fortification*, chapter 11.

18. Bonaiuto Lorini, *Delle Fortificazioni* (Venice, 1597).

19. Pagan, *Les Fortifications* (Paris, 1645), preface.

20. F. Blondel, *Nouvelle Manière de Fortifier les Places* (The Hague, 1684), and A. Tacquett S.J., *Military Architecture or the Art of Fortifying Towns* (London, 1672).

21. J. Ozanam, *Traité de Fortification* (Paris, 1694) and *Cours de Mathématiques Qui Comprend Toutes les Parties les Plus Utiles et les Plus Necessaires à un Homme de Guerre* (Amsterdam, 1699).

22. Many monographs on Vauban have been written. The most recent is M. Parent and J. Vernoust, *Vauban*.

23. His name was Clerville. See Augoyat, *Aperçu Historique*, vol. 1, pp. 75ff.

24. Cited by R. Blomdfield, *Sebastien le Prestre de Vauban*, p. 60.

25. Compare the opinions of his biographers: Rabelliau, *Vauban* (1932), and Ricolfi, *Vauban et le Génie Militaire* (1935).

26. Vauban, *Traité des Fortifications Attaque et Défense des Places*, in *Oeuvres* (Paris, 1771), introduction.

27. A complete bibliography of Vauban's writings appears in Rochas D'Aiglun, *Vauban, Sa Famille et Ses Écrits* (1910), pp. 81–100.

28. Cited by Blomdfield, *Vauban*, p. 116.

29. See Blomdfield, *Vauban*, pp. 143ff.

30. Vauban, *Plusieurs Maximes Bonnes à Observer pour Tous Ceux qui Font Bastir*, cited by Augoyat, *Aperçu Historique*, vol. 1, pp. 75ff.

31. Vauban, *Les Fonctions des Différents Officiers Employés dans les Fortifications*, cited by Blomdfield, *Vauban*, p. 81.

32. B. Fontenelle, *Éloge des Académiciens de l'Académie Royale des Sciences* (Paris, 1731).

33. Mentioned by Forest de Bélidor in *La Science des Ingénieurs* (Paris, 1729), and by Augoyat, *Aperçu Historique*, vol. 1, pp. 81ff. Vauban's tables are reproduced by Bélidor.

34. Cambray, *Manière de Fortifier de M. de Vauban* (Amsterdam, 1689); Anonymous, *The New Method of Fortification as Practised by M. de Vauban* (London, 1691); J. F. Pfeffinger, *Manière de Fortifier à la Vauban* (Amsterdam, 1690); L. C. Sturm, *Le Véritable Vauban* (The Hague, 1713); and C. Wolff, *Cours de Mathématiques* (Paris, 1747), 3 vols.

35. G. Le Blond, *L'Arithmetique et la Géométrie de l'Officier* (Paris, 1748), 3 vols., and *Éléments de Fortification Contenant la Construction Raisonée des Ouvrages . . . les Systèmes des Ingénieurs les Plus Célébres; la Fortification Irregulière* (Paris, 1775); *L'Ingénieur François par M.N. Ingénieur Ordinaire du Roy* (Lyon, 1748); and finally, Prevost de Vernoist, *De la Fortification depuis Vauban* (Paris, 1861).

36. B. Forest de Bélidor, *La Science des Ingénieurs, dans la Conduite des Travaux de Fortification et d'Architecture Civile* (Paris, 1830), pp. 2–3.

37. Ibid., pp. 6–7.

38. Ibid., p. 11.

39. Ibid., p. 12.

40. Ibid., pp. 13–14.

41. Bélidor, *Nouveau Cours de Mathématiques* (Paris, 1725), introduction.

42. Bélidor, *La Science*, p. 23n1.

43. Ibid., pp. 405–407, and see chapter 9 in the present work.

44. Ibid., p. 513.

45. Ibid., pp. 424–425.

46. Ibid., pp. 496–497.

47. Ibid., p. 425.

48. Ibid., p. 498.

49. Ibid., p. 497n1.

50. Ibid.

51. Ibid.

52. Ibid.

53. J. de Fallois, *L'École de la Fortification, ou les Elements de la Fortification Permanente, Regulière et Irregulière . . . pour Servir de Suite à la Science des Ingenieurs de M. Bélidor* (Dresden, 1768).

54. B. Palissy, *Recepte Véritable* (1563 ed.), pp. 118–119.

55. The *Ludi Matematici* was published for the first time by Cosimo Bartoli in 1568, but with many alterations. See L. Vagnetti, "Considerazioni sui Ludi Matematici," *Studi e Documenti di Architettura* 1 (1972):173. See also his "La Teoria del Rilevamento Architettonico in G. Guarini," in *Guarino Guarini e l'Internazionalità del Barocco*, vol. 1, pp. 497ff.

56. S. Belli, *Libro del Misurar con la Vista . . . Senza Travagliar con Numeri* (Venice, 1565). Other authors cited by A. Comolli in his *Bibliografia Storico-Critica dell'Architettura* (Rome, 1788), 2 vols., and by Vagnetti, "La Teoria del Rilevamento," in *Guarino Guarini*

e l'Internazionalità, vol. 1, pp. 497ff, are Guibert, Oronce Finé, and Capra. They all wrote pieces on mensuration or surveying during the sixteenth century.

57. G. Cataneo, *Dell'Arte del Misurare Libri Due* (Brescia, 1584).

58. S. Stevin, *Oeuvres Mathématiques* (Leyden, 1634).

59. Ibid., vol. 3, *argument*.

60. C. F. Milliet Dechales, *Cursus seu Mundus Mathematicus* (Lyons, 1674), 3 vols.

61. P. Casati, *Fabrica et Uso del Compasso di Proportione* (Bologna, 1664), and J. Ozanam, *Usage de l'Instrument Universel* (Paris, 1688).

62. G. Guarini, *Modo di Misurare le Fabriche . . . in Cui non vi è Corpo, e Quasi non vi è Superficie, Purche Godi di Qualche Regolarità, che Matematicamente non Resti Misurato* (Turin, 1674).

63. Lemonnier, *Procès-Verbaux*, vols. 1–3. See also Eric Langen-skiöld, *Pierre Bullet the Royal Architect*.

64. In June 1707 he presented a paper that compared different configurations of arches with regard to their resistances. See Lemonnier, *Procès-Verbaux*, vol. 3.

65. Pierre Bullet, *L'Architecture Pratique* (Paris, 1691).

66. See, for example, Jacques Androuet du Cerceau, *Les Trois Livres d'Architecture* (Paris, 1559, 1561, and 1582).

67. P. Bullet, *L'Architecture Pratique*, introduction.

68. Ibid. This may have implied a criticism of Perrault. See Langenskiöld, *Pierre Bullet*, chapter 1.

69. On this issue, he was criticized by Bélidor, who disagreed. See Bélidor, *La Science*, pp. 334–335.

70. H. Gautier, *Traité des Ponts* (Paris, 1727–1728). Gautier included in his treatise a section on bookkeeping for engineers.

71. See chapter 5 in the present work.

72. See, for example, C. D'Aviler, *Cours d'Architecture* (Paris, 1696); C. E. Briseux (?), *Architecture Moderne* (Paris, 1728); J. F. Blondel, *De la Distribution des Maisons de Plaisance* (Paris, 1737); A. Frezier, *La Théorie et la Pratique de la Coupe des Pierres* (Paris, 1737–1738); Jombert, *Architecture Moderne* (Paris, 1764); N. M. Potain, *Traité des Ordres d'Architecture* (Paris, 1767); and P. Patte, *Mémoirs sur les Objets les Plus Importans de l'Architecture* (Paris, 1769).

73. See chapter 3 in the present work.

74. See L. Perini, *Geometria Pratica* (Verona, 1727); C. F. Cristiani, *Delle Misure d'Ogni Genere* (Brescia, 1760); and T. Guerrino, *Opera di Geometria, Stereometria, Geodesia* (Milano, 1773).

75. G. A. Alberti, *Trattato della Misura delle Fabbriche* (Venice, 1757). Alberti discussed the measurement of vaults and translated some important papers on mensuration by De la Hire, Senes, and Pitot.

76. G. F. Cristiani, *Dell'Utilita e della Dilettazione de'Modeli ad Uso dell'Architettura Militare* (Brescia, 1765), preface.

77. William Halfpenny, *The Art of Sound Building* (London, 1725), preface.

78. W. Halfpenny, *The Modern Builder's Assistant* (London, 1747).

79. Albrecht Dürer, *Hierinn sind begriffen vier Bucher von menschlicher Proportion* (Nuremberg, 1528) and *Underweysung du Messung mit dem Zirckel und Richtscheyt, in Linien ebenen gantzen Corporen* (Nuremberg, 1525).

80. Mathurin Jousse, *Le Secret d'Architecture Decouvrant Fidelement les Traits Geometriques, Couppes et Derobemens Necessaires dans les Bastiments* (La Flèche, 1642), introduction.

81. François Derand, *L'Architecture des Voûtes ou L'Art des Traits et Coupe des Voûtes* (Paris, 1643), preface.

82. C. F. Milliet Dechales, *Cursus seu Mundus Mathematicus*, vol. 2.

83. François Blondel, "Résolution des Quatre Principaux Problèmes de l'Architecture," in *Recueil de Plusieurs Traitez de Mathématiques de L'Académie Royale des Sciences* (Paris, 1676).

84. G. Desargues, *Brouillon-Projet d'Exemple d'une Manière Universelle du S. G. D. L. Touchant la Pratique du Trait à Preuves pour la Coupe des Pierres en l'Architecture* (Paris, 1640), and A. Bosse, *La Pratique du Trait à Preuves de M. Desargues Lyonnois pour la Coupe des Pierres en l'Architecture* (Paris, 1643).

85. A. Bosse, *La Pratique*, introduction.

86. In March 1698, July 1701, and April 1703. See H. Lemonnier, *Procès-Verbaux*, vol. 2, particularly p. 297.

87. Amédée-François Frézier, *La Théorie et la Pratique de la Coupe des Pierres et des Bois, pour la Construction des Voûtes et Autres*

Parties des Bâtiments Civils et Militaires ou Traité de Stereotomie à l'Usage de l'Architecture (Paris, 1737–1738), 3 vols., vol. 1, dedication. Later editions were published in 1754 and 1768.

88. Ibid., pp. II–IV.

89. Ibid., *Troisième Discours*.

90. C. D'Aviler, *Cours d'Architecture Qui Comprend les Ordres de Vignole* (Paris, 1760).

91. See chapters 2 and 7 in the present work.

Chapter 7

1. Robert Boyle, *A Free Inquiry into the Vulgar Notion of Nature* in *The Philosophical Works* (London, 1738), 3 vols., Shaw ed., vol. 2, p. 133.

2. G. W. Leibniz, "Letter to Jacob Thomasius" (1669), in C. J. Gerhardt, ed., *Die Philosophischen Schriften von G. W. Leibniz* (Berlin, 1890), vol. 1, p. 25.

3. R. Boyle, *The Usefulness of Experimental Philosophy by Way of Exhortation to the Study of It* (1663), in *The Philosophical Works*, vol. 1, p. 123.

4. Galileo Galilei, *Discorsi e Dimostrazioni Matematiche Intorno à Due Nuove Scienze* (Leyden, 1638), dialogues I and II. For the history of statics and strength of materials see S. P. Timoshenko, *History of the Strength of Materials*, and Hans Straub, *A History of Civil Engineering*. Also useful is A. Wolf, *A History of Science, Technology and Philosophy*, vols. 1 and 2.

5. F. Blondel, *Cours*, chapter 4.

6. Carlo Fontana, *Il Tempio Vaticano e Sua Origine* (Rome, 1694).

7. Some of the important names worth mentioning in this regard are Jacob and John Bernoulli, Varignon, and Mariotte (who was instrumental in the introduction of experimental methods in French scientific circles). See Timoshenko, *History of the Strength of Materials*, chapters 1 and 2.

8. In the preface to his *Nouvelle Mecanique ou Statique Dont le Projet Fut Donné en 1687* (Paris, 1725), M. Varignon points out that by using the principle of geometrical resolution of composite forces, he was able to achieve a general understanding of mechanical action. This route facilitated the calculation of forces, their relations being immediately determined by the sine of the angles between their lines of direction. Varignon applied his geo-

metrical method to solve problems of statics through vectors, but his solutions did not allow for a consideration of friction or the internal cohesion of bodies.

9. Philip de la Hire, *Traité de Mécanique ou l'On Explique Tout Ce Qui Est Necessaire dans la Pratique des Arts* (Paris, 1695), p. 2.

10. P. de la Hire, "Sur la Poussée des Voûtes," in *Histoire et Mémoires de l'Académie Royale des Sciences* (Paris, 1712). Volumes are bound by years.

11. P. de la Hire, "Remarques sur la Forme de Quelques Arcs Dont On Se Sert en Architecture," in *Histoire et Mémoires* (Paris, 1702).

12. Pitot, "Sur la Force des Cintres," in *Histoire et Mémoires* (Paris, 1726).

13. H. Gautier, *Traité des Ponts* (Paris, 1727–1728). The first edition appeared in 1714.

14. Ibid., pp. 341ff.

15. Couplet, "Sur les Voûtes," in *Histoire et Mémoires* (Paris, 1730).

16. See *Histoire et Mémoires de l'Académie Royale des Sciences* (1707, 1711).

17. Jean-Rodolphe Perronet, *Description des Projets et de la Construction des Ponts de Neuilly, de Nantes, d'Orleans et Autres* (Paris, 1782), introduction.

18. J. Bertrand, *L'Académie des Sciences et les Académiciens de 1666 à 1793* (Paris, 1869).

19. J. R. Perronet, "Sur la Réduction de l'Épaisseur des Piles, et sur la Courbure Qu'il est Convenient de Donner aux Voûtes, le Tout pour que l'Eau Puisse Passer Plus Librement sous les Ponts," in P. C. Lesage, *Recueil de Divers Mémoires Extraits de la Bibliothèque Impériale des Ponts et Chaussées* (Paris, 1810), pp. 49–50.

20. Ibid.

21. J. R. Perronet, "Sur les Pieux et Pilotis," in P. C. Lesage, *Recueil de Divers Mémoires.*

22. Giovanni Poleni, *Memorie Istoriche della Gran Cupola del Tempio Vaticano* (Padua, 1748).

23. Ibid., columns 30–31.

24. Ibid., column 50 and plates XI–XIV.

25. "Parere di Tre Matematici sopra i Danni che Si Sonno Trovati nella Cupola di S. Pietro sul Fine dell'Anno 1742," in Poleni, *Memorie Istoriche*, columns 233–246.

26. Ibid.

27. Ibid., columns 366–368.

28. Ibid., columns 80–86.

29. Giovanni Bottari, *Dialoghi sopra le Tre Arti del Disegno* (Parma, 1846), pp. 79ff. The first edition appeared in Lucca in 1754.

30. Ermenegildo Pini, *Dell'Architettura, Dialogi* (Milan, 1770), pp. 18–19.

31. Francesco Ricatti, *Dissertazione intorno l'Architettura Civile*, in *Nuova Raccolta di Opuscoli Scientifici e Filologici* (Venice, 1761), vol. 8, pp. 435ff.

32. Nicola Carletti, *Istituzioni d'Architettura Civile* (Naples, 1772), pp. 9ff.

33. Francesco Milizia, *Principi di Architettura Civile* (Bologna, 1827), part I, pp. 260ff.

34. Ibid., pp. 340ff.

35. Ibid.

36. See J. Rykwert, *The First Moderns*, chapter 8, pp. 288ff.

37. Andrea Memmo, *Elementi di Architettura Lodoliana o sia l'Arte di Fabricare con Solidità Scientifica e con Eleganza non Capricciosa* (Zara, 1833), vol. 1, pp. 129–132. The first edition appeared in Rome in 1786.

38. Ibid., pp. 285ff.

39. Francesco Algarotti, *Saggio sull'Architettura*, in *Scrittori di Belle Arti* (Milan, 1881). The *Saggio* represents the first written formulation of Lodoli's principles. For its problems of interpretation, see Rykwert, *The First Moderns*, pp. 296ff.

40. A. Memmo, *Elementi di Architettura Lodoliana*, pp. 285ff.

41. V. Lamberti, *Statica degli Edifici* (Naples, 1781). Here Lamberti uses algebra, structured *more geometrico*, applying statics to all sorts of physical problems. Although his intention was to provide detailed simple instructions, Lamberti ignored the difficulties that

would have arisen in the application of these geometrical solutions to practice. He believed statics was the science of *firmitas* within the framework of a conventional theory of architecture. He depended on biblical archetypes and in the end thought that if the law of equality between action and reaction was not maintained, it would be impossible to achieve "correct proportions". Also worth mentioning is G. Borra, *Trattato della Cognizione Pratica delle Resistenze* (Turin, 1748). Although revealing an understanding of statics, Borra used geometry merely as a descriptive tool.

42. Memmo, *Elementi di Architettura Lodoliana*, p. 314.

43. Ibid., pp. 315–322.

44. This is the common understanding in most conventional books on the history of architecture of that period. See, for example, E. Kaufmann, *Architecture in the Age of Reason*, chapter 8, pp. 89ff.

45. See J. Rykwert, *The First Moderns*, pp. 296ff.

46. Memmo, *Elementi di Architettura Lodoliana*, vol. 2, p. 59.

47. See Giambattista Vico, *The New Science* (Naples, 1744). The first edition appeared in 1725. There is an abridged version of the 1744 edition translated by Thomas Goddard Bergin and Max Harold Fisch (Ithaca, NY, 1970), preceded by an excellent introduction. See also "Giambattista Vico", in Burton Feldman and Robert D. Richardson, *The Rise of Modern Mythology 1680–1860*, pp. 50–55, and Isaiah Berlin, *Vico and Herder*, pp. 1ff.

48. See J. Rykwert, "Inheritance or Tradition", in *Leonis Baptiste Alberti*, Architectural Design Profiles 21 (London), pp. 2–6.

49. Pierre Patte, *Mémoire sur la Construction de la Coupole Projetée de l'Église Sainte-Geneviève* (Paris, 1770). For a very well-documented account of the dispute, see M. Mathieu, *Pierre Patte. Sa Vie et Son Oeuvre*, chapter 4.

50. J. Monval, *Soufflot; Sa Vie, Son Oeuvre, Son Esthétique*, includes an appendix listing all of Soufflot's engineering works. For Patte, see his own *Mémoires sur les Objets les Plus Importans de l'Architecture* (Paris, 1769).

51. J. F. Blondel, *Cours d'Architecture*, volumes 5 and 6.

52. Patte, *Mémoires sur les Objets*, chapter 2. See chapter 2 in the present work.

53. Patte, *Mémoires sur les Objets*, p. 99.

54. Patte, *Monumens Érigés en France à la Gloire de Louis XV* (Paris, 1765), p. 4.

55. Patte, "Considerations sur le Mécanisme", in J. F. Blondel, *Cours*, vol. 6, pp. 1–2.

56. Ibid., p. 3.

57. Ibid., pp. 4–5.

58. Ibid., p. 5.

59. Ibid., pp. 5–6.

60. Patte, *Mémoires sur les Objets*, chapter 7.

61. J. F. Blondel, *Cours*, vol. 6, p. 36.

62. Ibid., p. 59.

63. Ibid., vol. 5, pp. 135–136.

64. "Patte Propose à l'Ex-Ministre de l'Interieur Benezec de Sacrifier le Dôme. Observations sur l'État Alarmant du Panthéon," *Journal de Paris* 245 (May 1797), and P. Patte, *Analyse Raisonnée de l'État Alarmant du Dôme du Panthéon Français* (1799), cited by Mathieu, *Pierre Patte*, pp. 273ff.

65. Emiland-Marie Gauthey, *Mémoire sur l'Application des Principes de la Mécanique à la Construction* (Paris, 1771), pp. 12–13.

66. Letter published in *Mércure de France* (August 1770).

67. E. Gauthey, *Mémoire sur l'Application*, p. 66.

68. Charles-François Viel, *Des Anciennes Études de l'Architecture* (Paris, 1807), p. 19n2.

69. After praising Euler's work as a vast analytical compendium, C. Bossut, for example, stressed its limited utility as a guide for practice. See S. Gillmor, *Coulomb and the Evolution of Physics and Engineering in 18th Century France*.

70. Charles-Auguste Coulomb, *Sur l'Application des Règles de Maximis et Minimis à Quelques Problèmes de Statique Relatifs à l'Architecture* (1773), in *Collection de Mémoires Relatifs à la Physique* (Paris, 1884), vol. 1.

71. Jean-Victor Poncelet, "Examen Critique et Historique Concernant l'Équilibre des Voûtes," in *Comptes Rendus Hebdomadaires des Seances de l'Académie des Sciences* (Paris, 1832), vol. 35, pp. 494–502. The translation is by S. Gillmor, *Coulomb*.

72. P. S. Girard, *Traité Analytique de la Resistance des Solides et des Solides d'Égale Resistance* (Paris, 1798), introduction.

73. Ibid., p. IX.

Chapter 8

1. Comte Laplace, *Essai Philosophique sur les Probabilités* (Paris, 1814), p. 2.

2. Ibid., pp. 3–4.

3. Ibid.

4. Laplace, *Exposition du Système du Monde* (Paris, 1813), p. 443.

5. Laplace, *A Treatise upon Analytical Mechanics, Being the First Book of the 'Mécanique Celeste'* (Nottingham, 1814).

6. See L. Brunschvicg, *Les Étapes de la Philosophie Mathématique*, pp. 243ff.

7. J. L. Lagrange, *Théorie des Fonctions Analytiques* (Paris, 1797).

8. J. L. Lagrange, *Mécanique Analytique* (Paris, 1811), p. I.

9. Lazare Carnot, *Principes Fondamentaux de l'Équilibre et du Mouvement* (Paris, 1803), pp. 3–4.

10. Auguste Comte, *Discours sur l'Esprit Positif* (Paris, 1844), p. XV.

11. I. Kant, *Critique de la Raison Pure* (Paris, 1905), French translation by Tremesaygues and Pacaud, pp. 5–6, 25.

12. A. Comte, *Cours de Philosophie Positive* (Paris, 1864), first lecture.

13. J. B. Delambre, ed., *Rapport Historique sur les Progrès des Sciences Mathématiques depuis 1789 et sur Leur État Actuel* (Paris, 1810).

14. E. Renan, "L'Instruction Supérieure en France," in *Questions Contemporaines* (1868), p. 71.

15. See F. A. Hayek, *The Counter-Revolution of Science*, pp. 105–116.

16. A. Fourcy, *Histoire de l'École Polytechnique* (Paris, 1828).

17. Pinet, *Histoire de l'École Polytechnique* (Paris, 1887), introduction.

18. "Loi Relative à l'Organisation de l'École Polytechnique de 25 Primaire, an 8 de la Republique," in *Journal de l'École Polytechnique*, vol. 4, *onzième cahier*, p. 2.

19. *Journal de l'École Polytechnique*, vol. 1, *premier cahier*, p. 15.

20. Ibid., pp. 16–37.

21. J. N. L. Durand, *Précis des Leçons d'Architecture Données à l'École Royale Polytechnique* (Paris, 1819), p. 5.

22. J. B. Delambre, ed., *Rapport Historique*, pp. 50–51.

23. Ibid.

24. Gaspard Monge, *Géométrie Descriptive* (Paris, 1795), pp. 13–14. See René Taton, *L'Oeuvre Scientifique de Monge*, for an extensive discussion of Monge's work.

25. Ibid., p. 20.

26. Auguste Comte, "Philosophical Considerations on the Sciences and Men of Science," in *Early Essays on Social Philosophy* (London, 1825), p. 272.

27. *Journal de l'École Polytechnique*, vol. 2, introductory remarks.

28. Ibid., vol. 1, pp. 1–14.

29. M. Chasles, *Aperçu Historique sur l'Origine et Développement des Méthodes en Géométrie* (Brussels, 1837), pp. 189ff.

30. Ibid., pp. 189–190.

31. Ibid., pp. 190–191.

32. Ibid., pp. 208, 210.

33. Ibid., p. 199.

34. M. le Général Didion, *Notice sur la Vie et les Ouvrages du Général J. V. Poncelet* (Paris, 1869), and Tribout, *Un Grand Savant . . . Poncelet (1788–1867)* (Paris, 1936). See also J. L. F. Bertrand, *Éloge Historique de Jean-Victor Poncelet* (Paris, 1875).

35. See Ugo Cassina, *Sur l'Histoire des Concepts Fondamentaux de la Géométrie Projective*.

36. Jean-Victor Poncelet, *Traité des Propriétés Projectives des Figures. Ouvrage Utile à Ceux qui s'Occupent des Applications de la Géométrie Descriptive et d'Operations Géométriques sur le Terrain* (Paris, 1822), title page.

37. Ibid., p. XXVIII.

38. Ibid., p. XXXIII.

39. Ibid.

40. Ernst Cassirer provided this clear appreciation in *Substance and Function*, pp. 70, 78. See also William Ivins, *Art and Geometry*.

41. Robert Rosenblum made this point in *Transformations in Late Eighteenth Century Art*. See his comparison of Ingres's drawing *Room at San Gaëtano* (1807) to Matisse's *Red Studio* (1911), pp. 189–191, figures 214, 215.

42. Timoshenko, *History of Strength of Materials*, pp. 57–58.

43. Jean Rondelet, "Mémoire sur l'Architecture Considérée Généralement, avec des Observations sur l'Administration Relative à cet Art, et le Projet d'une École Pratique qui Serait Chargée de Tous les Ouvrages Publics," in Jean Rondolet, *Traité Théorique et Pratique de l'Art de Bâtir*, (Paris, 1830), vol. 3, pp. VIff. According to the editor, this "Mémoire" was printed in 1789.

44. J. Rondelet, *Traité*, introduction, p. IV.

45. Ibid., p. VI.

46. Ibid., p. XXII.

47. Ibid., p. XXVI.

48. Ibid.

49. Ibid., chapter 10, p. 273.

50. Ibid., p. 275.

51. "Rédigée par l'Auteur sur l'Invitation de M. le Comte Daru, Intendant des Bâtimens de la Couronne, 'pour servir de règlement sur la forme des devis que doivent dresser les architectes de l'empereur, et les soumissions des entrepreneurs qui voudront être chargés de quelque partie d'ouvrage' (. . . 6 septembre 1805). . . ," in *Traité*, p. 280.

52. Rondelet, *Traité*, chapter 9, p. 1.

53. Ibid.

54. "Éloge Historique," probably by Navier, in E. Gauthey, *Traité de la Construction des Ponts* (Paris, 1809), vol. 1.

55. Emiland-Marie Gauthey, *Dissertation sur les Degradations Survenues aux Piliers du Dôme du Panthéon François et sur les Moyens d'y Remedier* (Paris, an VI).

56. E. Gauthey, *Traité de la Construction des Ponts*, introduction.

57. Ibid., pp. 1–2.

58. Ibid., p. 3.

59. Ibid., pp. 174–175.

60. L. C. Boistard, "Expériences sur la Stabilité des Voûtes," in P. C. Lesage, *Recueil de Divers Mémoires des Ponts et Chaussées* (Paris, 1810), vol. 2, pp. 171ff.

61. K. Mayniel, *Traité Expérimental, Analytique et Pratique de la Poussée des Terres et des Murs de Revêtement* (Paris, 1808), p. XV.

62. Riche de Prony, "Mécanique Philosophique ou Analyse Raisonnée des Divers Parties de la Science de l'Équilibre et du Mouvement," *Journal de l'École Polytechnique*, vol. 3 (Paris, an 8), and "Discours d'Introduction aux Cours d'Analyse Pure et d'Analyse Apliquée à la Mécanique," *Journal de l'École Polytechnique*, vol. 2 (Paris, an 7).

63. L. M. H. Navier, *Résumé des Leçons Données à l'École des Ponts et Chaussées sur l'Application de la Mécanique à l'Établissement des Constructions et des Machines* (Paris, 1826), introduction.

Chapter 9	1. J. N. L. Durand, *Précis des Leçons d'Architecture Données à l'École Royale Polytechnique* (Paris, 1819), 2 vols., vol. 1, p. 3.

2. Ibid., p. 6.

3. Ibid.

4. Ibid., pp. 6–7.

5. Ibid., p. 8.

6. Ibid., p. 16.

7. Ibid., pp. 69–70.

8. Ibid., pp. 18–19.

9. Ibid.

10. Ibid., p. 21.

11. Ibid., p. 30.

12. See Vitruvius, *De Architectura* (Como, Italy, 1521), edited and illustrated by Cesare di Lorenzo Cesariano, pp. XLIX, L, and Philibert de l'Orme, *Le Premier Tome de l'Architecture* (Paris, 1567), foll. 228, 235. For De l'Orme's theory, see A. Blunt, *Philibert de l'Orme*, pp. 108ff.

13. See, for example, Bruno Zevi, *Architecture as Space*, the English translation of *Saper Vedere l'Architettura* (Turin, 1948).

14. Durand, *Précis*, pp. 32–33.

15. Ibid., p. 34.

16. L. A. Dubut, *Architecture Civile, Maisons de Ville et de Campagne* (Paris, an IX).

17. L. Lebrun, *Théorie de l'Architecture Grecque et Romaine Déduite de l'Analyse des Monuments Antiques* (Paris, 1807), introduction.

18. J. N. L. Durand, *Recueil et Parallèle des Edifices de Tout Genre, Anciens et Modernes* (Paris, 1801), introduction.

19. J. B. Fischer von Erlach, *Entwurff Einer Historischen Architectur* (Leipzig, 1725), preface.

20. This confusion was finally cleared up in Jean-Marie Pérouse de Montclos, "Charles-François Viel, Architecte de l'Hôpital Général et Jean-Louis Viel de Saint-Maux, Architecte, Peintre et Avocat au Parlement de Paris," *Bulletin de la Societé de l'Histoire de l'Art Français* (1966):257–269.

21. Charles-François Viel, *Principes de l'Ordonnance et de la Construction des Bâtimens* (Paris, 1812), vol. 4, pp. 53–97. Under this title, Viel had planned to publish his entire theoretical work. In fact, volumes 2 and 3 were never published, and the intended chapters appeared separately.

22. Viel, *Principes*, vol. 1, p. 13.

23. Ibid., pp. 18–28.

24. Ibid., pp. 46–49.

25. Ibid., pp. 51–52.

26. Ibid., p. 198.

27. Ibid., p. 199.

28. Ibid., p. 200.

29. Viel, *De l'Impuissance des Mathématiques pour Assurer la Solidité des Bâtimens* (Paris, 1805), p. 5.

30. Ibid., pp. 11–25.

31. Viel, *Dissertations sur les Projets de Coupoles* (Paris, 1809), p. 35.

32. Viel, *De l'Impuissance*, p. 74.

33. Viel, *De la Solidité des Bâtimens, Puisée dans les Proportions des Ordres d'Architecture* (Paris, 1806), p. 12.

34. Viel, *Dissertations*, pp. 19–20.

35. Ibid., p. 47.

36. Viel, *De la Solidité*, pp. 49–50.

37. Ibid., p. 50.

38. Viel, *Dissertations*, p. 48.

39. Viel, *Inconvéniens de la Communication des Plans d'Édifices avant Leur Exécution* (Paris, 1813), pp. 7–8.

40. Ibid., p. 25.

41. Viel, *Dissertations*, p. 47.

42. Viel, *De l'Impuissance*, p. 70.

43. Viel, *Des Anciennes Études d'Architecture, de la Nécessité de les Remettre en Vigueur* (Paris, 1807), p. 1.

44. Ibid., p. 5.

45. Ibid., p. 6.

46. Ibid., p. 2.

47. Ibid., p. 3.

48. Viel, *Dissertations*, p. 23.

49. Viel, *Principes*, vol. 1, pp. 96ff.

BIBLIOGRAPHY

Accolti, P. *Lo Inganno degli Occhi*, Florence, 1625.

Adam, Antoine. *Grandeur and Illusion*, London, 1974.

Agrippa, Cornelius. *De Occulta Philosophia*, Antwerp, 1531.

Alberti, G. A. *Trattato della Misura delle Fabriche*, Florence, 1822.

Alberti, Leone Battista. *Ten Books on Architecture*, ed. J. Rykwert, London, 1955.

Alembert, Jean D'. *Discours Préliminaire de l'Encyclopédie*, ed. Gonthier, Paris, 1966.

Alembert, Jean D'. *Oeuvres*, 5 vols., Paris, 1821–1822.

Alexander, Christopher. *Notes on the Synthesis of Form*, Harvard, 1964.

Alexander, Christopher. "A Much Asked Question about Computers and Design." *Architecture and Computer*, Boston, 1964.

Algarotti, Francesco. *Saggio sull'Architettura*, Milan, 1881.

Algarotti, Francesco. *Il Newtonismo per le Dame, ovvero, Dialoghi sopra la Luce e i Colori*, Naples, 1737.

Allbut, T. C. *Palissy, Bacon and the Revival of Natural Science*, 1914.

André, P. *Essai sur le Beau*, Paris, 1741.

Androuet du Cerceau, Jacques, the elder. *Les Trois Livres d'Architecture*, Paris, 1559, 1561, 1582.

Androuet du Cerceau, Jacques, the elder. *Leçons de Perspective Positive*, Paris, 1576.

Argan, Giulio Carlo. *L'Architettura Barocca in Italia*, Milan, 1957.

Arts Council. *The Age of Neo-Classicism*, catalogue of the 14th exhibition of the Council of Europe, London, 1972.

Augoyat, A. M. *Aperçu Historique sur les Fortifications*, 3 vols., Paris, 1860–1864.

Aurenhammer, Hans. *J. B. Fischer von Erlach*, London, 1973.

Aviler, C. D'. *Cours d'Architecture*, Paris, 1696.

Bacon, Francis. *Novum Organum*, Leyden, 1620.

Bacon, Francis. *Works*, ed. J. Spedding and R. L. Ellis, London, 1859–1870.

Bacon, Francis. *The Wisdom of the Ancients and New Atlantis*, London, 1905.

Baltrušaitis, Jurgis. *Anamorphoses ou Perspectives Curieuses*, Paris, 1955.

Baltrušaitis, Jurgis. *Anamorphic Art*, New York, 1976.

Barca, P. A. *Avertimenti e Regole circa l'Architettura*, Milan, 1620.

Barozzi, Giaccomo, called Il Vignola. *Le Due Regole de la Prospettiva Prattica*, Venice, 1743.

Barozzi, Giaccomo, called Il Vignola. *Regola delle Cinque Ordine d'Architettura*, Venice, 1596.

Batteux, C. *Les Beaux Arts Réduits à un Même Principe*, 2 vols., Paris, 1746.

Baudin. *Funerailles du Citoyen Boullée*, Paris, 1799.

Becker, Carl. *The Heavenly City of the Eighteenth-Century Philosophers*, London, 1973.

Belaval, Y. "La Crise de la Géométrisation de l'Univers dans la Philosophie des Lumières." *Revue Internationale de Philosophie*, Brussels, 1952.

Bélidor, Bernard, Forest de. *La Science des Ingénieurs*, Paris, 1739 and 1830.

Bélidor, Bernard, Forest de. *Nouveau Cours de Mathématique*, Paris, 1725.

Belli, S. *Libro del Misurar con la Vista*, Venice, 1565.

Berlin, Isaiah. *Vico and Herder*, London, 1976.

Bertrand, J. L. F. *Les Fondateurs de l'Astronomie Moderne*, Paris, 1865.

Bertrand, J. L. F. *L'Académie des Sciences 1666–1793*, Paris, 1869.

Bertrand, J. L. F. *Éloge Historique de Poncelet*, Paris, 1875.

Birch, Thomas. *The History of the Royal Society of London*, London, 1968.

Blomdfield, R. *Sebastien Le Prestre de Vauban*, London, 1938.

Blondel, François. *Cours d'Architecture, Ensigné dans l'Académie*, Paris, 1698.

Blondel, François. "Résolution des Quatre Principaux Problèmes de l'Architecture." *Recueil de Plusieurs Traitez de Mathématiques de l'Académie Royale des Sciences*, Paris, 1676.

Blondel, François. *Nouvelle Manière de Fortifier les Places*, The Hague, 1684.

Blondel, Jacques-François. *De la Distribution des Maisons de Plaisance*, Paris, 1737.

Blondel, Jacques-François. *L'Architecture Françoise*, Paris, 1752.

Blondel, Jacques-François. *Discours sur la Nécessité de l'Étude de l'Architecture*, Paris, 1752.

Blondel, Jacques-François. *Cours d'Architecture*, ed. by Pierre Patte, 9 vols., Paris, 1771–1779.

Blondel, Jacques-François. *L'Homme du Monde Éclairé par les Arts*, Paris, 1774.

Blunt, Anthony. *Philibert de L'Orme*, London, 1973.

Blunt, Anthony. *Art and Architecture in France 1500–1700*, Hamondsworth, 1953.

Boas, M. "La Méthode Scientifique de Robert Boyle." *Revue d'Histoire des Sciences*, 1956.

Boas. M. *Robert Boyle and Seventeenth-Century Physics*, Cambridge, 1958.

Boffrand, Germain. *Livre d'Architecture*, Paris, 1745.

Borissavlievitch, M. *Les Théories de l'Architecture*, Paris, 1951.

Borissavlievitch, M. *The Golden Number*, London, 1970.

Borra, G. *Trattato della Cognizione Pratica delle Resistenze*, Turin, 1748.

Borromini, Francesco. *Opera*, Rome, 1720.

Bosse, Abraham. *Manière Universelle de M. Desargues pour Pratiquer la Perspective*, Paris, 1648.

Bosse, Abraham. *La Pratique du Trait à Preuves, de M. Desargues Lyonnois pour le Coupe de Pierres en l'Architecture*, Paris, 1643.

Bosse, Abraham. *Moyen Universelle de Pratiquer la Perspective sur les Tableaux ou Surfaces Irregulières*, Paris, 1653.

Bosse, Abraham. *Traité des Pratiques Géométrales et Perspectives*, Paris, 1665.

Bosse, Abraham. *Traité de Manières de Designer les Ordres d'Architecture Antique*, Paris, 1665.

Bosse, Abraham. *Le Peintre Converty aux Précises et Universelles Règles de Son Art*, Paris, 1667.

Bossut, C. *Traité Élémentaire de Géométrie*, Paris, 1777.

Bossut, C. *Nouvelles Expériences sur la Resistance des Fluides*, Paris, 1777.

Bossut, C. *Cours de Mathématiques*, 2 vols., Paris, 1782.

Bottari, G. *Dialoghi sopra le Tre Arti del Disegno*, Parma, 1846.

Boullée, Etienne-Louis. *Essai sur l'Art*, ed. J. M. Perouse de Mont-clos, Paris, 1968.

Boyceau, J. *Traité du Jardinage*, Paris, 1638.

Boyle, Robert. *The Philosophical Works*, 3 vols., London, 1738.

Braham, Allan. *The Architecture of the French Enlightenment*, London, 1980.

Briggs, Martin. *The Architect in History*, Oxford, 1927.

Briseux, Charles-Etienne. *Traité du Beau Essentiel*, 2 vols., Paris, 1752.

Briseux, Charles-Etienne. *Architecture Moderne*, 2 vols., Paris, 1728.

Brognis, J. A. *Traité Élémentaire de la Construction*, Paris, 1823.

Brunschvicg, Leon. *Les Étapes de la Philosophie Mathématique*, Paris, 1972.

Buffon, G. L. L. *Essai d'Arithmétique Morale*, Paris, 1777.

Buffon, G. L. L. *Oeuvres Philosophiques*, Paris, 1954.

Bullet, Pierre. *L'Architecture Pratique*, Paris, 1691.

Burtt, Edwin. *The Metaphysical Foundations of Modern Physical Science*, London, 1972.

Busca, G. *L'Architettura Militare*, Milan, 1619.

Bÿggé, T. *Travels in the French Republic*, London, 1801.

Campbell Lee, D. *Desaguillers of No. 4*, London, 1932.

Camus, C. E. L. *Cours de Mathématique*, 2 vols., Paris, 1749–1752.

Carboneri, Nino. *Andrea Pozzo Architetto*, 1961.

Carletti, Nicola. *Istituzioni d'Architettura Civile*, 2 vols., Naples, 1772.

Carnot, Lazare. *Principes Fondamentaux de l'Équilibre et du Mouvement*, Paris, 1803.

Casati, P. *Fabrica et Uso del Compasso di Proportione*, Bologna, 1664.

Cassina, Ugo. *Sur l'Histoire des Concepts Fondamentaux de la Géométrie Projective*, Paris, 1957.

Cassina, Ugo. *Dalla Geometria Egiziana alla Matematica Moderna*, 1961.

Cassirer, Ernst. *Substance and Function*, Chicago, 1923.

Cassirer, Ernst. *The Philosophy of the Enlightenment*, Princeton, 1951.

Cassirer, Ernst. *The Philosophy of Symbolic Thought*, vol. 2, New Haven, 1955.

Castel, L. B. *L'Optique des Couleurs*, Paris, 1740.

Cataneo, Girolamo. *Dell'Arte Militare Libri Cinque*, Brescia, 1584.

Cataneo, Girolamo. *Le Capitaine*, Lyons, 1574.

Cataneo, Girolamo. *Dell'Arte del Misurare Libri Due*, Brescia, 1584.

Cataneo, Pietro. *I Quattro Primi Libri di Architettura*, Venice, 1554.

Caus, Salomon de. *Les Raisons des Forces Mouvantes*, Frankfurt, 1615.

Caus, Salomon de. *La Perspective avec la Raison des Ombres et Miroirs*, London, 1612.

Caus, Salomon de. *Hortus Palatinus*, Heidelberg, 1620.

Cavallari-Murat, Augusto. *Giovanni Poleni nel Bicentenario della Morte*, Padua, 1963.

Chambers, William. *A Treatise on Civil Architecture*, London, 1759.

Chambers, William. *A Dissertation on Oriental Gardening*, London, 1772.

Chasles, M. *Aperçu Historique sur l'Origine et Développement des Méthodes en Géométrie*, Brussels, 1837.

Chevallier, Pierre. *Les Ducs sous l'Acacia*, Paris, 1964.

Christ, Yvan. *C. N. Ledoux, Projects et Divagations*, Paris, 1971.

Cochin, Charles-Nicolas. *Voyage d'Italie*, Lausanne, 1773.

Collins, Peter. *Changing Ideals in Modern Architecture 1750–1950*, London, 1965.

Comito, Terry. *The Idea of the Garden in the Renaissance*, Hassocks, 1979.

Comolli, Angelo. *Bibliografia Storico-Critica dell'Architettura*, 2 vols., Rome, 1788.

Comte, Auguste. *Discours sur l'Esprit Positif*, Paris, 1844.

Comte, Auguste. *Cours de Philosophie Positive*, 6 vols., Paris, 1864.

Coppleston, Frederick. *A History of Philosophy*, vol. 4, Garden City, NY, 1963.

Cordemoy, Abbé J. L. de. *Nouveau Traité de Toute l'Architecture*, Paris, 1714.

Coulomb, Charles-Auguste. "Memoirs." *Collection de Mémoires Relatifs à la Physique, Publiés par la Societé Française de Physique*, vol. 1, Paris, 1884.

Courtonne, J. *Traité de la Perspective Pratique*, Paris, 1725.

Cristiani, G. F. *Delle Misure d'Ogni Genere*, Brescia, 1760.

Cristiani, G. F. *Dell'Utilita e della Dilettazione de'Modelli ad Uso dell'Architettura Militare*, Brescia, 1765.

Cristiani, G. F. *Della Media Armonica Proporzionale*, Brescia, 1767.

Cuvier, G. L. "De la Part à Faire aux Sciences et aux Lettres dans l'Instruction Publique." *Revue Internationale de l'Enseignement*, vol. 10, 1885.

Delambre, J. B., ed. *Rapport Historique sur les Progrès des Sciences Mathématiques*, Paris, 1810.

De L'Orme, Philibert. *Le Premier Tome de L'Architecture*, Paris, 1567.

Derand, François. *L'Architecture des Voûtes*, Paris, 1643.

Désaguilliers, John Theophilus. *A System of Experimental Philosophy*, London, 1719.

Désaguilliers, John Theophilus. *Physico-Mechanical Lectures*, London, 1717.

Désaguilliers, John Theophilus. *The Newtonian System of the World, the Best Model of Government*, London, 1728.

Desargues, Girard. *Oeuvres*, Paris, 1864.

Descartes, René. *Oeuvres*, 11 vols., ed. Adam and Tannery, reprint Paris, 1974.

Desgodetz, Antoine. *Les Édifices Antiques de Rome*, Paris, 1683.

Dézallier d'Argenville, A. J. *The Theory and Practice of Gardening*, London, 1712.

Diderot, Denis. *Oeuvres Philosophiques*, Paris, 1961.

Diderot, Denis. *Oeuvres Esthétiques*, Paris, 1968.

Diderot, Denis, and Alembert, Jean D'. *Encyclopédie ou Dictionnaire Raisonnée des Sciences, des Arts, et des Metiers*, 17 vols., Paris, 1751–1765.

Didion. *Notice sur la Vie du Général Poncelet*, Paris, 1869.

Dietterlin, W. *Architektura*, Nuremberg, 1593–1598.

Dijksterhuis, J. *The Mechanization of the World-Picture*, Amsterdam, 1961.

Dögen, M. *L'Architecture Militaire Moderne*, Amsterdam, 1648.

Drexler, A. *The Architecture of the École des Beaux-Arts*, New York, 1977.

Dubos, Abbé Jean-Baptiste, *Réflexions Critiques sur la Poésie et sur la Peinture*, Paris, 1715.

Dubut, L. A. *Architecture Civile*, Paris, An IX.

Dubreuil, J. *La Perspective Pratique*, Paris, 1651.

Dufrenne, Mikel. *The Notion of the A Priori*, Evanston, 1966.

Dufrenne, Mikel. *Le Poétique*, Paris, 1973.

Dupain de Montesson. *Les Connoissances Géométriques à l'Usage des Officiers*, Paris, 1774.

Dupain de Montesson. *La Science des Ombres*, Paris, 1750.

Durand, Jacques-Nicolas-Louis. *Précis des Leçons d'Architecture*, 2 vols., Paris, 1819.

Durand, Jacques-Nicolas-Louis. *Recueil et Parallèle des Edifices de Tout Genre, Anciens et Modernes*, Paris, 1801.

Dürer, Albrecht. *Hierinn sind begriffen vier Bücher von menschlicher Proportion*, Nuremberg, 1528.

Dürer, Albrecht. *Under weysung du Messung mit dem Zirckel und Richtscheyt, in Linien ebenen gantzen Corporen*, Nuremberg, 1525.

Edgerton, Samuel. *The Renaissance Rediscovery of Linear Perspective*, New York, 1974.

Ellul, Jacques. *The Technological Society*, New York, 1964.

Errard, J. *La Fortification Demonstrée et Reduite en Art*, Paris, 1619.

Euler, Leonard. *Lettres à une Princese d'Allemagne*, Saint Petersburg, 1770.

Encyclopedia of World Art, 15 vols., London, 1963.

Fallois, J. de. *L'École de la Fortification*, Dresden, 1768.

Feldman, Burton, and Robert Richardson. *The Rise of Modern Mythology 1680–1860*, Bloomington, Indiana, 1975.

Felibien, André. *Des Principes de L'Architecture*, Paris, 1699.

Fermat, P. de. *Oeuvres*, 5 vols., Paris, 1891–1922.

Fischer von Erlach, J. B. *Entwurff Einer Historischen Architectur*, Vienna, 1721.

Fischer von Erlach, J. B. *A Plan of Civil and Historical Architecture*, London, 1737.

Fontana, Carlo. *Il Tempio Vaticano e Sua Origine*, Rome, 1694.

Fontenelle, Bernard le Bovier de. *Entretiens sur la Pluralité des Mondes; Disgression sur les Anciens et les Modernes*, Oxford, 1955.

Fontenelle, Bernard le Bovier de. "Éléments de la Géométrie de l'Infini." *Suite des Mémoires de l'Académie Royale des Sciences*, Paris, 1727.

Fontenelle, Bernard le Bovier de. *Éloge des Academiciens de l'Académie Royale des Sciences*, Paris, 1731.

Fontenelle, Bernard le Bovier de. *Oeuvres*, 5 vols., Paris, 1825.

Fourcy, A. *Histoire de l'École Polytechnique*, Paris, 1828.

Frankl, Paul, and Erwin Panofsky. "The Secret of the Medieval Masons." *Art Bulletin*, XXVII (1945).

Fraser, D., et al., eds. *Essays in the History of Architecture presented to Rudolf Wittkower*, London, 1967.

Freart de Chambray, R. *Parallèle de l'Architecture Antique et de la Moderne*, Paris, 1650.

Frémin, Michel de. *Mémoires Critiques d'Architecture*, Paris, 1702.

Frézier, Amédée-François. *La Théorie et la Pratique de la Coupe des Pierres et des Bois*, 3 vols., Strasburg and Paris, 1737–1738.

Friedrich, Carl. *The Age of the Baroque*, New York, 1962.

Fuss, P. H. *Correspondance Mathématique et Physique*, 2 vols., Paris, 1843.

Gadamer, Hans-Georg. *Truth and Method*, London, 1975.

Gadamer, Hans-Georg. *Philosophical Hermeneutics*, Berkeley, 1976.

Galilei, Galileo. *Discorsi et Dimostrazioni Matematiche Intorno à Due Nuove Scienze*, Leyden, 1638.

Galilei, Galileo. *Dialogues Concerning Two New Sciences*, New York, 1954.

Gallet, Michel. "Un Ensemble Décoratif de Ledoux: Les Lambris du Café Militaire." *Bulletin Carnavalet*, 26 (1972).

Gallet, Michel. *Paris Domestic Architecture of the Eighteenth Century*, London, 1972.

Gallet, Michel. *Ledoux et Paris*, Paris, 1979.

Galli-Bibiena, Giuseppe. *Architetture e Prospettive*, Vienna, 1740.

Galli-Bibiena, Ferdinando. *Architettura Civile*, Parma, 1711.

Gassendi, Pierre. *Exercitationes Paradoxicae adversus Aristoteleos*, Amsterdam, 1649.

Gauthey, Emiland-Marie. *Mémoire sur l'Application des Principes de la Mécanique à la Construction*, Paris, 1771.

Gauthey, Emiland-Marie. *Dissertation sur les Degradations Survenues aux Piliers du Dôme du Panthéon François*, Paris, An VI.

Gauthey, Emiland-Marie. *Traité de la Construction des Ponts*, 3 vols., Paris, 1809.

Gauthey, Emiland-Marie. *Papers on Bridges*, London, 1843.

Gautier, H. *Traité des Ponts*, Paris, 1727–1728.

Gay, Peter. *The Enlightenment. An Interpretation*, 2 vols., London, 1973.

Gillmor, S. C. *Coulomb and the Evolution of Physics*, Princeton, NJ, 1971.

Giorgio, Francesco. *De Harmonia Mundi Totius*, Venice, 1525.

Girard P. S. *Traité Analytique de la Resistance des Solides*, Paris, 1798.

Godwin, Joscelyn. *Athanasius Kircher*, London, 1979.

Goldman, N. *La Nouvelle Fortification*, Leyden, 1645.

Guarini, Guarino. *La Pietà Trionfante*, Messina, 1660.

Guarini, Guarino. *Placita Philosophica*, Paris, 1665.

Guarini, Guarino. *Euclides Adauctus et Methodicus*, Turin, 1671.

Guarini, Guarino. *Modo di Misurare le Fabbriche*, Turin, 1674.

Guarini, Guarino. *Coelestis Mathematicae*, Milan, 1683.

Guarini, Guarino. *Architettura Civile*, Turin, 1737 and Milan, 1968.

Guarini, Guarino. *Tratatto di Fortificazione*, Turin, 1676.

Guernieri, J. F. *Disegno del Monte Situato Presso di Cassell*, Rome, 1706.

Guerrino, T. *Opera di Geometria, Stereometria, Geodesia*, Milan, 1773.

Guerry, L. *Jean-Pelerin Viator*, Paris, 1962.

Guillaumot, C. A. *Observations sur le Tort que Font à l'Architecture les Déclamations Hasardées et Exagerées*, Paris, 1800.

Guillaumot, C. A. *Essai sur les Moyens de Déterminer Ce qui Constitue la Beauté Essentielle en Architecture*, Paris, 1802.

Guillon, E. *Lecreulx, un Ingenieur Orleanais 1728-1812*, Paris, 1905.

Gusdorf, George. *Les Sciences Humaines et la Pensée Occidentale*, 8 vols., Paris, 1966–.

Gusdorf, George. *Mythe et Metaphysique*, Paris, 1953.

Habermas, Jürgen. *Toward a Rational Society*, London, 1971.

Hahn, Roger. *Laplace as a Newtonian Scientist*, 1967.

Hahn, Roger. *The Anatomy of a Scientific Institution: the Paris Academy of Sciences 1666-1803*, Berkeley, 1971.

Hale J. R. *Renaissance Fortification; Art or Engineering?* Norwich, 1977.

Halfpenny, William. *The Art of Sound Building*, London, 1725.

Halfpenny, William. *A New and Compleat System of Architecture*, London, 1749.

Halfpenny, William. *The Modern Builder's Assistant*, London, 1757.

Hallays, A. *Les Perrault*, Paris, 1920.

Hampson, Norman. *The Enlightenment*, Harmondsworth, 1961.

Harvey, John. *The Mediaeval Architect*, London, 1972.

Hautecoeur, Louis. *Histoire de l'Architecture Classique en France*, vols. 3-5, Paris, 1950-1953.

Hautecoeur, Louis. *Les Jardins des Dieux et des Hommes*, Paris, 1959.

Hayek, F. A. *The Counter-Revolution of Science*, London, 1955.

Hazard, Paul. *The European Mind 1680-1715*, Harmondsworth, 1973.

Hazard, Paul. *European Thought in the Eighteenth Century*, Harmondsworth, 1954.

Herrmann, Wolfgang. *The Theory of Claude Perrault*, London, 1973.

Herrmann, Wolfgang. *Laugier and Eighteenth-Century French Theory*, London, 1962.

Herrmann, Wolfgang. "The Author of the 'Architecture Moderne' of 1728." *Journal of the Society of Architectural Historians*, 18 (1959).

Honour, Hugh. *Neo-Classicism*, Harmondsworth, 1968.

Husserl, Edmund. *The Crisis of European Sciences and Transcendental Phenomenology*, Evanston, 1960.

Husserl, Edmund. *Phenomenology and the Crisis of Philosophy*, New York, 1965.

Husserl, Edmund. *L'Origine de la Géométrie*, Paris, 1974.

Ivins, William. *Art and Geometry*, Cambridge, 1946.

Ivins, William. *On the Rationalization of Sight*, New York, 1938.

Jammer, Max. *Concepts of Space*, Cambridge, 1970.

Jeurat, E. S. *Traité de Perspective*, Paris, 1750.

Jousse, Mathurin. *Le Secret d'Architecture*, La Flèche, 1642.

Jousse, Mathurin. *L'Art de la Charpenterie*, Paris, 1751.

Kant, Immanuel. *Werke*, Berlin, 1912–1922.

Kaufmann, Emil. *Architecture in the Age of Reason*, New York, 1955.

Kaufmann, Emil. *Von Ledoux vis Le Corbusier*, Vienna, 1933.

Kaufmann, Emil. "Three Revolutionary Architects: Boullée, Ledoux and Lequeu." *Transactions of the American Philosophical Society*, 42, part 3 (1952).

Kirby, J. *The Perspective of Architecture*, 2 vols., London, 1761.

Kockelmans, Joseph. *Phenomenology*, New York, 1967.

Koyré, Alexandre. *Metaphysics and Measurement*, London, 1968.

Koyré, Alexandre. *From the Closed World to the Infinite Universe*, London, 1970.

Koyré, Alexandre. *Newtonian Studies*, Chicago, 1968.

Lagrange, J. L. *Mécanique Analytique*, 2 vols., Paris, 1811.

La Hire, P. de. *Traité de Mécanique*, Paris, 1695.

La Hire, P. de. *Divers Ouvrages de Mathématique et Physique*, Paris, 1693.

Lamberti, V. *Statica degli Edifici*, Naples, 1781.

Langenskïold, Eric. *Pierre Bullet the Royal Architect*, Stockholm, 1959.

Langley, Batty. *Practical Geometry Applied to the Useful Arts of Building*, London, 1726.

Langley, Batty. *Gothic Architecture Improved*, London, 1747.

Langley, Batty. *A Sure Guide to Builders*, London, 1729.

Langley, Batty. *The Builder's Compleat Assistant*, 2 vols., London, 1738.

Langley, Batty. *Ancient Masonry Both in Theory and in Practice*, London, 1728.

Langley, Batty. *New Principles of Gardening*, London, 1728.

Laplace, P. S. de. *Essai Philosophique sur les Probabilités*, Paris, 1814.

Laplace, P. S. de. *Exposition du Système du Monde*, Paris, 1813.

Laplace, P. S. de. *A Treatise upon Analytical Mechanics*, Nottingham, 1814.

Laplace, P. S. de. *Oeuvres Completes*, Paris, 1878.

Laprade, A. *François d'Orbay*, Paris, 1960.

Laugier, Abbé Marc-Antoine. *Essai sur l'Architecture*, Paris, 1755.

Laugier, Abbé Marc-Antoine. *Observations sur l'Architecture*, The Hague, 1770.

Le Blond, G. *L'Arithmétique et la Géométrie de l'Officier*, 3 vols., Paris, 1748.

Le Blond, G. *Éléments de Fortification*, Paris, 1775.

Lebrun, L. *Théorie de l'Architecture Grecque et Romaine*, Paris, 1807.

Le Camus de Mezières, N. *Le Génie de l'Architecture*, Paris, 1780.

Le Camus de Mezières, N. *Traité de la Force de Bois*, Paris, 1782.

Le Camus de Mezières, N. *La Guide de Ceux qui Veulent Bâtir*, Paris, 1781.

Le Clerc, S. *Géométrie Pratique*, Paris, 1669.

Le Clerc, S. *Nouveau Système du Monde*, Paris, 1719.

Le Clerc, S. *Système de la Vision Fondé sur des Nouveaux Principes*, Paris, 1719.

Le Clerc, S. *Traité d'Architecture*, Paris, 1714.

Ledoux, Claude-Nicolas. *L'Architecture Considérée sous le Rapport de l'Art, des Moeurs et de la Législation*, 2 vols., Paris, 1806 and 1846.

Leibniz, Gottfried Wilhelm. *Philosophical Papers and Letters*, ed. and transl. L. E. Loemker, 2 vols., Chicago, 1956.

Lemagny, J. C. *Visionary Architects*, Houston, 1968.

Lemonnier, Henri. *Procès-Verbaux de l'Académie Royale d'Architecture*, 10 vols., Paris, 1911–1929.

Lenoble, Robert. *Mersenne ou la Naissance du Mécanisme*, Vrin, 1943.

Lesage, P. C. *Recueil de Divers Mémoires Extraits de la Bibliothèque Impériale des Ponts et Chaussées*, Paris, 1810.

Libeskind, Daniel. *Between Zero and Infinity*, New York, 1981.

Lorini, B. *Delle Fortificazioni*, Venice, 1597.

Lorrain, H. *La Pyrotechnie*, Paris, 1630.

Mahon, D. *Studies in Seicento Art and Theory*, London, 1947.

Malebranche, Nicolas. *Oeuvres Complètes*, 11 vols., Paris, 1712.

Manuel, Frank. *A Portrait of Isaac Newton*, Cambridge, 1968.

Marolois, S. *Fortification ou Architecture Militaire*, Leyden, 1628.

Marolios, S. *Fortification ou Architecture Militaire*, Leyden, 1628.

Marolois, S. *The Art of Fortification*, London, 1638.

Mathieu, M. *Pierre Patte. Sa Vie et Son Oeuvre*, Paris, 1934.

Mayniel, K. *Traité Expérimental, Analytique et Pratique de la Poussée des Terres*, Paris, 1808.

Memmo, Andrea. *Elementi di Architettura Lodoliana*, Zara, 1833.

Merleau-Ponty, Maurice. *Phenomenology of Perception*, London, 1970.

Merleau-Ponty, Maurice. *The Primacy of Perception*, Evanston, 1971.

Mersenne, Marin. *Harmonie Universelle*, Paris, 1636–1637.

Middleton, Robin. "The Abbé de Cordemoy and the Graeco-Gothic Ideal." *Journal of the Warburg and Courtauld Institutes*, 25 (1962) and 26 (1963).

Middleton, Robin. *The Beaux-Arts*, Cambridge, MA, 1982.

Middleton, Robin, and D. Watkin. *Architettura Moderna*, Milan, 1977.

Milizia, Francesco. *Principi di Architettura Civile*, Bologna, 1827.

Milizia, Francesco. *Memorie degli Architetti Antichi e Moderni*, Parma, 1781.

Milliet Dechales, C. F. *Cursus seu Mundus Mathematicus*, 3 vols., Lyon, 1674.

Milliet Dechales, C. F. *L'Art de Fortifier*, Paris, 1677.

Milliet Dechales, C. F. *Huict Livres des Éléments d'Euclide*, Paris, 1672.

Milliet Dechales, C. F. *The Elements of Euclid*, London, 1685.

M. N. *L'Ingénieur François*, Paris, 1775.

Mollet, C. *Theatre des Plans et Jardinages*, Paris, 1652.

Mollet, C. *Le Jardin de Plaisirs*, Paris, 1657.

Monge, Gaspard. *Géométrie Descriptive*, Paris, 1795.

Monte, Guidubaldo del. *Perspectivae Libri Sex*, Pesaro, 1600.

Monval, Jean. *Soufflot: Sa Vie, Son Oeuvre, Son Esthétique*, Paris, 1918.

Morris, Robert. *Lectures on Architecture*, London, 1734.

Morris, Robert. *An Essay in Defence of Ancient Architecture*, London, 1728.

Morris, Robert. *An Essay upon Harmony*, London, 1739.

Nagel, Ernest, and James Newman. *Gödel's Proof*, London, 1959.

Navier, Louis-Marie-Henri. *Résumé des Leçons*, Paris, 1826.

Newton, Isaac. *Principes Mathématiques de la Philosophie Naturelle*, 2 vols., Paris, 1759.

Newton, Isaac. *The Mathematical Principles of Natural Philosophy*, 3 vols., London, 1803.

Newton, Isaac. *Opticks*, London, 1721.

Niceron, J. F. *La Perspective Curieuse ou Magie Artificiele*, Paris, 1638.

Niceron, J. F. *Thaumaturgus Opticus*, Paris, 1646.

Nicolson, Marjorie. *Newton Demands the Muse*, Princeton, NJ, 1966.

Nicolson, Marjorie. *Science and Imagination*, Ithaca, 1956.

Norberg-Schulz, Christian. *Architettura Barocca*, Milan, 1971.

Norberg-Schulz, Christian. *Architettura Tardobarocca*, Milan, 1971.

Oechslin, Werner. "Pyramide et Sphère", *Gazette de Beaux Arts*, 77 (1971).

Oechslin, Werner. *Bildungsgut und Antikenrezeption des frühen Settecento in Rom*, Zurich, 1972.

Ortega y Gasset, José. *Idea de Principio en Leibniz*, 2 vols., Madrid, 1967.

Ortega y Gasset, José. *En Torno a Galileo*, Madrid, 1958.

Ortega y Gasset, José. *Some Lessons on Metaphysics*, 1974.

Osio, Carlo Cesare. *Architettura Civile*, Milan and Lyon, 1684.

Ozanam, J. *Perspective Théorique et Pratique*, Paris, 1720.

Ozanam, J. *Traité de Fortification*, Paris, 1694.

Ozanam, J. *L'Usage du Compas de Proportion*, Paris, 1688.

Ozanam, J. *L'Usage d'Instrument Universel pour Résoudre Tous les Problèmes de Géométrie*, Paris, 1688.

Ozanam, J. *Récréations Mathématiques*, Paris, 1696.

Ozanam, J. *Cours de Mathématiques*, Amsterdam, 1699.

Ozanam, J. *Géométrie Pratique*, Paris, 1684.

Pacioli, Luca. *La Divina Proporción*, translation of the 1509 edition by Ricardo Testa, Buenos Aires, 1959.

Pagan, B. F. *Les Fortifications*, Paris, 1645.

Pagan, B. F. *La Théorie des Planetes*, Paris, 1657.

Pagan, B. F. *L'Astrologie Naturelle*, Paris, 1659.

Pagan, B. F. *The Count of Pagan's Method of Fortification*, London, 1672.

Palissy, Bernard. *Discours Admirables de la Nature*, La Rochelle, 1580.

Palissy, Bernard. *Recepte Véritable*, La Rochelle, 1563.

Palissy, Bernard. *Oeuvres*, Paris, 1880.

Panofsky, Erwin. *Galileo as a Critic of the Arts*, 1954.

Panofsky, Erwin. *Idea: A Concept in Art Theory*, Columbia, SC, 1968.

Panofsky, Erwin. *Meaning in the Visual Arts*, New York, 1968.

Panofsky, Erwin. *La Perspective comme Forme Symbolique*, Paris, 1975.

Parent, M., and J. Vernoust. *Vauban*, Paris, 1971.

Paris, France. *Histoire et Mémoires de l'Académie Royal des Sciences*, Paris, 1702, 1704, 1712, 1719, 1726, 1729, 1730, 1769, 1774, 1776, and 1780.

Paris, France. *Histoire de l'Académie Royale des Sciences, (1666–1699)*, Paris, 1793.

Paris, France. *Journal de l'École Polytechnique*, vols. 1–7, Paris, 1795–1810.

Paris, France. *Journal de Paris*, No. 245, An V.

Paris, France. *Mércure de France*, Paris, August 1770.

Pascal, Blaise. *Pensées*, English translation, Harmondsworth, 1975.

Pascal, Blaise. *Oeuvres Complètes*, Paris, 1963.

Patte, Pierre. *Discours sur l'Architecture*, Paris, 1754.

Patte, Pierre. *Monumens Erigés en France à la Gloire de Louis XV*, Paris, 1765.

Patte, Pierre. *Mémoires sur les Objets les Plus Importans de l'Architecture*, Paris, 1769.

Patte, Pierre. *Mémoire sur la Construction de la Coupole de Sainte-Geneviève*, Paris, 1770.

Patte, Pierre. *Essai sur l'Architecture Théâtrale*, Paris, 1782.

Pedoe, Dan. *Geometry and the Liberal Arts*, London, 1976.

Pérouse de Montclos, Jean-Marie. "Charles-François Viel et Jean-Louis Viel de Saint-Maux." *Bulletin de la Societé de l'Histoire de l'Art Français* (1966).

Pérouse de Montclos, Jean-Marie. *Etienne-Louis Boullée*, Paris, 1969.

Perrault, Charles. *Parallèle des Anciens et Modernes*, 4 vols., Paris, 1692–1696.

Perrault, Charles. *Les Hommes Illustres qui Ont Paru en France*, 2 vols., Paris, 1696.

Perrault, Claude. *Essais de Physique*, 3 vols., Paris, 1680.

Perrault, Claude. *Oeuvres Diverses de Physique et de Mécanique*, 2 vols., Leyden, 1721.

Perrault, Claude. *Mémoires pour Servir à l'Histoire Naturelle des Animaux*, Paris, 1671.

Perrault, Claude. *Les Dix Livres d'Architecture de Vitruve*, Paris, 1684.

Perrault, Claude. *Ordonnance des Cinq Espèces de Colonnes*, Paris, 1683.

Perrault, Claude. *An Abridgement of the Architecture of Vitruvius*, London, 1692.

Perrault, Claude. *Voyage à Bordeaux*, Paris, 1909.

Perronet, Jean-Rodolphe. *Description des Projets et de la Construction des Ponts*, Paris, 1782.

Petot, J. *Histoire de l'Administration des Ponts et Chaussées*, Paris, 1958.

Petzet, Michel. "Un Projet des Perrault pour l'Eglise de Sainte-Geneviève à Paris." *Bulletin Monumental*, 115 (1957).

Petzet, Michel. *Soufflots Sainte-Geneviève*, Berlin, 1961.

Pevsner, Nikolaus. *Academies of Art*, New York, 1973.

Peyre, Marie-Joseph. *Oeuvres d'Architecture*, Paris, 1765.

Pfeffinger, J. F. *Manière de Fortifier à la Vauban*, Amsterdam, 1690.

Pinet. *Histoire de l'École Polytechnique*, Paris, 1887.

Pini, Ermenegildo. *Dell'Architettura, Dialogi*, Milan, 1770.

Piranesi, Giovanni Battista. *Della Magnificenza ed Architettura dei Romani*, Rome, 1760.

Piranesi, Giovanni Battista. *Prisions with the "Carceri" Etchings*, London, 1949.

Piranesi, Giovanni Battista. *The Polemical Works*, Farnborough, 1972.

Poleni, Giovanni. *Memorie Istoriche della Gran Cupola del Tempio Vaticano*, Padua, 1748.

Poncelet, Jean-Victor. "Examen Critique et Historique Concernant l'Équilibre des Voûtes." *Comptes Rendus de l'Académie des Sciences*, 35, Paris (1832).

Poncelet, Jean-Victor. *Traité des Propriétés Projectives des Figures*, Paris, 1822.

Portiez, J. *Rapport sur les Concours de Sculpture, Peinture et Architecture*, Paris, 1795.

Portoghesi, Paolo. *Bernardo Vittone*, Rome, 1966.

Portoghesi, Paolo. *Roma Barocca*, Rome, 1975.

Potain, N. M. *Traité des Ordres d'Architecture*, Paris, 1767.

Poudra, N. M. *Histoire de la Perspective Ancienne et Moderne*, Paris, 1864.

Pozzo, Andrea. *Rules and Examples of Perspective for Painters and Architects*, London, 1709.

Prado, Jeronimo, and Juan Bautista Villalpando. *In Ezechielem Explanationes*, Rome, 1596–1602.

Prevost de Vernoist, *De la Fortification depuis Vauban*, 2 vols., Paris, 1861.

Quatremère de Quincy, A. C. *Histoire de la Vie et des Ouvrages des Plus Célèbres Architectes*, Paris, 1830.

Quatremère de Quincy, A. C. *Dictionnaire Historique d'Architecture*, Paris, 1832.

Ramsay, A. M. *The Philosophical Principles of Natural and Revealed Religion, Unfolded in a Geometrical Order*, 2 vols., Glasgow, 1748–1749.

Ramus, P. *Collectaneae*, Paris, 1577.

Raval, M., and J. C. Moreux. *Claude-Nicolas Ledoux 1756–1806*, Paris, 1945.

Renan, E. "L'Instruction Supérieure en France." *Questions Contemporaines*, Paris, 1868.

Ricatti, Francesco. "Dissertazione Intorno l'Architettura Civile." *Nuova Raccolta di Opuscoli Scientifici e Filologici*, vol. 8, Venice, 1761.

Riche de Prony. *Notice Historique sur Jean-Rodolphe Perronet*, Paris, 1829.

Riche de Prony. "Mécanique Philosophique." *Journal de l'École Polytechnique*, vol. 3, Paris (An VIII).

Riche de Prony. "Discours d'Introduction aux Cours d'Analyse Pure et d'Analyse Appliquée à la Mécanique." *Journal de l'École Polytechnique*, vol. 2, Paris (An VII).

Ricoeur, Paul. *The Rule of Metaphor*, London, 1977.

Ricolfi, H. *Vauban et le Génie Militaire*, Paris, 1935.

Rigault, H. *Histoire de la Querelle des Anciens et Modernes*, Paris, 1856.

Rome, Italy. *Retorica e Barocco, Atti del III Congresso Internazionale di Studi Umanistici*, Rome, 1955.

Rondelet, Jean. *Mémoire Historique sur le Dôme du Panthéon Français*, Paris, 1797.

Rondelet, Jean. *Traité Théorique et Pratique de l'Art de Bâtir*, 3 vols., Paris, 1830.

Rosenblum, Robert. *Transformations in Late Eighteenth Century Art*, Princeton, 1969.

Rosenau, Helen. *Boullée and Visionary Architecture*, London, 1976.

Rosenau, Helen. *The Ideal City. Its Architectural Evolution*, New York, 1972.

Rossi, Paolo. *Philosophy, Technology and the Arts in the Early Modern Era*, New York, 1970.

Rossi, Paolo. *Clavis Universalis*, Milan-Naples, 1960.

Rossi, Paolo. *Francis Bacon. From Magic to Science*, Chicago, 1968.

Roszak, Theodore. *Where the Wasteland Ends*, London, 1973.

Rykwert, Joseph. *On Adam's House in Paradise*, New York, 1972.

Rykwert, Joseph. *The Idea of a Town*, London, 1976.

Rykwert, Joseph. "Inheritance or Tradition." *Leonis Baptiste Alberti, Architectural Design Profiles* 21, London.

Rykwert, Joseph. *The First Moderns*, Cambridge, 1980.

Saccheri, G. *Euclides ab Omni Naevo*, English translation, London, 1920.

Sardi, P. *Couronne Imperiale de l'Architecture Militaire*, Frankfurt, 1623.

Scaletti, C. C. *Scuola Mecanico-Speculativo-Pratica*, Bologna, 1711.

Schabol, R. *La Pratique du Jardinage*, Paris, 1770.

Schabol, R. *La Théorie du Jardinage*, Paris, 1771.

Schlosser, J. M. *La Letteratura Artistica*, Florence, 1956.

Schofield, P. H. *The Theory of Proportion in Architecture*, Cambridge, 1958.

Scholem, Gershom. *On the Kabbalah and Its Symbolism*, London, 1965.

Schutz, Alfred. *Collected Papers I. The Problem of Social Reality*, The Hague, 1973.

Scott, Jonathan. *Piranesi*, London, 1975.

Sedlmayr, Hans. *Art in Crisis*, London, 1957.

Sennett, Richard. *The Fall of Public Man*, Cambridge, 1977.

Shattuck, Roger. *The Banquet Years*, New York, 1968.

Shumaker, Wayne. *The Occult Sciences in the Renaissance*, Berkeley, 1972.

Simson, Otto von. *The Gothic Cathedral*, London, 1956.

Sirigatti, L. *La Pratica di Prospettiva*, Venice, 1596.

Soriano, Marc. *Les Contes de Perrault*, Paris, 1968.

Spicker, Stuart, ed. *The Philosophy of the Body*, New York, 1970.

Spiegelberg, Herbert. *The Phenomenological Movement*, 2 vols., The Hague, 1971.

Spon, Jacob. *Voyage d'Italie*, Lyon, 1678.

Sprat, Thomas. *The History of the Royal Society*, London, 1722.

Stevin, Simon. *Oeuvres Mathématiques*, Leyden, 1634.

Stokes, J., and W. Hurst. *An Outline of the Career of J. T. Désaguilliers*, London, 1928.

Straub, H. *A History of Civil Engineering*, 1952.

Stuart, James, and Nicholas Revett. *The Antiquities of Athens*, London, 1762–1816.

Sturm, L. C. *Le Véritable Vauban*, The Hague, 1713.

Summerson, John. *Architecture in Britain 1530–1830*, Harmondsworth, 1970.

Tacquett, A. T. *Military Architecture*, London, 1672.

Tafuri, Manfredo. *Teorie e Storia dell'Architettura*, Bari, 1968.

Tatarkiewicz, Wladyslaw. *History of Aesthetics*, 3 vols., Paris-The Hague, 1974.

Taton, René. *Enseignement et Diffusion des Sciences en France au 18ème. Siècle*, Paris, 1964.

Taton, René. *L'Oeuvre Mathématique de G. Desargues*, Paris, 1951.

Taton, René. *L'Histoire de la Géométrie Descriptive*, Paris, 1954.

Taton, René. *L'Oeuvre Scientifique de Monge*, Paris, 1951.

Taylor, B. *Linear Perspective*, London, 1715.

Tesauro, E. *Il Cannocchiale Aristotelico*, Turin, 1670.

Thieme, Ulrich, and Felix Becker. *Allgemeines Lexikon der Bildenden Künstler*, Leipzig, 1910–1950.

Thorndike, Lynn. *A History of Magick and Experimental Science*, New York, 1923–1952.

Timoshenko, S. P. *History of the Strength of Materials*, 1953.

Trevor-Roper, H. R. *The European Witch-Craze of the 16th and 17th Centuries*, Harmondsworth, 1969.

Tribout. *Un Grand Savant, Poncelet (1788–1867)*, Paris, 1936.

Troili, G. *Paradosi per Pratticare la Prospettiva*, Bologna, 1638.

Turin, Italy, Accademia delle Scienze. *Guarino Guarini e l'Internazionalità del Barocco*, 2 vols., 1970.

Turin, Italy, Accademia delle Scienze. *Bernardo Vittone e la Disputa fra Classicismo e Barocco nel Settecento*, 2 vols., 1972.

Tymieniecka, A. T. *Leibniz' Cosmological Synthesis*, Assen, 1964.

Varignon, M. *Nouvelle Mécanique ou Statique*, Paris, 1725.

Vauban, Sebastien Le Prestre de. *Oeuvres*, 3 vols., Paris, 1771.

Vauban, Sebastien Le Prestre de. *Oeuvres Militaires*, 3 vols., Paris, An III.

Vaudoyer, A. L. T. *Funerailles de M. Rondelet*, Paris, 1829.

Vico, Giambattista. *Opere*, Bari, 1911–1940.

Vico, Giambattista. *The New Science*, Ithaca, 1970.

Vidler, Anthony. "The Architecture of the Lodges." *Oppositions* 5 (1976).

Viel, Charles-François. *Principes de l'Ordonnance et de la Construction des Bâtimens*, vols. 1 and 4, Paris, 1797 and 1812.

Viel, Charles-François. *De l'Impuissance des Mathématiques*, Paris, 1805.

Viel, Charles-François. *Dissertations sur les Projets de Coupoles*, Paris, 1809.

Viel, Charles-François. *De la Solidité des Bâtimens*, Paris, 1806.

Viel, Charles-François. *Inconvéniens de la Communication des Plans*, Paris, 1813.

Viel, Charles-François. *Des Anciennes Études d'Architecture*, Paris, 1807.

Viel, Charles-François. *Décadence de l'Architecture à la Fin du 18ème Siècle*, Paris, 1800.

Viel de Saint-Maux, J. L. *Lettres sur l'Architecture*, Paris, 1787.

Vignon, E. *Études Historiques sur l'Administration des Voies Publiques en France au 17ème et 18ème Siècles*, 3 vols., Paris, 1862.

Visionary Architects, see Lemagny, G. C.

Vitruvius Pollio (Marcus). *Architecture ou Art de Bien Bastir*, translated into French by Jean Martin, Paris, 1547.

Vitruvius Pollio (Marcus). *De Architectura*, translated into Italian, with commentary and illustrations by Cesare di Lorenzo Cesariano, Como, 1521.

Vitruvius Pollio (Marcus). See Perrault, C. *Les Dix Livres d'Architecture*.

Vittone, Bernardo. *Istruzioni Elementari per Indirizzo dei Giovanni*, Lugano, 1760.

Vittone, Bernardo. *Istruzioni Diverse*, Lugano, 1766.

Vogt, Adolf Max. *Boullées Newton-Denkmal*, Basel, 1969.

Voltaire, F. M. A. *Lettres Philosophiques*, Paris, 1964.

Voltaire, F. M. A. *Oeuvres Complètes*, 52 vols., Paris, 1877–1885.

Vycinas, Vincent. *Earth and Gods*, The Hague, 1964.

Walker, D. P. *Spiritual and Demonic Magic from Ficino to Campanella*, London, 1958.

Walpole, Horace. *Essay on Modern Gardening*, London, 1785.

Ware, Isaac. *Complete Body of Architecture*, London, 1756.

Wilkins, J. *An Essay toward a Real Character and a Philosophical Language*, London, 1668.

Wittkower, Rudolf. *Architectural Principles in the Age of Humanism*, London, 1952.

Wittkower, Rudolf. *Art and Architecture in Italy 1600–1750*, Harmondsworth, 1958.

Wittkower, Rudolf. *Palladio and English Palladianism*, London, 1974.

Wittkower, Rudolf. *Studies in the Italian Baroque*, London, 1975.

Wolf, A. *A History of Science, Technology and Philosophy*, London, 1968.

Wolff, Christian. *Elementa Matheseos Universae*, 2 vols., Magdeburg, 1713.

Wolff, Christian. *Cours de Mathématique*, 3 vols., Paris, 1747.

Wolff, Christian. *Gesammelte Werke*, Hildesheim, 1971.

Wren, Stephen. *Parentalia*, London, 1750.

Yates, Frances. *The Theatre of the World*, London, 1969.

Yates, Frances. *Giordano Bruno and the Hermetic Tradition*, London, 1971.

Yates, Frances. *The Rosicrucian Enlightenment*, London, 1972.

Zanotti, E. *Tratatto Teorico-Pratico di Prospettiva*, Bologna, 1766.

INDEX

Royal Society of London, 22, 168

Saccheri, G., 103
San Francesco della Vigna, 255
Sardi, P., 207
Scaletti, C. C., 184
Schabol, R., 189
  La Pratique du Jardinage, 188
  La Théorie du Jardinage, 188
Scientific inquiry, 134
Sorcery. See Witchcraft
Soufflot, Jacques-Germain
  on beauty, 71
  Church of Ste. Geneviève, 68–69
  Durand on, 303
  mathematics theories, 69
  Mémoire sur les Proportions d'Architecture, 71
  and natural philosophy, 71–72
  and Patte's theories, 260–264
  on Perrault, 71
  on proportion, 69, 71
  on taste, 69
Space, use of, in seventeenth century, 175
Stage design
  Bibiena on, 191
  and perspective, 191
Statics, 238
  in construction, 217
  Coulomb on, 265–266
  De la Hire on, 241
  in eighteenth century, 244, 248, 258, 264–265
  empirical method in, 258
  Frezier on, 233
  Galileo on, 238–239
  Gautier on, 243
  Milizia on, 253
  in nineteenth century, 291
  Pini on, 251
  Pitot on, 243
  Rigoristti theories, 254
  in seventeenth century, 241
  Stevin on, 238
  Viel on, 318
Stereotomy
  Derand on, 228
  Desargues on, 229, 232
  in eighteenth century, 232
  Frezier on, 232–233
  Guarini's use of, 94
  in seventeenth century, 227–229
  in sixteenth century, 227
Stevin, Simon
  on mensuration, 222
  Oeuvres Mathématiques, 204, 222, 238
  on statics, 238
Stonecutting. See Stereotomy
Strength of materials

eighteenth century experiments, 196, 244
  empirical method in testing, 244
  Girard on, 266
  in nineteenth century, 291
  Poleni's experiments with, 250
  Rigoristti theories, 254–255
  Viel on, 318
Surrealism, 323
Symbolization, 159–160, 323–324

Taste, theories on
  Blondel, 67
  Briseux, 60
  Ledoux, 147
  Soufflot, 69
Techné, 171, 185
Technical problems. See Mechanics
Temple de la Felicité Publique, 298
Temple of Solomon, 126–127
Theology
  Descartes on, 23, 25
  Perrault on, 25
Theory and practice, 50, 82, 83, 103, 104
  Blondel, 68, 198
  Boullée, 135–136
  Briseux, 60
  Bullet, 225
  De la Hire, 196
  Desargues, 97, 100, 229
  in education, 200
  in eighteenth century, 190, 196–197, 225, 250
  Frémin, 50–51
  Frezier, 232
  Jousse, 228
  Langley, 127
  Ledoux, 146–147, 160
  in mensuration, 223
  Milizia, 252
  Navier, 295
  in nineteenth century, 285, 322
  Palissy, 168, 170
  Patte, 73, 262–263
  Perrault, 18, 26, 32, 38
  Rondelet, 287, 290–291
  Royal Academy of Architecture, 57–58
  Schabol, 189
  in seventeenth century, 222–223
  Viel, 315–316, 320–322
  Vittone, 109
Topography, in seventeenth century, 223
Tuscan order. See Classical orders

Universal method, of Desargues, 97–105

Vauban, Sebastien Le Prestre de, on fortification, 210, 212–213, 215
Versailles, 175

Vico, Giambattista, 325
Viel, Charles-François, 264
on Blondel, 319
Décadence de l'Architecture à la Fin du XVIIIème Siècle, 322
De la Solidité des Bâtimens, Puissé dans les Proportions des Ordres d'Architecture, 319
De L'Impuisance des Mathématiques pour Assurer la Solidité des Bâtimens, 317–318
Des anciennes études d' architecture, 320–321
devis, criticism of, 320
Dissertation sur les Projects de Coupoles, 318, 319
educational theories, 320–321
on eurythmy, 316–318
on harmonic proportions, 318–319
mathematics, use of, 317, 319
Principes de l'Ordonnance et de la Construction des Bâtimens, 315
on proportion, 316–317, 318–319
and relativism, 321
on solidity and stability of buildings, 317–318
on statics, 318
on strength of materials experiments, 318
theory and practice, 315–316, 320–322
Viel de Saint-Maux, Jean-Louis, 159
Boullée, criticism of, 144, 146
Visible beauty. *See* Beauty
Vitruvius, Pollio (Marcus)
and Bélidor, 218, 220
Laugier on, 61
optical correction theories, 32
proportion theories, 32
Ten Books of Architecture, 18, 27, 32, 35–36
Vittone, Bernardo
grid, use of, 109
and Guarini, 105
harmonic proportion theories, 109, 111
Instruzioni Diverse, 108, 109, 111
Instruzioni Elementari, 108
light, use of, 111, 112
and Newtonian philosophy, 108–109
theory and practice, 109
Voltaire, on Newtonian metaphysics, 272

Witchcraft
Palissy, accusations against, 171
in seventeenth century, 25
Wolff, Christian
Elements Matheseos Universae, 115, 116
on proportion, 116
Woodcutting. *See* Stereotomy